The Coolie Speaks

In the series

ASIAN AMERICAN HISTORY AND CULTURE

edited by Sucheng Chan, David Palumbo-Liu, Michael Omi,
K. Scott Wong, and Linda Trinh Võ

Robert G. Lee, *Orientals: Asian Americans in Popular Culture*

David L. Eng and Alice Y. Hom, eds., *Q & A: Queer in Asian America*

K. Scott Wong and Sucheng Chan, eds., *Claiming America: Constructing Chinese American Identities during the Exclusion Era*

Lavina Dhingra Shankar and Rajini Srikanth, eds., *A Part, Yet Apart: South Asians in Asian America*

Jere Takahashi, *Nisei/Sansei: Shifting Japanese American Identities and Politics*

Velina Hasu Houston, ed., *But Still, Like Air, I'll Rise: New Asian American Plays*

Josephine Lee, *Performing Asian America: Race and Ethnicity on the Contemporary Stage*

Deepika Bahri and Mary Vasudeva, eds., *Between the Lines: South Asians and Postcoloniality*

E. San Juan, Jr., *The Philippine Temptation: Dialectics of Philippines-U.S. Literary Relations*

Carlos Bulosan and E. San Juan, Jr., ed., *The Cry and the Dedication*

Carlos Bulosan and E. San Juan, Jr., ed., *On Becoming Filipino: Selected Writings of Carlos Bulosan*

Vicente L. Rafael, ed., *Discrepant Histories: Translocal Essays on Filipino Cultures*

Yen Le Espiritu, *Filipino American Lives*

Paul Ong, Edna Bonacich, and Lucie Cheng, eds., *The New Asian Immigration in Los Angeles and Global Restructuring*

Chris Friday, *Organizing Asian American Labor: The Pacific Coast Canned-Salmon Industry, 1870-1942*

Sucheng Chan, ed., *Hmong Means Free: Life in Laos and America*

Timothy P. Fong, *The First Suburban Chinatown: The Remarking of Monterey Park, California*

William Wei, *The Asian American Movement*

Yen Le Espiritu, *Asian American Panethnicity*

Velina Hasu Houston, ed., *The Politics of Life*

Renqiu Yu, *To Save China, To Save Ourselves: The Chinese Hand Laundry Alliance of New York*

Shirley Geok-lin Lim and Amy Ling, eds., *Reading the Literatures of Asian America*

Karen Isaksen Leonard, *Making Ethnic Choices: California's Punjabi Mexican Americans*

Gary Y. Okihiro, *Cane Fires: The Anti-Japanese Movement in Hawaii, 1865-1945*

Sucheng Chan, *Entry Denied: Exclusion and the Chinese Community in America, 1882-1943*

THE COOLIE SPEAKS

CHINESE INDENTURED LABORERS AND AFRICAN SLAVES OF CUBA

Lisa Yun

TEMPLE UNIVERSITY PRESS
Philadelphia

HD
4875
.C9
Y86
2008

Cover image: "A Chapter on the Coolie Trade" by Edgar Holden Harpers, *New Monthly,* June 1864, vol. 29, issue 169.

Publication of this book is made possible through the generous support of the Chiang Ching-Kuo Foundation for International Scholarly Exchange.

Temple University Press
1601 North Broad Street
Philadelphia PA 19122
www.temple.edu/tempress

♾ The paper used in this publication meets the requirements of the American National Standard for Information Sciences—Permanence of Paper for Printed Library Materials, ANSI Z39.48-1992

Library of Congress Cataloging-in-Publication Data

Yun, Lisa, 1963–
　The coolie speaks : Chinese indentured laborers and African slaves in Cuba / Lisa Yun.
　　p. cm.
　Includes bibliographical references and index.
　ISBN-13: 978-1-59213-581-3 (cloth : alk. paper)
　ISBN-10: 1-59213-581-1 (cloth : alk. paper)
　1. Indentured servants—Cuba—History.　2. Alien labor, Chinese—Cuba—History.
　3. Slave labor—Cuba—History.　4. Alien labor, African—Cuba—History.　5. Slaves' writings—Cuba—History and criticism.　6. Revolutionary literature, Cuban—History and criticism.　7. Cuba—Race relations—History.　8. Cuba—Emigration and immigration—History.　I. Title.　II. Title: Chinese indentured laborers and African slaves in Cuba.

HD4875.C9Y86 2008
331.6'25107291—dc22   2007020202

2　4　6　8　9　7　5　3　1

To the Yun and Laremont families,
whose heritage spans five continents

CONTENTS

Acknowledgments

I am indebted to many who have helped me bring this to fruition. I will first thank Gary Okihiro for encouraging me over several years. Without his support and the enthusiasm of David Palumbo-Liu, this book would not have materialized. My words are entirely inadequate to express my gratitude. For my research in Cuba, I thank scholars at the Fundación Fernando Ortiz, who pointed me in the right direction: Jesús Guanche Pérez, Sergio Valdés Bernal, and especially, José Baltar Rodríguez for many hours spent sharing his own insights regarding the Chinese community. Federico Chang at the Casa de Altos Estudios Don Fernando Otiz gave me what amounted to an intense tutorial. Yrmina Eng, founding director of Grupo Promotor del Barrio Chino, and Alfonso Chao Chiu, director of the Casino Chung Wah, welcomed and introduced me to barrio chino in Havana. Marta Moreno Vega, founder of the Caribbean Cultural Center in New York, introduced me to Yrmina and besides, greatly encouraged me at the beginning. My respect goes to the residents of barrio chino, members of the Chinese Benevolent Associations, and residents of the Residencia de Ancianos. Their stories and kindness, quietly yet generously shared, will never be forgotten. Mercedes, her sister Teresa, and Cora offered friendship and assistance. Abel Fung, who is the longtime editor of Kwong Wah Po, the oldest Chinese newspaper in Cuba, spent many days with me walking the streets of barrio chino and sharing community history. Manuel Millán Amador (Maike), the sculptor and miniaturist, shared his artwork and family history unreservedly. Carmen Eng shared her knowledge of the Chinese schools and art in the local community. My special thanks to journalist Silvia Johoy, whose aid I can never forget. I acknowledge these individuals while regretting that there are others who aided and befriended me but are not named here due to space limitations.

In my quest for primary materials in Chinese, my deepest gratitude goes to Xiuying Zou, librarian at the East Asian Library of the University of Pittsburgh and former Binghamton colleague, who provided patient assistance in my search and went further to help with the translations for this project. She is a friend and scholar in her own right, and we will collaborate on projects in the years to come. My great thanks to Chengzi Wang, the Chinese studies librarian who helped me with primary materials at the archives of Columbia University's C.V. Starr East Asian Library.

At my home institution, I am indebted to the invaluable assistance of exceptional students and highlight here their translation work on Chinese materials. They are: Kuo-I Chou, who will be graduating with her doctorate in Comparative Literature; Yuanhui Wang, who graduated with a degree in Philosophy, Interpretation, and Culture; Naixin Kang, who moved into medicine; and Yueting Zhang, who went into biomedical research. These four offered camaraderie, fortitude, and humor in the face of my obsession over details (the "master charts"!). I thank Gabriela Veronelli for translation work on Spanish materials. Completing her doctorate in Philosophy, Interpretation, and Culture, she is a passionate activist, and I learned from our discussions on Latin American philosophies of race, indigeneity, and nationalism. To former graduate student Ju Li, I give my appreciation for earlier stages of translation work, and to another former graduate student, Hetal Thaker, thanks to her for her preparation of the index and her assistance in my pursuit of arcane references. I am also blessed to have had the help of two Asian Studies colleagues. Historian John Chaffee gave an insightful reading of my manuscript and has been a wonderfully supportive colleague for several years. Literary scholar Zuyan Chen helped especially with translation and finer points of verse. With generous spirit, Zuyan read through the testimonies and translations more times than he would care to remember. I also benefited from the suggestions of Michael West and Bill Martin, who read chapters with care. Dale Tomich shared rich conversation with me over the years on sugar and labor. Thanks to Richard Lee, who provided me opportunities to present drafts at the Fernand Braudel Center. I was lucky to have the best dean one could hope to have in Jean Pierre Mileur, who made it possible (when it seemed impossible) for me to undertake this research. I am indebted to Ali Mazrui's unflagging interest over the years and am particularly appreciative of his comments on the project in regard to slavery and abolition. In countless ways, he and Pauline have been vital supporters in my journey.

Manning Marable and Shelley Wong gave me opportunities to present and get feedback on this work while it was evolving, as did Michael Turner, *mi tío* whom I respect and admire. Three scholars of philosophy read portions of the text and engaged me with sustained dialogue: David Haekwon Kim, Ronald Sundstrom, and Tommy Lott. To David, I am thankful for his early interest and solidarity. Jack Tchen gave positive reinforcement and read portions at various stages. Bill Mullen, Lisa Lowe, and Fred Ho read the work and gave hearty encouragement. Kathy Lopez shared my interest in Antonio Chuffat Latour and generously shared her remarkable work on the Chinese of Cuba. Victor Chang at the University of the West Indies encouraged my first article on Chuffat in the *Caribbean Quarterly*. This has been revised and expanded into a chapter in this book, as has an article on the coolie traffic that first appeared in the *Journal of Asian American Studies*. Russell Leong encouraged my first article on coolie ships, for *Amerasia Journal*, which led to my long-term interest in the passage. Years earlier, Lawrence Hogue introduced me to Frederick Douglass and the slave narrative, which led to my interest in the litera- tures of bondage. Dennis Kratz and Rainer Schulte influenced my move towards interdisciplinarity. Anthony Lee demanded a sharper critical eye, and most of all, Dachang Cong pushed me in diaspora studies at a crucial juncture. My friendships with activists John Tateishi, Dale Minami, and our mutual friend Suzanne Ahn, were a turning point, as their experiences with testimony/testifying moved me to consider histories of testimony in social struggles. With Suzanne, we shared a renewed sense of possibilities but she succumbed to cancer. Here I pay tribute to her.

I benefited from feedback of audiences who heard early drafts of my work at the University of San Francisco, Cornell University, Columbia University, University of California Los Angeles, Pitzer College, National Library of Singapore, and a lively audience of Kent Ono and his col- leagues at the University of Illinois at Urbana-Champaign.

Fine comments of anonymous readers helped make this a better book; and thankfully, Elena Coler and Michael Sandlin gave great efforts to this project at Temple University Press. All of this leads me to say I am eter- nally grateful to my editor Janet Francendese, who lent great support to this project.

I am thankful for dear friends in my daily life who tolerated my short- comings and encouraged me along the way, both in my professional and personal life and in the world of poetry. I hope they will forgive me for this unsatisfactory way of writing about them here (I could write volumes!). I think they know who they are, and I am privileged to be among them.

Finally, I am indebted to my parents, Bob and Linda Yun, who devoted their lives to their children. Providing unconditional love and affection, they are the most extraordinary parents. With a great capacity for idealism and belief in social justice, they inspired this work. I mention my quirky dear brother Michael, and my children, Liana and Ali, who bring immea- surable joy and mischief to my life; and lastly, though only due to conven- tion, I thank my husband and friend Ricardo Laremont, with whom I have made this challenging journey.

INTRODUCTION: CHALLENGES OF A TRANSNATIONAL HISTORY

> We all live by robbing Asiatic coolies, and those of us who are
> "enlightened" all maintain that those coolies ought to be set free;
> but our standard of living, and hence our "enlightenment" demands
> that the robbery shall continue.[1]
>
> —*George Orwell*

In a critique of enlightened and liberal attitudes, Orwell once commented upon the ambivalence surrounding the subject of the coolie. In metropoles and colonies of the nineteenth and twentieth centuries, African slave labor and Indian and Chinese coolie labor underwrote the standard of living. It was coolie labor, however, that would effect the world "transition" from slavery to free labor, from premodern to modern production. "Coolie" labor, or Asian indenture, emerged in the midst of contentious debates. British abolitionists decried the inhumanity of indenture; American politicians sought to protect white labor from a coolie invasion; Christian missionaries attempted on-site interventions; and the Chinese government responded with public executions of collaborators in the traffic.[2] The political maneuverings and debates that surrounded the coolie took place in the global theater of abolition, progress, and emergent nationalisms. The politics on all sides were multivalent, multilayered, and globally imbricated. These important multinational debates took place in a context wherein the British and Americans were the leading coolie traffickers to the Americas, along with the French and Spanish. From this maelstrom, a strange lacuna emerges. What did the coolies have to say? How did the coolies narrate their own experiences? How is this related to the ways in which they entered the international scene as mass labor to the Americas during this period? The perspectives of coolies themselves remain spectral and difficult to locate, overshadowed by intersecting discourses of abolition, racial imaginaries, and colonial administrations of knowledge production in the course of those debates. The coolies, ambivalently figured as transitional figures, take their place as helpmates to history.

Though hotly debated, they have been portrayed as having something to do but not having anything to say.

In this study, I examine the perspectives of 2,841 Chinese coolies in Cuba, all of whom left behind stunning accounts of their experiences in written and oral testimonies. They described their particular experiences *within a slave society in the Americas*. These testimonies, in whole and excerpted forms, constitute counternarratives to historical narratives that elided subjectivities of subjugated labor. This is the first time that a critical examination of these original materials is introduced to the scholarly public. My particular interests regard the perspectives and, indeed, *arguments*: those presented by coolies in relation to literary genres and also historical and philosophical debates of slavery and freedom. I propose, through a presentation of the coolies' historical context and their testimonies, that the coolies of Cuba suggested radical critiques of the contract institution, which was proffered by Enlightenment and abolitionist philosophers as the guarantor of free society. Thus, my investigation conducts a dialogue with history (of slavery and freedom), literature (of bondage), and philosophy (of the "contract"). How are concepts of slavery and freedom—the bases of American and Western exceptionalist arguments—challenged by the histories of Asian diasporas in the Americas? Secondly, how do transnational narratives of the first Asians brought to this hemisphere (in the eighteenth and nineteenth centuries) contribute to and revise the legacies of North and South American history and literature? The coolies in Cuba revealed their lives as intensely violent ones and as unrelenting struggles for not only freedom from bondage, but for transcultural practices and strategic language use, and for racialized and collective consciousness. The emergence of a subaltern body politic and their mass mobilization lends an added dimension to antislavery's history, i.e., an Asian resistance against slavery in the West that lasted several decades. Unlike literary-historical genres of the slave narrative and the immigrant narrative, the words of coolies have remained in the margins of literature and history.

I examine the global and local historical contexts that coolie testimonies speak to, and the production processes that shaped and disciplined their forms. I then undertake a close reading and analysis of the testimonies themselves. I argue that these testimonies can be read as "narratives" that display certain tropes and conventions and that also contain certain themes and arguments. Finally, I trace the subsequent submergence and eclipse of the coolie narratives through a Cuban communal biography. Thus, this study is divided into five main sections. In Chapter One, I provide an historical analysis and overview regarding Chinese coolie labor in Cuba as situated in the matrix of sugar and slavery. It would be impossible (or imprudent) to broach the coolie testimonies without first examining the historical context and significance, and the particularities of economy and Cuba. In this section, I foreground and frame certain historical arguments and comparisons. This synopsis highlights interpretive concerns that address Asian migration in relation to slavery and also offers an historical interpretation (and related data) that contextualizes key themes raised by the coolies in their testimonies. In Chapter Two, I examine the testimonies and writing as resistance. I first attend to the apparatus of production and questions of methodology particular to narratives produced in bondage. I look to methods and problems raised in treatments of testimony from Indian indenture and African slavery. This methodological discussion is followed by the reading and analysis of the testimonies in Chapters Three and Four, with special attention to a series of written testimonies that feature "perversions of the contract" and what I argue are themes regarding "the commodification of freedom." I present these written testimonies as literary protests that were fashioned within narrative conventions. The testimonies included features of verse, mythological allusions, literary and classical references, metaphorical and figurative speech, and conventions of classical Chinese. Following an examination of the written testimonies is an examination of the verbal testimonies, with focus upon a main theme of "race and resistance." In Chapter Five, I examine the eclipse of the coolie narrative under exigencies of progress and the next generation of Chinese in Cuba. This second-generation perspective is told via a rare communal biography by an Afro-Chinese author from Cuba, Antonio Chuffat Latour, who dedicated his work to the coolies and framed the overthrow of slavery and Spanish colonialism as an inseparable history of Chinese and African struggle. This critical examination of his text is the first that has been undertaken in any field of scholarship. Chuffat revealed the eclipse of coolie history in nationalist narrations and the rise of the merchant class amid imperatives of modernity and racial exclusion. The role of *los californianos* and American policies in that process would be revealed in his telling. Ultimately, Antonio Chuffat Latour provides a veiled and subversive narrative of color and class, conveyed through his strategic use of multitextual materials (such as newspaper articles, photographs, and letters) and his underlying tones of irony. Finally, in my conclusion, I examine how these earlier narratives connect to new narratives of global migrant labor and "new slavery." Included is a brief research note explicating considerations and limitations in these translations of the coolie testimonies (in Chinese) and the translations of the communal biography (in Spanish). Materials for this study have been examined in their original forms and languages, and this presentation of these materials has incurred the significant process of translating the materials into English beforehand, a process which has been naturalized in this study but needs address and an accounting of method. This note acknowledges the impossibility and undesirability of "equivalency" in translation, and acknowledges the process of translation as constituting a "third epistemological body." I also address special factors and concerns of translation that led to certain conclusions regarding the materials. This endnote also briefly elaborates upon research material and sources, with the intention of aiding others who might wish to undertake further investigation and future directions. The nature of an inaugural study of such materials is that only a few lines of inquiry could be pursued in the initial investigation, but there are a wealth of avenues that could be undertaken and many aspects that could be mined.

For now, I bring the reader's attention to some technicalities of reading this text. Translations of Chinese person and place names appear in this study in two forms: Wade Giles and pinyin. As needed, I provide both forms, as called for in a study consisting heavily of nineteenth-century materials. However, when only the Wade Giles is known, and no original Chinese is available (from which the pinyin translation can be formulated), then only the Wade Giles is provided. Wade Giles is used as the preferred form in a case where perhaps a famous figure of the nineteenth century has become historically and primarily known by his or her Wade Giles name.

As for translations of Spanish passages, I provide these alongside the Spanish terms, though for a few of the lengthier passages, I provide paraphrases. I have tried to make it easy to distinguish whether a translation or a paraphrase is being provided. Thus, the English-only reader should be entirely comfortable with this multicultural and multilingual text. In some cases, footnotes are provided, which help explain particular terms in the original testimonies featured in the text. Besides those instances, however, chapter endnotes are provided throughout this book.

TERMINOLOGY

A study of the coolie subject begs the question of terminology. What do I mean by "coolie"? The term "coolie" has been reclaimed and appreciated as one of deep cultural significance, such as by scholars and writers who have explored the "coolie odyssey" and the diaspora-related history and culture that it formed; but "coolie" has a long history of pejorative connotations.[3] Community histories did not necessarily feature the coolie, partly due to the fact that "coolie" is a classed term. Asian coolies were regarded as lowly laborers. Imagined communities of belonging and institutions of historical preservation were fashioned and supported by merchant societies, which also had the material means to record, preserve, and publicize their histories. On the public platform, coolie was indeed present but as a sensationalist stereotype of Asian labor. Anticoolie and moralist campaigns, along with abolitionist writings against coolie labor, all contributed to negative connotations associated with the term "coolie."

"Coolie" is also an expansive term, like "Asian" and "labor," and it has a varied application and etymology. In Spanish, the term *culi* came late in political and social discourses. The Chinese in Cuba were referred to as *los chinos* (the Chinese), *contratados* (contract labor), and *colonos* (settlers or colonists). The term *culi* did not appear in the authoritative Spanish-Chinese dictionary of the time, *Diccionario Español-Chino* (1915),[4] and its etymology neither stems from Iberian nor Latin American discourses but rather was adapted from the English. In 1956 the term made its appearance in the *Diccionario de la Real Academia Española*, the authoritative dictionary of Spanish language, which notes its origin in English and Hindi and its use for designating Indian or Chinese labor.[5] Definitions of "coolie" also have been said to emerge or originate from the Tamil, Portuguese (via Gujarati), Chinese, and Fijian.[6]

My use of the term "coolie" is deliberate and strategic. First, I proceed in recognition of a body of scholarly work that precedes and makes possible this work. Studies of nineteenth-century labor include scores of period monographs and recent scholarship devoted to Indian and Chinese "coolies," indenture, and historical particularities of nineteenth-century regimes that contextualized indentured labor.[7] Most relevant for this work are the studies of Cuba that focus upon *los culíes chinos*. The term "coolie" is used in this study with respect to a deep and particular history. Second, the term "coolie" is a socially and historically specific designation used here in distinction to the diplomat and merchant, for example, which bring particularized social histories that are classed and racialized in certain ways. Asian migrations were (and are) composed of heterogeneous political and social histories over centuries, including migrations of indentured labor, "credit-ticket" labor, the intellectual elite, the diplomat, war refugees, war brides, the merchant/businessman, the student, the hi-tech and middle-class transnationalist, "astronaut" wives, "parachute" kids, and multiple passport holders.[8] The Chinese coolies of Cuba identified themselves as unfree laborers located in structures of colonialism and extreme exploitation. Third, I use the term as one that calls upon a *racialized* labor history, as "coolies" especially referred to *Asian* bonded labor and no other.[9]

Finally, a certain paradox underlies the usage of the term "coolie" throughout my work. The interpretive basis for understanding Asian migration to the Americas rests most often on notions of "the contract," with its philosophical complement of consenting relations between equal parties, and a juridical structure of its interpretation. In effect, Western philosophies regarding the contract and individual have overdetermined and predetermined narrations of Asian migration, past and present. The assumptions of social progress, self-ownership, individual freedom, and consensual relations (even if these should lead to consensual exploitation, as Hobbesian philosophers might argue) frame immigrant history and its component of immigrant labor as ultimately "voluntary" movements. In the case of the coolie history of Cuba, I argue that the contract's particular use was to produce *mobile slaves*. Coolies were marketed, sold, re-sold, rented-out, lent-out, and named and renamed by owners, traders, and police. They were moved to plantations, prisons, depots, railways and listed as dead, disappeared, or hired all at the same time—coolies were owned for life by one and many. Thus, coolie history and its attendant narratives become a conundrum of contradictions: hypermobile yet immobilized, owned by one and owned by many, fluid yet enslaved. The very contradictory nature of their enslaved freedom is depicted by the Chinese coolies as a surreal and panoptic contract state. This was a state in which they were legally defined by colonial and legal discourses as free, yet were enslaved by (1) the very technologies of "voluntariness" (the contract), (2) the apparatuses of "protection" (the law), and (3) existing technologies of bondage (slavery). Some 10 percent of the testimonies examined in this study are from those who no longer called themselves slaves and who had been freed from bondage. Yet the most intriguing feature of their accounts is exactly what it meant to be "free" in a contract state bent upon enslavement. With this social constitution in mind, the term "coolie labor" here is used to apprehend a particular labor group under veiled institutions and racialized discourses that disciplined them alongside, within, yet *against* institutions and discourses of slavery. This use of "coolie" here posits a radical reexamination of liberal philosophies and assumptions regarding contracts and freedom, positing the coolie not only as comparable to the slave, but also as being enslaved by the very structures of "free" society and "contractual" society based upon concepts of self-ownership.

WRITING FROM LOCATION

My study, as any study or argument, is delimited by the situation of its author. My intentions, however, are *not* to recuperate the "coolie" of Cuba as a "minority American" subject, which rehearses a kind of cultural imperialism and enacts a naïve homogenization of experience, history, and identity politics in the Americas. Rather, my aim is to excavate and consider perspectives within the global and local context of slavery and nineteenth-century philosophical and political economy. The study, therefore, conjoins several areas of Asian, African, Caribbean, Latin American, and American studies. It is through concerns of racialization, subordination, and colonialism that this study intersects and converses with the interdisciplinary field of Asian American studies and its concerns of immigration, race, labor, citizenship, and empire. Furthermore, Asian American studies has broadened into a field that also looks at Asian "Americas" and that finds methodological currency in "diaspora."[10] Historian Evelyn Hu-Dehart's ground-breaking introductions to the Chinese of Latin America began that transformation for Asian American studies.[11] In addition, filmmaker Loni Ding and the scholars who contributed to her work provided a visual touchstone for this broadening with a documentary on Indian and Chinese coolie labor to the Americas.[12] Asian American writers and artists also have creatively addressed the subject of Asians in the Americas, such as novelist Karen Tei Yamashita who has written on Japanese Brazilians. Hu-Dehart's historical research, Ding's film representation, and Yamashita's creative writings pushed open the boundaries of the field. An increasing flow of work on the subject has been produced from the field of Asian American studies, including essays from people of Asian descent in the Americas in a volume by Roshni Rustomji-Kerns, Rajini Srikanth, and Leny Mendoza Strobel, and a recent collection on Japanese of the Americas by Lane Hirabayashi, Akemi Kikumura-Yano, and James Hirabayashi.[13] Most recently, Erika Lee has expressed the need for a hemispheric approach to Asian American studies.[14] While acclaiming these authors, artists, and scholarship, this is not to say that work on this subject has not been produced outside of the United States on the subject of Asians of the Americas. Relevant scholarship in this area certainly has been undertaken before, and, in fact, it has been studied for several decades. There is a large body of scholarship on the history and culture of Chinese and South Asians in the Caribbean, particularly regarding Guyana, Trinidad, and Jamaica. As strands of postcolonial histories often extend and cross, these diasporic formations and the related scholarship are often connected across the Americas. Especially germane to this study is the scholarship specifically regarding the Chinese of Cuba, particularly the work of three major scholars who drew from different archives and methods: Cuban scholar Juan Pérez de la Riva (especially *Los culíes chinos en Cuba*), Canadian scholar Denise Helly (especially *Idéologie et ethnicité: Les Chinois Macao à Cuba*), and Australian scholar Yen Ching Hwang (especially *Coolies & Mandarins: China's Protection of Overseas Chinese*). When considered in tandem, I found them to provide substantive basis for subsequent work on the Chinese of Cuba in both global and local perspectives. I owe a debt to their work and to the long-standing scholarship of Caribbean studies, African slavery, and sugar.

These studies from multiple disciplines and locations share a common attribute, which is the implicit unsettling of binaries that have subsumed multiple histories and representations. Conventionally, the Atlantic and the Pacific are perceived as discrete epistemological geographies. Transatlantic studies traditionally focus upon Caribbean, West Africa, North and South America, and Europe. Yet the dichotomy of "Atlantic-Europe-Africa-America" and "Pacific-Asia" as discrete bodies of knowledge and art needs to be reconsidered. Stuart Hall once exclaimed, "You *can* find Asia by sailing West, if you know where to look!" (his emphasis).[15] A creative linkage of transatlantic and transpacific epistemes brings to the fore the consideration of Atlantic and Pacific as being discrete yet co-constitutive. Questioning these binaries as they have taken shape over the *longue durée*, historian Gary Okihiro has revealed the deeply tied connections between them, resulting in startling revisions of racial and global histories. He also points out that trade with Asia was directly linked to transatlantic colonial and maritime systems, as does Herbert Klein, who notes that "it was no accident that the two most famous slave trade ports in Europe, that of Nantes in France and Liverpool in England, first achieved importance as international trades through their East Asian trades. It was their supplies of East Asian goods which allowed them to become early and effective competitors in the Africa slave trade."[16] Maritime records reveal that in fact, many Asians (including coolies) and Asian-based trades also came via transatlantic routes; "transpacific" would actually be a misnomer for essentializing Asian migration.[17] A long-term engagement with the subject of Asians in the Americas involves critical and creative dialogue that queries "Asian" subjects in the context of "African" and "Latin."

Returning to Hall, he pointed out the Asian presence, yet he also "collapsed" that presence due to limitations of existing cultural models. He remarked that an examination of the Caribbean is based upon "at least three 'presences'" as suggested by Aimé Césaire and Léopold Senghor's metaphors: *Présence Africaine, Présence Européenne, Présence Americaine.* As for the Asian presences, he noted that "I am collapsing, for the moment, the many other cultural 'presences' which constitute the complexity of Caribbean identity (Indian, Chinese, Lebanese, etc.)."[18] In profound concepts of cultural formation in the Americas, the subject of Asians and Chinese is thus "collapsed" into models of national cultures and post-slavery histories. In that awkward dissonance of "presence yet absence," apprehending the Chinese coolie becomes a deep and lengthy process of disclosure, one of unfixing entrenched binaries: slave versus free, black versus white, East versus West, Pacific versus Atlantic. This work contributes to that unfixing and also brings forward narratives that offer vital and fresh perspectives to understandings of the Americas.

1

HISTORICAL CONTEXT OF COOLIE TRAFFIC TO THE AMERICAS

> We heard that the Chinese government has reconciled with those big
> foreign countries and those countries have prohibited the trade of
> Africans; how come no one tries to save the Chinese in Cuba? Why?
> The officials have made ways to make us slaves over and over . . . In all,
> when we die, we will have no coffin or grave. Our bones will be burned
> and mixed with ox and horse bone ash, and then used to whiten the
> sugar (Petition 54).
>
> —*Ren Shizen, Dai Renjie, Liang Xingzhao (1874)*

THE NARRATIVE OF TRANSITION

In 1874 there were 2,841 Chinese coolies who stepped forward to give
written and oral testimonies of their experiences in Cuba. Of some quarter
million Chinese sent to Cuba and Peru in bondage, this would be one instance of their mass protest via testimony. The perspectives of those such
as Ren Shizen, Dai Renjie, and Liang Xingzhao complicate narratives of
slavery and freedom and can be placed in comparison to contemporary
historiographic interpretations on the subject of Asian migration. Their
accounts provide an alternate perspective to the "transitional" narrative,
which has facilitated the modern teleology of slave to free, black to white.
In historical analyses of mass Asian migration to the Americas, particularly that of the Chinese, a *narrative of transition* has provided currency
for explaining their emergence and function as subjects in slave and free
economies and as mediums for "progress" and modernization. The utility
of Asians in a "transition" narrative goes hand in hand with the racialized
figuring of Asians as functional "intermediaries" between slave and free,
black and white and has enabled the continued entrenchment of these binaries.[1] Manuel Moreno Fraginals's explications, which have served as a
linchpin of Cuban studies and studies of sugar economies, map one version

of the transition narrative in his portrayal of Chinese wage workers as constituting the transition from slavery to modernization. He came to the following conclusion:

> The slave trade did not allow for the modernization of productive mechanisms. Though this has been a highly controversial topic in modern historiography (especially since Fogal [sic] and Engerman's studies), a detailed study of sugar technology confirms that sugar mills were unable to take advantage of any of the new production techniques developed by their European counterparts . . . The most illustrious economists and industrial technicians of the time came to the conclusion that it was impossible to establish a scientific system of industrial production using slave labor. The sharp drop in Negro contraband and rise of the consumer market coincided with sugar's industrial revolution . . . The key to success was in Chinese immigration.[2]

At the same time, Moreno noted that the treatment of the Chinese was "a brand of slavery similar to that of the Negroes." But the dictates of this treatment, he explained, were determined by the economic necessities of production, and by neither the "philanthropic nor perverse" intentions of the owners. Moreno emphasized that "in the eyes of the owners, the men who came to work on their plantations were production factors."[3] While this analysis explicates the logic of transition to industrialization, it also reveals the tenuousness of the transitional narrative. The narrative rests upon the submergence of lived experience or at least some normative justification of that experience, as anything else would complicate the imperatives of "progress" and modernization. In the nineteenth century, narratives of "transition" also lent themselves to characterizations that supported the clarity of moving forward from slavery. In nineteenth-century Brazil, various factions saw Chinese labor as constituting the "step forward" from slavery to postslavery. Jeffrey Lesser has noted that rationales included those by "progressive plantation owners who saw the end of slavery approaching and looked simply to replace African slaves with another servile group, abolitionists convinced that Chinese contract labor would be a step forward on the path to full wage labor, and still others who fervently believed that Chinese workers had some inherited ability as agricultural laborers and would help make Brazil a more competitive player in the world market."[4]

Many critiques have been forwarded that implicitly or explicitly complicate a transition narrative. Some directly address Asians in the Americas, such as critiques by Dale Tomich, Rebecca Scott, and Gary Okihiro. In a critique of Moreno, Tomich argues that linear narratives of transition obscure the complex integration of world economy and reproduce a simplified dualism of slave labor and modern technological labor. Tomich also takes issue with the assumptions of African labor as "unskilled" and Chinese labor as "skilled," noting the essentialist undertones of defining racialized labor. He considers "the ways in which the opposed elements of capitalist modernity and slave labor are constitutive of one another."[5] In a study of slavery and abolition in Cuba, Rebecca Scott also disturbs entrenched categorizations of slave versus free labor and notes the underlying racism in assumptions regarding internal contradictions between advanced technology and slavery.[6] "Under the circumstances," she argues, "it is difficult to see in what way the economic motivations of planter and Chinese contract laborer, in their work relations, would have been substantially different from those of master and slave. If they were not substantially different, this casts doubt on the idea that juridically "free" workers—in this case the Chinese—were essential to mechanization. Indeed, many of the Chinese were not employed with machinery at all but were used as agricultural workers, performing precisely the same tasks as slaves."[7] She further notes that while "some of the Chinese became efficient workers is testimony to their own sense of order and hope for full freedom, combined with the effects of coercion, it was not inherent in their fictitious intermediate legal status, which often allowed them to be systematically reduced to virtual slavery. It would thus be misleading to place great weight on their formal status as wage laborers in an explanation of how they could help plantations mechanize."[8] Tomich and Scott point out the theoretical and methodological problems precipitated by ideological rigidities inherent in narrations of national and liberal progress. Though not examining sugar economies specifically, Gary Okihiro critiques representations of Asians-as-intermediates in a related context, in his examination of global histories of "East-West" binaries. He points out the ideological bases carried over several centuries in the constructions of Asians "as intermediate, not Black and not White, yet bearing resemblances to both the 'savage' African and the 'civilized' European."[9]

The three critiques—one of world systems, one of slavery and abolition, and another of global race discourses—help illuminate the stakes for a reading of Chinese coolie testimonies, with recognition that modern interpretations of Chinese migration speak directly to its ideological significance in liberal teleologies and theories of race and emancipation. The most thorough critique and historiography regarding Cuba's Chinese coolie labor comes via Cuban scholar Juan Pérez de la Riva, whose extensive studies of this subject and of African slavery conclude that ideologies of colonial slavery, the system of social legislation, and ingrained practices of sugar elites overtly colluded to coerce contract labor into a system of enslavement in perpetuity.[10] A "transition" in Pérez de la Riva's work emerges as a further extension of slavery. Scott arrives to a related though less unequivocal conclusion via different arguments, by noting that contract labor did not *necessarily* shorten the course to abolition. Scott also notes the resilience of slavery as a system with mixed and complementary labor forms, such as indenture.[11] Pérez de la Riva's examination of Cuba's legal codes, along with the similar studies of Denise Helly and Juan Hui Huang in this regard, offers a view of the structural and regulatory forces behind what would be called a "transition" from slavery to wage labor. In separate analyses, they similarly concluded that the Chinese were installed under codes that explicitly removed their civil rights and attempted to meld contract labor to slavery ideology. Pérez de la Riva points to the overall spirit of slavery that dominated the legislation or "*el espíritu esclavista que predomina en la legislación.*"[12] Comparing the slave codes and the Spanish regulations for Chinese, he emphasized that while Chinese were cast as free persons, or "*hombre libre,*" under contract, the legislation "effectively reduced the Chinese to perpetual bondage," or "*todo eso equivalía a reducer a los chinos a una esclavitud perpetua.*"[13] Juan Huang Hui also came to a similar conclusion with an analysis of Spanish legislation and notes that regulations for Chinese coolies were equivalent in substance to those applied to African slaves. Huang Hui's position concurs with observations of Roberto Mesa, who noted the similarities between the legislation regarding the Chinese laborer of Cuba in 1860 and legislation for African slaves in 1842.[14]

The Chinese codes included laws that required permission from the owner for coolies to marry, laws that designated the status of any children of a coolie to be inherited from that of the mother (thus the child of a coolie or slave mother would be born into bondage), laws that denied freedom to Chinese who completed their contracts or who arrived after 1860, with the latter laws being framed as "recontracting" regulations. The recontracting system emerged as one of the main preoccupations and themes in the coolie testimonies and presents a challenge to conceptual and philosophical arguments of freedom. I argue that these themes of the coolie testimonies concern a peculiar and efficacious perversion of the contract institution, producing "consent" based upon potentialities of "future" freedom in the context of a racialized social contract (see Chapter 3).

First, what were the conditions of "transition" for the Chinese and how is this significant to our present narratives of race and global labor? The first part of the question occupies us here, though it is a question that is necessarily contextualized by multinational, multiethnic, and transnational histories. What follows then is a situating of Chinese coolies in historical contexts, without which it would be impossible to understand how coolies' self-representations were and continue to be located.

THE EARLY EXPERIMENTS

Before mass Asian labor arrived on the coasts of North America and Hawaii, experiments with and the importation of Asian labor had occurred in colonies in Asia and would eventually would reach the Caribbean and Latin America. During the 1620s, Jan Pieterzoon Coen, governor of the Dutch East Indies (Indonesia), already considered acquiring Chinese for the Indies: "No people in the world can do us better service than the Chinese. It is requisite by this present monsoon to send another fleet to visit the coast of China and take prisoners as many men, women, and children as possible. . . ."[15] Later in 1662, Jan van Riebeeck, who founded "Cape Colony" of the Cape of Good Hope (South Africa), wrote to Dutch authorities that he wanted Chinese labor sent.[16] In the 1800s, however, Chinese labor began being exported in sustained efforts. Chinese labor arrived in the colonial Malay Peninsula, and by the mid-1800s the Chinese were the largest ethnic group of the former British colony of Singapore. In 1806 the Chinese were brought to labor in the Caribbean, with an early experimental group of 192 Chinese taken to Trinidad. This experiment did not take root, as only twenty to thirty of them stayed on into the 1820s.[17] In 1810 several hundred Chinese were brought to Portuguese Brazil to grow tea. Although for various political reasons in Brazil, a consistent Chinese migration "program" did not materialize.[18] In 1838, however, the British experiment to bring Chinese to the Caribbean took shape and lasted until the last shipments of Chinese labor came to the West Indies in the 1880s. Significantly, while mobilizing to abolish the transatlantic slave trade, the British were establishing themselves as dominant traffickers of Indian and Chinese coolies. The Chinese appeared in the West Indies in addition to a large majority of Indian coolies going to the West Indies, while British colonial control over India was consolidating. (The British East India Company arrived in India in 1784, and in 1858 Britain asserted official political dominion over India.) Following the British example, the French brought Chinese to the French Caribbean, though in markedly smaller numbers. During the nineteenth century, the traffic in Chinese labor to the Americas included destinations such as Cuba, Peru, Guyana, Trinidad, Jamaica, Panama, Mexico, Costa Rica, and Brazil. The traffic in Indian labor to the Americas, which extended into the early twentieth century, was directed to Guyana, Trinidad, and Jamaica, as well as to the islands of St. Croix, Guadeloupe, Martinique, St. Lucia, St. Vincent, Grenada, and Tobago.

During the same period that the initial "experiment" began in Trinidad, the British Empire, through its navy, began imposing a unilateral embargo on the transatlantic transport of African slaves in 1809. This embargo became more formal when England and Spain signed a treaty in 1817 aimed at abolishing the slave trade.[19] The British suppression of the transatlantic African slave trade did not fully deny Spanish access to African slaves, but it continued to force traders toward more clandestine methods, which drove up the purchase price of slaves. The increased purchase price of African slaves pushed Cuban sugar planters to search for alternate sources of labor and forced the Cuban planters to confront a fundamental production problem of cost. Despite increases in the production of sugar and their increased prosperity, Cuban planters were continually beset by the challenge of lowering their labor costs to remain competitive in world commodities markets. Slave imports dropped from 10,000 Africans in 1844 to 1,300 in 1845, and then to 1,000 in 1847—a 90 percent drop in the importation of African slaves. It was in the mid-1800s that the European and American powers undertook massive coolie trading to the Americas and to Africa. During this nadir in 1847, the intensive trafficking of Chinese coolies to Cuba began, and two years later, there would be coolie trafficking to Peru. For the next thirty years, just under a quarter million Chinese would be taken to Cuba and Peru as part of the coolie trade. There were 100,000 coolies taken aboard ships to Peru and 142,000 to Cuba, though with a mortality rate of 12 percent (a higher rate than the African slave trade) fewer actually landed. These numbers account only for those who were documented, with some studies indicating several thousand more shipped as contraband.[20] In the case of Cuba, coolies were directly installed into a social and economic system *where slavery had not been abolished*. In fact, African slave importation to Cuba *increased* during the coolie period, complicating any argument that the increased need for contract labor is predicated upon the absence of slave labor. When coolies were introduced to Cuba in 1847, slave importation had indeed reached a nadir. Yet as coolie imports commenced and increased after 1847, slave imports *also* greatly increased, with yearly as high as 30,473 in 1859 alone and continued highs in the 1860s.[21] The coolie was not simply a "replacement" for the slave. Coolie and slave economies were clearly concomitant and coproductive.

CHINESE AND INDIAN COOLIE LABOR

The history of the Americas, with its Spanish, English, French, and American colonial legacies, and the distinct histories of indigenous peoples, cannot be homogenized. Likewise, the subject of mass bonded labor in the Americas—in this case, both East Indian and Chinese—cannot be homogenized and oversimplified.[22] The experiments and sustained migrations of Asian labor involved multinational and multiethnic histories. For example, the conditions and types of coolie labor in nearby Jamaica, Guyana, or Trinidad, compared to Cuba or Peru, were not the same. What emerges is a widely varied picture of what "coolie" and "indenture" mean. The term coolie generalizes Asian laborers in a spectrum of ethnic cultures, histories, material conditions, and political contexts. Coolie labor was utilized not only in the Americas but also in other parts of the world, such as Mauritius, Australia, Fiji, and the former colonies of Malaysia and Singapore. The coolie trade was a global one, with Chinese and Indian labor sent to all regions of the world, with overlapping colonial trajectories of political economies and imaginaries, enmeshed in a world system of capital flows. An example of this overlapping is when Spain proposed importing time-expired Indian coolies from the British colonies of the West Indies to the Spanish colony of Cuba. This was rejected by the British for a host of reasons. Still, the fact that this idea was proposed and debated is an example of the naturalized linking of Asian subjects/subjection in colonial imaginaries and economies.[23] In some instances Chinese and Indians did meet on the same grounds, such as they did in South Africa. Great Britain imported 64,000 Chinese coolies to work the Transvaal gold mines in South Africa in 1904. The ensuing solidarity of Chinese labor with Indian labor, though still formulated along ethnic lines, led to a shared movement of Chinese-Indian passive resistance led by Leung Quinn and Mahatma Gandhi, who was in South Africa during this period.[24] Chinese and Indian labor also overlapped in parts of Caribbean, such as in Guyana and Trinidad. However, Indians comprised a significantly larger number of the coolies imported to the British colonies, with many also being sent to the French colonies. The Chinese were also sent to the British and French colonies, but were mostly sent to the Spanish colonies. The British dominated the Indian coolie trade, but American, French, Spanish, and Portuguese involvement, on the other hand, was most prominent in the Chinese coolie trade.

The contrasts between the Chinese and Indian coolie trades arise partly due to the demarcations of empire, labor economy, and local developments in emigration. While the British dominated the Indian coolie trade, the British, Americans, French, Spanish, Portuguese, and Dutch led in the Chinese coolie trade.[25] Different imperial agendas, systems of migration, and of course, cultural and local politics, created distinct coolie systems. Major differences arose in routes and destinations, labor conditions, transport economics, "contract" constructions and administration, and gender ratios. Whereas Chinese coolie ships took 99 percent males, Indian coolie ships, by contrast, brought men, women, married couples, children, and families. These different gender characteristics led to a host of social and cultural developments that mark the Chinese and Indian diasporic patterns as clearly distinct when examining the descendant generations of Chinese in Cuba versus, for example, those of East Indians in Guyana. The differentiation between Chinese and Indian coolie systems, however, does *not* easily correlate to normative judgments as to which system was necessarily "better or worse." The "better or worse" comparison incurs simplistic presumptions of what constitutes "force" and "coercion." Both the oppressive force of the British colonial system in the West Indies and that of the Spanish colonial system in Cuba emerged in particularized forms of coercion and were subject to contestation by laborers in bondage (and in some instances, were challenged by abolitionists). In some cases, narratives regarding Indian coolie trade revealed similarities with the Chinese coolie trade, wherein rationalized codes such as "contract," "indenture," "law," and "emigrant" were semantics for regularized systems of deception and fraud.

Narratives of the Indian passage reveal this kind of deception from the outset. In 1858 Captain and Mrs. Swinton brought the coolie ship *Salsette* from Calcutta to Trinidad and kept a journal. Their journal recorded the particulars of this voyage, during which over half of the 324 coolies died from disease and poor diet. When investigated, the Captain could not be reproached, as he unflaggingly observed British "codes" of safe passage during the voyage. Yet "regulations" did not necessarily translate to more humane conditions. Furthermore, Mrs. Swinton wrote that most of those aboard were lured with inflated "fine promises" and did not truly "know where they were going or what is to be their occupation." In her words, the Indian coolies were "emigrants" who "were entrapped."[26] The rationalized language of willing "emigrants" dissembles when assumptions of foreknowledge and consent are contradicted by practices of entrapment. The experience of passage was also a gendered one. In one example of the passage experience, colonial court documents reveal that a woman called "Maharani" died after being raped by the crew. Verene Shepherd points out that rape was just one of many exploitative practices that were regular features of the coolie passage.[27] On land, investigations, such as a commission (1870) investigation in Guyana, exposed contradictions and brutalities in the indenture system—a system designed to disempower Indian laborers supposedly "protected" by contracts and regulations. These inquiries, on the other hand, did not necessarily produce or lead to ameliorative steps, or did so with the effect of deferring or managing conflict.[28]

Indenture conditions changed over time and under various colonial offices. Practices and regulations were implemented, ignored, or revised. They were subject to conflicting interpretations, vested interests, and political debates. Chinese and Indian laborers confronted their predicaments with various means of resistance, such as withholding labor, desertion, violent retribution, organized strikes, and formal challenges to juridical bodies. Still, generalized understandings of indenture mask ironies and contradictions, and comparisons of Chinese and Indian indenture are useful but must be specified and contextual. While it is tempting to draw a broad equivalency among "Asian" labor histories, Chinese and Indian indentured migrations were rooted in cultural and political circumstances that reveal similarities as well as important differences. Besides the baseline comparative analysis of free and coerced Asian migration to the Americas by Walton Look Lai, a sustained comparative study of indenture is sorely needed in this respect.[29]

Types of labor also led to unique specificities of coolie experience. In Peru, for example, Chinese coolies labored on plantations and on mammoth mountains of Peruvian guano, contributing to the hugely profitable fertilizer market of which the Americans and others partook. As shippers waited in the harbor for their guano loads, Chinese coolies slaved amid poisonous fumes. As one American consul wrote: "I have been informed by American Captains, trading to the Chincha and Guañapa Islands that many of them too weak to stand up are compelled to work on their knees picking the small stones out of the guano, and when their hands become sore from the constant use of the wheelbarrow it is strapped upon their shoulders, and in that way they are compelled to fulfill their daily task . . ."[30] The same consul went on to describe the "constant employment of guards" to thwart the repeated suicide attempts of enslaved coolies.[31] For coolies of Peru, the struggle became a grim battle for daily survival that was also contextualized by the particular kind of labor that they were forced to undertake. While it is certainly possible and fruitful to compare Cuban and Peruvian coolie histories and experiences, this author cautions against homogenizing or occluding distinct national histories and conditions (Cuban history and Peruvian history) via a study of diaspora (Chinese). With an enduring politics of indigenousness and the legacy of Simón Bolívar, Peru had distinct conditions of race, labor, and postslavery politics and economy. Peru had its own unique relations to Spain, China, and South America (especially Bolivia, Chile, and Ecuador). Peru declared its independence from Spain in 1821, finally ousted colonial control in 1824, and declared the abolition of slavery in 1854. Yet Peru fought Spain again in 1863–66 and was deeply embroiled in struggles with and against its South American neighbors. Cuba underwent thirty years of war and became independent from Spain in 1898, but then came formally under American occupation in 1899. Cuba would not end slavery until the 1880s. Periodizing is not prescriptive of lived conditions; but the sequence of events and the local histories of nationalist projects had bearing upon the particular politics of race and labor in each location.

The type of coolie system and the conditions of labor in Cuba raise challenging questions, with features of hypermobility (with coolies often having several masters) and state ownership (with widespread use of coolies in public works and prison works), operating in the context of racial hierarchy in a slavery system (with contract coolies under the control of black overseers). Theoretical and philosophical questions arise regarding the hybrid marrying of contract and slavery. Cuba's Chinese coolies constitute a unique history of a mass movement of resistant labor being forcibly shipped to Cuba where slavery had not yet been abolished. Slavery did not expire until 1886 in Cuba, which was over forty years after the arrival of the Chinese. Cuba was second to last in abolishing slavery in the Western hemisphere, with Brazil ending slavery in 1888. Elsewhere, in Jamaica and Trinidad for example, coolie labor was installed after slavery had been abolished.[32] The fact that Chinese coolies arrived in the midst of an ongoing slavery system greatly affected their lived experience and motivated their considerable role as insurgents in the Cuban war for independence. Chinese coolies arrived when the politics of economy and labor and the politics of class and race converged during a critical period of history: the overlapping and then final dismantling of African slavery, the war for independence, and the beginnings of a Cuban nation.

CHINESE COOLIES AND "TEA WITH SUGAR"

On the Spanish side, coolie labor was desirable because of economic and production demands, but there were other considerations that made it attractive as well. While the higher costs of African slavery were the bane of planters' daily concerns, at the same time, the anxiety of the planter class grew as the numbers of Africans grew. As the African presence increased in Cuba, alarmist sentiments arose among resident whites concerning the color disparity. By 1841 the white population was in the minority.[33] The racialized revolution in French colonial Haiti that led to the overthrow of the white elite provided lessons to the Cuban landowning class. The spectre of another Haiti-like revolution, one led by a black majority population, never seemed far away. Planters thought that using coolie labor might help alleviate multiple problems, with the most attractive factor being the low cost and widespread availability of Chinese labor. The control of costs and the control of racial labor became dual concerns.

Before the Haitian Revolution (1791–1805), Haiti was the primary producer of sugar for the world market. Cuba seized the lead in sugar production after Haiti and other competing sugar producers emancipated slaves (or the slaves freed themselves) and competitors' sugar production dropped. The following table reflects changes in Haitian and Santo Domingan sugar production before and after the Haitian Revolution. After the Haitian slave revolt and revolution, European states imposed a punitive embargo on Haitian sugar, driving Haiti out of the sugar market. In 1791 Haiti's sugar production had reached 78,696 tons. After the revolution, sugar production steadily dwindled, down to a half ton in 1835.[34] With Haiti displaced, the colonized territories of Jamaica, Brazil, Cuba, and Puerto Rico rose in prominence.[35] At first, Cuban sugar production began modestly. During the 1780s Cuba produced only 18,000 tons of sugar per year. Sugar production in Cuba began in earnest in 1798.[36] The 1830s, however, revealed the flourishing of the sugar economy. During the mid-1830s, Cuba first obtained parity with Jamaica as a sugar producer and then surpassed Jamaica when that country emancipated its African slaves during the late 1830s.[37] The emancipation of Jamaican slaves drove up labor costs for Jamaican planters, placing them at a comparative disadvantage with Cuba's sugar planters, who still maintained access to African slave labor at this time. Because of its labor cost advantages, Cuba quickly outpaced Jamaica in sugar production. By the 1840s Cuba had become the preeminent producer of sugar in the world (161,000 tons), accounting for 21 percent of world production—outdistancing Jamaica, Brazil, and Puerto Rico. From the 1840s to the 1870s Cuba leapt forward with even more phenomenal growth precisely during *the period when Chinese coolies were introduced and installed on Cuban sugar plantations.* In 1830 Cuba produced 105,000 tons of sugar. Forty years later, Cuba produced almost seven times more sugar (703,000 tons) while its closest competitors produced approximately 100,000 tons. By this time, Cuban sugar accounted for 41 percent

TABLE 1.1   SUGAR PRODUCTION FIGURES FOR JAMAICA, BRAZIL, CUBA, AND PUERTO RICO (TONS)

	CUBA	PUERTO RICO	JAMAICA	BRAZIL
1830	105,000	20,000	69,000	83,000
1840	161,000	36,500	26,500	82,000
1850	295,000	50,000	29,000	110,000
1860	429,000	58,000	26,000	57,000
1870	703,000	105,000	24,500	101,500

Sources: Noel Deerr, *The History of Sugar, I* (London:Chapman and Hall, 1949), 112, 126, 131, 199; Alan Dye, *Cuban Sugar in the Age of Mass Production* (Stanford: Stanford University Press, 1998), 27; Manuel Moreno Fraginals, *El ingenio: complejo económico social cubano del azúcar,* 3 vols. (Habana: Ciencias Sociales, 1978), 3:36, 37; and Andrés Ramos Mattei, *La hacienda azucarera: Su crecimiento y crisis en Puerto Rico* (San Juan: CEREP, 1981), 33.

of world output.[38] During this period, Cuba used a substantial coolie system grafted onto a continuing slavery system that involved clandestine slave importation.

During this period, the British consumed approximately one third of the world's sugar and also were the dominant Western consumers of tea. It is a likely assumption that these two facts are linked, as the British always consumed their tea with sugar. As Sidney Mintz has traced in an examination of sugar in modern history, sugar was an item of mass consumption, and one of its major uses was for sweetening tea.[39] With some irony, the British predilection for tea and sugar led to a worldwide movement in capital and labor. "Tea with sugar" instigated a wide circle of capital flows and trade imbalances of the era, and involved competition over labor as well. Spanish Cuba benefited from Britain's "opening up" of a Chinese labor market. At the same time, Spanish Cuba chafed under British restrictions against African labor. While the British controlled access to a worldwide Asian coolie market, they implemented measures against the African slave trade in international waters. This dual approach enabled British maneuverings over labor and economy, ultimately affecting the price of labor. Denise Helly situates the Chinese coolie trade as a confluence and siting of global rivalries and alignments involving European nations, the United States, Africa, and China, and the control of slave and coolie labors, with a particular rivalry taking place between Britain and Spain in relation to Cuba and sugar.[40]

While Britain occupied a major role in the coolie trade (they began withdrawing from coolie trafficking to Cuba in 1858), they were not the only colonial interests involved.[41] The ease of introducing Chinese coolie trafficking into the world system was due to multicolonial access, domestic conditions, and control of labor migration. Beginning in the 1840s, Britain and its allies effectively "opened" a valuable labor market in southern China. Losing the Opium War and the subsequent Arrow War, China opened twelve major ports to the British, French, and American settlements and handed over Hong Kong to the British. One result of the wars was deregulation of Chinese emigration. From 1840 to 1875 approximately one million Chinese left Guangdong province (southern China) as part of Western labor traffic (not including numbers from other provinces), with just under a quarter million going to Cuba and Peru.[42]

COOLIES ON SHIPS AND THE PASSAGE: INTERNATIONAL TRAFFIC AND THE PASSAGE "UNDER THE LID OF HADES"

Early in their considerations, Cuban planters had discussed the immigration of free whites from Europe. When free white laborers from Europe proved unwilling to work in sugarcane fields, however, Cuban landowners opted to import labor from China. The Cuban sugar elite began seriously discussing the need to import Chinese laborers from British-controlled ports in 1844.[43] Initially, the Spanish bought Chinese coolies through British traffickers. Eventually, a multinational network emerged, consisting of shipping companies and agents, businesses, prominent families, and governing agencies. These varied entities turned to the trafficking of coolies and collaborated to realize enormous profits, while continuing to purchase—with increased difficulty and costs—African slaves from the complicated, "clandestine" African slave trade. The network of coolie brokers, shippers, buyers, and investors crossed lines of colonial empires, including moneyed interests of the British, Americans, Portuguese, French, as well as the Spanish Cubans. While original financing for this labor-acquisition venture originated in Cuba, supplemental financing came from a multinational network of banks and firms in New York, Boston, London, Paris, Amsterdam, and Liverpool.[44] Participating commercial interests were the same as those that financed the African slave trade.[45]

Therefore, the passage of slavery and "voluntary" contract labor were underwritten by similar sources and ensconced financial relationships. To launch the coolie trade in Cuba, Cuban planters used a company called the Real Junta de Fomento y Colonización. The Real Junta de Fomento then engaged Julieta y Cia of London, headed by cousins Julián Zulueta and Pedro Zulueta, who devised the plan to transport coolies from China to Cuba. Pedro was the son of the London-based banker/slave trader/planter Pedro Juan Zulueta de Ceballos who amassed such a great fortune that he died the wealthiest man in the entire Spanish empire. The aligned machinery of private ownership and colonial power was exemplified in the appointment of Julian de Zulueta as Mayor of Havana during the coolie era. Zulueta headed the most powerful Cuban family in the mid-nineteenth century, with a fortune built upon sugar plantations and railways, shipping and ports, and all industries fed upon slave and coolie labor. Not surprisingly, the Zuluetas were infamous slave traders. At one point, Pedro Zulueta was accused, tried, but acquitted of slave trading in London in October 1843.[46] Scheming to augment slave labor, the Zuluetas initiated the coolie trade to Cuba in 1847 and brought in the first coolie shipment, under the auspices of Zulueta & Co. of London and the Junta de Fomento. With representatives and offices in London, Liverpool, Spain, China, and Cuba, the powers of family and state were consolidated in global empires of political economy. The two main labor agents based in Asia were Fernando Aguirre based in Manila and a Mr. Tait based in Amoy (Xiamen).[47] The Zuluetas engaged Tait and Company and Syme Muir and Company, both based in Amoy (Xiamen) and Guangdong, to obtain the first set of Chinese coolies to be shipped to Cuba.[48] After first working with Aguirre and Tait, the Cubans replaced them in 1855 with their own labor agents and opened their own offices for this trade in Havana, London, Manila, Macao, and Amoy (Xiamen).

It was entirely plausible for coolie traffickers to criticize black slavery and condemn the coolie traffic while engaging in one or both of these activities. Nicolás Tanco Armero exemplified this kind of paradox, as he made public claims under the mantel of modern liberal tradition, however questionable his commitments. Tanco, originally from a prominent Colombian family, published an article condemning the coolie traffic, and he also published a book recounting his travels, with complete omission of the coolie trade or his role in it.[49] He further criticized black slavery and its inequalities, characterizing it as the inheritance of a backwards Spain left to an emergent modern *criollo* nation.[50] Tanco, partnered with Francisco Abellá Raldiris, was the most notorious of the coolie traffickers. From 1855 to 1873 Tanco and his partner oversaw the buying, selling, and exportation of over 100,000 Chinese coolies to the new world.[51] Most of the prominent slaveholding families on the island (including the Zulueta, Torices, Drake, Aldama, O'Donnell, Diago, Pedroso, Sotomayor, Baró, Ferrán, Colomé, Ibáñez, Pulido, Moré, Alfonso, Almendares, Francisco, and Morales families) were involved in the coolie trade.[52] Many of them operated plantations in Matanzas, the central part of Cuba, where the most coolies were sent. The finance and insurance firm La Alianza entered the coolie trade in 1859, providing much of the essential financing for Chinese coolie importation. La Alianza then formed a powerful alliance with the Empresa de Colonización (owned by Rafael Rodriguez Torices, Marcial Dupierris, Antonio Ferrán, and Juan A. Colomé). Together, these two firms (La Alianza and the Empresa de Colonización) dominated the trade along with the Zuluetas. Others in the Cuban sugar planting elite were heavily involved in Chinese coolie trafficking. Among those who were prominent in this "trade" were the firms (and families) of Villoldo, Wardrop y Cía, Pereda Machado y Cía, Don Santiago Drake y Cía, José Maria Morales y Cía, and du Pierris y Cía.[53]

On June 3, 1847, the ship *Oquendo* arrived in Havana after 131 days at sea. Its cargo hold contained 212 Chinese men. Upon disembarkation, they were sold for 170 pesos per head to their new masters, Cuban landowners.[54] This cargo of Chinese, brokered by British traffickers and Spanish Cuban buyers, constituted the first significant trafficking of coolies to Cuba. According to several sources, 124,873 to 150,000 Chinese coolies arrived in Havana on 342 ships from 1847–1873.[55] The money to be made was considerable. O'Kelly, the *New York Herald* correspondent, observed: "The 900 human beings brought to the market in the ship I visited were worth some $450,000 to the importers; and, as they had cost originally less than $50,000, the anonymous society (corporation) had some $400,000 as a result of the voyage to meet expenses. Never in the palmiest days of the African trade were such tremendous profits realized. . . ."[56] Travel writer Henry Murray observed speculation by mercantile houses and individuals on the coolie trade driven by incredible profits.[57] A ship of 500 coolies required an average investment of 30,000–50,000 pesos but yielded

TABLE 1.2   AVERAGE PRICES FOR COOLIES AND SLAVES, 1847–1875

YEARS	AFRICAN SLAVES (PESOS)	CHINESE COOLIES (PESOS)
1845–1850	335	125
1851–1855	410	150
1855–1860	580	370
1861–1865	585	310
1866–1870	450	410
1871–1875	715	420

Sources: Laird W. Bergad, Fe Iglesias Garcia, and Maria del Carmen Barcia, *The Cuban Slave Market, 1790–1880* (Cambridge: Cambridge University Press, 1995), 162–73; Du Harthy, "Une Campaigne dans l'extreme Orient" in *Revue des Deux Mondes,* T. 66, 1866, 417; J. Pérez de la Riva, "Aspectos económicos del tráfico de culíes chinos a Cuba, 1853–1874," 269; E. Phillip Leveen, "A Quantitative Analysis of the Impact of British Suppression Policies on the Volume of the Nineteenth Century Atlantic Slave Trade," in *Race and Slavery in the Western Hemisphere; Quantitative Studies*, eds. Stanley I. Engerman and Eugene D. Genovese (Princeton: Princeton University Press, 1975), 56 (51–81).

an average of 100,000–120,000 pesos, resulting in fantastic gains at the time.[58] Even with the costs and overhead of coolie procurement, coolie mortality, coolie shipping, and the overall profit from coolie sales to Cuba was tremendous, amounting to some 80 million pesos.[59] Furthermore, Murray argued that in addition to coolie labor, this influx of liquid capital was also a factor in helping to industrialize the Cuban economy. The coolie market took on wild characteristics, with investors taking advantage of this newest commodity. The financing of the slave and coolie trades was made possible by profits from the sale of sugar. Although sugar prices fluctuated wildly from 1855 to 1857, prices steadily climbed in the 1860s and 1870s, during the height of coolie trafficking.

In comparative cost terms, Chinese coolies were simply much less costly than African slaves. In crude terms, the coolies were easier to procure and cheaper to purchase, making them an enormously profitable commodities. Furthermore, they could be brought in as indentured laborers, but eventually used as slaves. The table above tracks the difference in prices between African slaves and Chinese coolies from 1847–75. As production at the sugar plantations and *ingenios* increased during this period, the demand for labor intensified, and the importation of African slaves resumed after initially having fallen. With the coerced labor of both coolies and slaves, the Cuban sugar economy boomed.

The "transition" narrative of slave to wage labor is one of great human cost. The Chinese coolie passage incurred a markedly higher mortality rate than the African slave passage, as ethnographer Jesus Guanche asserts.[60] The journey stretched from four to eight months. The British ship *Panama* provided an especially sobering example of the Chinese coolie middle passage to the harsh "new world": Of 803 coolies taken aboard, only 480 survived. The American ship *Challenger* took 915 coolies on board, but only 620 survived. These few facts merely scratch the surface of the Chinese coolie period in Cuba, which was a penetrating history of human loss for some and a time of profit for others. Approximately 16,400 Chinese coolies were documented as having died on European and American coolie ships to Cuba during a twenty-six-year period[61] with some ships formerly used as African slave ships.[62] Mortality rates hovered around 12–30 percent while sometimes reaching as high as 50 percent, which was the case of the Portuguese ship *Cors* in 1857. Rebellions, crew assassinations, suicides, thirst, suffocation, and sickness occurred upon the "devil ships," as the Chinese called them.[63] Writer Alexander Laing called the Chinese coolie passage "a Dantean dream: it had become the lid of Hades, and the damned were below . . ."[64] A table of the mortality rates for coolies from 1847–73 follows.

Names of coolie ships reflected the legacy of the African trade, such as *Africano* and *Mauritius.* Still others bore incongruous, and in retrospect, ironic names such as *Dreams* and *Hope* (British ships), and *Live Yankees* and *Wandering Jew* (North American ships).[65] Ships hailed from twelve European states (England, Spain, France, Denmark, Holland, Portugal, Germany, Austria, Italy, Norway, Russia, Belgium) and the United States. The six primary shippers of Chinese coolies (the French, Spanish, British, Americans, Portuguese, and Dutch) were the same top six leaders in the trafficking of African slaves.[66] The French and Spanish led in total numbers of coolies transported to Cuba and in numbers of coolie ships, though in the first half of the trade, the British and Americans led the trafficking, until they discontinued the practice.

Resistance and rebellion occurred on ships because methods of procuring coolies primarily involved kidnapping by force and deceiving individuals to board ships—then entrapping them. An overwhelming majority of Chinese coolies declared that "Spanish vessels come to China, and suborning the vicious of our countrymen, by their aid carry away full cargoes

TABLE 1.3   CHINESE BROUGHT TO CUBA, 1847–73

	NO. SHIPS	TONNAGE	CHINESE EMBARKED	CHINESE DIED	CHINESE LANDED	% DEATHS
1847	2	979	612	41	571	6.7
1853	15	8,349	5,150	843	4,307	16.4
1854	4	2,375	1,750	39	1,711	2.2
1855	6	6,544	3,130	145	2,985	4.6
1856	15	10,677	6,152	1,182	4,970	19.2
1857	28	18,940	10,101	1,554	8,547	15.4
1858	33	32,842	16,411	3,027	13,384	18.4
1859	16	13,828	8,539	1,332	7,207	15.6
1860	17	15,104	7,227	1,008	6,219	13.9
1861	16	15,919	7,212	290	6,922	4.0
1862	1	759	400	56	344	14.0
1863	3	2,077	1,045	94	951	9.0
1864	7	5,513	2,664	532	2,132	20.0
1865	20	12,769	6,810	407	6,403	6.0
1866	43	24,187	14,169	1,126	13,043	7.9
1867	42	26,449	15,661	1,247	14,414	8.0
1868	21	15,265	8,400	732	7,668	8.7
1869	19	13,692	7,340	1,475	5,865	20.1
1870	3	2,305	1,312	63	1,249	4.8
1871	5	2,820	1,827	178	1,649	9.7
1872	20	12,886	8,914	766	8,148	8.6
1873	6	4,786	3,330	209	3,121	6.3
Total	342	249,065	138,156	16,346	121,810	11.8

Source: Report of British Consulate General, Havana, September 1, 1873. (The table does not include figures through 1874.)

TABLE 1.4   CHINESE IMPORTED TO CUBA BY NATIONALITY OF CARRIER, 1847–73

	NO. SHIPS	TONNAGE	CHINESE EMBARKED	CHINESE LANDED	CHINESE DIED	% DEATHS
British	35	27,815	13,697	1,457	2,240	16.3
United States	34	40,576	18,206	16,419	1,787	9.8
Austrian	3	1,377	936	864	72	7.7
Belgian	3	2,482	1,199	1,182	17	1.4
Chilean	4	1,702	926	743	183	19.8
Danish	1	1,022	470	291	179	38.0
Dutch	19	14,906	8,113	7,132	981	12.1
French	104	64,664	38,540	33,795	4,745	12.3
German	8	4,207	2,176	1,932	244	11.2
Italian	5	5,586	2,832	2,505	327	11.2
Norwegian	5	2,296	1,366	1,104	262	19.2
Peruvian	6	4,979	2,609	1,999	610	23.4
Portugese	21	15,847	8,228	7,266	962	11.7
Russian	12	9,857	5,471	5,093	378	6.9
Spanish	78	47,604	31,356	28,085	3,271	10.4
Salvadoran	4	4,145	2,031	1,943	88	4.3
Total	342	249,065	138,156	121,810	16,346	11.8

Source: Report of British Consulate General, Havana, September 1, 1873. (The table does not include figures through 1874.)

of men."[67] Other candidates for coolie procurement included gullible young men who went to "recruitment agents" only later to discover that "we were not to be engaged as labourers but to be sold as slaves."[68] Numerous Chinese were so desperate to escape their fate that they committed suicide or jumped overboard. The forced passage and the later coercion of Chinese in Cuba are extensively recorded in *Report by the Commission Sent by China* (1876) and the coolie testimonies (see Chapter 2, "The Coolie Testimonies").

The unabated presence of coolie ships incensed the Chinese public, and rumors abounded that the white "barbarians" of Cuba not only abused the Chinese, but ate them as well (similar to African rumors of their fate during the slave trade). Beginning in 1858, the British began capitalizing on the popular outcry of southern Chinese against the coolie traffic to Cuba. In response, Chinese officials began executing Chinese "runners" who were collaborating with the trade to Cuba. The British eventually ceased their coolie trafficking to Cuba—a traffic that had significantly aided their rivals, the Spanish, in the world sugar economy. The British turned away Spanish coolie ships in Chinese ports and stopped sending British coolie ships to Cuba. While the demand for coolies in Cuba continued to rise, obtaining coolies was complicated by the new opposition to coolie traffic. As a result, coolies were smuggled out through the Portuguese and Spanish colonies of Macao and the Philippines, rather than from Hong Kong, Amoy (Xiamen), Swataw (Shantou), which were under British supervision. In 1859 records reveal this noticeable shift, with almost all ships departing from Macao. Coolie trafficking continued without apparent British participation—with ships hoisting different national flags. In 1865 the British publicly denounced the Spanish coolie traffickers for engaging in a coerced labor system.[69] Meanwhile, the British did not cease transporting Indian and Chinese coolies to their own colonial territories in the West Indies.

COOLIES ON AMERICAN SHIPS

By 1860 there were more Chinese in Latin America and the Caribbean than in North America.[70] American investors and American coolie shippers had much to do with that fact. In 1895 Senator Henry Cabot Lodge of Massachusetts proudly upheld the American record of expansion: "We have a record of conquest, colonization and expansion unequalled by any people in the Nineteenth Century. We are not about to be curbed now."[71] Lodge, a key figure in American political history, mapped a vision of "Americanism" as one of commerce, trade, and global dominance. This would be the age of "modern times," he noted. Those modern times had been underwritten by commerce and trade with Asia, and in fact, included American coolie trafficking. However, the Americans officially halted their Chinese coolie "trade" activities, though it would take an act of Congress that specifically banned the trading of Chinese coolies by American citizens on American vessels. This occurred only after a great amount of debate among vested parties and labor protectionists, and after protestations from American consular officials in China. The most vociferous critic was the U.S. Commissioner to China, Peter Parker, who demanded that the American government stop the trafficking.[72] The conflicted issue of "coolie labor" warranted mention in presidential addresses and Congressional debates during the late nineteenth and early twentieth centuries. With the mounting controversy, Congress enacted the Prohibition of Coolie Trade Act of 1862. Until that point, the Americans had taken the lead in Chinese coolie shipping, surpassing the British, Spanish, French, and Portuguese in the number of ships and coolies in the trade.[73]

The Asian laborer was a vexing figure for American politics: neither black nor white, Asian laborers were ostensibly voluntary yet involuntary. American politicians would engage in heated "coolie debates" against Chinese immigration to California, with anticoolie views stemming from labor platforms, nationalist politics, anti-Chinese sentiments, and paternalist arguments. The specter of Cuba and Peru served to liberalize American arguments, as it exposed the evils of coolie slavery in the "South" (Cuba, Peru, and elsewhere). The darker cousin of the Chinese coolie had been relegated to narratives of the Caribbean, Latin America, and South America—a constructing of the "Other." Still, plantation society of the American South became occupied with possibilities for Chinese labor, with the Caribbean Chinese coolies playing a significant part in the debates and in plantation cultural and economic logic. This has been elaborated in separate studies by Lucy Cohen, Matthew Guterl, Najia Aarim-Heriot, and most recently, Moon Jung Ho, who examines in depth the relation between the coolie debates and the events in Louisiana.[74] After the Civil War, some 145 Chinese coolies from Cuba and some 400 Chinese coolie laborers from China arrived in the New Orleans port between 1869 and 1870.[75] Cries of "coolie labor" sensationalized their presence.

Furthermore, the coolie's unique transnational history suggests an outlaw narrative of northern American modern identity, with the "North" actually having been the *proponent of* and participant in captive labor markets abroad, while hypocritically preparing for civil war to ban slavery within American borders. At stake is the recitation of an American North as exceptional and free, bolstered by the freely migrating Asian laborer that figures in contrast to the African slave (though with historiographic nuances made regarding the credit-ticket system to San Francisco and contract system to Hawaii).[76] In a little-known but detailed dissertation on the Chinese coolie traffic to Cuba (1953), Marshall K. Powers was the first to query what I have called an outlaw narrative of northern liberalism. He wrote, "A careful study of the reports of the American consuls in the treaty ports of China involved in the coolie traffic indicates a large number of American vessels of Boston and other New English registry, active in the Chinese coolie trade. The names of the owners correspond to the names common in the literature of the abolitionist movement in the pre–Civil War period. The evidence is purely circumstantial; however, the fascinating possibility that at least a portion of the financial reserve of the abolitionist movement came from profits earned in the coolie traffic, present an intriguing historical paradox."[77] Powers's query and period references to Northeastern participation in captive coolie traffic disturb a legend of abolitionist liberalism and citizenry.[78] Coolie labor was transported, sold, and utilized by American interests in an expanding empire outside country borders. Coolie trafficking by American firms saw prominent families reaping profits from shipping coolies to Cuba and Peru. This would not be surprising given that Americans were also underwriting the Cuban plantation economy. Franklin Knight noted that "in Cuba, planters soon found themselves heavily indebted not only to merchants in Havana and Matanzas but also to the large consortiums in New York and Boston."[79] Family businesses flourished through the shipping of coolies, such as Howland and Aspinwall.[80] The substantial interests of American firms in coolie trafficking resulted in frequent consular dispatches and protracted Washington maneuverings over how to handle (or not handle) the issue.[81] Regarding American profiteering in the whole affair, historian of consular relations Eldon Griffin noted:

Certain leading American merchants along the Atlantic seaboard who were financially interested in the business were no less quick to assert their moral convictions, but lacking personal touch and administrative concern with the immediate vexations of the business, they were more hesitant than officials in the Orient to recognize the evils to which these convictions were applicable. Hampered by uncertainty and hesitation at home, American mercantile agents and shipmasters in China—quite apart from the quality of their individual ethics—were placed in an ambiguous position when compelled to choose between orders from their owners and the counsel of the official representatives of their country.[82]

Americans weighed their conscience on one hand and the lure of profits on the other, against a backdrop of American abolitionist politics. Traffic in coolies, added to the transport chain of Chinese goods and trade, seemed to be a coeval twin of such profit that it could not be ignored. Apparently "profits to owners and associates were considerable. It is not possible to isolate and total up the profits made by Americans in this international enterprise, in which there were many hidden factors, but figures show that it produced a large income."[83] American consul William Robertson, corresponding with the U.S. Secretary of State, recorded coolie ships arriving at Havana port and the ships' owners being registered in New York, Boston, and Connecticut. He went on to insert his own sentiments: "For my part, I assure you that I regret very much to see vessels under our flag engaged in such a traffic."[84] Later he would write, "There seems to be a rage at this time for speculating in Chinese; and from recent developments, the trade, which gives enormous profits, is engaging the attention of the first commercial houses and the largest capitalists of this city. Chinese are coming in fast . . ."[85]

In 1860 the congressional Committee on Commerce pointed out American involvement in the coolie trade to Cuba and Peru, stating:

It is a mortifying fact that up to the present time American shipmasters and northern owners are found willing to connect themselves with a trade in many of its features as barbarous as the African slave trade. In one respect it is more abhorrent to an honorable mind than that trade which the civilized world condemns as piracy. The captured African is not made to believe that he is changing his condition for the better; but the Asiatic coolie is trapped and deceived by false pretences of promised gain into the power of men who, having cheated him of freedom, enslave him for gain.[86]

While states in the Union made slave trafficking illegal within the states, an arena remained open for ownership and investment in activity undertaken in non-American ports.[87] With ambiguous laws regarding the "carriage of passengers in American vessels from one foreign port to another foreign port," consuls and citizens entered a gray area of international trafficking.[88] This legal loophole left an opening for American involvement in trafficking captive labor that seemed unthreatening to the domestic identity of American exceptionalism, until brought to a head in 1862.

American officials in foreign service expressed confusion over how to deal with American coolie traffickers, and they also revealed anxieties about the meanings of an American antislavery stance in the face of American involvement in what many saw as another form of slave trade. The question of race and color shadowed their thinking. Peter Parker appealed to abolish the trade on grounds of *humanity* while his successor William Reed appealed to abolish the trade in terms of *legal* precedents regarding the slave trade (though it would be a mistake to misconstrue Parker's and Reed's sentiments as a desire to curtail American empire). Reed's analysis circled around questions of race and *color*. Regarding Chinese coolies, Reed concluded that they were "people of color" and were treated as slaves, like African slaves. Reed referred to the Slave Trade Act of April 20, 1818. The purpose of the act was to curtail slave traffic to American ports. The penalties applied to citizens who transported "any negro or mulatto or person of color" for the purposes of slave labor:

> *Any citizen or citizens of the United States, or other persons resident within the jurisdiction of the same, shall, from and after the passage of this act, take on board, receive, or transport from any of the coasts or kingdoms of Africa, or from any other foreign kingdom, place or country, or from sea, any negro or mulatto or person of color, not being an inhabitant, nor held in service by the laws of either the State or Territories of the United States, in any ship, vessel, boat, or other water-craft,*

for the purpose of holding, selling, or otherwise disposing of such person as a slave, or to be held to service or labor . . . [89]

Reed argued that such laws applicable to the African slave trade should then apply to the transport of unfree Chinese laborers and defined Chinese as "persons of color." He wrote the following in 1858:

In the act of 1818 the words 'person of color' is used as distinguished from negro or mulatto. In the act of 15th May, 1820, the words 'person of color' are omitted. If, instead of the question arising on the modified color of the Chinese, it arose on a cargo of the black sepoys one meets in the streets of Hong Kong, or the Malays and Javanese of the Archipelago, there could be little doubt about it. They would be clearly within the act of Congress. The Chinese cooly, is to the sense at least, a person of color. As to the tenure of labor or service for which these poor people are destined there is still less question . . . The word by which the cooly is described in this ordinance [Spanish] is equivalent to 'laborer' in English, or it may mean 'imported laborer.' It does not mean 'free day laborer,' for which another term is used, or slave. They are imported under a contract for a term of years. They are the subject of transfer, with no volition of their own, and no provision is made for their return to their native country. To this time none have returned. All these elements combine to make the Chinese coolly a man of color, to be disposed of to be held to service in Cuba . . . I have thus considered the trade only in its relations to the laws of the United States.[90]

Reed's argument pointed to Chinese coolie traffic as "clearly within the act of Congress," noting that "The Chinese cooly, is to the sense at least, a person of color." But his writing exposed the ambivalent and conflicted core of American worldviews toward free and unfree people. The "problem" of the coolies was a problem of *racial perception*, exacerbated by "the modified color of the Chinese." Reed compared the Chinese to "black sepoys one meets in the streets of Hong Kong, or the Malays and Javanese of the Archipelago," and concluded that in the latter cases, there "could be little doubt about it." Yet weighed against those examples, the Chinese raised the "problem" of racial definition. In Reed's writing, *racial definition,* "to the sense at least," is revealed as the most challenging problem for Americans in formulating global policies on slavery. In political history and racial imaginary, debates regarding the coolie in the Americas were intimately entangled with the impulse to define, fix, contain, and maintain the borders of "blackness" and "whiteness," historically efforts that would be continually disturbed and frustrated by Asian bodies.

The impulse to contain color, and the practicalities of subduing involuntary bodies of color, were manifested in the transformation of slave ship to coolie ship. The new ships to China were celebrated for their speed, heralded as symbols of modern progress and achievement, and linked to manifest destiny upon the seas. The American public heralded the next finest and fastest ship, as each builder tried to outperform the other. Captains were treated as celebrities of the day.[91] The American maritime economy reached its halcyon days in the mid-nineteenth century with ships being launched to China from the coasts of New England, New York, and San Francisco. The Chinese trade of tea, spices, silks, porcelain, woods, and dry goods had not only a shadow market of opium but also a market of labor and materials stemming from the highly profitable guano and sugar trades—made possible by Chinese coolie labor. Shipping goods *and coolies* to the Caribbean and South America, American ships were registered and built in the North, and continually refined for transport and speed.[92] One of the refinements to new American ships, however, had nothing to do with enhancing speed: rather, it made holding coolies in captivity easier. The infamous iron hatch was utilized to imprison coolies below the deck and to insure the protection of the armed crew above. The hatches were symbolic of Chinese coolie traffic as pirated slave traffic. Like other coolie ships, the American ship *Kate Hooper* was renovated with hatches and more at the cost of over twelve thousand dollars.[93] Obviously its owners, a prominent Baltimore family, predicted that the profit from coolie labor would more than make up for the cost.[94] The hatches in coolie ships were reinforced by bars, grating, cage doors, and barricades. Maritime historian Basil Lubbock noted that

> *a rising of the coolies was the one terror that ever stalked behind the captain of a Chinese coolie ship . . . the decks and hatchway openings were barred and barricaded like the old convict ships. Over each hatchway a semi-circular grating of stout iron bars was bolted to the coamings. In the centre of this there was a circular opening 8 or 9 inches at*

the most in diameter, and through the cage door was the only was on deck for the coolies below. In many ships a barricade was built athwartship from rail to rail a few feet in front of the break of the poop, which was some 10 feet high, and thick enough to stop a bullet. On top of this barricade it was often necessary to post an armed sentry.[95]

As one example of ship modifications, the coolie ship *Norway* left the port of New York loaded with coal for a U.S. naval squadron and returned with a cargo of Chinese under the hatches. A ten-foot-high barricade was built that stretched from rail to rail, with an armed guard to prevent against coolie rebellion. Despite having barricaded themselves in with firearms, the crew of sixty was overwhelmed when the 1,037 Chinese undertook a violent and sustained mutiny at sea.[96]

The "transition" to free labor was a violent one, and the implied mythology of liberal "progress" and willing participation is contravened by accounts of the passage. The captive Chinese violently resisted their circumstances, causing embarrassing reports that were published and sensationalized in publications such as *Harper's* and *Cornhill* magazines. During this period, both slaves and coolies were linked in their quest for freedom on land and at sea. A fitting illustration is provided by foreign policy scholar Gaddis Smith who once compared the ships *Amistad* and *Robert Browne*, one containing kidnapped Africans and the other containing kidnapped Chinese, both bound for the Americas.[97] The Chinese mutinied on the American ship *Robert Browne* in 1852, killing the captain and crew, and were eventually captured and brought to trial. Britain's Sir B. Robertson declared that Chinese coolie mutinies at sea were "a fearful record . . . I venture to say it could not be matched in the palmiest days of the slave trade."[98]

COOLIES ON LAND: COOLIE SLAVERY

In 1923 Persia Campbell offered the first global examination of Chinese indenture under British imperial rule.[99] She detailed British administrative politics and the Chinese coolie systems that arose in Cuba (since the British were active in the trafficking to Cuba), Canada, Australia, New Zealand, Guyana, South Africa, Samoa, and Malaysia. Campbell concluded that under certain circumstances, the indenture system should be abolished: "The story of the past makes it apparent that this system is subject to abuse. . . . It may be questioned whether, under such circumstances, the indentured labour system should be allowed to continue if the end to be attained through social organization is the welfare of man rather than the accumulation of 'cities and money and rich plantations.'[100] Campbell's criticisms of the system, especially Cuba's system, were based upon her assessment of abuses in the coolie system and violations of the contract. Yet she did not reject the contract system as being inherently problematic. In her analysis, the system in Cuba emerges as a special example of egregious abuse. I argue, nonetheless, that the Cuba case reveals that the *contract institution* itself, if taken to its logical extreme, is capable of being one of enslavement (see Chapter 3).

The Chinese coolie situation was desperate—in surface terms, the Chinese coolie was a contract laborer, with Cuban contracts lasting for "eight years."[101] Yet, experts on Cuba and slavery, such as Philip Foner and Franklin Knight, respectively conclude that "the Chinese and Yucatecan workers were bought, sold, and transferred like slaves, and treated as slaves," and "Chinese labor in Cuba in the nineteenth century was slavery in every social aspect except the name."[102] The coolies endured slave conditions, due to the unenforceability of a contract that provided for certain conditions of "employment" subject to the interpretation of the master. The coolie therefore could be exploited with little investment in maintenance. In 1860 the women's rights activist and abolitionist Julia Ward Howe commented insightfully on the coolies in Cuba: "men will treat a hired horse worse than a horse of their own."[103] Contemporary Cuban scholars further concluded that the treatment of a Chinese coolie was worse than that of an African slave.[104] Because of malnourishment and abusive conditions, or because of their disposability, over 50 percent of coolies died *before* their eight-year contract ended.[105] The average life span of an African slave on a sugar plantation was twenty years. The percentage of coolie attrition due to voluntary exit (coolies who were able to exit Cuba) was negligible.[106] Furthermore, the "eight-year" limit was illusory. "Indenture," in this case, was undermined because of the unenforceable nature (or acceptable violation) of the "contract." The coolie contract was routinely ignored in Cuba. The gap between theory and lived experience disturbs North American paradigms of "contract," "coolie," "slave," and "indentured labor." The "contract" behaved as a globalizing institution that punitively enslaved new global labor: the coolies. How does the experience of Chinese coolies in Cuba bring into question and politicize notions of language—what is the meaning of *contract, slave, coolie?*

The 1854 regulations concerning the Chinese permitted them to purchase the remainder of their contract at any time—but only after they had compensated their master for the purchase price. The worker was responsible for value added since the time of their purchase, which meant any clothing, loss of labor time due to sickness, and the inconvenience of finding a replacement for the Chinese laborer. Of course, these conditions were subject to interpretation by the master. Through legal sophistry and machinations of the contract and its ostensible representation of consent, the planters created a hybrid slave system involving Chinese coolies who worked in tandem with African slaves. The contracts with Chinese coolies were patently deceptive. Coolies supposedly were paid four pesos monthly. From this four peso "salary," deductions were made by the master for the cost of travel from China, provisions like clothing and food, sickness or lost labor time, and a host of other "costs" to the master. Therefore, by the time a coolie's eight-year term expired, if he survived (over half perished), the coolie wound up owing his master. It is no wonder that few Chinese coolies could discharge this cost for the purchase of freedom. The 1860 regulations explicitly closed off options for freedom and forced Chinese into sequential slavery, under the guise of "recontracting" rules. Those who did not re-sign would be arrested. The master could invoke a "renewal" clause in the contract, thus keeping the coolie unfree until his death. The notion of the Chinese coolie in Cuba being described under the generic term of "indentured labor" (meaning labor stipulated by legal contract and terms, with the possibility of freedom upon the end of the term) becomes problematic if terms for "indenture" were illusory or patently engineered to prevent the possibility of freedom. The folly of quoting contracts as actualized history is revealed. Contracts were, in fact, veiled representations beholden to empowered institutions and persons. The coolie experience in Cuba exposes the nature of language, historical terms, and legal categories as contingent—the varied conditions of "slave," "coolie," and "contracts" need greater examination.

"Recontracting" at the mercy of the master was not exceptional but was common. In rare instances, some indentured coolies did manage to escape the island. Caribbean historian Walton Look Lai notes that "there was even one unusual case of a Chinese man who found his way to Trinidad in 1866 all the way from Cardenas in Cuba, after having escaped an attempt to reindenture him."[107] Coolies, who were thought to be passive, also displayed a defiant nature and resorted to plantation rebellions, cane field burnings, assassination of overseers, escape, or suicide. While Cuban laws stipulated "rules" or guidelines for the treatment of African slaves and Chinese coolies, and whereas methods of resistance (and even attempted legal recourse) were undertaken by slaves and coolies, clearly they were disempowered under the Cuban slave and coolie systems. Those coolies who attempted escape were arrested and punished. The condition of the African slave in Cuba and the servitude of the Chinese coolie in Cuba resulted in deprivation of liberty and life. The standard labor contract also provided for the sale of a labor contract. Coolies could then be sold as property or recontracted without recourse. The coolie contract also involved rampant misrepresentation of the coolie, with said coolie being put under contracts and renewed contracts under different names. Planters could also divert contracts by false claims that the coolie under contract had died; the "now-dead" coolie could then be resold to another Cuban employer under another name. Chinese coolie runaways, called *cimarrones* (like their African counterparts), could be captured and sold by the Cuban police. Also similar to their African counterparts, Chinese were sold at marts and auctions.[108] Chinese coolies repeatedly testified to being kept and treated as slaves. Typical of the coolie testimonies was one by Wen A-fa who asserted, "After eight years are completed they refuse us the cedulas and we are forced to remain slaves in perpetuity."[109] Among many eyewitness accounts of the treatment of coolies was one from *New York Herald* correspondent in Cuba, James O'Kelly, who observed that a Chinese coolie "contrary to the representations made about the traffic in Asiatics was treated in every respect the same way as his sable companions in misfortune."[110]

Given the condition of being "contracted" at the mercy of the master, the Chinese coolie became maximally exploited, and the meaning of "contract" became illusory. The Chinese coolie could be disposable or unfree at any time, depending on the vagaries of the system and the master. [111] The innocuous description of coolies as supposed "contract employees" or "Asiatic colonists" neatly allowed coolie traffickers to sidestep accusations of slave trading. Noel Deerr, technologist and historian of sugar,

TABLE 1.5   CHINESE POPULATION IN CUBA (BY REGION), 1861–77

PROVINCE	1861	1872	1877
Pinar del Rio	2,221	3,396	3,137
Havana	9,456	11,365	10,108
Matanzas	15,782	27,002	20,054
Santa Clara	6,274	15,878	13,301
Puerto Principe	341	297	94
Santiago de Cuba	754	462	422
Total	34,828	54,400	47,116

Sources: 1861: Cuba, Centro de Estadística, *Noticias estadísticas,* "Censo de población segun el cuadro general de la Comisión Ejecutiva de 1861"; 1872: Expediente General Colonización Asiática, AHN, Ultramar, leg. 87; 1877: Iglesias, "El censo cubano."

made this observation: "To avoid the charge of slavery[,] the coolies before sailing signed a contract of eight years indenture, and on arrival at Havana or Lima they were sold in a way differing in a manner but little from a public auction and were at once reduced to the status of slavery."[112] An in-depth examination of these conditions follows in the subsequent chapters, with analysis of testimonies and arguments presented by the coolies themselves and of materials disclosed by other relevant sources of the period.

Throughout the 1860s and 1870s Chinese were prevalent in the *ingenios* or sugar mills. On the smaller plantations, Chinese sometimes accounted for 50 percent of the labor force. However, on the larger plantations they constituted a smaller percentage.[113] In Cuba, Chinese coolies were a minority in a larger population of African slaves and were concentrated in the sugar plantations of Matanzas, the central province of Cuba, and secondly in Las Villas.

One might assume that coolie history occupies a lesser role in the history of labor and production in Cuba, given the total number of Chinese coolies versus the overwhelming numbers of African slaves. However, this assumption has been complicated by the recognition that coolie labor was a critical force in reorganizing the Cuban sugar economy and its systems of production, and furthermore, constituted an implicit challenge to entrenched paradigms of race and nation. Some scholars, such as Evelyn

Hu-Dehart, have examined the coolies in terms of their relation to racial constructions in Cuba.[114] Others, such as Moreno, emphasize coolie labor as crucial to an economic transition from slavery to wage labor. [115] Scott asserts, on the other hand, that the use of coolies as slavelike property in Cuba could have aided in prolonging the institution of slavery.[116] It is generally agreed, however, that coolie labor was significant in a political economy that was moving toward different modes of production and capital acquisition. In effect, the use of coolie labor contributed to the industrialization and mechanization of the *ingenios*, though the question here is how paradigms of "transition" are explanatory yet lacking in a more thorough accounting of ideological and material complicities and of living history.

One aspect of this "transition" was the major insurgency of Chinese and Africans in the wars for liberation, during which Chinese escaped the plantations and made the "transition" to free labor through mass rebellion and war. Two major events disrupted the coolie labor on plantations. The first was the coolie/slave insurgency in the wars for liberation that began in 1868. At one time, Madrid itself called for an end to coolie imports because coolies were aiding rebels in eastern Cuba.[117] The Cuban patriot Gonzalo de Quesada wrote the most enduring words about the Chinese freedom fighters of Cuba, recalling that there was never a traitor or deserter among them: "*No hubo un chino cubano traidor; no hubo un chino cubano desertor.*"[118] His words are inscribed on a still-extant black marble monument in Havana. This monument is a dark obelisk that is distinctive yet mysterious. Little is known about the coolies' ages, names, or the plantations they came from.[119] The Chinese participation in the wars for liberation spanned a remarkably long period of thirty years: with their role in the fighting beginning with *la Guerra de los Diez Anos* (The Ten Years' War of 1868–1878) through *la Guerra Chiquita* (The Little War of 1878–1879), and to the end of *la Guerra de Independencia* (The War of Independence 1895–1898).[120] Testimonies of commanders and comrades, interviews with survivors, memoirs by Cuban insurgents, and newspaper accounts of the period help reconstruct what amounted to the extraordinary history of Asians who took up arms in a prolonged battle to overthrow a colonial system of slavery in the Americas. For the Chinese, the struggle for Cuban liberation was the struggle for freedom from slavery, and their stake in it was on grounds mostly linked to their own emancipation. In 1870 the

Cuban rebel government promised liberty to any *chinos* and *negros* who
joined the insurrection against Spain. Before the 1870 declaration, however, both coolies and slaves were already escaping the plantations to join
in force. Despite the *ranchadores*—ubiquitous man-hunters whose job
was to capture runaways—*los chinos* responded to the call for insurrection within the first days.[121]

A second event, occurring after the advent of the insurrectionary wars,
was the historic investigation of coolie conditions in Cuba by a commission sent by China in 1874. The report of the commission led to the eventual banning of Chinese coolie traffic to Cuba. The subsequent section is
devoted to this episode. The cessation of coolie traffic to Cuba, and later,
the United States barring of Chinese immigration to their shores under the
Chinese Exclusion Act of 1882, resulted in a marked decline in Chinese
migration to the Americas. In Cuba, the cessation of Chinese coolie traffic
after 1874 and the additional costs of Cuba's independence wars had an
impact on the Cuban economy. With developments resulting from the long
wars, labor restrictions, and important advancements in technology, slavery would finally be dismantled, though planters hung on via a patronage
system, which bound slaves and coolies to their masters as apprentices.
Because of ingrained attitudes towards slavery, planters found it difficult
to change their ways. Also, most of the available free white laborers were
unwilling to do the hard work on the sugar cane plantations. That work
was to be left for slaves and coolies, those still bonded or formerly bonded.
Besides the unavailability of free wage laborers, the planters lacked sufficient capital to finance a transition to free labor. The engagement of free
labor on the sugar plantation would have driven up labor costs at a rate
higher than the planters could have withstood. The transition to free labor,
therefore, was a risky venture for planters who were accustomed to the old
way of engaging labor. In this economic context, Chinese had begun brok-
ering coolie work gangs called *caudrillas*, which filled a need for controlled, contracted labor, though these would eventually be banned by the
colonial government because the *caudrillas* became sanctuaries for runaways. But moreover, as I suggest in the following sections, they constituted competition for the most profitable brokers of Chinese labor on the
island— the officials and police themselves.

The factors of production in the sugar economy continued transform-
ing, and large sugar plantations were slowly breaking up by the 1880s. The

large landowning families either sold their properties to newcomers or began entering the business of processing sugar only, which they did in *cent-
rales* (large scale sugar mills). The cultivation of sugar cane was then
turned over to sharecroppers who replaced the slaves and the coolie system. By the beginning of the twentieth century, even more efficient refining machinery was introduced to the Cuban sugar industry, leading to
economies driven by technological innovation. New technology lowered
the cost of production, leading to renewed profitability in the sugar industry and the recovery of the efficiencies lost when coerced labor was elimi-
nated in Cuba.

Today, it is the images of the Chinese freedom fighter and the Chinese
merchant that are generally known by the Cuban people, with the coolie
being a more distant historical figure in the national memory of labor and
independence. There are multiple histories of nineteenth-century Chinese
Cubans that follow hybridized lines of class, culture, and race (mixed race
and "pure" Chinese). However, the initial histories of the Chinese in Cuba
were composed by Chinese Cuban clan associations and a generation of
entrepreneurs.[122] As the makers of social representation, they necessarily
interpreted their history by focusing on the accomplishments of their
communities and their contemporary relevance. As a result, the history of
the coolies and the context of their bondage have been dimmed by the
more recent narrative of the Chinese immigrant struggles and contributions. Consequently, the coolie story has been called "la historia de la
gente sin historia" (a history of a people without a history).[123] This work
revisits the coolie story, an extraordinary story of people who endured and
overthrew one of the last standing systems of colonial slavery in the Western hemisphere.

THE COOLIE TESTIMONIES

Remarkably, of the 125,000 Chinese who were trafficked to Cuba, there were 2,841 coolies who left behind an astounding body of written and oral testimonies that described their descent into a hellish system of bondage. One group came together to write a lengthy testimony of their experience, which opened with: "We are sinking in a strange place and living in a hell on earth" (Petition 25). Based upon these testimonies, a report was issued in 1876 entitled "Report of the Commission Sent by China to Ascertain the Condition of Chinese Coolies in Cuba." The report chronicled the abuse of the Chinese and ultimately led to abolition of the coolie trade to Cuba. A treaty was ratified in December 1878 to that effect.[1] This dismantling of the coolie trade to Cuba was concomitant with the erosion of the slavery system in Cuba. In 1870 the Moret Law had been enacted, granting freedom to children born after 1868 and to slaves over age sixty (though one travel writer dryly observed: "In the first place, few hard worked slaves survive to sixty; and in the second place, the children have no one to look after or to enforce their rights."[2] In 1880 the patronage system was implemented, and in 1886, an end to the slavery system was officially proclaimed. The nineteenth century in Cuba saw four decades of temporal overlapping of the slave and coolie bondage systems. Therefore, the perspectives and narratives of bondage that arose from this period necessarily arose from the crucible of bondage in several forms and colors. The perspectives as presented by coolies in their testimonies provide a rare glimpse into the overlap of slavery and indenture.

At times, testimonies have played a crucial role in liberatory politics. In this regard, the Chinese coolie testimonies shared historical parallels with another body of testimonial literature, that being African slave narratives. Though discrete in their forms and historical particularities, both the Chinese coolie testimonies and the slave narratives would be used to overthrow the respective systems of their bondage. Today, however, little is known of the Chinese testimonies. This section offers a reading of the testimonies, which ultimately reveal radical visions of "freedom" and the "contract" institution. There are two main bodies of narrative that stem from this historical episode of bondage, one being the *testimonies* by the coolies and the other being the *commission report*, which excerpted the testimonies and provided official reportage and recommendations. An engagement with the testimonies and the commission investigation raises questions regarding testimony procurement and production. What were the politics and histories (including abolitionism and nation-state interests) that framed the gathering of such testimonies? How was the commission formed? How was the commission's report constructed, and how did it make use of the testimonies? What of the testimonies behind the report—what materials are extant from this investigation? How were these testimonies actually obtained? What did the Chinese say and how? How do we account for the politics of translation and language? The *report* offers a point of reference for examining how the testimonies were produced and taken up, and for examining the historical and political context of their production. The *testimonies* offer a basis for examining perspectives of bondage, albeit produced within these constraints of the inquiry. For this study, the latter (a close, critical reading of the testimonies themselves) is prioritized. This task, though, is prefaced here by at least identifying key aspects of the commission investigation that inform such a reading.

THE COMMISSION INVESTIGATION: "THEY FORBADE ME TO SPEAK UP."

While a treaty was ratified in 1878 for the abolition of the coolie trade, coolies already in bondage would remain so, along with black slaves, until the 1880s when Cuba entered its final dissolution of slavery.[3] Nevertheless, the commission and its report played the pivotal role in marking the beginning of the end of coolie trafficking to Cuba. The formation of the commission took place in a distinctly diplomatic context involving the direct participation of four nations and the indirect though significant involvement of additional nations.[4] Beyond a bi-national dispute, the investigation into Cuba involved interests of sovereignty and the entwined economies of slavery, abolition, and contract labor. The inspection by the commission at the site of contention and the uniquely multinational nature of the effort is historic, perhaps one of the first instances of an investigation led by multiple nations, which precedes such multinational undertakings later sponsored by the United Nations (and its forerunner, the League of Nations). Initiated outside of Cuba, involving China and the Allied powers, the commission was charged with investigating "conditions" administered under Cuba's colonial government, Spain. The five leading foreign powers in nineteenth-century China were Britain, the United States, France, Germany, and Russia. The commission comprised representatives of China, Britain, and France. In the nineteenth century, it was unusual for a commission to be formed and dispatched to investigate on-site conditions in the territory of another major world power.

The commission was formed during a period of anti-Western protests, rebellions, and riots among Chinese who became inflamed over the Opium Wars and foreign incursions. In 1872 tensions were exacerbated with bitter conflict between China and Spain concerning conventions of emigration, the treatment of Chinese emigrants, and reports of extreme abuse in Cuba. Further pressure was brought to bear by public outcry and official reports of abuse in Cuba. Newspaper publicity and interventions by missionaries also contributed to raising the profile of the coolie traffic.[5] Though the Spanish denied the charges against them, they were subject to mediation by foreign powers. Not surprisingly, parties on all sides were vested in the concerns and profits of Chinese trade and export, and one of those major concerns was the access to and control over labor. Economies among several nations were connected via trade with China, and labor recruitment and emigration were important issues. The British, Americans, French, Spanish, and Portuguese had the most obvious stake in the export of Chinese labor to the Americas. From the 1840s through the 1870s alone, some quarter million Chinese were sent to Cuba, Peru, and other parts of

Caribbean and Latin America. The Americans, like their British and French counterparts, were major coolie traffickers and were deeply involved until the eve of American Civil War. At this point, Congress was forced to confront the contradictions of American involvement in coolie ("slavelike") labor abroad while going to war over slave labor at home. Although the Americans did not have a seat on the commission, the United States would be of consequence in the balance of power among the negotiating nations. Robert Hart, the British official and influential Inspector General of China's Imperial Maritime Customs Administration pondered the role of the Americans in private correspondence to his secretary in London (with reference to tensions with Francisco Otin, the Spanish envoy in China): "Otin just in. He talks of striking his flag and putting Spanish affairs in the hands of the Admiral. But as the matter is Cuba, and as America might probably side with China on Coolie questions, and so get the island, he hardly knows how to turn. So far, it seems that the Cuban expedition will be knocked on the head and that Huber and Macpherson will not have the trip. The Yankees have a splendid card in their hands: I wonder will they play it? Confound this country: one never knows where one is from day to day!"[6]

The Americans were the first to propose the formation of a commission to resolve contention concerning coolie trafficking. Samuel Wells Williams, secretary and interpreter to the American legation, proposed an onsite review of conditions in Cuba (although despite their call to examine conditions, it must be noted that the Americans eventually sided with Spain).[7] Given its deteriorating relations with China, and with designs on gaining further access to Chinese labor, the Spanish finally accepted the formation of a commission. In September 1873 the Chinese court sanctioned an investigation. To their dismay, the Spanish did not get a seat on the commission itself, despite their efforts to make the commission binational. A three-member commission was composed instead, led by Chen Lan Pin (Chen Lanbin) with assistance from a British and a French representative: A. Macpherson, Commissioner of Customs at Hankow (Hankou), and A. Huber, Commissioner of Customs at Tientsin (Tianjin) respectively. While there are official records of the commission, a composite background on the commission's operation can be drawn from newspaper articles, and from writings of Edward Rhoads, Robert Irick, Yen Ching Hwang, and Charles Desnoyers. While the British representative Macpherson and the French representative Huber also contributed to the commission, Chen took the lead. Modern scholarship and period newspapers referred almost exclusively to Chen, who was understood to be *presidente de la comisión china*.[8] At the time, Chen was posted in Connecticut as co-commissioner of the first Chinese Educational Mission to the United States. Apparently, Chen drew upon his staff and work in Connecticut to form his team that would travel to Cuba: Included were Yeh Yuanchun, a language teacher;[9] a student in Hartford named Chan Lun;[10] Mr. H. L. Northrop, an interpreter of Spanish;[11] Mr. H.T. Terry of Hartford;[12] plus several assistants.[13] Apparently before heading to Cuba, Chen sent a trusted emissary, Tseng Lai-shun (Zeng Laishun), to make arrangements. Zeng was a Chinese-Malay originally from Singapore.[14] Chen then arrived in Cuba with his team of teachers and translators. According to the Cuban newspaper *Diario de la Marina*, ten individuals assisted Chen's commission.[15] Of those, Zeng and Yeh would emerge as having the most significant roles.[16]

After first making a stop at the White House, Chen arrived in Cuba on March 17, 1873, on the German ship *Strassburg*.[17] After gathering the testimonies, Chen returned to the States on May 8. In the following months, he composed his report, and toward the end of 1874 he continued on to China with the copious compilation of materials.[18] A much smaller and unofficial (without imperial sanction) investigation of coolie traffic to Peru also took place via Yung Wing (Rong Hong), the co-commissioner of the Chinese Educational Commission, at the personal request of the Chinese viceroy. Yung, along with two Americans, his friend Reverend Twichell, and his future brother-in-law Dr. Kellogg, traveled to Peru for a short investigation in September of 1874.[19] Following the coolie investigations, Chen and Yung were offered a historic opportunity to head the first Chinese embassy to the United States. In 1878 Chen was appointed the first-ever Chinese minister, and Yung was named the assistant minister. Chen also brought with him members of his staff who had served him well in Cuba. Thus, Chen and Yung's rise in stature and their roles in international and American politics involved Chinese, American, Cuban, and Peruvian experiences. And their exposure to very different kinds of social histories involved not only bureaucratic and scholarly interests, but also the struggles of common labor in bondage. The divergent social roles of Chinese in the Americas were signaled in a year of ironic coincidence. In

1847 Yung Wing had arrived in New York and eventually became the first Chinese graduate of Yale. And in 1847 Chinese arrived in Cuba to be sold as coolies. While these historical details are of general interest, it is the sequence of particulars that deserve attention in contextualizing the testimonies and lead to insights into their composition. The biographies of those such as Yung and Chen offer not only a mapping of diasporic heterogeneities, but they also show how these diasporas intersect.

In Chen's past, we find details that have bearing on how testimonies evolve as forms in dialogic and cultural context. Chen and his diplomatic corps of Chinese came to their statesmanship via two separate missions in the Americas: The first mission brought them in contact with privileged social circles in Connecticut, and the second was a tortuous encounter with exploited labor in Cuba. As co-commissioner of the newly established Chinese Educational Commission, which brought Chinese students to study in American schools, Chen and the Chinese were exposed to patrons at colleges, schools, and churches of New England. Scholarship suggests that Chen was selected by the Chinese government for a variety of reasons, one of which was his disposition as a loyal Sinocentric bureaucrat. This impression of cultural opposition also was popularized during that period by Yung Wing, who became the most well-known Chinese to have resided in nineteenth- century New England and who made plain his antipathies toward Chen.[20] The portrait of Chen as a staid and loyal bureaucrat was consistent with Chen's past service. He served for decades on the Board of Punishment, one of six Chinese ministries under the Qing. A senior secretary, Chen was highly educated, having *juren* and *jinshi* degrees and having been admitted to the Hanlin Academy.[21] Attaining *jinshi* status meant that Chen was a member of a tiny elite who had passed the highest-level exams in the imperial system—exams that required extensive study of history, politics, and literature. Chen apparently functioned as counterweight to Yung Wing, who was deemed overly influenced by Western thinking, though modern scholars have made problematic the constructed binaries in such interpretations.[22]

There is, however, a curious aspect that complicates the staid biography of Chen.[23] Chen was involved in organizing a militia in Guangdong, and it was through his militia experience in that region, Charles Desnoyers argues, that he gained recognition.[24] The idea that Chen was not only a bureaucratic man, but was also involved in a militia, might be of passing interest. But for a critical reading of the testimonies, such details of Chen's life take on greater importance in understanding how the testimonies might be understood as culturally based forms. In organizing a militia, Chen would have had exposure to commoners and nongentry people. This militia experience took place in Guangdong, the province from where the majority of coolies came, and the province in which there had been mass unrest among the populace against coolie traffic, opium traffic, and Western incursions. This composite biography of an elite scholar, bureaucrat, and militia organizer—one who had exposure to both elite and nonelite classes—makes Chen an intriguing figure in the investigation of bondage abroad. Besides being chosen for more obvious reasons of social class, loyalty, and bureaucratic experience, he had a past that would have been better suited than most officials to procuring testimony from mass labor in an international context. His past may have had direct bearing on *how the testimonies were procured* and *how the coolies might have viewed the possibilities for their testimonies.* The procuring of a massive number of testimonies in Cuba, obtained under strenuous and politically tenuous conditions abroad, was an impressive feat. Besides the obvious negotiations of language and local politics, the gathering of testimonies required Chen and his team to travel to various provinces of Cuba and included visits to *barracones*, prisons, and plantations. The mammoth undertaking would have required a highly qualified person who could successfully administer such proceedings in an unfavorable foreign environment, and most of all, someone who understood regularized conventions for obtaining and recording testimonies—rendering them usable to an official inquiry. Evidently, Chen had such capabilities. With his background in the Board of Punishments, he would have had exposure to juridical procedures applied to various social classes. And Chen would have been aware of the forms of civilian complaints, written with particular conventions and processed in a regularized manner. In a history of the Chinese civil system, John Watt notes that "The Board of Punishment . . . recommended that local officials be ordered to examine the pleas drawn up and sealed by the authorized office clerks (*tai-shu*)" with *tai-shu* "designated to take down the depositions of plaintiffs."[25] According to legal tradition in China, complaints to officials were presented in a formalized procedure and played a crucial role in the systemization and management of Chinese civil society.[26] Complaints in China were submitted to clerks and local courts on publicly announced days for their submissions. Legal scholars have noted that an actual petition in the Qing dynasty contained four parts: First, there was the petitioner's name, age, and residence; second, there was the text of the plea; and third, came the rescript by the magistrate, which contained his understanding of the case; lastly, there was the record of judgment, which contained the magistrate's judgment.[27] The existence of petitions as a written and systematic form of complaint, and as a social convention of Chinese society, would have been culturally familiar to Chen and the coolies of Cuba. Additionally, given clues to Chen's background, it is possible to consider that the manner of processing for the testimonies may have efficaciously followed a procedure based upon established Chinese practices. The civil system of complaint was already imbedded in social practices in Chinese society before and during the Qing period.

The form and forum of civilian protest were, of course, linguistically and culturally based, as was the case in 1874. Of relevance is the fact that Chen Lanbin was a native of Guangdong, and his first language was Cantonese—one of the many Chinese dialects. But more importantly, Cantonese was the dialect of the majority of the coolies in Cuba. This fact would have influenced how the oral testimonies were received and interpreted. Chen also brought with him a staff of teachers that spoke subdialects of Guangdong. Some dialects in China were (and still are) so different from each other that Chinese from different provinces (and sometimes even those from the same province) would not necessarily understand one another. Their dialects entail different phonetics, tonal structure, and physiological articulation. Chen and his staff were prepared for linguistic comprehension of the coolies and their testimonies; thus, they would have a better understanding of cultural codes, references, and potential subtexts in the testimonies. While exact particulars of Chen's or his staff's biography and credentials may not have been known to the coolies, there would have been enough cultural and social prologue, from the point of view of the coolies, which would have affected their *approach* to the testimony forum, their *composition* of the testimonies, and their estimation of the testimonial *possibilities*. This helps explain the astonishing depth, graphic nature, and outspokenness in many of the testimonies, despite their being given while the coolies were in bondage and under punitive circumstances.

A long social and cultural history of "petitioning" suggests a comparative and contextual basis for examining the coolie petitions. In addition to the practice of petitioning in China, petitioning occurred in other parts of the world. Peasantry, clergy, landowners, and merchants petitioned their rulers regarding a range of agendas, social grievances, and favors. Complaints ran the gamut, such as protesting taxation, seeking laws favorable for particular guilds, even petitioning to have a street name changed.[28] One of the most commonly cited episodes of the petition being employed and appropriated by various parties is that of *les cahiers de doléances*, the French "notebooks" of complaints by the three estates in 1789. One historian makes the following pertinent assertion: "Petitions have been used throughout history to voice demands, including those of working class and middle class citizens . . . from Egyptian building workers in pharaonic times to illiterate Ecuador Indians in 1899, from anti-Catholic English women in 1642 to French workers asking for the repeal of the *livret ouvrier* ["worker's booklet"] in 1847, from Italian peasants complaining about noble banditry in 1605 to Brazilian slaves vindicating their rights against their owners in 1823, from Western European early modern guild members to German Democratic Republic workers demanding improvement of economic efficiency or voicing consumer demands."[29] Petitions and "petition-like" materials have provided a wealth of insight into social relations and power. However, the petitions of 1874 need to be differentiated from a long view of petitions generally. The long view includes social histories of citizenry petitioning their governments for more favorable land rights and the protection of trades. The 1874 petitions are more comparable to testimonies of African slavery, which call for foregrounding of colonialism, bondage, race, and resistance. Unlike petitioners of other "petition" histories, the Cuba coolies were not citizenry making complaints to a local standing government. Rather, they were people forcibly transported overseas and sold into a state of bondage. They were people petitioning for their freedom.

The testimonies exhibit characteristics linked to unique factors of forcibly transported people in bondage who faced constraints and reprisals because of their testimony. Chen and his commission came and left each town after a few days, and the coolies who testified had a constricted window of time to submit their testimonies. It was not possible to engage in any ongoing appeals to the commission. Combined with the transience of the commission was the transient nature of the coolies' lives. The moment of testimony was broached by the coolies as possibly the last recording of their lives, with almost all the testifiers describing heightened awareness of their days being numbered. Witnessing the high mortality rate of the majority of their fellow coolies, the testifiers conveyed sentiments of mourning coupled with urgency. Further heightening this urgency was the struggle to circumvent immediate obstacles to testifying. Not surprisingly, the coolies' testimonies were treated by local authorities as seditious. Their testimonies were an indictment of an entire system of labor and social organization. While there was no legislation that stated coolie testimony was sedition (and in fact, coolies could make complaints and appeals to the island administration, as some persistently did), their testimonies revealed the punishments meted out to those who were caught testifying. Several obstacles lay in the path of coolies who attempted to get their testimonies heard. First, the Spanish exerted influence in the process via control over the commission's itinerary and its access to coolies. Second, the Spanish attempted to prevent coolies from submitting testimonies. In a reading of the testimonies, pervasive coercion becomes significant in appreciating the coolie testimonies as acts of resistance and as veiled narratives.

Coercion took place on several levels, with restrictive maneuverings or "procedures" at the official level, not to mention outright intimidation. The commission was required to make local travel arrangements via letters, issued ahead of time from Havana, that were "addressed to the Sub-Commissions of Colonization established in the chief town of each jurisdiction."[30] Also briefly noted was that these "letters of permission" would be issued by a "Señor Zulueta," the Governor of Havana. The brief mention of Zulueta needs critical commentary. "Señor Zulueta" actually referred to none other than Julián de Zulueta, who was chief trafficker of slaves to Cuba. Upon perceiving the erosion of slavery under increasing antislavery sentiment, he also became the leading proponent of importing coolies and was their chief trafficker.[31] Having amassed a family empire from the conjoined enterprises of slave and coolie trades, sugar plantations, and railroad development, Zulueta was the most powerful and wealthy man on the island and was hardly a colonial functionary. The Italian writer Antonio Gallenga once said this of Zulueta: "He is the heart and soul of every public institution, political or social, in Havannah. He is president of the *Casino Español*, that *Imperium in imperio*, which as I have often said rules the Island in the interest of the Peninsular and slave-holding party . . . the will of Don Julian de Zulueta is supreme."[32] As Presidente de la Comisión Central de Colonización (President of the Central Commission of Colonization), Zulueta presided over a body that supervised all coolie-related matters, and its membership was constituted by at least two-thirds planters.[33] Given Zulueta's influence, planters' interests naturally impinged upon the commission visit at the outset. A logical assumption would be that Zulueta and the planters would have made whatever interventions necessary to present Cuban conditions in the best possible light. Coolies' testimony revealed that many testifiers were preselected by their masters. With this in mind, the overwhelmingly resistant testimonies of the coolies, which were vigorously hostile toward their masters and local officials, are even more remarkable.

On one hand, the commission acknowledged the gracious hospitality of their plantation hosts. Yet in terse understatements, the commission commented upon the embedded role of administrators and planters in their itinerary. The commission's site visits were

> *only received after arrangements had been entered into between the local official and the proprietor. . . . The hours of visiting the plantations were settled in advance by the local officials, and by them the Commission was occasionally accompanied. To the proprietors of some plantations the Commission is indebted for the providing of carriages and hospitality, but the request that the common labourers should be produced for interrogation was constantly met by the excuse that they were in the fields, and the cooks and other domestic servants, in all an inconsiderable number, were offered in their stead, and when after a long delay a few of the class desired were brought forward, it was urged that their absence was productive of harm and the examination should in consequence be as brief as possible. Ordinarily, too, the administrators and overseers stood by whip in hand; but fortunately they attempted no more overt intimidation.*[34]

The commission's comment of "no more overt intimidation" leads one to read the passage with some skepticism, given the intimidation tactics described in the testimonies, including the ubiquitous "whip in hand." The local administration presented a plausible choreography of diplomatic protocol, gracious hospitality, and coercion. Intimidation included the normalized and totalizing threat of retaliation to come, inherent in the "ordinary" presence of overseers with whips. Not surprisingly, certain coolies were selected to appear while others were prevented from appearing. Some communicated this coercion from overseers with veiled statements that signaled the subtext of their testimonies: "I was *picked out* by people at the official workshop for your honor to ask questions" (my emphasis) (Deposition 159). Pan Duoli, Wang Shuzhao, and Chen Jing similarly stated, "We are *especially picked to be here* to report our situations to you" (my emphasis) (Petition 50). You Asi called attention to appearances: "A few days ago, they heard some Chinese official was coming, so they let us sleep on wooden beds and gave each of us a set of clothes" (Deposition 240). Han Qingze explained, "Knowing your honor is coming today; we sneaked out secretly to meet with your honor. We don't know whether we will be beaten or locked up when we go back" (Deposition 717). Coolies pointed to restrictive measures and yet circumvented them, in person or by submitting clandestine testimonies in writing. Liang Ade wrote, "Last night I tried to see your honor in person, but my owner caught me and made me wear shackles, so I could not see you. Thus, I especially send this written piece and report my condition to you" (Petition 35). The testimonies reveal that the coolies considered the punitive consequences of testifying, and evidently, their desire for freedom and the desire to *tell* trumped any fear of punishment (Depositions 173–225). The potentially dire consequences of giving testimony underscore the very *acts of speaking or writing* as acts of resistance.

Still, regretfully little is known regarding the actual onsite proceedings for the testimonies. It is known that the testimonies were taken at a range of sites in several cities and towns in several provinces. The testimonies were given in the coolies' native tongue before the commission. A team of translators and secretaries accompanied the commission. Overseers or administrators were present, "whip in hand," and testifiers were prevented from giving testimony or attempts were made to intimidate testifiers, including those caught and dragged back to the plantation or those who were actually beaten in the presence of the commission.[35] The "Despatch" of the three commissioners states that "these men were seen

by us all, and these words were heard by us all," indicating that all commissioners were present, though we have no way of knowing for sure.
The commission managed some physical examinations of the testifiers, as it
listed coolies' evident wounds and disfigurations in one part of the report.
As one Liang Ahua urged, "You can still examine our scars" (Deposition
734). As to additional descriptions of what went on in the interrogation itself, this is not known. Such details have rarely been recorded for histories of testimony given in slavery. Some testifiers succinctly addressed
onsite labor conditions, whereas others gave either long, meandering
tales of hellish odysseys or melancholic meditations on their experiences.
Some gave extremely brief testimony. It is possible to imagine that each
site offered different kinds of delimitations and dialogic circumstances in
the giving and receiving of testimony. Outside the testimony forum, perhaps coolies conveyed additional information to the commission, though
it is impossible to conclude in what manner; the commission made curious reference to information exchanged outside the purview of local officials, "in the places where we stayed, as well as on the road, independent
enquiries were instituted."[36]

The commissioners concluded that the coolies "on arrival to Havana . . .
were sold into slavery—a small proportion being disposed of to families and shops, whilst the large majority became the property of sugar
planters . . ." They concluded that the coolie system was rigged so that it
would be nearly "impossible" for the coolies to get free; and, on this basis, the commission condemned the coolie system. Once the report was
composed, the Spanish accused the commission of making the report in
bad faith and obstructing the possibilities of goodwill negotiation.[37] Their
report was organized around fifty questions or concerns that the commission was charged with investigating, using coolie testimonies to illustrate
the commission's conclusions. The report began circulating in 1875 and
was officially presented in 1876, though prolonged wrangling and dispute
occurred over the report, with acrimonious protestations from the Spanish. A treaty to end the coolie traffic was not signed until November of
1877 and ratified in December of 1878. Despite appearances, the Chinese
offices were frustrated by the British and European powers, which were
ultimately reluctant to further embolden the Chinese in the balance of
power.[38] Ultimately, the report reflected the Chinese government's heightened interest in Chinese abroad, marking a historical moment when Chi-

nese attitudes of sovereignty acquired a distinct ethnic transnationalism with the claiming of subjects overseas. This case involved not only responding to or criticizing overseas conditions, but also involved effecting significant changes in Chinese extraterritorial policies toward transnational subjects.[39]

METHODOLOGICAL CHALLENGES OF READING TESTIMONIES: "BENDING CLOSER TO THE GROUND"

In a reading of testimonies in colonial India regarding the death of a woman named "Chandra," Ranajit Guha critiques juridical discourse as functioning through the delimitation of legal narrative, characterizing it as "a matrix of real historical experiences [is] transformed into a matrix of abstract legality." In examining the "Chandra" case, Guha makes transparent his purpose "to reclaim the document for history," and he counters abstract legality with an examination of testimony in the context of Chandra's nineteenth-century rural community. At the same time, he acknowledges that such documents are named and claimed for a variety of purposes, whether they are "anthropological, literary, administrative, or any other." Therefore, while his approach is interventionist, it is another renaming and reclaiming of materials, though one made "by bending closer to the ground in order to pick up traces of a subaltern life in its passage through time."[40] Guha's disclosures on intervention and claiming, and the specter of Gayatri Spivak's concern about speaking for the subaltern, need to be addressed.[41] While an apprehension of the testimonies might be interventionist, it is necessarily interpretive, as are all claims to materials. The purpose of this study is not to convey a pure, transparent, or essentialized record of experience. Rather, it is an effort to read testimonies with attention to what apparently were previously obscured radical and dissonant views. The messiness of these perspectives becomes subsumed in global enterprises specifically formulated to locate, represent, and archive "truth." State enterprises for "truth" normatively subsume dissonant perspectives to the will of consensus, as commissions are most often initiated out of the very need to manage dissonance and conflict. The commission, as an institutional form that shapes global relations and knowledge production, is framed by a long-running global history of consensus-building productions.

The 1874 testimonies represent an early instance of collecting mass testimonies via commission, though it is not clear what impact this episode had on the longer history of testimony production. Beyond the testimonies of 1874, the contemporary task of collecting mass testimony has transformed the way in which the world interprets, copes with, and manages human atrocities on a large scale. After World War II, commissions were formed to hear testimony regarding the Holocaust. And in recent decades, there are ongoing efforts to institutionally preserve survivor accounts. Another commission formed decades after World War II to hear testimony of Japanese Americans who endured the American internment camps, and survivor accounts have also been collected. Since World War II, commission investigations calling for testimonies include those mobilized in response to atrocities in Africa, Latin and South America, Eastern Europe, and Southeast Asia, with some commissions initiated but stalled for decades. The acts of managing and creating forums for testimony, the historicizing of speaking and witnessing, the public enactment of processional, and the archives produced by these acts, all provide highly charged enterprises of knowledge and collectivity in the tensions of social consciousness and the politics of memory.[42] However, commission interrogations of indenture precede the contemporary history of commission interrogations of mass atrocities, and precede forms of testimonies given in forums for human rights and self-determination, "truth and reconciliation," and prosecution before international tribunals. These carry contemporary (and not any less opaque) discourses on human rights, crimes against humanity, international and local community sanctions, mandates for healing, and in some cases, transnational juridical power and enforcement.[43] Not surprisingly, the nineteenth-century commission on Cuba did not undertake "human rights" and the duties of prosecution. Its jurisdiction and enforcement of any amelioration were limited. The mandates, procedures, ambitions, and discourses that have driven and shaped inquiry-testimonies, whether they are from contexts of atrocities, apartheid, slavery, or indenture, are ideologically grounded and specific. For this study, treatments of testimony from Asian indenture and African slavery of the nineteenth-century Americas provide the most salient methodological comparisons for examining the coolie testimonies from Cuba.

The episodic deployment of commissions and committees in regard to Indian indenture-related crises was not unusual, though extensive gathering of "native" testimonies was fairly uncommon. British administrations called up a committee process as a method of reconfirming their authority—particularly their moral authority—in the British territories. Examples of these commissions include the one formed in 1870–71 to investigate Indian indenture in Guyana (or what was then British Guiana), which was spurred by criticism from colonial administrator George William des Voeux.[44] The investigation included examinations of forty-six witnesses and visits to fifty-five plantations.[45] Three decades earlier, a committee had formed to investigate indenture in Mauritius and submitted a report in 1840.[46] In reference to such state inquiries into Indian indenture, Madhavi Kale, Radhika Mongia, and Marina Carter have produced separate critiques.[47] Radhika Mongia and Marina Carter's arguments and conclusions are rooted in the history of Mauritius, and Madhavi Kale draws her analysis from the history of Guyana (and, to a lesser extent, Trinidad and Mauritius).[48] Looked at together, their approaches highlight different aspects that could be considered in apprehending commission-testimony history.

Kale and Mongia critique state politics and Carter focuses upon a reading of subjects' testimonies, though all explicitly recognize the imbrications of state and subject. Kale analyzes "imperial knowledge" and the ways in which employers, antislavery activists, imperial administrators, and Indian nationalists wrote about labor.[49] In her approach, "labor is a *category*, a role and not people, and so I focus here on describing how that category was elaborated in the mid-nineteenth century and beyond, rather than on the people cast in it" (her emphasis).[50] Kale's elaboration of imperial knowledge establishes labor as a category "made known and accessible through the mediation of British industry and enterprise."[51] Kale's concerns are related to Mongia's examination of discourses created by British colonial inquiries. Mongia foregrounds the imperatives of modernity and liberalism that affect "the inquiry," and argues that instead of effecting change, such investigations actually enabled a state system of indenture and abuses. Referencing Foucault's notion of a "regime of truth," Mongia examines rituals of "the inquiry" with focus upon administrative writings and decisions. She argues that such processes often operated as a means of deferring demands upon the state. Inquiries produced "impartial" and "expert" knowledge in "majority" reports, and inquiries either precluded "native" testimony, or employed it on a selective basis.[52]

"Native" testimony was deemed essentially "unreliable." Both Kale and Mongia, in separate approaches, critique the colonial production of knowledge as discounting some perspectives while privileging others under the guise of objectivity. The colonial production claimed to represent the best interests of "natives," since they could not ostensibly represent themselves.

A critical engagement with coolie testimonies lies in undressing the complicities of colonial economics and liberal ideologies that structure productions of knowledge, such as in representations produced by administrators and authorities. At the same time, a critical engagement also can be found in close-reading the testimonies themselves. Writing from a different perspective, Marina Carter examines representations of bondage by bonded labor, as conveyed in letters and testimonies from Indian indentured laborers of Mauritius. Others such as Khal Torabully (Mauritius), David Dabydeen (Guyana), Noor Kumar Mahabir (Trinidad and Tobago), and Brij Lal (Fiji) have attended to perspectives from indenture as expressed in mediums such as poetry, folksongs, and memoir. Carter describes her intervention as "shifting the focus of historical attention from the macro to the micro level: in other words, away from official perceptions and the administrative concerns of contemporaries, and the appraisal of causes and functions of migration schemes by historians, towards closer analysis of the preoccupations and problems articulated by indentured and ex-indentured Indians . . . "[53] She stresses that a significant but relatively unexamined source of materials regarding Indian indenture comes from the depositions of returnees. Indian migrant terms of service, although often extended, were legally finite; and they returned home in significant numbers, comprising some 30 percent of migrants.[54] The "macro" structures and "micro" experiences of indenture for Indian and Chinese laborers have as much in common as in contrast, as evident in the testimonies. Carter's foregrounding of Indian indenture testimony provides an apt comparison to Chinese indenture testimonies. While clearly noting the limitations of testimony, Carter at least proffers the reading of testimony as a step toward engaging perspectives of marginalized people and argues, "The study of petitions is important because of the opportunity they offer to visualize immigrants not as objects of analysis by colonial officials but as individuals articulating fears, disappointments and expectations in their own manner and idiom."[55] While Kale and Mongia examine the institutionalization of knowledge by the administering bodies, Carter examines perspectives via the mediated form of testimony. The separate arguments presented among these approaches are complementary and useful to the subject of testimonies from Cuba.

Postcolonial critiques of "inquiry" engage testimony as it has been produced under colonial regimes of "truth"-getting. In another vein, human rights approaches to testimony have included notions of testimony as it appeals to "western sensibilities," as anthropologist Meg McLagan notes: "Rooted in dual Christian notions of witnessing and the body as the vehicle of suffering, testimony is a deeply persuasive cultural form that animates and moves western sensibilities."[56] The contours of the coolie testimonies in Cuba suggest another dimension of testimony production. For Chen, it is language and the Chinese tradition of petitioning that complicate critiques of inquiry focused upon established forms of "western" juridical "process" and "witnessing." True, the British and the French were part of the 1874 commission, and the commission's political viability was directly linked to interests of Western powers. Furthermore, the commission was asked to respond to a list of questions posed by Robert Hart, regarded in modern scholarship as the "most influential Westerner in all of China" during the nineteenth century.[57] Yet one might also consider the testimonies as Chinese cultural and social forms appropriated by the coolies. This is not to naïvely suggest that a social history of Chinese petitioning is any less subject to ideological politics and administrative management and mediation. Rather, it is possible to say that the coolies transformed the petition to a subversive cultural form of protest to challenge a colonial state. The content and styles of the testimonies suggest that the coolies were using conventions of the Chinese petition, but more interestingly, they creatively transformed and exceeded the form of complaint. These were testimonies that creatively and graphically described slavery, indicted a system of human traffic and bondage, and sought freedom.

This study's priorities are exploring and close-reading the testimonies themselves as remnants of self-representation produced within certain constraints. This study recognizes co-constitutive considerations of the testimony-gathering process and comments on the inseparable intimacy of inquiry-testimony; but it also foregrounds the testifiers and testimonies themselves. In this case, the testimonies suggest that coolies seized the venue of testimony as an expression of resistance en masse. Such an argument suggests that the nature of "inquiry" is clearly not impervious to appropriation from below. The coolie testimonies suggest the possibility of state inquiry processes being seized upon by subaltern agendas. The seizure of the "testimony" form by thousands of coolies who utilized it as an expressive and elastic form, foregrounds strategic forms of resistance that mobilize one institutionalized form (of knowledge production and legal process) to overthrow another institutionalized form (of bondage). Therefore, this reading of the testimonies acknowledges the hegemonic imperatives of inquiry but also acknowledges the collective and creative force of subjects who seized the opportunity to change the dynamics of power.

COOLIE TESTIMONIES AND AFRICAN SLAVE NARRATIVES: METHODS FOR READING WORDS IN BONDAGE

The theorizing of "testimonies" as "narratives" has been most consistently and thoroughly raised in regard to testimonies associated with African slavery and in regard to testimonies of the Holocaust.[58] For the coolie materials, the treatments of slave materials offer the most salient comparison. The study of slave writings and the analysis of over 2,300 oral testimonies by ex-slaves are two main bodies of scholarship attending to the politics of narrating bondage.

The rise of coolie labor in Cuba from 1847 onwards coincides with the appearance of some of the most influential slave narratives of the nineteenth century. Frederick Douglass's *Narrative of the Life of Frederick Douglass* (1845) and Harriet Jacobs's *Incidents in the Life of a Slave Girl* (1860) are just two examples of the slave-autobiography genre that has been studied at great length for decades. Over one hundred book-length slave narratives were published in Europe and the Americas before 1865.[59] As examples, slave autobiographies from the Americas include the narrative of Mary Prince (Bermuda), *The History of Mary Prince* (1831); the narrative of Juan Francisco Manzano (Cuba), *Autobiografía* (1840); also from Cuba, there is the narrative of Esteban Montejo (Cuba) as told in *Biografía de un cimarrón* (1966) by Miguel Barnet, an example of a related but different genre, the *literatura testimonial*; the narrative of Mahommah Baquaqua (Brazil), *Biography of Mahommah G. Baquaqua* (1854); and of James Williams (Jamaica), a former slave who wrote of extended slavery under "apprenticeship" in *A Narrative of Events Since the First of*

August 1834 (1837). The body of slave narratives, with these works as prime examples, share literary expressions and formalized strategies employed in the particular contexts of slavery and abolition. Racialized politics of authenticity emerged as a primary influence in the composition of slave narratives, which included conventions such as testimonials by white abolitionist friends, prefaces by a white editor, chapters narrating slave experience, and appended supporting materials.[60] The narratives of Douglass, Jacobs, Prince, Williams, Baquaqua, and Manzano, for instance, were all introduced to the public by white sponsors. In fact, Manzano's narrative was initially published and contextualized in English by an abolitionist sponsor in London in 1840, and the narrative was not published in Spanish (and wasn't released in Cuba) until almost a century later in 1937. Language, mediation, and political debates of slavery contributed to the production and transmission of slave writings; and in different ways, these factors contributed to the production of the coolie testimonies. Distinctive thematic patterns marked the slave autobiographies, such as reading and writing as acts of resistance and self-realization. Douglass's autobiography prominently featured this trope of literacy and charted the course of his eventual journey to freedom. Literary scholars such as Henry Louis Gates, William Andrews, Robert Stepto, and James Olney have examined the tropes of literary and narrative conventions, motifs, and traditions that were employed in slave writings. These included religious and biblical forms, song, folklore, motifs of journey and quest, and tropes of the "Talking Book."[61] Others such as John Blassingame and Jean Fagan Yellin have also demonstrated the importance of the slave narratives in the historiography of slavery. With its deep literary and historical significance, the slave narrative calls for dual or combined approaches, as Charles T. Davis and Henry Louis Gates have emphasized.[62]

Slave narratives involved creative negotiation with what Dwight McBride calls an "imagined horizon" or the discursive reader in the context of both antislavery and proslavery debates.[63] Slave narratives were sited in the historical context of these debates and were featured before antislavery audiences, though they were accessible to the wider reading public and continued being produced for decades. Since that period, the narratives have been studied and recirculated today. In comparison, the coolie testimonies also were historically situated in relation to coeval slavery debates and liberal narrations of progress. The coolie testimonies were sited in the concomitant institutional and governmental struggles over the definition and institutionalization of "free" labor and migration. On the other hand, the testimonies have not been studied as a narrative body and are not circulated today. Their exposure was circumscribed by the state bodies that archived them, their primary readership being diplomats, officials, and civil servants involved in assembling or presenting the case. As a result, cultural legacies of coolie testimony materials are difficult to compare to the pervasive cultural impact of African slave narratives. While the coolie testimonies would have historic import and political utility in the ending of coolie traffic to Cuba, the substance of these testimonies are little known today to scholars, artists, and the general public.

On the surface, slave narratives are not necessarily a logical comparison in terms of their conditions of production and the making of a genre. Despite the historical linkages between slave and coolie, the comparison of their testimonial productions has obvious limits. After all, slave narratives mainly encompassed pamphlet and book-length authored productions that were published and sold to the public, mostly narratives by slaves who had either escaped slavery or had been freed. However, the treatments of slave narratives and the narrative tropes that appeared provide useful comparison to the coolie testimonies, both in terms of strategic uses of language and cultural expressions under social hierarchies and oppressive technologies of slave societies. The critical questions and methodologies raised by treatments of slave writings are entirely useful in an interrogation of the written testimonies by Chinese coolies in Cuba, which featured verse, literary allusions, historical references, cultural metaphors, and repeated tropes of witnessing, veracity, and resistance. Like African slaves, the great desire of the coolies *to tell* was limited by oppressive circumstances, material deprivation, social hierarchies, and of course, the punitive force of their owners and a "plantocracy" that oppressed the coolie through manipulations of the "contract." Furthermore, the majority of coolies who testified were in the service of their masters at the moment of testimony. Despite the inadequacy of words and the repercussions of testifying, Chinese inscribed searing impressions of their lives and simultaneously shouldered the burden of authenticity. The coolie testimonies share with African slave narratives the quality of being *transpirational*— to make known what was suppressed or secret, to exhale, to leak out what had transpired. The transpirational nature of the coolie testimonies, and in this case, the great risks taken to testify, call for a reading of their testimonies focused upon *exposing* suppressed facts of their enslavement. In a system of subjugation, coolies demonstrated an awareness of the burdens of veracity and epistemic authority. "Everything I have said is truth, nothing I have said is false," wrote Li Chengxun, a former teacher abducted into the coolie traffic (Petition 21). Other petitioners wrote, "(We) truly saw this with our own eyes and grief" (Petition 64). Dai Risheng and Pan Acong emphasized that "we were personally on the scene and truly witnessed everything with broken hearts. We have to tell the truth" (Petition 64). Others who appeared in person, such as Zeng Qingrong, pointed to their bodies as evidence, saying "I still have scars on my body" (Deposition 225)[64]

Some coolies, such as Xu Axiang, detailed not only "what I saw," but emphasized being criminalized and punished by authorities for describing what he witnessed (Petition 49). The language of witnessing and truth in the face of subjugation was a repeated feature of the testimonies, similar to patterns of African slave narratives. Like African slaves who gave witness to their experiences, the coolies addressed concerns of truthfulness. Some coolies further attempted to establish veracity through the use of formal language and literary forms, which indicated a certain social status and education, and thus, an assumed moral character. Using the Chinese language as a veil, coolies subverted their Spanish-speaking authorities in the testimony process and used particular tropes to depict their situations both poetically and graphically. In the midst of a slave society, coolies attested to their experience through creative expressions fashioned in resistance and in some cases, with lengthy arguments and analyses regarding the system of their exploitation. Thus like slave writings, the coolie testimonies demand attention as strategically formed, argued, and signified narratives.

The coolies made known their struggle in oral form as well, in 1,176 oral testimonies. Given in person before the commission, these oral testimonies are qualitatively different from the written testimonies. The written and oral testimonies constitute distinct bodies of testimony that suggest different considerations, due to their forms. Methodological questions regarding spoken testimony in a history of racialized bondage have been raised in treatments of an extensive body of testimonies regarding the experience of African American slavery. In particular, over 2,300 oral testimonies by African American ex-slaves were gathered in 1936–38 by the Federal Writers Project under the aegis of the Works Progress Administration. These were later collected by George Rawick in *The American Slave: A Composite Autobiography*. Contemporary scholars of race and slavery, and American history, emphasize the singular importance of these testimonies to understand what it was like to be a slave. Clearly, these testimonies were given under different circumstances than the coolie testimonies. The ex-slaves gave their recollections in the 1930s, a time lapse of several decades after emancipation. The coolies of 1874 testified in the moment of their bondage. Neither instance could be (or should be) said to be qualitatively more "authentic" or "true," but there are distinctions related to the purpose and timing of the testimony given. Nonetheless, the scholarly treatments of the WPA material raise concerns germane to the Cuba materials, such as the peculiarities of procuring and transcribing oral statements, the role of the "interviewer" or interrogator, the coded nature of language, cultural and colloquial expression, and the gaps and silences stemming from not only politics of memory but also politics of racialized interrogation. Norman Yetman and John Blassingame give attention to variance in interview methods and assess the potential for qualitative and quantitative analyses.[65] Blassingame notes that methodologies must take into account whether samples were representative of the larger population of ex-slaves. Additionally, he contrasts interviews involving black interviewers versus white interviewers, and notes racialized formalities and cultural contexts of the formerly slaveholding South as considerable factors in the testimony process. Coded speech patterns, vernacular expressions, and folklore emerge as important features of expression and veiling in the interviews. Paul Escott also notes the balance needed in methodological approaches to the testimonies, with both quantitative analysis and humanistic approaches being necessary.

The oral and written ex-slave narratives have been characterized as "narratives" and "testimonies," and as "literary" and "historical" material, and these documents have yielded a breadth of quantitative and humanistic insights.[66] The double assignations of "narratives" and "testimony" most importantly call attention to accounts in the first person and their employment as conscious acts of articulation and witnessing. With their testimonies, former slaves recounted their experiences of slavery, an institution that banned black testimony in the courts.[67] Apprehending testimonies as "narratives" brings attention to the expressive forms of their representations under oppressive structures. In a similar vein, the Chinese in Cuba gave witness to their experiences of another kind of slavery and provided "testimonies" that can be apprehended as "narratives." Like the slave testimonies, the testimonies of the coolies bring perspectives from their individual and collective experiences and provide grounds for examining their relationships to power and social order. What were their relationships with each other, with African slaves, with their owners? What were their relationships to family? How did they express their cultural and political views? As subjects of an official inquiry, they certainly were not naïve participants in the representation of their experiences within a coercive environment, and furthermore, they were aware of the transformative possibilities of their testimonies. Managing to combine urgency with deliberateness, the coolies provided testimony indicating that they were by no means passive subjects under examination. Their responses, while diverse and "polyvocal," demonstrate patterns that belie any assumptions of coolies as uninformed "victims" in the testimony process.

On one level, the coolie testimonies are individual accounts. On another level, they form an overall body of accounts with shared documentary and creative tropes. Their testimonies reveal strategies undertaken by coolies, individually and collectively, to communicate specificities of their lives; but the coolies' testimonies also reveal a shared subjugation. Rather than reading the testimonies before a commission as simply legalistic artifacts, reading their testimonies as narratives—as a form calling for both literary approaches and quantitative analyses—acknowledges the subversive agency of subjects whose creative articulations and representations of their experiences took place in both individual and collective struggles for power. Mark Sanders, critical scholar of South African testimonial literature and testimony given before the South African Truth and Reconciliation Commission, views testimony beyond the vein of "legal purism" or forensic necessity.[68] He points to the "tired oppositions of law and literature found in both legal purism and literary exceptionalism" and stresses the limitations inherent in reading testimony with this engrained binarism.[69] The giving and receiving of testimony, and its "reading," is marked by what Sanders calls an "enfoldedness" of the testifiers, questioners, and readers, and furthermore an "enfoldedness" of the living and the dead, exemplified by appeals seeking justice for the dead, burial rites and exhumation.

His theorizing of "enfoldedness" accounts for the nature of testimony as also "literary."[70] Given this compelling argument regarding testimony as being "literary" and given germane critiques regarding testimonies of African slavery and Indian indenture, the 1874 depositions and petitions are apprehended here as narratives of bondage that transcend the immediacy of an investigatory procedure.

WHO WERE THE COOLIES?

The following conclusions regarding the testimonies are taken from a 100 percent sample. There were 1,176 Chinese coolies who gave oral testimonies (depositions) and 1,665 Chinese coolies who gave written testimonies (petitions). The different forms of depositions and petitions call for a heterogeneous rather than uniform methodological approach. Besides the more obvious differences in oral-versus-written forms, the depositions and petitions differ in terms of singular versus collective representation. The depositions are uniformly individual statements attributable to particular individuals who each gave testimony in person. In contrast, petitions were submitted by individuals, small groups, and sometimes by groups of over a hundred. The collective will of these groups and its effect upon writing and representation needs to be considered in a reading of the petitions. With these large group petitions, certain kinds of analyses would be inaccurate or inappropriate, given the impossibility of determining which of the signatories (in mass petitions) were claiming any particular aspects of the petition. This is not to say that the depositions are a more "transparent" or conclusive body of representation. Rather, the qualitative and quantitative conclusions drawn from the depositions are distinct from those drawn from the petitions, due to certain consistencies of one genre of testimony versus the other. As a result, the following conclusions are drawn from either the deposition materials, or the petition materials, or both. Conclusions drawn from either or both sources will be so indicated. The testifiers were mainly located in three provinces: Havana, Matanzas, and Santa Clara (the latter comprised present-day Villa Clara, Cienfuegos, and Sancti Spiritus). These provinces are contiguous and central to the island and they were the most accessible to the commission because of their location. In these provinces could also be found the main sites of sugar plantations and *ingenios* (sugar mills), and included the largest populations of Chinese and Africans. These areas also accounted for over 70 percent of the sugar production in Cuba.[71] The testifiers were a subset of a larger Chinese population on the island, which numbered 68,825 at that time (this census number did not include the numbers of Chinese who were in the insurrectionary forces).[72] Of the total Chinese population, 20 percent were free and 80 percent were either in bondage or in prison. The enslaved Chinese amounted to some 55,000, according to Cuban census data.[73] The testimonies reflect perspectives from both free and enslaved Chinese. Of the deponents, 9 percent were free and 91 percent were enslaved at the time of testimony.[74] That a certain number of Chinese were "free" is a point of considerable interest, especially given their perspectives on *what it meant to be "free"* (see Chapter 3).

As a point of comparative interest, many blacks in Cuba were also categorized as "free." Of Cuba's total population in 1860, 30 percent were slaves and 20 percent were free persons of color.[75] Of Cuba's total persons of color in the 1860s, some 70 percent were slaves and 30 percent were free.[76]

The testimonies provide portraits of bondage spread over various economic and social spaces, involving more than just sugar plantation sites. Coolies described bondage in urban and rural sites, in diverse types of labor, such as railroad labor. A group of coolies sold to a railroad company in Guanabacoa wrote the following: "Although we have completed the contract for several years, they still refuse to give us the proof and freedom paper. And they even force us to sell our bodies again and continue working for them. It is extremely painful to be a contract laborer here" (Petition 18). In Oscar Zanetti and Alejandro García's important study of the Cuban railroads, is evidence that the coolies, at times, accounted for 50 percent of Caminos de Hierro's workforce. And by 1865 coolies were the main labor source for Ferrocarril de La Bahia, which reported having one slave and 446 Chinese coolies. In their study of conditions and mortality, Zanetti and García concluded that "the treatment meted out to both (coolie and slave) indicated no substantial difference. Nor should it be surprising that the demographic profile of the Chinese 'colonists' and African slaves manifested great similarities."[77] Other Chinese in bondage included those sold to small businesses and family households. Ou Rong was sold to a family in Havana that beat him and locked him up when he proved insubordinate (Deposition 776). A former tailor named Huang Qiutai recounted how he was sold to a candy shop and kept in bondage (Deposition

885). And a former grocer named Wu Asi was sold to a tailor's shop where the manager would abuse him and tie him up (Deposition 227). Chinese as waitstaff are preponderant in the history (and images) of the Chinese diaspora in the Americas, as Chinese were often portrayed as disadvantaged immigrants. Yet the typology of the disadvantaged immigrant falls short in addressing dimensions of the *captive* body and urban slaves, as exhibited in these accounts. The Chinese "shopkeeper" behind the counter, in such instances, was actually a slave.

The commission went to sites in or near the cities of Havana, Cardenas, Sagua la Grande, Matanzas, Colon, Guanajay, Guanabacoa, Cimmarones, Cienfuegos, and San Antonio. Based on the testimonies, the Chinese were forced into labor or labor sites that included, among others (as literally described by the coolies): bakery, beggar, blacksmith, building bridges, building lighthouses, butcher, carpenter, cement, cleaner, coal factory, construction, cook, cowherd, doctor, gardener, haircutter, horse-herding, official workshop, road construction, plant tobacco, plant vegetables, railroad company, rolling cigarettes, servant, small business, shoe shop, slater, stone cutter, sugar plantation, sugar refinery, woodcutter. The largest numbers testified to labor in sugar sites and "official workshops," described by the testifiers as sites of imprisonment and forced work administered by local officials. Testimonies were also taken from prisons and *barracones*, where Chinese were waiting to be sold. The testimonies, however, did not include two groups of Chinese: rebels and women. Due to the difficulties of travel and the unrest from civil war, the commissioners did not travel to Oriente, the eastern part of the island where rebellion was taking place, and consequently, were not exposed to rebel elements. If they had been able to do so, this would have yielded valuable information on coolie politics from the perspectives of runaways and rebels, or *chinos cimarrones* and *mambíses*. Although the commissioners noted that they were not able to interview rebels, they speculated that "the probability is that the Chinese are unwilling to take part in aiding the insurrection; minute details could only be ascertained by reference to sources of information—the camps of the insurgents—which could not be reached."[78] While making this speculation, the commissioners readily admitted that they could not know for sure if the Chinese were helping the insurrection. In all likelihood, another reason rebels were not interviewed was because of the commission's political concerns. If the commission was perceived as associating with insurgents, the investigation and subsequent negotiations on behalf of the coolies would have been compromised. The coolies did indicate, on the other hand, their dread of being forced to fight in defense of the Spanish: "Until the first moon of the Tongzhi, local officials and rich businessmen posted official notice and wanted to arrest us and force us to serve the army to fight in the mountains. Whenever we hear about this incident, we tremble with fear. Later they heard that Chinese officials would visit here so we escaped from being forced to serve the army. . . . We are afraid that we will be arrested and sent to serve the army after your honor goes back to China" (Petition 10).

Also missing are the perspectives of bonded Chinese women in Cuba. While there is scant evidence of their presence in the testimonies, the depositions and petitions reveal one case of their signatures appearing together on a mass petition (Petition 15), with their gender indicated by Chinese traditions of naming for unmarried and married women. Occasionally, testifiers made mention of Chinese women headed for bondage, such as a former bricklayer He Asi who mentioned traveling with twelve women during the passage (Deposition 376). While not mentioned in the testimonies, advertisements in Cuban newspapers also revealed the sale of Chinese girls and women. One such advertisement indicated the sale of a "Chinese woman of twenty one years" and another announced the sale of "a Chinese girl."[79] Glimpses of the traffic in Chinese girls emerge in episodes documented by Persia Campbell, Juan Pérez de la Riva, and Juan Jiménez Pastrana. Campbell noted the discovery of forty-four young Chinese girls imprisoned under deck of the British ship *Inglewood* bound for Cuba. Crew members reported being overwhelmed by the sickness and stench of the child captives, the eldest of whom was eight years of age.[80] Pérez de la Riva noted that in Cuba, José Suarez Argudin, a well-known Spanish Cuban slaver, was known to keep Chinese girls.[81] And Jiménez documented the open sale of Chinese in Cuban newspapers, including girls.[82] Furthermore, the treaty to end the coolie trade (ratified in 1878) made mention of China's demand for the return of Chinese women to Cuba. Despite indications of their presence, Chinese females did not have the opportunity to articulate the particularities of their bondage experience to the commission. This raises critical questions regarding narration and representation as well as certain testimonial omissions along gender lines. Given these limitations, the perspectives offered in the testimonies were almost entirely male, yet brief mentions of women hint at their presence in the coolie traffic. Even *before* the advent of mass coolie labor to Cuba, there is evidence of Chinese girls being sold in the Cuban market. In the main newspaper, *Diario de la Habana*, nine days prior to the first coolie ship arrival (the *Oquendo*), one ad read as follows: "For sale: A Chinese girl with two daughters, one of 12–13 years and the other of 5–6, useful for whatever you may desire. Also one mule . . ."[83]

Besides this significant gap in information regarding the earliest Chinese women trafficked to Cuba, the testimonies do reveal a significant amount of other information on the social diversity of the coolies. The evidence of great social diversity, and of a relatively privileged and educated segment among the coolies, runs contrary to generalizations of "coolie." The long-standing definition of "coolie" has been generic, usually marked by implications of workers being poor, unskilled, and uneducated. In push-pull analyses, nineteenth-century Chinese migrant laborers have been typecast as displaced, manual laborers, and often "working class." And there were those pushed to migrate because of droughts, floods, overpopulation, and political turmoil.[84] Zanetti and Garcia put it this way: "The economical advantage of the Chinese derived from his exploitation. Taking advantage of the extremely low living standards in their native country, the Cuban contractors subjected them to working conditions that white workers refused to accept."[85] From these historical mappings, Chinese migration to the West has been cast as a movement propelled from poor, inferior conditions of the native Old World to better opportunities in the New World. This modeling of Asian migration lends itself to periphery-core, Third World–First World paradigms, the bedrock of transnational labor systems analyses. Compounding the poor native model are nineteenth-century anticoolie discourses of morality, with coolies cast as not only poor but also as characters with "evil habits." The specter of poor hordes with evil habits occupied American congressional and British parliamentary debates and was sensationalized via journalistic representations of labor and shadowed public imaginaries of the Americas.[86] The commission report similarly made reference to slipshod characteristics of coolie types:

> *Industrious men who work willingly and well, can support themselves at home, and do not emigrate voluntarily. . . . The depositions, on the*

other hand, show that men have gone abroad to escape the results of crime and gambling, but even these did so in complete ignorance of the suffering which was before them, whilst, tempted by lotteries, etc. they adhere to their evil habits in their new place of residence, and are unable to lay by a single cash. From the moment of their falling into the snare, an existence of suffering is the only one known to both the stupid who are kidnapped and the clever who are induced to embark under false pretences.[87]

The commission's casting of wayward Chinese was likely a gesture to the prevailing attitude of the Qing government at the time, which had nominally prohibited Chinese subjects from going abroad. Until 1893 the official though unenforced law in China declared that those who clandestinely went abroad would be punished. The assumption on the side of the Chinese government was that only those of questionable character would be forced to such undesirable options of migrating to Cuba. The Qing government's view of coolies as undesirable—and as marginal and poor Chinese—converged with "yellow peril" discourses that underwrote a host of cultural and popular perceptions of "Asia" and Asian migrations.[88] The typology of the coolie reveals a construction based upon multisited and multinational convergences of stereotypes and rationales, with the coolie being cast as vagrant, morally marginal, and thus, exploitable and exploited. Interestingly, scholar Fernando Ortíz, often regarded as the preeminent narrator of Cuban history, likewise reinscribed negative stereotypes of Asians, despite his transformative theory of transculturation that accounted for the cultural formation of Cuban identity drawn from Africans, Europeans, and indigenous people. He added to that list, somewhat inconsequentially, the "Yellow Mongoloids" (in reference to Chinese in Cuba), bringing to mind yellow hordes. As Frank Scherer pointed out in his study of Ortíz and orientalism, Ortíz's uncomplimentary views were further expressed in his casting of subsequent Asian migrants as "spies": "The Mongoloid immigration, now as merchants, fishermen, garderners, and probably as spies, of many Asiatics from China and Japan continues."[89]

The scholarly generalizations regarding social origins of Chinese migrant laborers and period presumptions regarding "coolie hordes" are greatly disturbed by the testimonies. In fact, the testimonies reveal coolie labor to be drawn from widely diverse professional fields, including academia, medical practice, civil service, and business. Class-based notions of privilege and freedom, (i.e., peasants were indentured migrants, scholars were free migrants), are complicated by the fact that even highly skilled or educated workers were in bondage. In fact, not only Chinese but also Indian indentured laborers were from widely diverse social backgrounds. Upon examination of social origins of Indian indentured labor in Fiji, for example, Brij Lal concludes the following: "It is obvious that the evidence calls in question assertions about the predominantly low caste origins of the indentured migrants. Low castes, of course, contributed a large percentage of the total numbers migrating, but the proportion of high and middling castes is noteworthy."[90] Li Yingsong referred to the diversity of coolies' social origins, exclaiming that Chinese of all classes were falsely told that in Cuba "the payment is very high and no matter scholar, farmer, craftsmen or merchant, people will be asked to work based on their different talent" (Petition 6). In 62 percent of the depositions, it is possible to infer the deponents' occupations in China *before* their arrival to Cuba. A statistical breakdown reveals the largest labor group in the coolie demography to be farmers, comprising 17.4 percent of the indentured workforce. In addition, there were others who made their living selling farming goods, such as vendors who sold vegetables, eggs, fruit, and chickens (and who also could have been farmers themselves). *Still, some 80 percent were not farmers or sellers of farming goods*. The great diversity of the coolie class undercuts homogenizing assumptions of the socioeconomic background of "labor" and reveals that the bondage system ensnared doctors and farmers alike. The table below includes some of the testifiers' occupations based upon their self-descriptions, with some descriptions being easily recognizable, some general, and others more arcane.

Studies indicated that the coolies were craftsmen (such as glassblowers, silversmiths, engravers, and chair makers) and wage laborers (such as waiters, cooks, clerks, and office workers). A large number made their primary living selling and trading goods (such as coal, wood, salt, and sugar) and making products (such as wine, silk, cloth, and paper). Numbers included business owners (including those owning a jewelry store, a dye workshop, an herb shop), and some were in the fields of medicine, the arts, the military, and civil service (doctors, scholars, students, actors, soldiers,

TABLE 2.1   OCCUPATIONAL BACKGROUNDS OF CHINESE COOLIES AS
INDICATED IN THE DEPOSITIONS AND PETITIONS OF CUBA 1874

OWNER OF:

"After-life" shop	Herb shop	Rice shop
Bowl store	Incense shop	Shoe shop
Chair shop	Jewelry store	Silver shop
Cloth shop	Oil and wine shop	A shop (general)
Coal shop	Paper store	Tea/Food shop
Dye workshop	Pawn store	Tofu shop
Firewood store	Paper-fan shop	
Grocery store	Restaurant	

MAKER/SELLER OF:

Baskets	Lamps	Vegetables
Buckets	Leather	Wine
Candy	Milk	Wood
Canvas	Oil	Chairs
Chicken	Opium	China
Coal	Pastry	Gold thread
Crystal sugar	Pork and mutton	Machines
Eggs	Pottery	Materials for making paper
Fences	Salt	Mirrors
Fish	Salty fish	Paper
Fruit	Sausage	Silk
Goods made in kiln	Seafood	Thread
Grocery	Shoes	Tobacco
Hats	Tea	
Herbs	Tofu	

PROFESSIONS AND LABOR:

Actor	Blacksmith	Butcher
Aristocrat	Boat poler	Carpenter
Animal driver	Boat rower	Carrier (general)
Bamboo craftsman	Bricklayer	Civilians (general)

(continued)

TABLE 2.1   (*CONTINUED*)

Cloth weaver	Military officer	Wine steamer
Cook	Military soldier	Woodcutter
Copper forger	Naval officer	Worker in a bookstore
Cotton fluffer	Navy soldier	Worker in a dye shop
Court official	Odd jobs	Worker using water mill in
Craftsman	Official	glass shop
Doctor	Painter	Worker in grocery store
Engraver of patterns and	Palanquin lifter	Worker in jade shop
designs	Pole carrier	Worker in a paper store
Farmer	Porter	Worker in a restaurant
Fisherman	Servant	Worker in a silk store
Flax weaver	Silversmith	Worker in a tea shop
Gardener	Student	Worker in uncle's silk store
Glass blower	Tailor	Worker on a small boat
Government worker	Teacher	Worker, laborer (general)
Grinder of rice	Theater manager	Worker in Tong Ren Tang
Haircutter	Translator	Herb Shop
Herder	Water mill operator in a glass	
Jade shaper	shop	
Japanner	Wine brewer	

SMALL BUSINESS:

Business (general)	Paper and material business	Suitcase business
Currency exchange business	Pharmacy business	Tobacco business
Firecracker business	Ship/boat business	
Hemp/flax/jute business	Store (general)	

sailors, and officials). Interestingly, some testifiers indicated that they were recruited to use their skills in the coolie passage; but after providing service, such as interpreting or doctoring, they were sold off with the rest of the cargo. Zhan Tailong recounted being hired on a ship in Jakarta as a translator, for his abilities to speak Malay. He was promised a return passage and given an "official document" that ostensibly protected him. Instead, Zhang was sold off upon arrival in Cuba. He declared with some irony, "I did not understand the local language, so only later did I know that the captain sold me. How miserable it is!" (Petition 80). One doctor, Yao Wenxian, was recruited to care for the sick on a coolie ship; but upon arrival, he suffered the fate of being sold "to work in wards in a sugar plantation" (Petition 57). Another doctor, Chen Ming, wrote of being entrapped after running into an ill-intentioned acquaintance "Yang," who was purchasing herbs:

> *I trained to become a doctor since I was young. [. . .] Mr. Yang said a foreigner asked him to find a doctor to treat people on a foreign ship until it arrived at the city.*
>
> *I then went to Xinhe Hang with him.[i] After I negotiated with the owner of the ship, he promised to pay all the expenses including salary, traveling fee and others. On the fifteenth day of the eighth moon, I signed a contract, which stated that I was responsible for medical treatment on the ship, and after arriving the destination, I could return by taking the same ship; if not I would be compensated for one hundred and eighty yuan and I could take another ship as I wish. After arriving at Havana city, I took out the contract; however, the owner of the ship was evil! He tricked me to give him the contract, but he refused to give me any money. Moreover, since I did not speak the language, I did not know where to go. The suffering and humiliation I experienced cannot be described with words.[. . .]Whoever hears about our experience of being hired labor will cry, and whoever sees us being hired labor will grieve. As quoted. (Petition 9)*

One physician, De Situ, petitioned from a cigarette workshop in jail and complained of not being able to practice medicine (Petition 3).

The coolies came from a rich diversity of social lives, and rural and urban economies, as different as the "scholar" who indicated the level of imperial exams he had passed; the "theater manager" who likely worked with an opera troupe; the commonly known "cotton fluffer" who plied his trade in the streets by calling out and offering to fluff cotton comforters

---

i. Xinhe Hang was likely a foreign firm.

with his simple tools; the "after-life shop owner" whose artistic paper houses and symbolic figures were central to the rituals of death and worship; the "poling boat" man who ferried people across water; the "aristocrat" whose once-vaunted status meant nothing in bondage; the army "officer" who was betrayed by fellow soldiers and sold; the "teacher" who was lured into a tutoring job for a rich family, only to discover that he was being sold into bondage. The style and writing of the petitions reflected the social class of their writers, including well-educated persons who denounced injustice through references to literature and history, former businessmen who analyzed the political and economic predicaments of bondage, or farmers who wrote plainly and astutely about their dire fates and the nature of systemic exploitation.

Eighty-nine percent of the testifiers were from Guangdong, but their testimonies nevertheless indicated coolies originating from at least *fourteen* provinces of China, including inland provinces and some near Mongolia, in descending order: Guangdong, Fujian, Hunan, Jiangxi, Zhejiang, Guangxi, Jiangsu, Jiangnan, Anhui, Sichuan, Tianjin, Henan, Hebei, and Shanxi. The testimonies also reveal that the coolie population included Vietnamese, Filipinos, and Manchu bannermen, who were a highly privileged ethnic group in China.[91] As Bai Yongfa stated proudly, he was of the "red-border banner Manchu people" and personally knew of "other Manchu people" who were enslaved in Cuba, such as one "white-border banner Manchu, his name is Huang" (Deposition 204). Bai's testimony harkened back to the tribal, militarized organization of the Manchus who had ruled during the Qing Dynasty and were given special legal and economic privileges in China. They had become organized under four plain and four bordered banners of yellow, red, blue, and white. Zhang Yi, who was taken on a coolie ship from Macao to Cuba in 1864, noted that "there were several Vietnamese people who came with me on the same ship from Macao" (with reference to what was then Annam) (Deposition 555).

The testimonies also reveal the presence of very young migrants. Rarely have studies of early Asian migration included the testimony of extremely young laborers. However, 20 percent of the deponents admitted being taken to Cuba at ages under twenty. Some of these 20 percent were abducted at ages of eight, nine, eleven, twelve, and thirteen. One twenty-two year old named Lai Chuanshou recounted his abduction at age thirteen. Tempted into a gambling game, he lost money and was ashamed to go home. He suffered unexpectedly terrible consequences (Deposition 690). Yet, the young were not necessarily pliable. One Huang Achai, age thirty-one, revealed himself to have been a fierce nine-year-old who was entirely uncooperative while kidnapped. His abductors had to "soak me in water for two days" to induce him to sign a contract. He was sold to a military official in Havana and then resold into mountain labor at age eleven; but apparently, he remained unbroken. He had the gumption to attempt to sue his "manager." The boy was subsequently punished. Even then, he refused to cooperate: "I didn't have enough food. The manager was mean and hit me a lot; I wanted to sue him. Once he found out I wanted to sue him, he made me wear shackles while working. I suffered a great deal. After eight years, my owner wanted me to sign a new contract, but I refused; then he sent me to the official" (Deposition 16). Amazingly, the boy lived to give testimony at age thirty-one. Chen Afu pointed out that "Somebody kidnapped me to a 'pig building' in Macao when I was 11. They gave me a contract, but I didn't understand the meaning of it" (Deposition 12). Zhang Er, however, was the oldest of the testifiers, and at age seventy-two, gave one of the briefest testimonies. He concluded: "I am too old" (Deposition 43).

3

THE PETITIONS:
WRITING AS RESISTANCE

Edward Jenkins, a British barrister, noted that during a commission investigation into indenture in Guyana, he received petitions from Chinese that came in a variety of forms: "Besides the many deputation of Coolies [*sic*] from the estates, all persons who were in any way connected with the Commission became the suffering recipients of many letters and petitions. Some of these in Chinese I still possess, written on all sorts of paper—brown, straw, candle-box, cartridge, etc., one on a tiny slip of scarlet torn off a wall or cut from a book. The woes contained in such documents were naturally unfathomable to me, but I sent them to the Commission, on whose application the government interpreter translated them into English."[1] It is not difficult to imagine that those Chinese in the former British Guiana wrote their petitions on whatever materials available. In Cuba, given the conditions for coolies, it would have been a challenge for the coolies to find the means and opportunity to write. Materially impoverished, with restricted freedom, under a brutal regime of labor extraction—how did the Chinese manage to write petitions? How did they get the time and materials to write them? Most certainly the petitions were written in secret. The commission made note of the petitions as clandestine testimony:

The following extracts from petitions supply additional information. Liang A-te, in service at Matanzas, declares, "I last night intended to in person lay my story before the Commission, but I was dragged back and placed in irons by my employer, and I am in consequence compelled to hand in this written statement." Pan To-li and 2 others in service in the neighborhood of Cardenas declare, "hearing of the inquiry which you are instituting we intended to in person present our statement, but our employer said he would only allow (other) eight men to visit you, and as his severity is great we did not dare to disregard the order and therefore transmit this written petition.[2]

Those coolies who were chosen to appear may have, in all likelihood, later informed their fellow coolies of the procedures and makeup of the commission, the demeanor of the members, and their discovery that commissioner Chen and members of his team were natives of Guangdong, the home province of the majority of coolies. Those who were prevented from appearing would have become further emboldened to send in petitions. How were the petitions delivered? Exactly how the petitions got from plantations (or labor sites) to the commission is unknown. It is likely that coolies discovered when the commission was arriving and passed on information about the commission's itinerary. Potential petitioners aimed to get their petitions delivered on the exact dates when the commission was stationed nearby. Dates and location of submission are indicated on each petition, with one or two petitions trickling in on some days, but as many as eight were submitted on another day. The petitions then were transcribed by a Chinese secretary, whose role was made transparent by the uniform opening and ending affixed on all transcriptions, opening with "According to the petition of . . ." and ending with "as quoted."[3] "As quoted" could also be translated as "et cetera." Either translation, "as quoted" or "et cetera," indicates the possibility that information was omitted from the petitions. Some petitions came to abrupt endings, either due to circumstances or decisions of the writer or the transcriber. Also it is possible that human errors were made in the transcription process. Yet for some petitions, there would have been limits to rescripting them, particularly with regard to those with sections in poetic verse. In some cases, rescripting one detail or word would have meant rearranging and rewording sections of the petition with considerable effort. The rhyme, rhythm, length of lines, word order, caesura, and tone (as Chinese is a tonal language and rhetorical phrases were fashioned with this in mind) maintain the integrity and meaning of passages particularly in instances of verse. Changing or omitting a word would have meant rewriting and recreating the structural integrity.

Each petition reflected the unique voice, style, and peculiarities of the authors, though not all petitions displayed wholly complex compositions. Some petitions were written in a more literary style and some displayed a more vernacular style. Some were lengthy and well crafted, others were short and pithy. Overall, however, all were written in forms reserved for formal writing, different than spoken Chinese; and commonly, many employed terms that no longer appear in the modern Chinese language lexicon. The testimonies also employed terms that were created by the coolies to address their unique situation. And some terms were phonetically transliterated forms, such as terms for Spanish-language and English-language places and names, such as the much mentioned "dou la zha" and "cou la zha," which apparently meant *La Trocha* in Spanish, literally meaning "the trail." Apparently, this forced labor site entailed the clearing of forestry and constructing a railway, and was especially dangerous. Coolies spoke of it with dread, noting the high attrition rate and their overexposure to the elements. As one coolie explained, "There was no house so I had to live in the forest. I had to chop trees, dig ditches, and construct the railway" (Deposition 244). Some terms were conceived to describe their particular conditions, such as "Washing Head" to denote baptism, "Selling People House" to denote the place of coolie auctions, "Runaway Company" to denote the detention and forced labor of Chinese who were deemed runaways, and "Official Workshop" to denote a place of forced labor run by officials and local government. As expected during this period of the Qing dynasty, the testimonies were written using traditional Chinese characters, a form no longer in use and now supplanted by simplified Chinese and the modern lexicon.

In his report, Chen referred to the coolie testimonies as *bing* (禀). *Bing* was a term used to denote a report from subordinate officials to their superiors.[4] However, the term can also be used as noun and verb. As a verb, "bing" could also mean "telling" and the giving of information from people of lower social status to those of higher status (this was a term that once caused a diplomatic dispute in British-Chinese relations).[5] As one coolie stated to the commission, "I came especially to tell you my poor condition here" using *bing* to denote the social context of his telling (Deposition 19).[6] One petition, for example, was composed by four military officers who began their petition with the term *zhi deng* (职等), a term used when lower-level officers or officials reported to higher-level officials (Petition 11). Such Chinese called upon their previous knowledge of *how* epistemic authority could be established in testimonies. The four military officers, now reduced to coolies, made clear their former status: "Zhang Luan, a military officer from Guangdong, former Commandant of the Right Brigade in Tingzhou City who was awarded the rank of Brigade Commander because of military merits; Cheng Rongling, a Jiangsu native and Expectant Appointee for Police Chief; Mo Rongxian, a Commandant in the Jinxian County, Guangdong; Chen Xuezhou, a Squad Leader by Recommendation from Guangdong Province . . ." The first, Zhang Luan, held significant rank as commander of a brigade, a unit of some 500 soldiers in the Qing army. Their petition bore the perspectives of officers, as they presented views regarding principles of both good and bad governance. They deplored the collusion of both Chinese and foreign agents in the trafficking of coolies and lamented the costly losses to Chinese society and kinship. In their new world of bondage, scholarly and official rank, not to mention achievements in literature and martial arts, were treated with disrespect, they wrote. They also offered some brief comments relating to Cuba's civil war. Zhang, as it turns out, also appeared and testified orally. His testimony revealed careful attention to details that would affirm his identity. He stated, "In the eleventh year of Xianfeng (1861), I went to suppress the bandits in Jiangnan with Officer Zhenhai Lai; then I went to Fujian and worked with Officer Zuo. In the eleventh year of Tongzhi (1872), I went home to see my father, Yong Zhang. Then I met a soldier, Xiong Zhu, who was in my old troop. He invited me to Macao; however, I was abducted into Tong Fa Pigpen and locked in it by him" (Deposition 1050).

How a deposition was stated or how a petition was written, was as important as its factual content, as was the social rank of the person testifying. These factors determined whether the testimony would be seriously considered by the magistrate. The testimonies demonstrated types of formal address and conclusions that were customary in address to a Chinese juridical body and included expressions of humility and respect to the reader. Florid and respectful writing, seemingly excessive in a modern English translation, was not unusual in Chinese address to superiors. But this flowery writing was also part of the coolies' strategy to establish epistemic authority and persuade elite authorities to read their petitions. Some gestured to the commissioner or to the emperor with respectful homage, such as the ninety-six petitioners who closed their petition with "His Majesty's kindness is like a wide ocean, extending to corners of the world. We are like grass and trees that benefit from his rain-like generosity, which is a rare grace in thousands of years. We, as ordinary civilians, are humble and foolish laborers with misfortune. Youths trapped in a land faraway from home; adults wasting their lives in a foreign country. We regret that we are poor and sickly. We feel woeful that the harsh government here is making more cruel policies. That is why we dare to voice our grievance to you" (Petition 25).

Despite limitations of language and of not knowing "where to bring an action against them [masters]," the Chinese attempted to take the juridical route in Cuba before appealing to the commission. The testifiers made it clear that previous to the commission's visit, they felt themselves to be law-abiding persons and had sought justice through local law and government in vain. Their challenges to authority followed four main actions: on-site resistance, running away, and appealing to local officials (and joining the insurrectionary wars, though not mentioned). Yet they understood that the juridical system was entwined with colonial business interests against Chinese labor. There were 131 petitioners who asserted, "Officials never hear the case. Even if they try to appeal, officials never look at the case" (Petition 55). Seventeen petitioners protested, "If we report an incident to the government, no one cares. We hate them but we are helpless" (Petition 38). Another four coolies wrote, "We appeal to the mayor; however he does not care at all. When we report to the government, officials do not look at the case. We are fined and have no place to voice our grievance" (Petition 43). Others observed that "policemen and officials are bent solely by profits" (Petition 53) and "the government has made ways to make use slaves over and over" (Petition 54). Officials obstructed and deferred cases, and used some cases to arrest and re-bond Chinese. The former military officers of Petition 11 said, "On top of it all, most of the Cuban officials are businessmen; sugar plantation owners always collude with the government officials. If owners apply brutal punishments, officials pretend that they do not know anything about it. If owners beat laborers to death, officials do not ask about it."

Many petitions contained direct appeals for rescue. "I now appeal to you to save my life" was a typical appeal, like that of Lu Aguang (Petition 7). Small groups such as Diao Mu, Li Xiang, Liu Quan, and Jiang Jiu, similarly pled, "We are hoping that your honor has a plan to save our lives" (Petition 53). Others begged plainly, "We beg your honor to show pity on our ant-like lives. Save us and right this injustice" (Petition 84). Yet others went farther and aimed at *systemic change*. This type of testimony correlated with a unique aspect of the petitions, which is the presence of not only group signatories but also mass signatories indicting the bondage system. These groups seized the opportunity to speak out on a range of subjects beyond their immediate, individual fates. Reflecting the imprint of collective protest, these petitions contained larger arguments that analyzed systemic exploitation and sought to abolish the coolie system. Thirty-four percent of the petitions were signed by ten or more coolies and 12 percent were signed by groups of eighty or more. The petitions from the largest groups came with signatories in the following numbers: 90, 95, 97, 107, 124, 129, 131, 131, and 164. The writing of a petition not only represented a way to voice their grievances, but in the case of group petitions, also incurred collective action via the clandestine writing and signing of these petitions. The feature of raising consciousness and forming resistance via writing is especially significant given the repressive measures to sever Chinese from communication with the outside world and prevent them from forming alliances *with each other*. Group actions or attempts to organize were treated as seditious acts. In dozens of petitions and depositions, coolies described the retributions for speaking, congregating, and walking in groups of two or more. There were 124 petitioners who repeated the common refrain, "if several Chinese talk in the street, the police will claim that they are planning a riot" (Petition 55). Zheng Amao and others wrote, "We were not allowed to gather three or five people together to talk" (Petition 85). Likewise, another coolie bemoaned the restrictions against Chinese as preemptive, declaring that even "the ones who are not supposed to be locked up are all locked up; the ones who did not run away are accused as runaways" (Petition 11). Fourteen petitioners noted that "we always think of writing letters to warn other Chinese not to be deceived into coming to Cuba again, but we find no way to send them out" (Petition 2). Another 159 petitioners ended with the following: "Since we cannot send letters back to our families, we have no way to voice our grievance" (Petition 80).

The surveillance of coolies was accomplished not only via the collusion of local officials and owners but also via collusion of foreign consular officials such as those from Portugal. Profiting from the coolie trafficking through their colony of Macao, the Portuguese also profited from recycling coolies in Cuba. Captured Chinese were accused of planning "revolt," and as such, could be turned in by almost anyone and then resold. Describing these suppressions and alliances, the Chinese indicated awareness of their subject positions as imbedded in multisided collusions and conflicts. The Chinese described their attempts to form organizations for collective action and the retaliatory measures against them. They sought out non-Cubans, such as British and Americans, who might be sympathetic to their cause, while consistently referring to Portuguese as local conspirators with the Spanish. However, it should be noted that testifiers also indicated that the British, Americans, and Europeans were active slave and coolie owners. One coolie recounted: "My owner is British, who treated me badly. After working for one month, eighteen people and myself killed a white overseer, who is a native. We couldn't bear his bullying and torture anymore, so we tried really hard to kill him" (Deposition 436). Coolies demonstrated an awareness of being sited in a multinational field of strategic alliances and rivalries. Thirty-one petitioners stated with mounting anger the following: "Several years ago, because of no doctors for the ill, no graveyards for the dead, no way to send letters home, and no definite date to return home, with donations from every county and from righteous foreigners, the Chinese planned to set up an association and elected leaders. Unexpectedly, the Portuguese government wanted to break the morale of the Chinese. They colluded with Chinese traitors and accused the Chinese of revolt. Later, Portugal's vice-consul lured the Chinese with fake freedom papers in Cardenas. At the same time, he secretly contacted patrols to check their papers and extort them" (Petition 11). Another eleven petitioners described similar failed efforts to organize: "British and American officials saw the hardness we have been through and tried to help us set up an organization. By the time the organization was almost set up, the local thugs framed us by accusing us of trying to help the rebellion, so the organization was disbanded" (Petition 84). There were 133

petitioners who declared that British and Americans "negotiated with local officials so that we can still be alive" (Petition 15). Alliances with British and Americans were also mentioned in Petitions 2, 10, 25, 37, 40, 53,
84, and in the one below:

> *In the night of the tenth day of the ninth moon in 1871, tyrannical local*
> *officials arrested all of us who had completed working contracts,*
> *whether or not we had freedom papers. Later we were all sent away and*
> *locked up in official workshops and jails. Fortunately, officials from*
> *Britain and the United States could not bear to sit back and watch with-*
> *out doing anything, so they went to negotiate with local officials; there-*
> *fore, we were released gradually. Yet, local precinct chiefs often spy on*
> *us. If we stay in a house or gather together and chat in a group of three*
> *or five, precinct chiefs would accuse us of gambling, or smoking, and*
> *then demand that we turn in our freedom papers. We are bullied, black-*
> *mailed and punished. If we refuse to be extorted, they arrest us and lock*
> *us up or make us work. During that time, a morally courageous Ameri-*
> *can named "Langluofu"[i] could not bear to stand idly by and donated*
> *money to help us set up an association to mediate disputes. However,*
> *the rich and powerful local thugs ganged up and wrongly accused us of*
> *using that money to help rebels. As a result, the association was broken*
> *up. We are still bullied by those rich and powerful locals. The bullying*
> *seems to last forever; we utterly detest it. Nowadays, every county has*
> *set up official workshops. People who are about to complete contracts*
> *are either sent to those official workshops to work, sent away to work in*
> *mountains, or forced to sign another contract. They are fed like fowls or*
> *dogs, reprimanded and forced to work like oxen or horses. The misery*
> *and sorrow are extremely unbearable. As quoted. (Petition 23)*

Some petitioners even asked the commission to get local foreign consu-
lates to take them in, such as those in Petition 10: "We beg earnestly to be
taken care of by the embassies of other countries so that we can escape
from this disaster. Please save our lives." The petitioners also mentioned
strategic attempts to obtain papers through British and Portuguese consu-
lates by claiming that they were formerly residents of Hong Kong (British

---

i. Transliteration.

colony) or Macao (Portuguese colony), though the responses of the Portuguese were portrayed by the coolies as decidedly unfavorable. The depiction of alliances, in the face of retribution, reveals an avenue of resistance fashioned beyond the plantations. By describing such avenues of resistance, the Chinese brought into the open an awareness of their cause as directly linked to rival views concerning coolie labor in Cuba. The petitions emerge here as protest literature situated in the context of multilateral disputes and negotiations; and at minimum, the testimonies offer a portrait of migration and bondage as regionally and globally entangled. The petitions and depositions referred to the following cities and countries: Britain, United States (San Francisco and New York), France, Spain, Portugal, Macao, Philippines, Vietnam, Hong Kong, Singapore, Indonesia (Jakarta and Semarang), Malaysia (Kuala Lumpur), and Australia (Melbourne). Aside from the strategic alliances sought by coolies, the trajectories of diaspora and imaginaries associated with going abroad led to easy deception of those such as Li Wencai, a former fish seller who said, "They did not translate the words in the contract to me, and I thought it was only something about working in San Francisco" (Deposition 116).

THE WITNESS PETITION: SHOUTING OUT THE NAMES

Some Chinese articulated their experiences by writing in the tradition of witnessing. Some expressed themselves by writing poetically of spiritual and emotional trials and others by presenting an analytical argument. These types of written testimonies—the witness petition, the verse petition, the argument petition—represent some of the diverse and strategic approaches undertaken by the coolies who adapted the testimony platform to suit their own purposes. We begin by reading examples of witness petitions, which are then followed by verse petitions and argument petitions.

Yuan Guan submitted a brief but exacting "witness petition" in Colon. He utilized a form of listing and bluntly enumerated the injustices he witnessed. He boldly named names and particularized incidents. Yuan Guan's testimony focused upon seeking justice by presenting oneself as a witness to "unrighted wrong" as visited upon others. His and others' similar testimonies forced the inquiry into facing the most extreme consequence of the coolies' "conditions": the violent loss of human life. The coolies described kidnapping, beating, torture, murder, suicide, and psychological terrorism that had gone unpunished. Yuan Guan stated that he was kidnapped and sold, and he gave the names of his owner and plantation in transliterated terms known among the coolies. The petition by Yuan Guan, Yong'an County, Guangdong Province reads as follows:

> *In the year of 1858, I was kidnapped to Macao. There were more than a hundred people on the ship. The ship arrived in Havana in April of 1859. Until mid-June, we were sold to a white foreigner named "Lang Bei Lu" and then we were brought to a sugar plantation named "Jiu Bi Jia Shan A Huai." Until 1860, the owner had bought sixty Chinese to work for him. Unexpectedly, in 1864 the old owner died and all the managers and overseers were changed. The new ones are as vicious as wolves and tigers. Their hearts are like snakes. There was a person named Chen Azao in the plantation. He was so depressed that he jumped into the sugar hot pot and died. Another person named Lian Axing had weak-foot illness. But he was forced to work. Later he hung himself. Another person named Liu Bairen was beaten by the overseers till he spat blood and died.[7] Another person named Hong Afu did not do enough work and tried to escape secretly. However, he was caught by the overseer at night. He was beaten to death in the house with the big chimney. Later he was burned. People from outside didn't know about it until someone saw the human figure inside the window. Another person named Zhang Abing was sick and took poison to kill himself. Another person named Zhou Shilan was beaten to death by the overseer on the fifteenth day after he reached the sugar plantation. As quoted. (Petition 60)*

Like African slave narratives, the coolie petitions were a *writing into history* of a previously suppressed history. In Petition 60, Yuan's *naming* and writing about the fates of his fellow countrymen—"Hong," "Chen," "Lian," "Liu," "Hong," "Zhang," and "Zhou"—demonstrated that he was keenly aware of his pressing role as the surviving witness who would be inscribing an otherwise suppressed history. Yuan's petition is a brief history of lives otherwise expunged from colonial records and colonial language. His petition was more about other people and his observations of them, than about himself. Without Yuan's intervention, the fate of Hong, who was tortured and burned in the "house with the big chimney," would have gone unrecorded.

The witnessing testimonies take on significance in the context of a system wherein simply giving testimony could be deadly for the Chinese. The Chinese who informed were punished. As noted in Petition 20, "No one goes to the law against the owners. Even so, government officials merely come to take a look and get through it perfunctorily. Some of us, who . . . have witnessed a murder, do not dare to tell the truth. If we ever do so, we would be killed immediately." The witnessing petitions emerge as acts of intervention and resistance in the official record of history that was part of a system obstructing coolies from "informing." One petitioner wrote that he could not tell of the crime and have it recorded, even though the crime was known unofficially: "Last year, laborer Zeng Aji was beaten to death. I couldn't inform. Yet we knew about it far and wide" (Petition 33). A deponent typically described a coolie being beaten to death and made sure to note, "No one knows that dead person's name is Afu" (Deposition 225). While only remembering the first name, a common name "Afu," the deponent made the point of claiming it, nonetheless. Some testifiers desired to "inform" even if they did not know the names at all, revealing the existence of "someone": "I do not remember his name, but I remember he was clubbed to death using a wooden rod" (Deposition 877). Another declared, "Two people could not stand the torture and hanged themselves, which happened when I had been on the sugar plantation for two months. Although I could not remember those two person's names, I saw it happen with my own eyes" (Deposition 244). Wen Azhao said with anguish, "I couldn't remember these dead people's names, for I was almost dying at that time, and I was too collapsed to remember. I could only remember two dead acquaintances' names. One is Ah-Lai who was locked up, beaten with a handspike, poked with a knife, and beaten to death; the other is Ah-San who hanged himself. Both of them couldn't take the misery anymore and gave up their will to live" (Deposition 50). The importance of remembering and reclaiming history as a witness, even the act of stating "I do not remember the name," is a recurrent trope of the testimonies. Despite not remembering "the names," the reiteration of "someone's" existence calls attention to the politics of claiming identity and memory in histories of bondage and resistance. As can be found in histories of African slavery, Chinese coolies were either re-named with Spanish names, or they bore some appellation assigned to them by sellers, owners, or overseers. The naming and renaming of coolies take on a more perverse significance in references made by coolies to their being forced to take *names of the dead* (see further elaboration in "Chasing Freedom"). Repeatedly, the Chinese mentioned being forced to take on another name. As narrated in Petition 41, "I was whipped many times; my name was changed." The renaming of Chinese appeared in Cuban newspapers that regularly advertised Chinese for sale and posted runaway notices. Even in the months during and after the commission visit, newspapers continued to run ads offering cash rewards for turning in or providing information on the whereabouts of Chinese runaways. A perusal of *Diario de la Marina* reveals the regular advertisements for Chinese runaways alongside those for escaped slaves, such as a Chinese named "Fernando," described as an escaped cook of approximately eighteen to twenty years of age, having large eyes, and bearing a scar on his head now covered over by hair.[8] Another advertisement offered a reward for a Chinese named "Largio," described as hairless, of regular stature, having a lesion on one leg, and having just escaped from the *barracón*.[9] Another advertisement listed "Ramon," a Chinese escapee aged eighteen.[10] The colonizing practice of renaming, and the nature of subordination through renaming, such as in the cases of "Fernando," "Largio," or "Ramon," raises the practical epistemological question of how history is remembered, how it was recorded, and how it might be reconstructed.

The advertisements, which exhibit the public renaming of Chinese, contrast with the testimonies by the coolies who instead referred to each other as Yuan did: "Hong," "Chen," "Lian," "Liu," "Hong," "Zhang," and "Zhou." The trope of naming in the testimonies—purposefully naming names, reclaiming one's name, or conversely, emphasizing the importance of naming and the acts of forgetting/remembering/renaming of names—brings to mind the motif of naming in African slave narratives. For example, Olaudah Equiano recounted his being renamed "Gustavus Vassa" (a Swedish name) by his first master, in Equiano's narrative *The Interesting Narrative of the Life of Olaudah Equiano, or Gustavus Vassa the African* (1789). Frederick Douglass described being renamed several times under different masters until he escaped slavery and named himself, in his *Narrative of the Life of Frederick Douglass* (1845). Naming also figured into Douglass's rhetorical strategy of establishing the authority and veracity of his narrative. He purposefully affixed names and places throughout his autobiography. And at the same time, he indicated that had he been prevented from knowing certain markers, such as his birthday. "Naming" and the listing of events emerged as sites of struggle and reclamation in slave narratives. Likewise, naming and listing emerge in the coolie testimonies as tropes of struggle and reclamation.

The witnessing-style testimonies also are contextualized by a pressing condition that underwrote the coolie predicament, that being *expendability*— a theme that runs throughout both Yuan's petition and throughout the majority of coolie testimonies. Coolie life was filled with brutality although ubiquitous in the testimonies, this brutality seemed mundane and routine. Take this statement by Liang Yayou, for example: "unexpectedly, the owner locked me up and cut off my left ear" (Petition 68). A statement such as "the overseer took a knife and chopped four of my fingers off," was also commonplace in the testimonies (Deposition 1035). Death and torture appear as the main themes in Yuan's petition, conveyed in a numbing litany. His petition reflected the coolies' expendability in daily life, as the attrition rate for Chinese was extremely high. In addition to death from beating and torture, the death rate from coolie suicides alone resulted in Cuba having the highest suicide rate in the world.[11] From 1850–1860 suicides per million inhabitants in Cuba included 5000 Chinese, followed by 350 Africans, and 57 whites.[12] The battle to survive under ubiquitous deadly conditions and the heightened awareness of expendability were consistent themes in the testimonies. Besides the petitions, the theme of death was dominant in the depositions, with an emphasis on death appearing in 953 of the 1,176 oral testimonies. In one petition, 164 petitioners described the precariousness of their lives: "We do not know in the morning what may happen in the evening; we do not know when our lives will be ended" (Petition 20). In another, ninety-eight petitioners declared that arbitrary violence pervaded their lives: "you could die easily like an ant" and "no one knows what is going to happen to us . . . the police are bent solely on profit and oppress the Chinese" (Petition 40). Other statements such as "you could die easily like an ant or cricket" (Petition 80), and coolies admitting to being "treated as dogs and pigs" (Petition 26), stood out as the most common self-descriptions of the Chinese in the testimonies, conveying their owners' disregard for their lives. "Pigs" and "pigpens," *zhuzai* and *zhuzai guan*, had become common terms in Chinese for the pig (coolie) trade and pens that imprisoned the Chinese to be shipped and sold.

Being exploited and disposable, the coolies were "boiling with resentments" (Petition 40). The entwined factors of expendability and anger contribute to the themes and tropes of the testimonies. One theme concerned the burning desire to inscribe their fates before arbitrary death should occur. The witness-type testimony represented an alternate means of protest in a context wherein urgent appeals to the Spanish juridical system were unheard or dealt with punitively. The Chinese repeatedly challenged the system, though the stipulated route for complaints operated as a system of obfuscation and was entirely unfavorable to the Chinese. Perez de la Riva notes cases in 1852–1854.[13] The first case brought to trial by a coolie occurred in 1852 and was initiated by a Chinese laborer named Pablo who filed suit in an effort to gain his freedom, only to lose the case and take his own life in protest. Four others would follow with similar legal action in 1854, and this time the coolies were successful. And still others continued to press for freedom and were successful due to a fortunate confluence of circumstances, including a sympathetic Captain General who heard the cases. However, in 1858, the colonial government began establishing rules to close off legal loopholes and routes to freedom for the coolies, followed by the 1860 legislation written for that purpose. The apparatus of "protection," to which the coolies were supposed to appeal, was described by coolies as a system of surveillance and exploitation, a different perspective from that of colonial government, which couched the need for "protection" in paternalistic phrasing such as "for their good government and for their police supervision."[14] Procedures of complaint required coolies to apply to the "Protector" of the Chinese, who was actually the island's colonial administrator and policing agent, the Captain General, who would decide whether the complaint had merit or not, as stipulated in the Royal Decree of 1860, Section III.[15] The Captain General's office was the same office that meted out punishment to coolies. When punishments from employers "prove insufficient" for coolies and "when immigrants on the estate mutiny, or offer an active and united resistance to the orders of their superiors . . ." the Protector implemented discipline.[16] The Protector of the Chinese was not, by any means, an office that protected the welfare of the Chinese. According to regulations, the penultimate route of complaint was through the employer: "The representatives of employers are empowered to exercise a similar disciplinary jurisdiction . . ." and "In all cases of liability under criminal or civil law in which the competence of employers to act as judges ceases, the ordinary tribunals shall be resorted to . . ."[17] The "competence" of employers and ordinary tribunals offered little assurance to the Chinese. Besides, legislation plainly stipulated that all Chinese laborers entering the island *must forfeit their civil rights*, a point already underscored by Pérez de la Riva, Denise Helly, and Juan Hung Hui, in their separate critiques of Cuba's legal codes vis-à-vis Chinese coolies. In fact, the decree of 1860 stipulated plainly that "immigrants, when signing and accepting their contracts, renounce all civil rights which may not be compatible with the accomplishment of the obligations . . ." and required permission from the "employer" to marry. The decree also stated that if children were born to a mother under contract, they would also be considered bonded until the age of eighteen.

Another example of the witness petition is that of Xu Axiang. Unlike the listing style of Yuan Guan's petition, Xu Axiang's witness petition conveyed a sense of dread more reminiscent of a ghost story. His account concerned a gruesome death and its cover up, which doomed the victim and witnesses to unrest in this world and the next. Xu described the discovery of a murdered coolie who had been secretly buried in a forest. A "loathsome smell" floats in the wind, and "flocks of crows" appear near a forest. The petitioner and a fellow coolie have the premonition of "something dead over there." A crowd gathers. The victim's hat is found on the ground. Soon thereafter, a band of coolies begin digging and discover the victim's body only a few inches under the ground. By focusing upon this tale of secrecy and murder, Xu specifically located the treatment of coolies as *criminal*, thus turning the commission's investigation of labor "conditions" into a confrontation with "crime." Despite all methods used to silence him, Xu Axiang was determined to testify, as he gave both a petition and a deposition (Deposition 282). Added to his account of murder was his added attention to the criminalization of those who witnessed and spoke the truth. Xu himself was imprisoned for trying to "report the injustice." Xu's testimony underscored the acts of coolie-witnessing and speaking as perilous and resistant acts. Thus, his memorable testimony mourned the unjust death of his acquaintance; but moreover, he portrayed coolies as resistant subjects, not silent victims.

On the second day of the third moon, according to the petition by Xu Axiang from Kaiping County, Guangdong Province: In the eighth year of Tongzhi (1869), I was abducted by a villain and was sold to a sugar plantation in Cuba named "Luo liang ji li du."[ii] The injustice I suffered starts from an incident in the tenth year of Tongzhi (1871). An acquaintance of mine, named Li Aliu, started working in the morning and did not come back until late at night. We could not find him anywhere and the crowd started to discuss and guess about it. After ten days, one day on my way taking the ox back to the sugar plantation, I ran into a Chinese named Ali, who pointed to a forest not far away. The wind carried a loathsome smell. Flocks of crows gathered. Something dead seemed to be there. Then I walked another mile or so and ran into the other workers who gathered together. I told them and a man named He Zhangyou what I saw. He went to the forest right away. He recognized Aliu's hat there and reported it to the deputy. He then led some Chinese and dug only a few inches before finding Aliu's body. The deputy reported it to the official in the town immediately, and then the official came with some soldiers to arrest and investigate us. The official asked, "The body was buried under the ground. Who knew about it?" People pointed to me, and then I was interrogated and tortured. They accused me of murdering for money and did not allow me to explain. I was escorted back to the yamen with He Zhangyou. Without any investigation and interrogation, I was sent to prison in Cardenas. I tried to report the injustice many times, and it has been two years already, but my case has not been decided. I thought painfully: if I didn't report the evidence of this injustice, then the murder would be covered up forever. I reported this murder, and I almost got myself killed. Looking into the sky, I cannot reach it. Looking down at the ground, I cannot rest in peace. My gut is being cut by knives. My heart is being burned by fire. How sad and desperate I feel. As quoted. (Petition 49)

THE VERSE PETITION: "THOUSANDS OF WORDS ARE UNDER THE SWEEP OF OUR BRUSHES"

Petitioners wrote poignantly of the difficulty of describing their experiences, sometimes expressed in lyrical and poetic ways and sometimes in lengthy verse forms. Thus, while crafting their testimonies, petitioners

---

ii. Luo Liang Ji Li Du is a transliterated name of a sugar plantation.

were acutely aware of the power of language, but they also became more aware of its limits. They described the painful challenge of comprehending, defining, and articulating what had befallen them. Almost at a loss to describe their predicament, Huang Fengji provided a terse petition, and summed up his testimony as follows: "We have experienced astonishing calamity" (Petition 75). "It is difficult to vent our grievances; it is impossible to pour out our woes," wrote He Aying in his verse petition (Petition 73). Liu Ashou and his four companions graphically articulated their painful experiences, but what had occurred was beyond comprehension: "The overseers are like wolves and tigers. If we slow down a bit, they lash our backs or let big dogs bite us. Blood and flesh are dripping. We wonder why we have to bear this misery. There is no response if we cry to the sky; there is no reply if we beseech the earth. Some could not bear the suffering and committed suicide. Some are dead from injuries. It is really hard to describe" (Petition 79). Fang Tianxiang also wrote of the difficulty in putting his experience to words: "I was abducted and sold to Cuba and the harshness cannot be fully described by words" (Petition 45). Chen Ming similarly wrote that "the suffering and humiliation I experienced cannot be described with words" (Petition 9). As a theme, the struggle with language displayed itself in several forms: the limits of linguistic representation in the face of trauma; oppression due to foreign language barriers; and the profound instability of language as a stable signifier of "contract," consent, and agreement—the basis for a free labor market. The frustration with language was most keenly expressed in anger regarding hierarchy and justice. "Lots of us don't know the language," one verse petition typically stated, "and don't know where to bring an action against them" (Petition 40). Likewise, Li Yisong declared, "Because we did not know the language, we could do nothing about the injustice" (Petition 6). Another coolie expressed outrage and regret that he could not appeal for the dead, because he did not know the language (Deposition 178). Lin Jin and his companions lamented, "We suffer great injustice without chances to express ourselves" (Petition 14). The oral testimonies similarly expressed the sense of powerlessness due to "not knowing the language."[18] Zhang Luan described this disempowerment as one of the biggest obstacles in his struggle to *inform*: "I do not know foreign language, so I cannot tell the name of the sugar plantation, the owner or the manager" (Deposition 1050).

Despite their struggles with language and material deprivation, some petitioners were more attuned to the persuasive possibilities of literary composition. These authors produced verse petitions, which exhibited a range of literary allusions, historical references, antitheses, parallelism, metaphors, colloquialisms, and rhetorical constructions. The use of poetic forms and the stylistic diversity of the petitions illustrate how these individuals thought of themselves as more than passive respondents to an inquiry. The verse petitions featured literary references and figurative language to a greater extent than others, with a few petitions being entirely or mostly written in verse, or with some containing a few sections in verse. Two attributes that appear in verse petitions are antithesis and parallelism. These literary devices generally take subtle forms in colloquial and written Chinese, but appear in the petitions as chief features. Because of their cadence and affected language, the verse petitions were some of the most effective appeals. Antithesis and parallelism in Chinese are somewhat different than their rhetorical applications in Western literary traditions. Antithesis in Chinese literary composition, as in "对偶" or *dui ou*, requires the same number of words and matching grammatical structure in two sentences to express opposite or similar meanings (whereas in English literature, antithesis is only related to oppositional meanings) and requires a strict accounting of rhythm and tones (as Chinese is also a tonal language). Parallelism, as in "排比" or *pai bi,* is composed of a series of phrases or sentences that have the same grammatical structures, line lengths, related meanings, and similar moods.[19] Shi Zhihe and his fellow petitioners provided these antithetical verses: "Thousands of words are under the sweep of our brushes, but they are too many to be put down in writing. Whips lash our backs; shackles chain our bodies. The young and strong can merely live with starvation; the old and weak die with unrighted wrong. From now on, if we remain alive, we will be cold and hungry men; if we die, we will be ghosts of the starved" (Petition 4). A group of 133 coolies, including seven women, also provided verses to describe their bondage and deprivation:

What kind of crime have we committed to deserve being chained when we repair the roads? What kind of deed have we done to deserve being stoned when we walk the street? We are humiliated but whom can we appeal to? Food is no better than plantain and corn; person is no better than ox and horse. Pause for a moment, and they lash and reprimand us; stop for a rest, and they surely lock us up. We are birds in a cage that cannot fly with wings; fish in a net that cannot swim in a deep lake. People commit suicide by hanging themselves, by drowning themselves, by swallowing opium, by jumping in the hot sugar cauldron. Misery is beyond language. We hope your honor can control Macao, prohibit abductions, release our souls. If so, you will open a new world for us. (Petition 15)

The verse-type petitions appealed to the reader aurally and emotionally in different ways than the witness petition. Rather than focus upon naming names, listing incidents, or detailing specific crimes, the verse petitions relied more upon figurative language, poetic effect, cadence, rhyme and rhythmic construction, images of suffering, motifs of captivity, and the coolies' desire to be set free. Distilled in the above Petitions 4 and 15 are some of the most oft-repeated figures of speech used in the testimonies. In Petition 15, the analogy to "birds in a cage" and "fish in a net" emphasized their captivity, and their acute desire to be freed was expressed in "release our souls," a phrase originating from the Buddhist saying, "Release my soul from purgatory." Often, the testifiers made analogies to themselves as domesticated and enslaved beasts of burden, or "oxen and horses," as in Petition 15. Their anguished refrain, "Misery is beyond language," appears in several of the petitions. The "whips and shackles" in Petition 4, and the "suicide by hanging themselves, by drowning themselves, by swallowing opium, by jumping in the hot sugar cauldron" are litanies in the testimonies that present their most common forms of punishment and suicide. Complementing such images of suffering are motifs that contrast the "predators" from the "prey," which appear throughout the petitions. The coolies repeatedly referred to their oppressors as ruthless "wolves and tigers." Cai Heng and his co-petitioners wrote, "Some of us chop trees in the forests; some of us cut cane in the fields. Toil by wind and frost; errand into day and night. Moreover, when we work, the overseer watches us with whip and club in his hands and machete and gun on his belt. When he yells, his voice is like thunder and lightning; when he raises his hand, he is ferocious as a tiger and wolf. He relies on the owner's power and considers us as horses and sheep. People whom he likes will live; people whom he hates will die" (Petition 67). Chen Gu described his oppressors in the following terms: "Managers and overseers, who are like wolves and tigers, hold machetes and carry guns all the time. If we worked a bit slower, we would be lashed till our blood stains the ground. Some people, who run away and are caught later, are locked up with no faint hope of being released; some are forced to starve to death in the mountains, and others hang themselves or throw themselves into rivers. The misery is too great to be described with mere words" (Petition 22). One group of coolies described Cuban government officials as mythological beasts of terror, *qiongqi* and *taotie* (Petition 25). *Qiongqi* appeared in Chinese mythologies in protean guises: as a fearsome beast, shaped like a cow, with hedgehog hair, making noises like a wild dog; as a beast shaped like a tiger with wings that eats humans from their heads, with another name *congzu*; and as an evil god who encourages bad deeds. *Taotie* has appeared as a terrifying figure since the Shang Dynasty. Associated with eating and satisfying the dead, the image of the *taotie* has graced sacrificial vessels and has also appeared as a greedy human-eating monster, having a goat's body, a human face, eyes under its armpits, tiger teeth, and human fingers.

The motifs of suffering and captivity, and the desire to be freed, are most poignantly expressed in Petition 41, which included the extended metaphor of birds being caged. The author wrote the following: "My flying wings were pinned down" and "I couldn't escape even if I had wings on my back." The only thing that flies in his depiction is "ashes." In fact, of all the petitions, Petition 41 and Petition 21 provide the most useful illustrations of the verse form used to very different effects. The former was written by a feng shui expert, Ren Shizen, and the other was written by a teacher, Li Chengxun. Ren Shizen's long petition is one of the most heartrending of the testimonies, as it poetically communicates spiritual anguish and emotional intensity. Abounding with evocative metaphors and references to legendary figures, Ren's writing reveals that he was an educated man. Ren crafted his petition entirely in parallelisms, with matching line lengths and word order, in the basic unit of four characters per clause. Reminiscent of the *fu*-style poetry of Han Dynasty, his petition reads like a prose poem. Ren's parallelisms may be poetic, but they are also imperfect. At times, his composition lacks the consistency that Li Chengxun displayed in Petition 21. However, while Ren's testimony is sometimes irregular in the formalist sense, it is powerful and emotionally affecting. His is a narrative of trauma that, in the end, does not make a plea for help. Instead, his testimony describes the piercing realization that no one would likely be coming to his aid. He wrote of "crying and gazing at the end of the world" and lamented that no one "could possibly know about my situation from the beginning to the end." Ren's petition is filled with images of irreversible loss, though he displayed a flash of anger when vowing to "stay with hatred in the netherworld." His writing was despondent, yet Ren was also tenacious. Ren turned in two petitions—he was author of 41 and coauthor of Petition 54—in which his name appears first. In the latter submission, Ren and two fellow Chinese, who were former business owners in China, submitted a critique of the coolie system from a distinctly business point of view, emphasizing rights of ownership and property. The threesome weighed coolie contributions against extreme losses and abuse, making similar revelations as the groups of coolies from Petition 40 and 43, who attested to becoming small retailers yet found "free" life to be one of persecution and torment. But it is Ren's solely authored petition that most directly addressed the question: What does it feel like to be in bondage?

Ren's vision of Spanish Cuba, or the "Lusong" colony, was of a dark frontier that lacked morality. "*Lüsong*" and "small *Lüsong*" appeared in the testimonies as appellations for Cuba, and the term "big *Lüsong*" apparently referred to the Philippines. Undoubtedly, the term for Cuba was conceived in reference to the Spanish colonization of the Philippines. Luzon is the largest island in the Philippines and historically where the greatest number of ethnic Chinese were (and still are) concentrated in the archipelago. Ren's themes were of colonial expansion, extraction of natural resources, the drive for profit, religious coercion, and human exploitation. Profiteering from the land was described by Ren as not simply an enterprise driven by sugar barons but one marked by widespread systemic corruption. Regardless of the existence of contracts, Ren described himself and fellow Chinese as being forcibly and systemically worked to death. Writing of hypocrisy at the highest levels, Ren pointed to the government and a paternalistic church. He protested coerced baptism and conversion as a mode of controlling the Chinese, noting that "we always have to get our heads washed and become Catholic. We have to prepare gifts for (the godfathers) in order to be our 'relatives' or 'elders.' If we do not follow this rule, we will be accused of committing a crime and will not be able to get away with it." Meanwhile, Ren noted that the most sacred of rites, the burial, was disregarded for the coolies, as "bones of Chinese pile up like a small hill." Similarly, other testimonies stressed religious coercion, such as that by Zhang Yuan and his group: "We had to beg for a godfather to keep ourselves safe. We had to get a document for going to church to chant and wash heads. Then we had to go to a foreign officer to sign a proof so that we could work in other places to make a living. The owner would send people who did not get their heads washed to the government. Those people would be forced to work in an official workshop with no payment but endless misery" (Petition 59). Furthermore, Ren denounced the government as enforcing laws that bound Chinese in perpetuity, noting that "some of us were fortunate enough to survive after eight years and were looking forward to escaping from this disaster. Government officials locked us up and forced us to be slaves forever."

Most striking are Ren's expressions that convey the smallness of human life, which was compounded by consignment to an island across the ocean and an agonizing desire to escape to freedom: "The beach is so wide and boundless that a single person cannot be seen. Seawater surrounds the city. Trees grow wildly and form a canopy . . . Now I try to gulp down my sobs. My life is held in the manager's hand. In this dense forest and remote mountains, thousands of people are being whipped . . . The ocean is boundless and the sea is vast. I could not escape even if I had wings on my back." Nature is portrayed as overwhelming and endless to those who labor under the lash attempting to tame it. Similarly, the poetic writing of Xie Shuangjiu and certain other fellow coolies described their suffering and vulnerability: "We worked under the canopy of the stars and the moon; we were washed by the rain and combed by the wind" (Petition 69). Complementing the overpowering landscape of nature is Ren's landscape of spiritual desolation, with the "dry grass and flying ashes." Witnessing the insignificance and disposability of their lives, Ren, like many others, would have had to struggle for hope. Images of hunger, thirst, ghosts, graveyards, sobbing, and weeping fill Ren's soliloquy. His images are linked to the upturning of a social order as he knew it. Emphasizing the degradation of his position, Ren wrote, "My hair is disheveled and my face is dirty. My pants are worn-out and my shirt is moldy. When I am alive, I work like a bull or a horse; when I am dead, I am worthless as mole crickets and ants." The theme drawn by Ren concerned demoralization

arising from dehumanizing circumstances of slavery. Implements associated with slavery—chains, shackles, rods, and whips—were always
present, while food was not. He exclaimed, "There are shackles around
my ankles and chains about my neck. I had to carry dirt and fill up holes.
I drew cakes to allay hunger and thought of sour plums to quench my
thirst." Drawn from Chinese classics, Ren's cakes and plums refer to an
antithetical idiom in Chinese that reads as follows: "Hope to stop hunger
by drawing a cake; wish to stop thirst by thinking about plums." Ren's reference refers to the power of imagination, although it also implies the
chasing of illusion. Both contribute to Ren's saving grace but also to his
extreme depression. In a classic Chinese text, *Romance of the Three Kingdoms*, the drawing of cakes appears as false and fleeting: "We should not
recommend anyone for official service just because he has fame, for fame
is like a cake drawn on the ground, which is inedible." The fantasizing of
plums appears in a legend regarding Cao Cao, a military commander. Cao
Cao's troops were suffering from unbearable thirst due to a long march
with no water in sight. At one point Cao Cao inventively declared there was
a plum orchard ahead. Imagining sour plums, the troops began salivating,
thus quenching their thirst. They marched farther, eventually reaching a
water source. In Ren's petition, however, hunger and thirst are not only
deprivations of food, but also deprivations of dignity and freedom. The
promise of freedom seems hopeless and illusory. Ren depicted the bleak-
ness of mere survival and wondered "where good things will ever come
from." Symbolic staples of daily life, such as a "lamp oil and a bowl of
rice," were stripped away, as were familial bonds. Families disintegrated
and bonds broke like "rotten trees, which do not have any leaves or branches
in this world." Wives, children, parents, and brothers are like one's own
"feet and hands" yet would never know "whether we are alive or dead."

It is no small detail that Ren mentioned the loss of his name. The loss
of name, the certainty of unmarked death, the impossibility of preserving
his family and lineage, is the loss of future for Ren. His allusions and references convey the erosion of spirit and cultural traditions due to the
breaking of familial and cultural bonds. The traumatic rupture of familial
and cultural bonds is figured in Ren's references to historical figures associated with exile, Li Ling and Su Wu (or "Ziqing"). Li Ling and Su Wu
were trapped in territory of the Xiongnu, a nomadic tribal people who
dominated northern China during the second and third century B.C.E.

Li Ling was a general in the Han Dynasty who was captured by the Xiongnu and eventually became a collaborator. As punishment for this, Li Ling's mother, wife, and children were executed under orders of the Chinese emperor. While there are several versions of the episode, all emphasize that Li remained in Xiongnu territory for the rest of his life, unlike his countryman Su Wu, who was an ambassador detained by the Xiongnu for nineteen years. Unlike his peer Li, Su Wu refused to collaborate despite various forms of hardship and deprivation placed upon him. The final parting of Li Ling and Su Wu, the former who remained in exile and the latter who finally returned to his homeland, was dramatically portrayed in literary and historical narrations. Ren's references signaled his knowledge of literature and history but were also deployed in ways that underscored themes of captivity, betrayal, and exile. Betrayal marked the coolie experience, as close friends and relatives sold their loved ones into the traffic, and "wicked civilians" colluded with foreigners. "These wicked grew a lotus under their tongues but hid a sharp blade in their stomachs," Ren wrote. The lotus flower, symbolic of beauty and purity in Chinese classical poems, is subsumed into an image of greed and corruption. From Ren's perspective, the tenets he most identifies as inviolate have been violated: family ties, honorable behavior, bravery, and loyalty. And in his eyes, cultural models of strength and intelligence have been rendered powerless. "At this place," he lamented, "even Wu Huo could not use his incredible strength; even Yan Yan could not use his extraordinary intelligence." Wu Huo was a brave warrior during the Warring States period in China who was known for legendary strength (it was said he could lift a ton), and Yan Yan was Confucius's best student in literature and was a famous scholar during the Spring and Autumn period in China (770–476 B.C.E.).

By drawing upon such inspirational figures, Ren expressed his profound disillusionment and despair, implying that even such heroic figures would be diminished under brutal enslavement.

On the first day of the third moon in the thirteenth year of Tongzhi (April 16, 1874), according to the petition by Ren Shizhen, Nanhai County, Guangdong Province: I was deceived into going abroad. I regret it all year long. So I write down my experience of going abroad in short: The beach is so wide and boundless that a single person cannot be seen.

Seawater surrounds the city. Trees grow wildly and form a canopy. Look around in the mountain: laborers are needed to cut trees and open wasteland for development in the border regions. There are thousands of sugar plantations here that need laborers. This is why the Lüsong people are hiring laborers. They are crafty in their hearts and greedy and cruel in their nature. Since the land is vast and scarcely populated, they are rich and deceitful. Their ships go into China and collude with wicked civilians. Their companies are in the district of Macao and recruit foolish people. China's population is growing day by day; China's trading with other countries is growing day by day. Some people used up thousands of gold pieces and were ashamed to go back to their hometowns. Some people were very poor and looked for a job alone. They met friends on their way. Some of these friends were heartless. These wicked people pointed falsely at a gold mountain and promised to show the way. They tricked many people, no matter who were their close friends or relatives. They grew a lotus under their tongues but hid a sharp blade in their stomachs. They deceived people into traps in order to make a profit. They lured people to a foreign land and didn't care about family loss and lineage. I didn't realize that I was tricked until the ship sailed to the middle of the river. It is difficult to pull back your horse if you are on a plank road along a cliff. At this place, even Wu Huo could not use his incredible strength; even Yan Yan could not use his extraordinary intelligence. Once I entered the cage, my flying wings were pinned down for eight years. Once I was victimized by the scheme, I could not return love and care to my parents in the remaining years of my life. Even if my body should be sold, my parents' signature should have been required. I try to gulp down my sobs. My life is held in the manager's hand. In this dense forest and remote mountains, I was whipped many times; my name was changed and I had to suffer many sicknesses by wearing shackles. Countless people were persecuted to death or ran away. Every meal is less than two dishes. I am fed with yam, corn, and green bananas all year long. All the salary for the day is not even enough to buy lamp oil and a bowl of rice. Li Ling could not go back to his country; Su Wu was trapped in a foreign land for a long time. My parents must be longing for me at the entrance of their alley every day. They will never know that their efforts are futile. Who will take care of my wife and children? Who will care whether they have enough food or clothes? There are hundreds of thousands of Chinese laborers in Lüsong, while there are hundreds of thousands of sorrowful families in China. Some of us are fortunate enough to survive after eight years and are looking forward to escaping from this disaster. However, government officials lock us up and force us to be slaves forever. There are shackles on my feet and chains around my neck. I have had to carry dirt and fill up holes. I have drawn cakes to allay hunger and thought of sour plums to quench my thirst. If I give something as a bribe to the overseer, he will allow me to slow down; if I give nothing to him, he will beat me with rods. My hair is disheveled and my face is dirty. My pants are worn-out, and my shirt is moldy. When I am alive, I work like an ox and a horse; when I am dead, I am worthless like crickets and ants. When my life reaches an end, who will pity a hungry ghost with no coffin? Where is the graveyard? All I will have is dry grass and flying ashes. I will remain with hatred in the netherworld. Bones of Chinese pile up like a small hill. We always have to get our heads washed and become Catholic. We have to prepare gifts for the godfathers in order to be our "relatives" or "elders." If we do not follow this rule, we will be accused of committing a crime and will not be able to get away with it. Only if we spend hundreds of gold on them, would we be safe. All my savings in years will be gone in one use. Every year, we have to renew our freedom paper with great effort. Whatever we do is restricted, who wouldn't feel sad? Sigh! We were all good civilians. Who didn't have parents? Their guidance, support, love and care. We fear they cannot live long. Who didn't have brothers, who were like feet and hands? Who didn't have spouses, who were like friends and guests? Is there anything good about being alive? What did we do so wrong that we were all deceived? Whether we are alive or dead, our families do not hear anything about it. Maybe someone will pass a little information about us to our families, who would half believe and half doubt. Everything is pitiful and tragic; who wouldn't weep sorrowfully? Our messages don't reach them at all; we are crying and gazing at the end of the world. Goods here are as expensive as jewelry. If I stopped working, I would have nothing to eat. I am like a rotten tree, which does not have any leaves or branches in this world. I wonder where good things will ever come from. I am just waiting for my death to come. Who in China would know about my situation from the beginning to the end? The ocean is boundless and the sea is vast. I couldn't escape even if I had wings on my back. I just hope that one of my peers can be fortunate enough to go back to China and deliver my message to everyone: Don't be deceived into coming here. As quoted. (Petition 41)

According to Ren's petition, enslavement was constructed upon a host of conditions: corporal punishment and restraints, extortion, religious conversion, and state-enforced slavery, under collusion of business, church, and state. Notably, the wage was barely mentioned. Ren's brief mentions of the wage were only in the context of starvation and extortion. Having a wage did not seem to help the coolie's position, but only led to further extractions of labor under punitive circumstances. His most intriguing point referred to the constant "renewal(s)" for freedom papers, resulting in exorbitant and seemingly endless payments. What were these renewals about? Ren's petition suggests that *getting nominally free from under contract-bondage* was a small possibility, but *remaining free* seemed to be impossible. As verse petition #4 stated, "Even if the contract is finished, we will still not be released." In another verse petition, He Aying wrote, "People who finished their contracts would be humiliated for no reason or be caught for no reason" (Petition 73). What was the experience of "freedom" as experienced by the Chinese coolies? The role of the contract, the basis of "free" labor and liberal philosophies, and the twin challenges of getting free and remaining free, are more deeply and extensively displayed in the petitions of the "paper chase" (see "The Paper Chase Petition").

Taking a different strategy, the teacher Li Chengxun focused upon establishing authority and veracity by making moral character the focal point in his Petition 21. Li Chengxun exhibited refined restraint and crafted his petition entirely in pentameter, with five characters per clause, and two clauses per sentence. Like *yuefu* poetry, this form of writing would be called "pentasyllabic ancient song," which refers to the poetic style popular before the Tang dynasty (618–907). Unfortunately, a translation cannot capture the rhythmic (and difficult) construction of this style. Instead, the translation provided here effects a representation of content. Thus, the admirable movement and effects of its narration are entirely lost. Told that he would be employed as a teacher for a wealthy family, Li recounts that he was deceived and forced abroad at knifepoint. Li goes on to say, "Since I

arrived in the island of Cuba/I have become the same as other slaves."
Still, he dedicates only three lines relating to his condition in Cuba. Instead, Li's rhetorical strategy was to emphasize his proper upbringing and
social standing, and key aspects of virtue and respect in Chinese traditions. The beginning of his petition acknowledged his father's strict teaching and his father's passing. Li recounted great sacrifices to provide his
father with a proper funeral. The mention of borrowing money for the funeral is important, as it indicated dedication to one of the most important
aspects of proper Confucian upbringing. According to Mencius, "The funeral of a parent is an occasion for giving of one's utmost," and according
to Tseng Tzu (Zeng Zi) one should "serve your parents in accordance with
the rites during their lifetime; bury them in accordance with the rites
when they die; offer sacrifices to them in accordance with the rites; and
you deserve to be called a good son."[20] Like many of the testifiers, Li
stressed unfulfilled responsibilities to an "old mother" and his "wife and
children," and the breakdown of social cohesion, families, and friendships. An "old acquaintance" of Li's sold him into the coolie trade: "He
took out a sharp dagger/saying that if I didn't obey, I would lose my life/I
thought about my old mother at home/and my wife and my children./If I
lost my life/who could my entire family depend on?/I was forced to obey/
sighing and weeping that I had such misfortune." Similarly, Ren Shizen
had written the following in his petition: "My parents must be longing for
me at the entrance of their alley every day. They will never know that their
efforts are futile. Who will take care of my wife and children? Who will
care whether they have enough food or clothes? There are hundreds of
thousands of Chinese laborers in Lúásong, while there are hundreds of
thousands of sorrowful families in China" (Petition 41). Yao Wenxian was
preoccupied with his inability to care for his mother: "I came to this foreign country at the age of fifty-five. I am sixty-three now. I have an old
mother in my home. Right now, whom can my eighty-four-year-old mother
depend on?"(Petition 57). As shown in previous examples, broken family
and social disintegration were major preoccupations in the testimonies.
The Chinese expressed grave concern over obligations to parents (particularly those mentioning aged and infirm parents), children left behind, loss
of communication with family, betrayal by friends, loss of names, collapse of lineage, and the denial of death rites.

These thematic threads regarding social cohesion and continuity raise the possibility of testimony as a vehicle for preserving family history and for communication with family. The testimonies suggest that coolies viewed the inquiry as not only an instrument of investigation but, more importantly, as a potential instrument of communication. Through the coolies' testimonies, it was hoped that news would reach their loved ones and also the world. Teacher Li focused upon his father, mother, wife, and children, rather than on his peers in Cuba. Like many of the testifiers, Xian Arong took the opportunity to give the exact address of his shop in China, his family status, the name of the person who sold him, and a host of specificities of his conditions: names, dates, locations, a description of his owner, the owner's brother, hours of work, types of torture, and so on. He ended his testimony with what may have been his last known words: "My Father's name is Axing Qian. This sugar plantation is in Cardenas and the name is Recreo" (Deposition 297). The intended audience was most immediately the commission, but implicitly, the hope was that the audience would eventually include families and villages. As the coolies commonly stated, they were expendable and their chances of getting back to China were slim. Their responsibilities to family weighed heavily upon them. Conveying news of their fates to their families weighed just as heavily on their minds as protesting their circumstances and contemplating the slim chance of being saved. "After the abduction, for tens of years, our families have no idea of whether we are alive or dead and of our whereabouts," wrote one Li Zhaochun. "Our families do not know about it; the government does nothing about it. The society is so decadent that even relatives and friends try to cheat each other. The Spanish are destroying human relations and rotting people's sympathy in China. This peril has no end and is no trivial matter" (Petition 20). Ren Shizen maintained that "whether we are alive or dead, our families do not hear anything about it" (Petition 41), and in his second petition with Dai Renjie and Liang Xingzhao, he declared, "Nobody in our family will have the chance to know where we are" (Petition 54). Another group of petitioners despaired that families had not heard of their fates: "We cannot even send letters back to our families. We cry to heaven, but there is no reply; we appeal to earth, but there is no entry" (Petition 80).

The coolies transferred to the commission the responsibility of making public what was previously unknown, and placed special importance on the fact that their families did not know what had happened to their missing and dead. Sanders puts forth a notion of "transference" in his study of the Truth and Reconciliation Commission of South Africa. In a close reading of testimony, he notes that "replying to the questioner, the witness seems not only to address him or her as another but to address an other, or others, *in* the questioner . . . The Commission acts, so to speak, as an engine of 'transference.' "[21] Sanders's notion of transference applied to a particular historical moment when a "truth commission" was charged with restoring "the human and civil dignity of such victims." Sanders suggests the meaning of transference is related to responsibility and ethics, as in commission responses to petitions for funeral rites and to the need for special women's hearings. This notion of transference is helpful, as it regards the power of testimony to engender collaborations and complicities. Compared to the South African Truth Commission, the 1874 testimonies emerge from a different era and with different delineations of a commission's power and purpose, yet the testimonies bear out coolies' strategies of pushing the investigation of labor "conditions" into a confrontation with losses to the fabric of larger society. The "family" appealed to an extended sense of social responsibility and social cost. In fact, Li's petition mentioned much more about his family than about his own immediate suffering. At one point, he wrote, "If I can go back to my country to see my mother and my children/All my descendants will be grateful to you." Li's overall petition limned "transference" as a strategy, as he addressed traditional "values" that would speak directly to the moral duties and sympathies of a Chinese commissioner: lineage, family, filial duty, education (the "teacher"), and social standing. Li's petition was not focused on the unrighted wrongs done to others (such as Yuan Guan's and Xu Axiang's witness petitions), nor the trials endured in slavery (such as Ren Shizen's verse petition), but dwelled more on the concerns of social virtues and stability. By displaying virtuous traits and by crafting an entire petition in verse, Li demonstrated his respectability as a teacher—a profession linked to substantial social status in China. Poor but virtuous, Li displayed a proper humility, modestly writing "I am sorry that my pen is short and my writing is poor." Notably, Li elaborated upon his social standing as it once was and refrained from elaborating upon the humiliations of what his station had become, which he briefly summarized as like a "dog" and like "other slaves." By underscoring the fact that this humiliation could happen to a person of correct upbringing, such as a teacher, Li emphasized injustice in terms of social class. Li's petition implicitly argued that it was Li himself who was most deserving of respect and whose petition should be taken seriously. Other petitioners also stressed social standing and pointed out that their groups included the relatives of officials: "We could not appeal this misery; we could not voice this injustice. Moreover, Wu En, who is the nephew of former Governor of Hubei and Hunan Provinces (who was also from the Imperial Academy in Guangzhou), is now in 'Shahua' Sugar Plantation; Ye Shengzu, who is the nephew of Ye Qianlan from the Imperial Academy, is now in 'Simalongpu'; Yang Yujing, who is the nephew of Yang Yi from the Imperial Academy in Gaozhou Prefecture, is now in an ironworks. Three of them cannot come and see your honor in person" (Petition 67).

Due to his preceding emphasis upon Confucian virtues and social standing, Li's closing claim to truthfulness, "Everything I have said is the truth/Nothing I have said is false," is made more persuasive. Rhythmically and admirably crafted, Li's long verse provided little elaboration upon the structures of exploitation that he faced. Yet his strategy was prescient due to the fact that after the commission inquiry, the Qing government inquired after any coolies who were of scholarly standing.

On the eighteenth day of the second moon of in the thirteenth year of Tongzhi [April 4, 1874] according to the petition by Li Chengxun, Xinhui County, Guangdong Province:

When I was young, my family was poor/I followed my father's strict teaching.

When I was eighteen years old I became a teacher in Jiangmen County.

In the year of Ren Shen (1872), my father passed away/It was mid-May.

I asked for help from fellow villagers/I received 3000 wen I thanked them at the alley/and went back home for my father's funeral.

Because of my father's death, I lost my teaching job/My family became
so poor that we didn't even have a grain of millet for food.
I was willing to go to a relative's place/just to find a place to stay.
I met Agao Liang on the way/He was a civilian in Xiaoze County.
We were old acquaintances and talked about the past/We chatted hap-
pily and inquired after each other's family well-being.
He told me that there was a dragon family in Macao[iii]*/The family was*
quite wealthy.
They would pay eleven yuan/for a family teacher.
I believed in him/and followed him to the port of Macao.
He pointed at a foreign ship/saying that my employer was on the ship.
To get to the ship, I took a small boat/On the way, (he) revealed his real
purpose.
He said that the ship was going to Lüsong/I didn't want to listen in the
beginning.
He took out a sharp dagger/saying that if I didn't obey, I would lose my
life.
I thought about my old mother at home/and my wife and my children.
If I lost my life/who could my entire family depend on?
I was forced to obey/sighing and weeping that I had such misfortune.
Since I arrived at the island of Cuba/I have been the same as other
slaves.
The work is extremely heavy/Oxen and dogs are ten times better off
than I am.
I am sorry that my pen is short and my writing is poor/I cannot tell ev-
erything from the beginning.
I sincerely hope that your honor has a little mercy[iv]*/and can save me*
and other fellow Chinese.
If I can go back to my country to see my mother and my children/all my
descendants will be grateful to you.
Everything I have said is the truth/Nothing I have said is false.
As quoted. (Petition 21)

---

iii. Dragon family: The name for families living on boats in Southern China.
iv. "Your honor" is not literally present in the sentence but is inserted here, as in other translated
petitions of this study, to signal the markedly humble and respectful address, which would indicate
"your honor," "your eminence," or similar address. The simple address of "you" would not suffice.

二月十八日據廣東新會縣李承訓稟稱竊我幼家貧謹承父嚴訓行年十八歲吞耕江門鎮壬申歲父歿五

月之中旬求施於鄉黨得錢三千文叩謝乎閭里歸家議葬親因喪而失館家無粒粟願往親友處覓枝

以棲身路遇梁阿高小澤鄉中民舊識談往事復假間寒溫云澳一蜑戶其家頗稱殷修金一十圓邀我爲

西賓我信以爲然隨到澳門津伊指一洋船云即我東人乃用小艇往半海露情眞云往呂宋國我初不願

聞伊出鐵利器不從定喪身念家存老母妻兒女成羣若然身喪後合家靠誰憐迫得乃從權泣歎生不辰

到此古巴島與奴隸爲倫工夫苦異常牛犬勝十分惜短杆拙筆難盡錄由根萬望發慈悲早救我輩人旋

邦見母子萬代共沾恩所稟盡實情無半點虛陳等語

PETITION 41.
Source: Testimony of Chinese Laborers in Cuba, National Library of China in Beijing

THE ARGUMENT PETITION: RADICAL VISIONS OF THE CONTRACT AND FREEDOM

In the commission's report, section thirty emerges as the report's guiding principle and poses this question: "The contract coolie is a man who has pledged himself to work according to contract for a term of years: he is not a slave. Is he treated as a man who consented to be bound by a contract, or as a slave? Are there slaves in Cuba—or were there, and what is or was their treatment?" The question bears the imprint of liberal philosophies of freedom and contract, with the contract presumably the line of demarcation between slavery and freedom. The question bears some similarity to the differentiation made between indenture and slavery in the *Report of the Commissioners Appointed to Inquire into the Treatment of Immigrants in British Guiana* written in 1871, which differentiated between indenture and slavery based upon civil rights: ". . . practically, the obligations of the slave are enforced with violence, and of his rights, such as they are, the law is an inadequate protector; while the obligations of the indentured labourer, like those of the free labourer, are only to be enforced by law, and his rights he is invited and encouraged to defend."[22] Significantly, the overall focus of the fifty questions designed by Hart and the commission was on whether or not the contract had been abided by. The commission's findings and replies implicated Spanish slavery and added fuel to rival criticisms of Spanish Cuba, with the testimonies being the damning evidence. As a philosophical, political, and juridical basis, it was the "contract" that became the strategic rationale for intervention in Spanish Cuba. The main focus of the report concerned specific violations, with the contract being upheld in this case as the sacred guarantor of bona fide transition from slavery. The commission's examination of "contract" assumed an a priori discursive and materialized concept of contract (and consent) that could be transnationally understood and implemented. This nineteenth-century case could be viewed as a massive landmark test case of not only transnational contract rights but also a test of the contract institution as a globalizing exercise.

The report reveals two main bases for intervention: sovereign rights and contracts. The first is the state's right (China's) to interests in the emigration of its subjects and related state conventions that could be entered into, or that were violated, as a result. But the commission report was almost entirely based on arguments focused upon the proper (or improper) administration of contracts. The commission examined emigration in the context of *the contract*, based upon notions of consent and rights of the individual. Furthermore, the investigation and its arguments implicitly acknowledged the rights of subaltern individuals in extraterritorial residence. Chinese coolies of Cuba were regarded as social detritus; but in this case, they still retained rights implied by the contract. Arguments made regarding contract administration and violations implicitly recognized the normalizing of "contract" discourse in the wake of abolition. Slavery, abolition, and liberal construction of the "contract" formed a formidable background upon which the coolie testimonies unfolded.

As liberal abolitionists saw it, the voluntary selling of one's labor via the contract would effect the transition from slavery to free labor, and thereby, laborers such as coolies would materialize this transition. The commission *report* revealed the massive violations of contract, but the coolie *testimonies*, however, reveal more radical views than those of the commission. The report, though impressive for the sheer amount of detail that it includes from the coolie testimonies, obscured the testimonies as whole narratives fashioned by the coolies regarding their lives, their backgrounds, and their views. The coolie testimonies trouble the very presumptions of the "contract" as the guarantor of free and consensual relations. Their portrayals of the contract upend a casting of their role as intermediating "unfree" and "free" labor economy. In effect, the coolies offered rival and radical views of the contract that trouble the imperatives of Hart's questions, which found credible evidence that the contract system was not being faithfully abided by, but did not question the sacredness of the contract itself. Viewed in hindsight, the testimonies speak to a long debate on modernity, freedom, and slavery. Here, special attention will be given to four key arguments—with attention to philosophies of contract, freedom, and narrations of modernity—that are then followed by radical testimonies of the coolies themselves.

PHILOSOPHICAL PRELUDE

As a preface to presenting coolies' views of the "contract," briefly addressed here are specific critiques on the liberal contract. Arguments forwarded by historian Amy Dru Stanley, legal scholar Robert Steinfeld, and philosophers Carole Pateman, Tommy Lott, and Charles Mills, provide relevant reference points and contradistinctions for taking up recurrent themes in the coolie testimonies and their address of the contract as a system. This philosophical grouping is more catholic than "in like," as each undertakes distinct approaches and stakes different views. Their arguments are not taken up here as ideological prescriptions for how the coolies should or should not have made their representations regarding the contract; but rather, they are contemporary meditations that aid in apprehending the testimonies as narratives that *also present their own arguments*, apparently broached in the midst of a new experiment on the contract.

In addition to the views initiated by philosophers and politicians, "rival understandings of the free contract" already existed among the actors of "free labor" themselves, as Amy Dru Stanley argues. In her tracing of liberal abolitionism and contracts, Stanley exposes the different strategies taken up by different actors who navigated in the postslavery, contractarian world.[23] Freed slaves, married women, wage labor, and vagrants presented different challenges to the coercive nature of the contract. "Almost invariably," Stanley argues, "contract was contrasted with bondage . . . [but the] contract served as a legitimating symbol for social relations in which inequality was either cloaked by exchange or said to arise from consent."[24] Following Stanley's stress upon the cloaking of contract and the multiple challenges to it, the Chinese in Cuba were indeed historical actors who displayed rival understandings of the liberal contract and whose writings could be read in this vein. With their testimonies, they exposed fraudulence and the ambiguousness of basic contract tenets that gird modern conceptions of freedom, such as temporality and consent. The coolie testimonies, as narratives fashioned in direct confrontation with the contract system, also are narratives that implicitly confront philosophies of modernity and the "contract" as derived from Hobbes, Locke, Mill, and Rousseau. Temporality, ownership, property, rights, and consent were among the foundational concepts that defined and framed the bases of "freedom" and yet, were among the conceptual traps deployed to subordinate the Chinese. Problems with the temporal fixedness of the contract figured prominently in the coolies' testimonies, complicating notions of the contract as a static and distinguishing marker of free labor. The term limit was disregarded for the coolies, and was more the rule than the exception, and the notion of "consent" was portrayed as problematic. As coolie Zeng Ashi maintained, "Many of us asked the owner the exact date when we can stop working; however, the owner not only refused our quest, but also shackled our feet immediately and forced us to keep working like slaves. Freedom paper was not issued; payment was not raised. Not until we *consented* to keep working were we released from shackles. I am not afraid of the machete or ax; giving you my words and telling you the truth, I beg you with my heart to save all of us, so that we do not end up being slaves for the rest of our lives" (my emphasis, Petition 34).

While the contract gave semblance to temporal fixedness, the colonial government further imposed rules of "good government" to especially "protect" (exploit) the Chinese as supposedly term-limit, contract laborers.[25] As colonized labor within a colonial Cuba, the Chinese emphasized that they were, in effect, held hostage by the contract system. In a critique of contractarian theories and the "sexual contract," philosopher Carole Pateman makes arguments regarding the "extreme fragility of the criterion of temporal limitation of the employment contract as a distinguishing mark of a free worker" and further distinguishes between libertarian representations of the contract and the nature of subordination under paternalism. "The question central to contract theory," she argues, "does not involve the general liberty to do as you please, but the freedom to subordinate yourself in any manner that you please."[26] Pateman's critique of subordination involves the radical reconsideration of basic distinguishing markers of free labor, including the markers of temporality, the wage, "equal footing" of worker and employer, and contracting of labor power but not the person.[27] Her critique unveils these basic tenets as partial and slippery mechanisms of a patriarchal contract institution that achieves subordination through exceptions, exclusions, and gendered power relations. The four basic tenets and Pateman's argument regarding subordination via hidden social mechanisms situate a distinct pattern that appears in the testimonies. The coolies directly or implicitly address these four tenets of "free labor" in a manner demonstrating how these principles were patently violated. While the material contract itself operated as a signifier of fair wages and equal footing, the coolies of Cuba described it instead as a mechanism for instituting enslavement and inequalities. Moreover, they addressed mechanisms of subordination, some of which operated not through hidden exclusion but through *particularizing* and *singling out* the

Chinese as racialized contract labor to be held hostage by contract rules and manipulations. In short, the coolies were super-controlled.

The second principle of contract theory rests upon some measure of voluntariness, the notion that an agreement is made by consenting parties. Voluntariness is foundational to creating tropes of consent and individualism as a pattern underlying interpretations of Chinese and Asian migration: voluntary and "transitional" forces. The coolie testimonies suggest a counternarrative to this interpretation. What is meant by "voluntary"? Legal scholar Robert Steinfeld critiques what is meant by *voluntary* and examines the nature of coercion under economic and legal pressures in an examination of wage labor in the nineteenth century. Unique combinations of pecuniary and legal enforcements effected coercions that upturn the "conventional narrative of free labor [that] continues to rest on the assumption that labor falls into discrete, discontinuous types—wage labor, contract labor, indentured servitude, serfdom, slavery—each having its own natural set of characteristics that define it as either free or unfree," according to Steinfeld.[28] He argues that "the issue of whether a contract has been entered into voluntarily or involuntarily suffers from the same logical difficulty discussed at some length. . . . It is not possible, as a logical matter, to distinguish difficult choices that give rise to 'voluntary' decisions to contract from difficult choices that give rise to 'coerced' decisions to contract." Steinfeld's strategy is to move away from measuring the voluntariness of *entry into* a contract and examine the freedom of *withdrawal from* the contract system.[29] On this point, the coolie predicament with the contract comes into bold relief. The circle of bondage and the violent struggle to *get free* from the contract system, and the repressive measures to effect a hostage contract system, form an equation of "in/voluntariness." Withdrawal from the contract system is complicated by coolies who described being released only to be forced to find another owner, forced into another contract, or risk being brutally apprehended. Steinfeld's calling into question the meaning and measure of "voluntariness" is especially relevant to the coolie representations of force, as this question relates to the unstable demarcation of what is "free" and what constitutes the experience of so-called freedom. Steinfeld's strategic focus is helpful in teasing out the slippery construct of consent and coercion, and thus, the slippery construct of contract. Still, his main arguments about coercion do not address the contract as possibly *creating* conditions of slavery, such as suggested by the Chinese coolies in Cuba.

Philosopher Tommy Lott's arguments highlight the inherent problems in defining "servitude" and "slavery," especially given rigid perceptions of what constitutes "slavery." His argument could be taken up as prologue for considering the contract an extension of slavery or as an overlapping condition. In his treatment of Hobbesian and Lockean constructions of slavery, servitude, morality, and corporeal liberty, Lott argues that "servitude and slavery" are overlapping institutions, both historically and philosophically, with special attention to African American slavery. Discerning the problematic distinctions between servitude and slavery, he attacks the notion that "slavery is, b*y definition*, always harsher than servitude—an idea that has created a conceptual barrier that prevents the application of reasons for condemning slavery to sufficiently similar instances of servitude."[30] Lott's arguments pivot upon questioning notions of corporeal liberty and consent, as in his reading of Harriet Jacobs, in which he concludes that Jacobs reveals domination and subjugation as conditions under a spectrum of slavery, in which supposedly benign forms of slavery existed as *extensions* of harsher forms of slavery that "constantly loom in the background as negative incentive." [31] The house slave and the urban slave, he argues, have been figured as supposedly more benign forms of slavery compared to the field slave, when in fact, these forms constitute related kinds of violation and coercion. The idea of a spectrum of slavery in Lott's argument is especially relevant in this reading of coolie writings that pointed to the contract as an institution separating them from slavery yet reproducing slavery. The appearance of corporeal liberty under contract— that is, the notion that they supposedly were not *bodily* enslaved—is thoroughly undermined by the very use of contract technology to particularize and mobilize Chinese precisely as bodies to be enslaved.

Lott, Steinfeld, Pateman, and Stanley all foreground philosophical and legal problems in the contract's philosophical and political genesis and its historical deployments in the creation of "free" relations. In the coolie testimonies, the labor contract and *de jure* contract emerge as masked systems of oppression that not only coerce the Chinese but also work to inscribe and reinscribe a patently false narrative of the "social contract." Philosopher Charles Mills makes a penetrating observation regarding a patent disingenuousness inherent in the social contract, which he argues is, in fact, a "racial contract." He argues that its continued ameliorations and codes simply mask the underlying and continuing imperatives of subordination: "Indian laws, slave codes, and colonial native acts formally codified the subordinate status of nonwhites and (ostensibly) regulated their treatment, creating a juridical space for non-Europeans as a separate category of beings. So even if there was sometimes an attempt to prevent 'abuses' (and those codes were honored far more often in the breach than the observance), the point is that 'abuse' as a concept presupposed as a norm the *legitimacy* of the subordination. Slavery and colonialism are not conceived as wrong in their denials of autonomy to persons, what is wrong is the improper administration of these regimes."[32] Though Mills footnotes that he is not totally dismissing the potential of "contract" in theory, he critiques its historical institution as corrupt.

In the testimonies, the contract emerged as the main tool for creating and maintaining the coolies' enslavement. The contract, a representation of their allegedly voluntary participation in a scheme of labor, suggested the elusive promise of eventual freedom yet created conditions for continual bondage. Their testimonies, which emerge over a century before the arguments of Mills, Lott, Steinfeld, Pateman, and Stanley, provide grounds to be further considered in deliberations of a contractual system, its manipulations, and its potentialities. According to the coolies, the brevity of their lives and their hyperexploitation was related to a pervasive system of exploitation *that was organized around the contract and a "paper" system.* Contracts and related "paper" generated the interests of profit and further bondage. This notion is especially illuminated in the petitions with large group signatories. These petitions reveal technologies of enslavement and exemplify a *narrative of the "paper chase."*

CHASING FREEDOM: "IT IS LIKE A CIRCLE WITHOUT ANY END"

The contract and the paper system emerged as the most heightened and visible representation of *relations* between two or more parties; thus, the battle with paper became a struggle over representation and the relations of power. In these testimonies, subordination and enslavement are described as being exercised via the very instruments of ostensibly free relations: the contract and "papers." Images of entrapment, tropes of chasing paper, and motifs of the hypercircularity of paper and bodies emerge as a dominant pattern. As the Chinese in Petition 65 stated, "It is like a circle without any end, no matter how many times." Papers—contracts, certificates, permissions, permits, passes, passports, identification papers—were not so much things being *referenced* as they were *commodities* to be endlessly pursued, as described by the coolies. One Xie Qiren described his desperate chase upon hearing that some "official" was partial to granting him a freedom paper. He was reduced to begging his master for the documents: "I begged the master to write down my name and to ask for a paper." Xie chased his prospects until "unexpectedly" discovering that, in fact, the official would not issue him a paper (Petition 71). The "paper chase" is one of the most powerful themes drawn in the coolies' representations of their struggle for freedom. Among the oral testimonies, 641 coolies featured the paper chase as their preoccupation. Featured here are written testimonies that most clearly featured the paper chase: Petitions 2, 11, 20, 25, 54, and 65. As conveyed in the testimonies, these papers granted *temporary* freedoms of various *degrees* that could only be had for fees that varied wildly according to the local market (and extortions) of officials, police, and planters. The extent of the freedoms, the application, the temporal limits, and the restrictions by locality of those freedoms were purely arbitrary, subject to the whims of profit-seeking local authorities and any seller or buyer in the market. The coolie contracts apparently emerged in different forms, and so did their freedom papers, which were obtainable through fees and were only valid for a month, sometimes six months, or a year at most. A lexical tracing of their "papers" in the testimonies reveals that contracts and papers included various types, with some categorized under the same term but deployed in multiple ways:

- "Contract" (卖身纸, *mai shen zhi*) Literally means "sell body paper." Denoted a coolie contract.
- "Contract" (合同, *hetong*) Most often referred to as the first contract that Chinese signed upon being detained at port in China. Sometimes referred to recontracting in Cuba, in relation to "Tie Up" contract (*bangshen*) (see "Tie-Up").
- "Contract" (约券 *yuequan*, as in 以身拘约券 *yi shen ju yuequan*) A term for an agreement.
- "Contract" (工券, *gongquan*) A term for a labor agreement.

- "Five-year contract" (五年工满合同, *wu nian gongman hetong*) Contract signed upon being detained at port in China, which indicated a five-year term.
- "Eight-year contract" (分符执据八年为期 (*fenfuzhiju ba nian weiqi*) Contract signed upon being detained at port in China, which indicated an eight-year term.
- "Bondage, Tie-Up" (绑身, *bangshen*) The reselling of Chinese, which entailed the forced resigning of another contract called "Tie-Up" or *bangshen.*
- "Freedom paper" (满身纸, *manshen zhi*) Paper that literally means "completion of body paper," and means the "completion of contract." In the context of the testimonies of Cuba, this term assumed much greater significance than simply completion of a contract. It became an intensely desired yet elusive promise of freedom from bondage and captivity. This freedom paper could not be obtained without first procuring two other papers, a "Proof" and a "Guarantee."
- "Release from Contract Paper" (脱工文凭, *tuogong wenping*) Means "release from labor diploma." This paper was issued by officials.
- "Complete contract/contract expires"(工满, *gongman)* A paper indicating completion of contract.
- "Redeem oneself/buy back one's freedom" (赎身, *shushen*) To buy back one's freedom and get a paper, a term that rarely appeared in the testimonies. Mentions of *shushen* were in the context of coercion, of not getting a release paper, unless paying for it.
- "Guarantee Paper" (凭据纸, *pingju zhi*) First type: A paper/proof of "washing head" (baptism) from godfather or sponsor. Needed in order to obtain a freedom paper.
- "Guarantee Paper" (凭据纸, *pingju zhi*) Second type: A paper from the master, as proof of finishing the contract. Needed in order to obtain a Freedom Paper.
- "Guarantee Paper" (凭据纸, *pingju zhi*) Third type: A preliminary paper, obtained from officials or police, needed for subsequent kinds of papers.
- "Proof" (非马, *feima*) First type: A paper, obtained from officials or police, needed for subsequent kinds of papers.
- "Proof" (非马, *feima*) Second type: Like *pingju zhi.* A paper from the master, as proof of finishing the contract.

- "Walking Paper" (行街纸, *xingjie zhi*) Paper allowing Chinese laborers to walk in the street. If one only had a freedom paper but no walking paper, one would be arrested by police or patrols. However, in order to obtain a walking paper, one had to have a freedom paper first, which could not be obtained without a proof and guarantee paper. Thus, more money was needed for additional freedom to walk.
- "Begging Paper" (乞丐纸, *qigai zhi*) For those exiled or discarded by owners and official workshops, due to being maimed, sick, or old. This paper had to be bought, needed constant renewal (for a fee), and allowed one the freedom to beg.
- "Go-to-Another-County Paper" (过埠纸, *guobu zhi*) If a Chinese laborer wanted to go to another town, city, or county in Cuba, he or she had to obtain a go-to-another-county-paper from local officials, like a travel pass. However, in order to obtain this paper, one needed paper and permission from the master.
- "Go-Abroad-Paper" (出港纸, *chugang zhi*) Like a passport or visa. Considered the penultimate step toward escape. This paper ostensibly allowed a Chinese coolie to get out of Cuba. It was extremely expensive, as it was obtained only after first obtaining a proof, guarantee, freedom paper, and residence paper, and required the presence of a sponsor or godfather. Most Chinese could not afford this or could not amass the required papers. However, some managed to procure the paper. Still, testimonies indicated that the paper itself did not guarantee *actual exit* from the country and did not preclude return to bondage.
- "Residence Paper" (文凭, *wenping*) A residence paper was required to get a go-abroad-paper. According to testimonies, this part of the paper chase was filled with irony—coolies dreamt of getting a *residence* paper in order to increase their chances *of leaving*. However, this paper could only be obtained with a freedom paper.
- "Open-store Paper" (开铺纸, *kaipu zhi*) This paper was obtained by some Chinese laborers. They saved enough money to buy their freedom paper and attempted to operate small businesses, such as vending and selling vegetables. They had to buy the "Open-Store Paper" and constantly "renew" it, with risk of confiscation. This paper did not protect them from seizure and being returned to bondage.

• "Doctor's License Paper, Doctor Paper" (行医纸, 医生纸, *xingyi zhi, yisheng zhi*) This paper was needed for Chinese doctors to practice medicine. Several Chinese doctors testified to being abducted into the trade. Large fees were required to obtain a doctor's paper and needed constant "renewal," with risk of confiscation. This paper did not protect them from being returned to bondage, where they could be forced to continue providing services.

Sometimes the testimonies simply indicated the existence, proffering, or need of some "paper" (any paper that seemed to grant some type of freedom at any given time). The "paper chase" turned out to be a paper hell in which several participants at any given moment wielded power over the "paper." Wu Aguang protested, "It has been eight years till now, but the owner still refused to issue me the *proof*, so the local official refused to issue the *freedom paper*. Without *freedom paper*, we would be arrested and shackled up in official workshop, whether we have fulfilled our *contract* or not. And we would be forced to work for free day and night, with supervisors riding on horses, holding guns and watching us! If no Cuban people bail us out, we will be shackled until the day we die. I have already worn the shackles for years. My feet festered severely because of wearing shackles for years, and I became handicapped with incomplete limbs" (my emphasis, Petition 7). Junctures of "paper" represented multiple opportunities to further bond Chinese, who could be sent back to square one: a state of bondage, until the owner decided to sell, at which point the cycle would start again. Chen Gu described the arbitrary withholding of freedom by owners, police, local officials, and the humiliation of having to beg on his knees:

After the completion of eight-year contract, we were forced to renew our contract, and we were turned down when we asked for our freedom paper. Without freedom paper, we could not leave and work as contract labor in other neighboring districts. If the precinct chief caught us, we would be detained in the official workshop, where we would have to work and suffer indefinitely; there would only be death waiting for us. Last year, on the third night of the eighth moon local officials and precinct chiefs personally inspected us and arrested us regardless of us having freedom paper or not. We were sent to excavate and chop down trees at a place called by the natives, La Trocha. The limit of working time is six months, and after finishing, people who have freedom papers would be returned with their freedom papers; others who do not have freedom papers would be given one. Until the second moon of this year, I have worked for six months, so I begged them on my knees to return my freedom paper and send me back to the town where I used to work, so that I could find a new job there. However, they lied to us. They took me along with others to the official workshop in Havana and forced us to work for the government. As quoted. (Petition 22)

In scenarios described by the coolies, Chinese were resold into bondage at any time, and papers went to the higher bidders. In this scenario, the promise of freedom from bondage operated as the master tool of systemic exploitation, with freedom not a static principle but as a segmented and fluctuating state. There were degrees of freedom that coolies could ostensibly obtain and that officials marketed, rationed, segmented, or sold in degrees on a contingent basis.

A literary-economic approach to slave narratives was called for by Houston Baker, in his reading of the "economics of slavery" and the "propertied self." And the "financial and imaginative currency" of paper and slaves is provocatively and extensively examined by Ian Baucom in his study of the slave ship *Zong* and the conditions of speculative finance capitalism. His investigation of the commodification of slaves, and the system of slave credit and exchange, leads to his argument that the *Zong* event illustrates but also led to a universalizing of modernity. Baucom's study is more than logbooks, accountants, and insurance policies, as he teases out a phenomenology of "transactions, promises, character, credibility" and most of all, he examines imaginative and cultural questions that arise when using human beings as commodities. The testimonies of 1874 bear out a further scenario of slavery economics and the propertied self, in which coolies described being sold, circulated, exchanged, loaned out, resold, but also described their (the coolies') simultaneous investment in the schema. The rub here is that coolies became recast as consumers and investors in their own slavery. Commodities of freedom, represented by a paper instrument, could be sold to the Chinese in degrees. According to the testimonies, "freedom" from bondage could be granted or rescinded arbitrarily, and buying one's freedom, however tenuous and fleeting, was offered to the coolies as an option.

The coolies' freedom to beg exemplifies freedom as commodity and recast as purchasable privilege. In the quest for begging, as portrayed in the testimonies, the paper instrument ultimately functioned as the most powerful commodity of racialization and social hierarchy (a hierarchy reenacted in public spectacles such as whites, blacks, and children throwing stones at coolies).[33] Perhaps the lowest of the low were Chinese who were deemed unusable. One travel writer observed the Chinese as "lame, half-starved, ragged mendicants, numbers of them blind," whereas the able-bodied Chinese were surviving in cigar workshops or vending fruit.[34] Beggars in the streets of Cuba were not exclusively Chinese, certainly. Those needing papers, passes, identification, were also not exclusively Chinese. However, the conditions of contract labor exacerbated conditions of exploitation, given the hyperdisposability and circularity of contract labor, conditions of language, and the perverse situation of racialized contract laborers dependent upon contracts. In the scenarios described by the Chinese, they were discarded by owners when they became incapable of producing enough labor (they were old, sick, or disabled). Begging emerged as means of survival. Their begging was premised upon *applying for* and *purchasing that particular freedom (to beg)*. Yuan Aishan's petition offers a typical example of the begging theme that recurs in the testimonies. His last words to the commission were a plea to get a begging paper. The regularizing of begging emerges as an extension of the freedom papers, as a means of consolidating control over coolies who were close to being free. Yuan was discarded due to age and disability: "I am sixty-six years old now. I am begging your honor to apply for a begging paper for me, so that I can beg on streets. If you can grant my wish, you will be giving me a new life" (Petition 77). The most impoverished coolies, begging to survive, needed to first apply and buy this privilege, materialized via a purchasable "begging paper." Thus begging was converted to a "productive" act, since coolie beggars must *pay* for a paper. If one did not have money to afford begging, then perhaps one would be reduced to "begging" for the right to beg. Zhang Luan and his fellow petitioners wrote the following: "the old and weak often beg for begging papers to become beggars" (Petition 11). One Zhang Shilian begged the commission to get him the begging paper: "I do not have the begging paper right now.

I came to petition sincerely for this begging paper" (Petition 83). The coolies of Petition 2 railed against the supremacy of paper:

> *If a Chinese did not have the "Proof" issued from the owner, he could not apply for "Freedom Paper" from official. If he did not have the "Freedom Paper," the patrol could force him into the official workshop whenever they wanted to. In Cuba, the official workshop is no different from prison. They just make a conspiracy to trap the Chinese workers to work at the official workshop forever since they do not need to pay us anything and also they can skim profits by binding us. Apart from the "Freedom Paper," there is the "Walking Paper," which requires a fee to renew every year. Without that paper, one could not walk on the street. If one wanted to travel to another town, one would have to ask the local officials for "Traveling Paper"; otherwise, one could be put into prison.*

Any Chinese who are handicapped and cannot work, or are expelled by the sugar plantation, or are very sick in the official workshops, need a "Begging Paper" in order to become a beggar. The "Begging Paper" cannot be obtained without a fee.

> *As to the "Go Abroad Paper," the fee depends on how much money one has in savings. It ranges from ten yuan to several hundred yuan. How dare a Chinese worker dream of going back to China?* (my emphasis).

Begging here was converted to a "productive" act profiting others (officials); yet in histories of labor, begging has been looked upon as nonproductive, parasitic, and as a refusal to join the contract society. As one measure for halting this kind of activity, begging was criminalized. In an examination of begging and its economic and moral contexts, Amy Dru Stanley examines begging in nineteenth-century North America as a challenge to abolitionist views and to the contract as the basis of a free-market society. As Stanley asserts, the "hireling abided by the obligations of contract; [but] the beggar eluded them."[35] Beggars were therefore criminalized and imprisoned or forced back into the labor contract, thus reinsuring the sanctity of the wage and contract society. Saidiya Hartman, in her study of racial "subjection" in American slavery and its aftermath, also calls attention to Stanley's analysis and to what Hartman calls the compulsion of the poor, who were "literally forced to participate in the world of exchange."[36] Remarking upon contract enforcement in Trinidad, Viranjini Munasinghe notes that in the history of East Indian indenture, a scheme was implemented to discourage vagrancy among the coolies—they would be fined if they did not have a contract, though the scheme was later abandoned.[37] K.O. Laurence noted that imprisonment became the penalty instead.[38] Fining and imprisonment were meant to force vagrants back into the contract system. But rather than fine, imprison, or force the beggar into labor for a wage, a type of freedom was regularized and marketed to the beggar in Cuba, as a privilege granted in the transaction of paper and money. The poorest could get the begging privilege and continually pay to renew it.

The coolies' representations of freedom amount to a reversal of Enlightenment and humanist philosophies, in which freedom is ostensibly a condition, not a commodity. The commodification of freedom, represented by multiplying papers, dominated the lives of coolies and would become the construct of psychological and physical enslavement. The notion of freedom as commodity implied that freedom could be had, if only transiently. While simple extortion might be a means for describing this state of affairs, it does not account for systemic exploitation and the psychosomatic investment in such a system. Implicated in the coolie representations is their awareness of themselves as coerced participants of the system, notwithstanding their expressed disillusionment and resentment of the system. As subjects being recruited into a system of *freedom deferrals*, the coolies both struggled with and participated in this schema of paper. The production of "freedom" and the profusion of rules did not guarantee liberties (whether purchased or not), but instead operated to segment and diffuse avenues of power and possession. The commodification of freedom, in the form of a paper system, structured a field of possibilities within a coercive market, and to a certain extent, structured the field of action.[39] The wielding of paper—by officials, police, owners, and middlemen who produced and circulated such papers—emerged as a supreme method of control. Coolies described this system of control as a paper system combined with characteristic features of a slavery society: corporal punishment and physical containment by masters. Therefore, the possibility of getting free and staying free from bondage was signified by the act of purchasing something within a slavery society—in this case, a symbolic paper instrument—yet being subjected to punitive measures within that society. The authors of Petition 54, formerly businessmen in China, narrated the paper chase in a way that implicitly indicated not only their participation in the system but also their resistance to it. They expressed indignation over the transfer of capital in a contract system that "robbed" money from the laborer and redirected it to the officials and police. They linked this to their reduction in status to that of slaves and animals, reified as commodities to be traded: ". . . the Walking Paper, the Open-Store Paper, the Doctor's Paper, the Go Abroad Paper, the Begging Paper, and the renewal for all these papers, how much money have they got from us Chinese laborers? And it is needless to mention the rapacity and robbery from the police and precinct chief. Though the officials and the businessmen in Cuba have gained so much money from the Chinese laborer, they don't know how to appreciate us; instead, they humiliate us, trample on us and insult us by making us slaves and treating us like animals." More intriguing is that the paper system involved direct participation in the market. Value and profit was created through the demands of the coolie seeking freedom from bondage and through owners and officials who wielded, accumulated, sold, and circulated papers. Hailed as "contract holders," the Chinese identified and believed themselves (at least *initially*) as distinct from slaves, despite their treatment as chattel. The deceitful pact here is not only a deceitful contract of labor but also a deceitful social contract: presumably, Chinese *would not be slaves, would never be black; they could possibly escape that predicament, if only because they had "contracts."* The proximity to slaves, and precisely the use of chattel slavery's implements against coolies, seemed to only heighten the allure of holy grail–like paper. As Zhang Dingjia and his fellow coolies typically described, they suffered all the implements of chattel slavery:

> We were all naked when we were inspected by buyers. We never saw
> people being humiliated in such a terrible way. We were sold to sugar
> plantations and treated worse than dogs and oxen. Foreign overseers
> rode on horses, with cowhide whips and guns in their hands. Regard-
> less of our speed or quality, they lashed us from a distance; they hit us
> with clubs within reach. Some of us had bones broken and some spat
> blood right away. People with cracked head and broken legs still had to
> work instead of being sent into a ward. Countless people died of injury
> within eight years. If one went out into the mountain without permis-

sion, overseers would release several big dogs to bite that person. There were cells in each sugar plantation with numerous instruments for torture. The heaviest chain was more than fifty jin and the lightest chain was at least twenty jin. Sometimes, they randomly put chains on one or around one's ankles, even to one's hips, and one still had to work with these heavy chains. Everyday we had only a couple of corns and plantains for meals. I saw that dogs and oxen could have enough food and rest. We were treated even worse than livestock. As quoted. (Petition 80)

The contract represented racialized possibilities for bettering a dire situation. The enlisting of Chinese as "contract holder" and the clear racial symbolism of this—with Chinese being "contract labor" and Africans being "slaves"—appears to have been an effective mechanism of maintaining social control of a multiracial multitude, effectively dividing Chinese from African. In confronting the folly of the contract, the Chinese described their status in reference to a social hierarchy: At the top there were whites, then blacks, then animals. The "racial contract" shadowed their understanding of contract and its possibilities, and is directly revealed in the repeated comparisons to their black counterparts. As 131 Chinese stated in Petition 55, "Since we were abducted to Cuba, no matter we have the freedom paper or not, we Chinese are bullied and humiliated here. We cannot go to the first class carriage in a train and cannot sit at the first class table in a restaurant. We are treated the same as black slaves." The Chinese of Petition 2, after lengthy discussion of the contract system and its perversions, asked why contract laborers were relegated to lesser social status than slaves: "Why are the Chinese inferior to Blacks?" Nowhere do the Chinese refer to themselves as occupying an intermediary position between white and black. Echoing the sentiments of other testifiers, one coolie emphasized that "here, whites and blacks often bully the Chinese; they hit us without any reason and throw stones at us."[40] The Chinese repeatedly described their reduced social status in antithetical phrases, not only as less than white, but as equal to, or "less than black," and more often, as "less than animals." Black slaves and animals were, in these writings, the most relevant comparisons in terms of social status and "property." Coolies called themselves "pigs" being sold (or *zhuzai*) and called their confinement in barracones as "pigpens" (or *zhuzai guan*). They were confounded by being denoted "contract labor," yet treated as less than "slave labor." As one coolie stated, "People in Cuba already got used to enslaving the blacks but they treat Chinese worse than black slaves. This does not make any sense" (Deposition 855). Seventeen Chinese of Petition 38 perceived their status as lower than blacks and more equivalent to animals. They were "looked upon as livestock like cows, sheep, dogs, and horses." There were 159 Chinese in Petition 80 who thought themselves to be even less than animals: "We saw that dogs and cows could have enough food and rest. We were treated even worse than these livestock." Through these negative comparisons, the Chinese described their new status as the lowest possible existence, not only lower than whites, blacks, and animals, but, as phrased repeatedly, "less than ants." Being presented with a contract that could possibly lead to freedom from bondage, the coolie predicament reveals dimensions of psychological enslavement via instruments of "voluntariness," such as the contract. The varied rhetoric of being legally different from African "slaves," yet in practice regarded as "less than slaves," led the Chinese to resist but also invest in the paper concept and system. Whereas Lai Zhizhi and his group dissected their injustice by underscoring presumptions regarding the inviolability of contract, they also illustrated its failures and violations point by point:

> On the day when we signed the contract in Macao, we heard that the employment period for working was eight years according to the clauses of the contract. Unexpectedly, the foreigners were deceitful and the clauses of the contract were all empty talk. Even though the contract expired after eight years, we would still be forced to work for another eight years. If we did not work, we would be either beaten or shackled. If we argued with him, we would be sent to the officials immediately. We worked as government labor with no payment year after year. In the day, we did not take a hearty meal; at night, we did not get a sound sleep. If we got sick and could not work, we would be lashed immediately. If we escaped in protest, once we were caught, it would be hard for us to bear the corporal punishment. We suffer from dispossession of document papers and infinite work. The best way to describe this: it is difficult to leave the tiger's mouth if one enters the tiger's den. As quoted. (Petition 32)

The coolies' vigorous protests against their enslavement included a conflicted and tortuous intimacy of survival in capitalistic schemas of self-enslavement, with the chasing of paper being the main trope: the power of paper, the strategy to obtain paper, the struggle to hold onto the paper, the elusive meaning of paper, the relation of paper to self and identity, and the fetishistic aspects of paper. The testimonies reveal resistance to the contract system, but their confessions also revealed a troubled complicity with the very same system.[41] The pervasive struggle over paper appears not only as an operational means of getting "free," but also as a struggle over identity and representation, as contract and paper became the concentrated *representation* of the *relations* of power.

The coolies, not simply passive subjects of the contract, were obviously actively engaged in an intense struggle with paper, and they wrote from the complex position of being against their enslavement while simultaneously being enfolded as participants in the system of their oppression. The trope of the paper chase occurs most intensively in testimonies from Chinese who held onto the belief that there was still some slim possibility of obtaining freedom through still-extant legal loopholes. However, the Royal Decree and Regulations of 1860 closed off avenues to freedom for Chinese and were designed to implement virtual slavery. Chinese were still able to occasionally obtain papers, though with great difficulty and with no guarantee of freedom from bondage, according to the testimonies. Nevertheless, the tightening of the paper system correlates with a heightened pattern of open violence against authority, including increased patterns of the Chinese killing their overseers, apparent in testimonies of Chinese *who arrived after 1860–1862*. It is after 1860 that flurries of legislation were enacted in a series of colonial codes to increase repressive measures against Chinese labor and to further articulate (yet obfuscate) the contract system. The testimonies from post-1860 Chinese coolies seethe with anger.

Althusserian and Gramscian approaches to coercion take into account the ideological recruitment of subjects (and in Gramscian terms, cast more dynamically as ongoing sites of struggle among contradictions), and are of relevance in locating the workings of power in the paper system. Yet these theoretical lenses, which emerged from a distinct set of historical contexts, leave more to be desired. The Cuba episode raises conceptual challenges regarding the subject's relation to a melded system of mechanisms traditionally associated with a free labor economy (cast as modern) with those mechanisms traditionally associated with a slavery economy (cast as premodern). Coolies in the market were mobile, with some modicum of wages (however severely or impossibly limited), yet had to be continually disciplined via brutal mechanisms to keep them enslaved as long as possible. Such apparent contradictions, appearing in high relief in the localized particularities of coolie lives, can be considered in relation to Dale Tomich's view of contradiction on the global scale and his conceptualization of the "second slavery." He argues that "both the capitalist character of slavery and the slave character of capitalism emerge from the historically evolving relations among the various forms of production and exchange within this totality," and *"conceived of in this way, the historical hierarchy among forms of labor is not, and cannot be, the same as the theoretical hierarchy"*[42] (my emphasis). And as Lott argued, the theoretical fixities of "slavery" and "servitude" occlude conceptual considerations of their shared philosophical bases and problems. Tomich's argument on "second slavery" envisions contradiction as integrative, and Lott's argument on "slavery-servitude" envisions contradiction as a spectrum. Given the arguments of the historian Tomich and the philosopher Lott, whether integrative or spectrum, there still remains the question of what mechanism functions as the axis of social control in a historical moment of antinomy for the Chinese. The testimonies point to mechanisms of profit and social control located in the act of *transaction*, which in this history, emerges as moments of *racial inscription*. Papers emerged as a pervasive and consistent measure of exploitation through racialized market relations.

The testimonies describe uneven, multisited resistance (see Chapter 4), but more clearly, they point to the subordination of Chinese persons via racialization. For the Chinese, racialization appears as a mechanism that advanced "second slavery." Legislation explicitly articulated specific policies, regulations, and disciplinary actions for the "Chinese." This in itself, however, does not account for the unique form of coercion used on the Chinese. One might say the coolies' descriptions are of freedom as a state directly related to a market, which continually inscribed racial marking in acts of market exchange. This market was pegged to *racialized* mechanisms of power. Take the simple (and typical) statement from a testimony, "I bought a Walking Paper from a white man" (Deposition 79). The "freedom" to walk in the street, not available to a coolie, was sold by a "white man." "Freedom" emerges as a racialized transaction in the marked inscription of one man of color buying some degree of freedom via its paper representation from a white man with the power to grant it. The reinscription of racial hierarchy becomes repeated via innumerable transactions that followed (or came before) this moment, revolving around paper.

A crystallizing instance of transaction being the pivot of racialization and control is more clearly illustrated in the use of a *dead person's papers to extract forced labor.* Petition 20 signed by 164 Chinese, the largest group to send in a petition, describe dead persons' contracts being imposed upon living persons as a means of seizing labor. The death of a coolie constituted another layer of marketability. Death did not "end" the potentiality for extracting labor. Apparently, paper identity could be imposed from a dead person to a living one as a means of forcing Chinese persons back into bondage. The coolies state the following: "As to the contracts we signed at Macao, most of them were taken away by the owners of the plantations when we entered the plantation. The plantation owners can negotiate with officials and substitute a dead person's contract with another living person in the official workshop." These papers could be reassigned, others could be accumulated. The confiscation and accumulation of contracts (and freedom papers), and the imposition of a dead person's contract onto a living person, led to *procurement* of Chinese and led to a paper market for procuring labor.

Testimonies reveal that over 200 Chinese specifically described the practice of being forced to take another person's name (a condition distinct from being given a Spanish name). One deponent named Tan Achin was subsequently contracted under two names, with the first instance being under Lan Ahou, and the second under the name Li Asi (Deposition 1151). Another deponent in his forties dryly stated, "I was given a contract, which said the age of the person is twenty-eight years old" (Deposition 1112). Zhang Luan exclaimed that upon being abducted, "I was forced to meet with a western official and sign a contract. But the name on that contract was not mine but 'Gui Chen'" (Deposition 1050). A former bricklayer and the only son of a sixty-six-year-old mother described betrayal by his cousin and being forced to take another name: "My cousin A-an Li asked me to work in Macao. When I arrived at Macao, I stayed at my cousin's home for two days. Then he asked me to take over someone's name and sign another person's contract. But then I was forbidden to leave"

(Deposition 1114). And still more coolies described the trickery of being recruited to help sign a contract on behalf of a sick person who was physically unable to sign. In return, the signer was promised some remuneration (usually money or clothes). "They asked me to help a sick person, take over his name and sign his contract," Cai Xiang recounted. "They said after I boarded the ship, they would send someone to bring me back. I believed their words. Then I met with a western official and signed a contract. They gave me eight dollars and two sets of clothes" (Deposition 1054). Xu Axiang similarly described the ruse: "The manager in the Pigpen told me to sign the contract for a sick person, stay on the ship for one day, and then he would bring me off the ship the next day. Because I believed him, I saw a foreign officer, signed a piece of contract, got eight dollars and two suits of clothes" (Deposition 965).

The abduction of Chinese, the imposition of papers and new names—and on the other hand, the confiscation of these very papers deemed "fake"—offer a glimpse into the profound struggle of coolies over identity and liberation. Historically, the forgery of papers has been engaged as a weapon of the subaltern, as in histories of illegal immigration.[43] In the testimonies, occasionally the "Penman" appeared, often a local Cuban or foreigner who could be paid to fill out an application for a paper, or perhaps, to compose a fake one. On the other hand, the testimonies underscore the pervasive fakery of paper by *administrators* and those in power. Coolies were also forced by officials or police to buy freedom papers with someone else's name on the paper. As one deponent pointed out, "The paper used to belong to a person who was already dead, so the name on the paper was not mine" (Deposition 354). At the same time, Chinese also stated they were frequently forced to relinquish papers, which were deemed fake, by officials and police. As one coolie described it, "Officers in official workshops would take away Chinese's freedom paper, if they had one. And if the Chinese died, the officer would sell his freedom paper to other people. And that freedom paper would go under another person's name" (Deposition 251). The use of dead persons' contracts illustrates what might be best described as a mobile contract and mobile slave. The chattel went with the conveyance, so to speak, but the conveyance could be attached to numerous chattels and operated with a cumulative value. Contracts and *cedulas* (identification papers) were held by the owners (not the coolies) according to colonial regulations, yet there was a noticeable omission in the laws as to what should happen to a dead coolie's papers. They could, in effect, be accumulated. It is only in the colonial "Rules of 1873," that some stipulation appears regarding dead-coolie papers, in which the "employer" needed to deliver the deceased coolie contract and *cedula* to local officials, who would then be required to turn them in to district authorities, "by whom they are to be cancelled."[44] The legislation appears almost thirty years after the coolie labor in Cuba had been already installed, and the degree to which it was enforced is unknown. The coolies of Petition 20 expose a public circulation of bodies and contracts, in which a contract *accumulated* value to the property owner, profiteering official, the state, or an enterprising entrepreneur. The idea of dead persons' contracts accumulating and pinned onto freedom-seeking Chinese is not surprising if examined within the logic of a market in which papers accumulated value precisely from the power to acquire, discipline, and force persons to perform in a racialized economy. The coolie testimonies reveal that besides being the *representation* of property relations, a contract circulated as an enforceable means of sequentially pressing particular persons into service and as a means of accumulation. The power of enforcement could be applied to anyone *appearing to be Chinese*. The contract's value and use thus turned upon the *racialization* of the contract and the particular *racializing* power of contract. In other words, a white person, for example, could not be seized under a coolie contract. But persons of Chinese appearance could be arbitrarily seized. The case of the Chinese coolie in Cuba emerges as a history of the contract as a transparently racialized instrument, which fed upon and reinscribed subordination of particular people through labor and profit. The contract, supposedly the instrument of free and consensual relations, thus functioned as an instrument of surveillance that apprehended particular people and contributed to their enslavement by making bodies highly visible as property. The contract as ideological and racializing instrument refines observations of conflicts in the labor force, as directly tied to the racialized construct of contract and its divisive use by owners (see further discussion of race and resistance in Chapter 4).

From the coolies' narratives, one may consider this a case of the racial contract transparently materialized, as it has been theorized from various intellectual standpoints, such as that articulated by Charles Mills in his critique of the "social contract." Mills argues that the "racial contract" reproduces hierarchy and exploitation with particular mechanisms of ideology, force, and moral psychology.[45]

A paper system—dead persons' papers, fake-name papers, confiscation of papers, resale and transfer of papers—operated as the linchpin of enslavement, rather than as a linchpin of free labor. The "value" of paper functioned upon transactions that determined the relative freedom of Chinese, which in the moment of transaction wielded punitive force over Chinese. This was clearly manifested in the power of *verification*. The determination of a paper's value, as the symbolic arbiter of social status (being degrees of freedom), depended upon its verifiability. Coolies who acquired papers were confronted with the next hurdle: Was the paper "real" or "fake"? The possibility for freedom was dependent on the temporal exchange value of the paper, producing uncertainty for the Chinese, who were confounded by the shifting *procedures* for verification and eligibility. Papers were confiscated, declared fake, declared inapplicable to the coolie, while being completely useful to noncoolies. Dai Risheng and Pan Acong described the arbitrary yet particular function of paper with this example: "People without paper would be arrested and extorted. People with paper would be coerced and punished" (Petition 64). The acquiring of papers took on certain value at a given moment, depending on whether the user was a coolie, an official, a policeman, a businessman, or some enterprising individual. As examples, five statements from different testimonies illustrate a few of the many examples of "verification":

— "I do not have a freedom paper now. I bought one before, but officers in the official workshop said the paper was useless and took it away" (Deposition 438). (Obtaining freedom was contingent upon the transaction. It could be bought some times and could not be bought other times.)

— "I was told that my freedom paper was not issued from this area, so the local officer took it away and changed it to another person's name. Therefore I do not have the freedom paper anymore" (Deposition 71). (Freedom status was entirely contingent upon locality.)

— "There were several times when patrols wanted to make money, so they forced Chinese to hand over their freedom papers and threatened Chinese to give them money. If the Chinese refused, his paper would be torn apart and he would be escorted to the official"

(Deposition 207). (Freedom involved a triple transaction or seizure of paper, money, and body.)

— "Chinese people's freedom paper is issued by foreign official, and I cannot tell what is real and what is not. Foreign officials here are calling a stag a horse, and cannot tell good from bad" (Petition 46). (The value of paper is determined by unpredictable systems of verification in the moment of transaction.)

— "Local officials and precinct chiefs inspected us and arrested us regardless of our having freedom papers or not." (Petition 22) (Verification served as a pretense for seizure.)

With the paper medium, the power of verification and its ever-shifting grounds produced the key to perpetually bonding persons who were supposedly not slaves. The testimony by Li Zicheng and his three peers, who hired themselves out into a work gang, is representative of those who described the experience of being "free":

We civilians have finished our eight-year contract for years. Thanks to the owner, we got the freedom paper. We are law-abiding people and worked as contract labor in order to live. Last year, several of us planned to work in a sugar plantation, and Fang Tianxiang held our freedom papers and planned to show them to the local official first. However, he lost direction on the way and was caught by some white people from another sugar plantation. He was accused of forging fake freedom papers and arrogating names. Then Fang Tianxiang was arrested and sent to the prison, and our freedom papers were handed to the foreign official. The official tricked us to meet with him in order to get our freedom papers back. We fell in his trap and were all escorted to the official workshop. We were forced to work there without any payment; it has been already more than three months! We kept begging but he refused to release us. As quoted. (Petition 44)

The hapless Fang Tianxiang wrote a petition as well, further elaborating upon this incident, with the confiscation of ten freedom papers and subsequent forced labor (Petition 45). The Chinese clung to their contracts and freedom papers in a state that marketed freedom as paper, yet contract laborers could not simply get "free" upon fulfilling the contract. First, one had to be verifiably *eligible* for freedom and even then, it was transient freedom contingent upon city or town or encounter, as one Yu Aqia protested: "I wanted to go to another place, but was afraid that the owner would find out. If so, he would beat and lock me up. Now, those who have paper in this city cannot travel to other places. They are afraid that the foreign soldiers would arrest and lock them up" (Petition 82).

The coolies became preoccupied with the conditions through which they regarded the "contract" as a legal document—what was "real" and not real, what was "true" and not true. Coolies clung to notions of fixedness bestowed by contract ("We have contracts to prove our words," as the Chinese in Petition 23 state), yet they were confronted with the contract's slippery and manipulative nature. The contract seemed to have no fixed meaning, and it bewildered coolies who identified the contract as institutionalized text construed to be fixed and extended in its meaning. Gu Qiaoxiu protested that "contracts" and associated freedoms were contingent and shifting: "The local official could not distinguish 'good from evil, blue from white' " (Petition 62). Diao Mu and his group similarly asserted that "Cuban soldiers could not tell the difference between jade and stone, and arrested Chinese all at once" (Petition 53). Deng Asi recounted his experience of being "free" as entirely contingent and also illustrated the dark turn of paper as a weapon of the disempowered, as Chinese turned against Chinese. An acquaintance of Deng's, "Tang," was accused of bearing false papers. Nursing a longtime grudge against Deng, Tang took the opportunity to turn against Deng and accused him of forgery instead. Thus Deng was recaptured into bondage by soldiers. Deng recounted the following: "A Chinese person's freedom paper is issued by foreign officials. I cannot tell what is real or not. Foreign officials here are swearing 'a stag is a horse,' and cannot tell good from bad" (Petition 46). Deng referred to a Chinese idiom that originated from the infamous history of Zhao Gao, chief eunuch of the second Qin emperor, who staged a test of loyalty by presenting a stag before the court and deliberately (and falsely) declaring that it was a horse. While some ministers were savvy enough to quickly agree that the animal was a horse, others were not. Zhao executed all who did not agree with him. The coolies described their problems with the paper system as no less arbitrary, with the contract—the reading and wielding of the most crucial "text"—becoming the centerpiece of their intense struggle with those in power.

The proliferation of paper and proliferating sites of verification resulted in a contract perversion, a psychology of mortgaging oneself: Rather than desert the paper system, one would return to it, even cling to it, and claim oneself as a papered (contracted) person rather than a paperless (contract-less) person. Thus, one would rather go *back into bondage* as a way of preserving the *future possibility* of being eligible for freedom, when *chances* might be better. As one deponent typically described, losing one's paper (in this case, the contract) became one of the worst predicaments: "After working for eight years, I was asked to work for a few more years. I refused, so they took my contract away and gave it to the local official" (Deposition 235). In contract perversion (or perhaps, a case of hypercon-tract state), the threat of losing the contract was used to coerce *further bondage* beyond what was stipulated in the contract itself. Losing the contract meant the foreclosure of obtaining a freedom paper, *since one needed to be bonded (have a contract) in order to get free (with a freedom paper)*. Moreover, one would have *to actively seek* bondage, find an owner, or turn oneself into a prison laborer, because one could not *afford* freedom. If one could not buy freedom, one would be forced to actively find another owner. Said one coolie, "The officer said if I had three gold dollars, I could get the freedom paper; if I did not have gold dollar, I had to go find another owner or get into an official workshop"(Deposition 354). Coolie Chen Ay-ing indicated the perverse circularity another way: "Because I didn't have a freedom paper," he says, "I was sent to the local officer to renew my contract . . ." (Deposition 37). Chen did not have a freedom paper. Further-more, Chen would not "qualify" for such a paper without yet another paper in the first place, which would be a contract for bondage. Freedom could not be gotten unless he gave up whatever freedom he had, thereby rebond-ing himself. It is a dizzying scenario, to say the least. Chen rebonded him-self in the hope of attaining some future freedom. The paper chase thus enacts a perpetual mortgaging of freedom with the hope of actually acquir-ing freedom in a system that continually defers it. In a surrealistic perver-sion, the *imagining* of future freedom became the most powerful mechanism for perpetuating enslavement. In this case, paper provided a symbolic and material means for displacement and deferment of hopes.

The coolie struggle with the proliferation of the contract and paper sys-tem was doubly confounded under another set of papers—that of chang-ing sets of rules, regulations, and contracts. These were presented as a function of colonial morality and paternalism directed at Chinese coolies. Government regulations described the overall objective as "the improving of the morality and the regularizing and utilizing of Chinese immigrants."[46] The "contract" is generally understood to be a stable narrative for a given term, theoretically making possible the moment of "agreement." For indentured labor, "contract" would be historically understood as a regularized agreement, or a mass narrative. For the coolies in Cuba, however, there were at least eight versions of "contracts" known to have existed within a short period.[47] This count does not include versions for "re-contracts." Multiple versions of the contracts and recontracts, compounded with frequently changing laws and instructions, not to mention a seemingly endless system of freedom papers in a foreign language, preoccupied the Chinese in a system of obfuscation. Dozens of rules and regulations were issued to specifically address and amend the status of Chinese and the disciplinary measures to control them. These regulations took several forms: colonial government decrees, orders, rules, regulations, instructions, supplements, and modifications. The most significant of measures would arise from legislation directed specifically at Chinese in 1849, 1852, 1853, 1854, 1860, 1862, 1868, 1871, 1872, and 1873.[48] The Royal Decrees in 1854 and 1860 were the most extensive, with the latter closing loopholes for coolie freedom and creating more measures for perpetual bondage.[49] The Royal Decree of 1860 was reinforced with yet another decree in 1862. This legislation was followed by the promulgation of laws and regulations for Chinese in 1868, 1871, 1872, and 1873. In some years, multiple changes to Chinese regulations were made within the same year, such as in 1872, when new orders, amendments, and reversals were made on January 16, February 5, May 17, July 3, July 18, September 14, and December 13.[50] The testifiers stressed these seemingly arbitrary changes by highlighting years of sweeping police raids, seizures of contracts, and seemingly unpredictable measures that were used to conduct repressions en masse. The years 1860, 1861, 1862, 1870, 1871, and 1872 were most frequently described by the coolies as marked by mass coolie hunts and seizures. Specific rights stipulated in contracts for the Chinese, such as the payment of a wage and temporal limit, were simply amended or negated by raids, seizures, and by still more rules.

Furthermore, the Chinese were faced with Spanish as the language of colonial power and as a tool of deliberate obfuscation. Legislation reinscribed the already normalized practice of *cloaking* the contract in Spanish, making the use of language a *legal* matter. This practice ensured that most Chinese would be unable to read the terms of their own contract, as in the rather transparent Regulations of September 14, 1872: "The contract shall be made out in Spanish, and in it the immigrant shall declare his acceptance of the wages stipulated—although they may appear lower than those earned by other labourers—in consideration of the exceptional advantages secured to him." The "exceptional advantages" of contract led to a sense of powerlessness and frustration among the coolies and to the creation of slavery for the market.

SLAVES OF THE MARKET

Pérez de la Riva argues that the forcing of Chinese into public works amounted to yet another condition of slavery. Not only were the Chinese turned into slaves for life, or "*es evidente que se lograba a la perfección el propósito de convertirlo en esclavo por vida*" but they also became slaves in public works, or "*se convertía en esclavo publico.*" In effect, they became slaves of the state, he argues, "*convertir al culí en esclavo perpetuo del Estado.*"[51] The testimonies bear out Pérez de la Riva's assertions, as the testifiers made repeated reference to forced labor in "official workshops" and prisons, as well as forced labor to build roads, clear land, and even build churches.[52] The testimonies, however, go beyond depicting slavery of the state. They depict slavery of the market. The state's key role, as understood in the testimonies, could be seen not only in terms of punitive authority but also in terms of circulating bodies (rather than immobilized bodies). This is evident in the descriptions of the "official workshop," which was depicted as administrator of forced public works and also as clearing-house for marketing and reselling coolies. The coolies' observations and arguments take on an ultimately radical dimension when depicting a market experiment on the *mobile slave*. The official workshops functioned as profitable clearinghouses for further buying and selling of Chinese, who would be deposited there by former owners and police and then resold to private owners in a hypermobile cycle. As witnesses in Petition 20 described, the Chinese would be sold to private owners, who in turn would recirculate the Chinese to the state workshops. Then these workshops would resell the coolies to other interested parties, who would then send the Chinese back to the workshops, and so on. The mobile slave, as drawn by the coolies, was related to the confiscation of wage as profit and the confiscation or resale of bodies by owners, brokers, and the state. The stipulation in the contract that Chinese be paid was manipulated to the point that a more novel kind of profit circulation took place, wherein the "wage" was confiscated by owners, police, and businessmen, all of whom took a cut: "We had to wait for businessmen to select and to negotiate the price. We did not know how much we were sold for or who shared the ill-gotten gains. We had thought that we were born in China, educated by our parents and finally grew up. To our surprise, we are cheated and sold by foreigners in a steady stream, who keep the bondage money. . . . Most of the salary is submitted to the officials, according to the policy." Laws indicating that direct pay to the coolie would be "permissible" only appear in 1871. Yet there is evidence that the Chinese coolies attained enough currency and wages, however minimal, for them to subsequently describe their descent into paper chase hell. The wage, in this sense, emerged as a key component of the paper chase. The coolies talked of scraping together just enough to buy papers from officials. Later it was found that these papers would not protect the coolies as much as *target* them, doubly as bodies to be exploited and as holders of "papers,"—papers being commodities to be confiscated, reassigned, exchanged, or sold by the next official.

According to legislation on the coolies, their circulation was boosted by the practice of public postings for those who had just completed a contract: "Immediately after a Chinese who has completed a contract and who has not made a fresh engagement with his employer, has entered a depot, the facts of his being open to engagement shall be made public in the local journal, or in the absence of such journal, notices to the same effect shall be posted in the most populous localities of the district."[53] Ideally for the local administration, contract labor would be effectively bought, sold, bonded, and circulated until death. Thus, coolies underwent a condition of hypermobility. As one coolie described, "I was resold six times in two years" (Deposition 556). Given the mortality rate of *50 percent attrition within eight years of arrival* for coolies in Cuba, the following numbers take on certain significance.[54] This study reveals the following breakdown, based upon the 1,176 oral testimonies: There were 42.4 percent who indicated that they already served three different owners, 24.4 percent served four or more owners, and an additional 4 percent served seven or more. One coolie, Wang Dacheng, expressed his hypermobility in these simple terms: "I worked in many places." He was transferred twelve times over a ten-year period, working on plantations, and in workshops, prisons, and mountains located in Havana, Colon, Sagua la Grande, and Guanajay. When caught while attempting escape, he was put in stocks. "They locked my feet for four days using a strip of board and two iron hoops," he says. "I could not move; I could not sleep, either. Four days later, they opened the hoops and changed to chains" (Deposition 526). Han Yanpei was moved seven times in fifteen years, finally ending up in shackles as prison labor, after he attempted to sue his penultimate owner (Deposition 219). These predicaments reflected the resistance and resilience of coolies who lived long enough to testify. This accounting refers only to those who cared to or had the opportunity to explicitly describe each of their transfers in their testimonies. The aforementioned calculations would be conservative estimates. There were 107 Chinese who signed a petition describing this process of hypermobility as being moved from private slavery to *market slavery*, that is, they became hypermobile slaves made forcibly available to a broad market of owners: "They will put you into prison or the official workshop doing non-paid work with your feet and neck chained. This will last until some rich businessmen comes to declare you an escapee and claim you in a casual manner" (Petition 65). The casualness of claiming any Chinese coolie as property (and under any name) is made more surreal by its circularity, as expressed in the following testimony:

> *Even if one had all the papers that one needs, the patrols on streets could always stop him; precinct chief could always intrude and search one's home. Sometimes they say that the paper is fake and take it away or tear it apart. Later, they will put one into prison or the official workshop, doing non-paid work with one's feet shackled. Until some rich businessmen lobbies the officials into pretending those Chinese are escapees, then they would claim and take those Chinese with them. Those Chinese then would be forced to sign another contract called bondage. Most of their payment would be taken away by government officials. After the completion of contract, they would be sent back to the official workshop to work for some time. Then they would be forced to sign*

another contract, and then sent back to official workshop again. It is like a circle without an end. We Chinese do all the work on the island of Cuba without any payment. Businessmen gain lots of profit by trading labor that has finished the first contract. The more associated the businessmen and the officials are, the more suffering the Chinese labor get. Originally we were only one owner's slaves, but now in the official workshop, we are forced to be slaves for all. We are slaves for them for the rest our lives! (Petition 65)

In some petitions and depositions, the Chinese described their detention with the term "Runaway Company." Any Chinese coolies who were not bonded could be seized and categorized as escapees or runaways. And in a sense, they *were* fugitives, trying to escape the contract system. Transformed into slaves for many buyer-sellers, the coolies described the contract pact as a tripartite force of police, business, and officials: "They have expanded the police department and have had patrols to hunt for Chinese everywhere. If a Chinese is caught, they force him to sign a contract to work. Government officials do so as a favor for the businessmen, as well as getting a share of the bondage money. These officials circulate the Chinese laborers to gain pure profit. In this way, the Chinese pass through many hands and become all Cubans' slave forever, without any hope for life again" (Petition 11).

However, there was one circumstance in which coolies would be transferred within a single household. The death of the "employer" incurred a transfer of inheritance. According to colonial laws, the bonded Chinese would pass to heirs like property: "in the event of death of the employer the contract may pass to his heirs with his other rights and property." Though couched in language of free labor, as in "the contract may pass," it is clear that the body was passed as chattel. Some indicated foreclosure, as their owners had died and they passed as property to the state, such as one sixty-one-year-old Zhang Meng, who was turned over to the state as a prison laborer when his owner died: "The owner died and I did not receive freedom paper. I was asked by soldiers for the paper, but since I had no papers, I was put into prison. Every day I have to sweep streets. I work but receive no payment or clothes" (Petition 66). In the Chinese testimonies, *release* from bondage seemed not a measure of freedom, in terms of rights and liberties, but was entirely contingent and reversible. Furthermore, the coolies' release operated as a public means of inserting Chinese into a slavery market. The contract thus emerged as only one paper in a proliferating system of papers and circulation.

The following section deals more extensively with a "paper chase petition." This lengthy discussion in reference to Petition 20 puts forward several themes that appear throughout the petitions as a whole. Paper chase petitions 2, 11, 20, 25, 54, 65 are then presented in the Addendum.

THE PAPER CHASE PETITION

Petition 20 was crafted with an analytic approach and takes up the task of defining the coolie's position within a system of slavery. Submitted in Havana, the petition is particularly interesting for its lengthy and detailed analysis of how the contract system worked. With 164 signatories, this petition represents the largest collective petition, and is an example of those that used collective means to establish a far-reaching argument marked by veracity and authenticity. The range of experiences marshaled to form an argument is demonstrated in its broad overview of exploitation and its mechanisms. The writer appears to be a "Li Zhaochun." Though none of the coolies were ever identified as "the writer," in cases of large group petitions, the writer can be inferred through a combination of features. One pattern that emerges from the testimonies is a priority listing in the signatories. In some cases the first one, two, or three persons were clearly identified with greater elaboration, whereas the remaining petitioners were simply listed by name. The narrative of the petition would open with more information on the priority signatories—where they were educated or how they attained their status, and how they were individually brought into their present fate. Then the petition would proceed in apparent third person plural point of view. Some petitions did not highlight any particular signatories and did not single out anyone above the others. The petitions with clearly indicated writers include those written by officials, scholars who had passed certain exams, and literate students. The writer in this case was a teacher and first-degree licentiate who graduated from Zhang Baikui Institute, an institute of education and politics, named after a high governor of Guangzhou, Zhang Baikui. It is striking that Li was only twenty years old when involved in writing the petition. As a first-degree licentiate, Li would have passed the first level of exams in the imperial system (the civil service examination system), with the first level being county, the second being provincial, and the top level being national. Satisfactory completion of these exams required a thorough knowledge of the Four Books and the Five Classics, which were classic Chinese texts of Confucianism that laid out philosophies and principles of governance and society. Literary and political analyses were also part of the exams. Legendary for their severe requirements, the exams were gateways to prestige and positions in official institutions, and were passed only by a small percentage of those who attempted. The total number of scholars (including lower level scholars such as Li, called *shengyuan*) were a respected minority that did not exceed 1 percent of China's population at any given time, and yet here, they were found among the coolies.[55] There are no indications that Li and his group express any hope for being saved and little in this petition suggests any redress for themselves. Their petition is presented as an intervention and as protest against a system. The coolies understandably feared that future generations could become similarly enslaved. After laying out arguments against the Cuban system, the petition ends with the following: "We just hope that this peril can be terminated so that Chinese won't ever come to Cuba again to suffer. Then we can die with our eyes closed." Li made reference to an idiom regarding the belief that people die with their eyes open because of uncorrected wrongs or unfulfilled obligations. With their eyes open, Li's group provided insight into the nature of becoming slaves. Li pointed to the contract as the contradictory signifier that most dominated their lives, and he methodically described stages of exploitation under auspices of the "contract" institution: from the initial abduction, to the Pacific passage, to coolie auctions, to enslavement by business, colonial government, and a network of profiteers.

Stressing the gap between the rhetoric of the contract institution and its application as a system in practice, Li located the contract predicament in its bad-faith conversion of contract labor into slave labor: "We did not know we were sold to Cuba to be slaves, suffering hardship for the rest of our lives from that time on. . . . From ancient times to the present, is there anything that is more unpredictable than this? Cubans claim that they are merely hiring and recruiting people, or trading contracts. They never say that they were selling people to be slaves! . . . How can the Spanish even deny the fact that they trade us as slaves? . . . No matter where you work, no matter how long you work, you have to work until you die. . . . The Spanish sell us for slaves and make a way to tie us up for the rest of our lives . . ." Li further emphasized, "We think that you need permission from the owner of the goods if you want to sell the owner's goods, but the Spanish collude with gangsters, trading Chinese freely." It is possible to argue that Li's concept of self-"ownership" in this petition was more likely to stem from Confucian principles of parental obligation, and thus "ownership" really referred to cultural notions of parental rights over their children and not self-ownership. This context was implied in some of the testimonies. However, the entire petition undermines this assumption. There is enough in the petition to suggest that Li and his group also incorporated distinctions made between freedom and slavery as rooted in liberal debates, and that ownership in this case referred to the differentiation between wage labor and slave labor. As in the case of Li, who made clear distinctions about self-ownership, a deponent who managed to get free stated emphatically, "I own myself." Though despite owning himself, he went on to indicate the fleeting nature of self-ownership under the omnipresent contract. His freedom papers would expire after only one year and were dependent upon locality and sponsorship, which if lacking, would cause the freedom paper to "no longer be eligible and the person (he) will be forced to sign another contract" (Deposition 73).

Li's petition presented two discourses: the disingenuous *representation of freedom* as contract and the actual *practice of slavery* via the contract. Li's petition recounted their passage to slavery as hellish and deadly. Those who refused to cooperate were tortured or put to death. Others were put on board and "shut in the cabin," in bamboo cages, or locked in irons. Li's short description of imprisonment under deck is further elaborated in other petitions, such as that by Ye Fujun and his group of fifty-four petitioners, which described the infamously narrow hatches of coolie ships: "We were all locked up in the cabin with an entrance that merely allowed one person to go through. And the smell there was terrible. Lots of people died of diseases and their bodies were thrown into the sea" (Petition 74). Torture, beatings, disease, thirst, and throwing oneself overboard during the passage were common occurrences described in the testimonies. Qiu Bishan and his group described the passage as follows:

We were all tricked to Macao and sold to pigpens. Later, we were
forced to work abroad, and some of us were threatened by being locked
in the sewage closet. Whenever torturing any of us, they forced the rest
to witness the whole process and made us scared, so that we did not
dare to resist. Then we were forced to board the ship. If the ship owner
was nice, people would merely get serious and protracted illness; if not,
people would be tortured and tormented terribly. More than half of the
people on ship died during several months sailing on the ocean, which
was tremendous suffering. After arriving in Havana, we were put into
the Pigpen in Havana, where Chinese laborers were seen and treated
as dogs and pigs. There were people who oversaw and tended us, peo-
ple who locked and imprisoned us, people who fed us, and people who
patrolled and investigated us. After staying in the Pigpen for a few
days, we were sold to a sugar plantation; every twenty-five people were
sold together for several ten thousand silvers. As quoted. (Petition 26)

Chen Ahe also indicated that their passage as captives began in "pig-pens" waiting to board ship, made worse by the seeming ineffectiveness of an inspection: "They heard some Chinese officials were coming to investigate, and they forbade me to speak up" (Deposition 599). Oral testimonies exhibited a wealth of accounts on the abductions and passage, such as that of a former chair maker, Tang Acheng: "I knew they sold people to foreign countries as Pigs, so I refused to work abroad. And the Pig Gangster just beat me and asked one person to hustle me down to a ship. I jumped into the water, but a foreigner pulled me up onto the shore and beat me brutally. I was beaten and fainted; afterwards, the foreigner tied me up and took me to the ship. The ship set off right away. My feet were shackled during the whole voyage, and I was not released until the arrival at Havana" (Deposition 1117).

In his petition, Li also described the coolie mart. Chinese were physically inspected upon arrival and sold at the "Selling People House." Other petitions provide greater detail of the coolie mart, such as that by Ye Fujun, whose testimony recounted the following: "We, several hundred people, were all put into the Selling People House, sorted into three classes, upper, middle, low. Our clothes were taken off, and we were examined by buyers so that they could appraise and fix a price. They (the buyers) did not have a sense of shame at all. How humiliated we were" (Petition 74).

Another 159 petitioners stated that they were "all naked when we were examined by buyers" (Petition 80). Significantly, upon arrival, the Chinese's queues were cut off, as described by Li and by others (such as Petition 2). The cutting off of queues—long braided hair worn by Chinese men during this period—would have been the source of deep cultural humiliation, as the queues symbolized loyalty to the Chinese government.

Li himself was first "sold to be a slave in a tobacco shop," while others were sent into other kinds of labor, including sugar labor. Li listed the widespread use of Chinese in varied sites, and he noted that all sites shared a common feature with plantations: They were all systems of corporal punishment against the Chinese. Once "peasants, scholars, woodcutters, fishermen, or small retailers," Li stated that the Chinese shared the common lot of becoming an enslaved labor group in Cuba and noted their common subjection to the lash, chain, and attack dogs—disciplinary measures commonly associated with chattel slavery. From Li's perspective, the contract emerged as a punitive force that channeled these abuses. Li explained that the contract could be completely disregarded or amended, replaced, revised, and "renewed." Contracts could be sold at the will of the owner, police, and local officials, all of whom were in collusion with each other—especially in the case of owners who were "also officials in government." As Li described, "There are official workshops . . . After several years, they sign bondage contracts with rich businessmen to enslave the Chinese again. After the expiration of these contracts, they again use these tricks." Li underscored the systemic obfuscation and manipulation of supposed rules and agreements, which included disregard for wages and periods of labor obligation; but he also revealed that slavery also was enabled by an impoverished subsistence *with* a wage, just enough to feed the imaginative desire for freedom deferred. Li's petition provides insight into the nature of "contract" as the basis for the married contradiction of the "free slave." While abducted and forced to labor against their will, the most powerful mechanism for continued psychological and physical bondage in Li's and other testimonies emerges as the *contract*.

Li's observations regarding the cloaking of contract and its deployment as a tool of slavery are deepened with observations regarding social measures of racial oppression coupled with the wage. He deplored the promotion of gambling and drugs, arguing that these were mechanisms sustained by the "police" and the "rich people" to control the minds of Chinese.

Li pointed to these mechanisms as social measures that, most importantly, both stoked and sabotaged hope. Li observed that "the Spanish government emphasizes gambling like 'The Game of White Dove' and has tickets sold everywhere. If one won a prize, called 'Heaven Prize,' one would be allowed to buy back freedom. Therefore, everyone puts their hope on the game without knowing that this makes them even poorer!" Li further reasoned that "police use opium houses to make money and use opium-smoking to extort people. So they are glad to let Chinese smoke opium. Rich people believe that if the Chinese get addicted to opium, they will not desire to go back to China because of lack of money and aspiration. That is why they like to lure the Chinese to smoke opium. The Chinese would think that their bodies are not owned by themselves, and the money is not owned by themselves." Similar remarks were made by Zheng Amao and his group of eighty petitioners (Petition 85). Li's argument and Zheng's remarks regarding gambling and drugs as officially promoted social practices are interesting given the coolies' views that these activities stem from an ideology of slavery and can reproduce a kind of psychological slavery.

Young scholar Li and the other 163 of his group included members from three provinces of China: Jiangsu, Fujian, and Guangdong. We do not know what became of them. They presented themes common to the petitions, which included unique analyses of freedom and slavery and narratives of the profound struggle for liberation from exploitation. Moreover, their struggle to survive was also a struggle to comprehend a brand of slavery that was based upon representations of "agreement." For them to make sense of such a predicament would have required a seismic shift in their worldviews. Articulation of their experiences would have required an uncommon agility for making sense of what transpired. In Li's case, it further involved the narration of experience as intimately linked to a systemic analysis. "Is there any more brutal and vicious thing in the world that is worse than that? Would there be a tragedy worse than what we face?" Li asked. There is no evidence that indicates Li or any of the testifiers from 1874 were actually rescued as a result of their testimony. Li starkly noted that "we do not have any hope of surviving." Tracing Li would be difficult; we have no idea what his Spanish name was.

4

THE DEPOSITIONS

A Chinese glowered like a spark of fire amid gray ashes; his usual
expression of sullen insubordination being sharpened by the pressure of
physical suffering. One of these sat on the edge of his bed, with a swollen
and bandaged limb drawn up beside him—the very incarnation of
impotent hate and rage. The mayoral laid a firm, detaining grasp on his
shoulder, under which I could see the man wince and shiver, while the
official told me how he had run away weeks ago, and hidden in the woods,
leading a sort of highwayman's life, and baffling all pursuit, until he
cut his foot badly on a sharp stone, in jumping a stream; which wound
festered and gangrened, and so disabled him that he could no longer
procure food, nor drag his wasted body from one hiding place to another;
when he was found—half-dead, but untamed in spirit—and brought back
to prison. Since which time, he had twice attempted suicide. The Chinese
meanwhile regarded us with a look that would have stabbed us both to the
heart, if looks were available for such a purpose. Plainly, he felt himself at
war with the whole tyrannous universe; and especially resented the
indignity of being exhibited and commented upon as if he had been a wild
beast.[1]

—Julia Louisa M. Woodruff (pseudonym "W.M.L. Jay")

In 1871 Julia Louisa M. Woodruff published her observations of her time
in Cuba. Included was her visit to the Santa Sofía sugar plantation, where
she encountered a recaptured coolie. Her description touched upon the
power struggle inherent in domination and daily resistance. "Half-dead and
untamed in spirit," the coolie represented a continual challenge to management and its drive to maximize output through captive labor. While coolies
appeared in observations of white travelers and journalists of the time, what
did the coolies themselves say about these daily struggles? On the whole,
the depositions did not usually present the sort of lengthy arguments presented in the petitions. However, they provided detailed accounts of the
coolies' daily trials and conditions, and revealed startling views of how systemic subjugation was designed yet resisted. Some coolie deponents

expressed intense resentment and described the planned murder of their overseers. Others relived their humiliation, such as one who described being forced by the manager to bark like a dog and bleat like a sheep. And there was another who numbingly declared, "I just cannot stop crying" (Deposition 938). Those such as Wu Axiang plaintively yearned to return to their families: "I really want to go back to China and see my mother" (Deposition 114). Occasionally, others revealed moments of youthful naïveté. One Californian named Yang Atian, age twenty-six, was rueful about his situation. He had lived in San Francisco since he was fourteen years old. After working on the railroad in California, he took work on a ship, with a misguided sense of adventure. To his dismay, he lost his earnings by gambling at the port of Havana and was forced into bondage. He concluded, "My four brothers and my parents are still alive, but they do not know I am here. I really walked right into the trap myself!" (Deposition 1036) The texture of individual experiences ranged from this naïve youth to the sixty-six year old Yuan Aishan who recounted his escape attempt and his capture by soldiers (Deposition 378). The rawness and spontaneity of the depositions contrast with the deliberate, collective writing of the petitions.

Of the 2,841 testifiers, 1,176 gave oral testimonies, and some explicitly named their masters or their plantations, such as the plantations of "San Antonio," "Recreo," and "Esperanza" (in Cardenas); "Juniata" and "Candelaria" (in Cienfuegos); "Espana" and "Flor de Cuba" (in Colon); "Santa Catalina" and "Las Canas" (in Havana); "Armonia," "Concepcion," and "San Cayetano" (in Matanzas); "Santa Ana," "Capitolis," and "Santa Isabella" (in Sagua la Grande). Each of the oral testimonies were unique yet bore out shared themes. One common thread concerned the micro view of daily survival, portrayed as tenuous and unpredictable. The acute conditions of deprivation and the nature of resistance within those conditions were described by the coolies in the context of *expendability* and *racialized conflict*. How coolies resisted their forced bondage, in the midst of shifting political conditions and uneven relationships to power, can in some ways be compared to forms of resistance that emerged in histories of oppression and labor. Coolie resistance manifested itself in passive recalcitrance and covert sabotage, as well as overt individual and group rebellion. Explications and arguments on what constitutes (or what can be read as) "resistance" especially appear in treatments of resistance of peasantry, contract labor, and slavery. These treatments help highlight the particularities of coolie resistance in

Cuba. James Scott's foregrounding of covert forms of peasant resistance, "weapons of the weak," has expanded what were conventional narrations of resistance as open, collective, or large-scale revolts.[2] By attending to the local specificities that shape the overriding concerns of the oppressed, Scott raises questions regarding how we define resistance and how local conditions make those forms particular. Howard McGary also undermines conventional definitions of resistance through a philosophical critique of the emphasis upon "intent" as the measure of resistance. He notes, "We often associate acts of resistance with courage, but it would be a mistake to claim that every act of resistance is an act of courage."[3] As a case in point, he examines slaves stealing from their masters as a form of resistance. Scott's and McGary's conceptions of resistance extend to subversive actions beyond overt acts of rebellion and beyond acts deemed "courageous." In a history of plantation labor of Hawaii, Ronald Takaki also drew attention to forms of resistance manifested in daily acts. Workers organized strikes, but according to Takaki, they also employed forms of daily resistance, including intentional laziness, inefficiency, and work slowdowns.[4] Scott, McGary and Takaki assess the different histories of peasantry, slavery, and contract labor, and present "resistance" as a range of actions. The critical interventions on resistance mitigate what George Rawick once called the "entire view of the slave as Victim and Object."[5]

However, these analyses assume certain continuities and foundations. The peasantry in Scott's study is grounded to the land, and wedded economically and socially to the village. McGary's critique refers to the "peculiar institution," an institution characterized by generations of slavery and an equally long history of slave resistance. Contract labor in Takaki's study was relatively rooted, in comparison to contract labor in Cuba, and was shaped by planters' designs to form a stable (and hypothetically less volatile) labor pool. The extensive presence of contract labor families on the Hawaiian plantations led to social and cultural patterns of continuous plantation and migrant life that markedly differentiate the Hawaiian history of contract labor from the Cuban history. The constellation of examples and arguments regarding resistance exposes a problematic lacuna for grappling with representations of resistance in the coolie testimonies of Cuba, in which resistance was presented under the chief conditions of high attrition, disposability, and hypermobility. As one Liu Arui declared, "The owner often said to the overseer, 'I only care about how much sugar they (Chinese) can make, and you don't have to treat them well. If you beat one Chinese to death, I still can afford to buy ten more next year.' " (Deposition 244) Coolies were mobile slaves with short life spans, and mobility appears as a main trope of their testimonies. Contrary to liberal narratives of mobility (which emphasize physical and social mobility as basic features of free society), the combination of mobility with disposability emerged as a form of enslavement. Narrations of resistance in the depositions were shaped by this condition of mobile enslavement and, furthermore, shaped by the racial hierarchies that structured this very condition.

RACE, RESISTANCE, AND SPECTACULAR SUBORDINATION

Overt resistance, including heightened and deadly conflict, emerges as a distinct and pervasive feature of the testimonies. The divisions between yellow, black, and white, and survival under extreme exploitation, were revealed in the testimonies as everyday struggles that often led to deadly consequences. For the treatments of Asian and African histories, this aspect reveals a unique dimension to histories of resistance, racial conflicts, and collaborations. Here, more attention is paid to overt resistance in the testimonies, though some attention is paid to representations of passive and covert resistance. The testimony of twenty-three-year-old Ou Rong, abducted and shipped to Cuba at age fifteen, offers an example of mixed forms of resistance deployed by the coolies, such as running away, altercations with owners, refusal to work, and taking sick:

In the fifth year of Tongzhi (1866), someone invited me to see a performance in Macao, but I was taken to Xinhe Pigpen. I lived there for two weeks and met with a foreign officer, signed a contract and was given eight dollars. The ship set off in the ninth moon (October, 1866). Two months after arriving at Havana, I was sold to a family in the city as a waiter. I worked there for nine months. Later I had a quarrel with the son of the owner, so I was locked up while working for three weeks and got fiercely beaten. Then I was sold to a sugar plantation where I was treated badly. I did not want to work there, but the manager told me if I did not want to work, I would be locked and put in chains. I said, "I am not afraid of wearing chains. I am not afraid of you stabbing me with a

knife. I don't want to stay here." So he sold me to this sugar refinery in
Cardenas. This sugar refinery treated me badly too. The food was not
enough and the work was toilsome and difficult to do. In the sugar refin-
ery, I knew eight people who hanged themselves. I got sick a few months
ago. I told the overseer I was sick, but he just beat me. Then I ran away.
I stayed outside for three weeks but then was captured. I have been
chained for a long time since they caught me. (Deposition 776)

Within seven years, Ou was sold into a family household, then to plantation labor, and later to a refinery. With each type and location of bondage, Ou Rong resisted in different ways, including his striking description
of speaking out. His recounting of passive and overt disobedience demonstrates various forms of resistance on Ou's part; but his testimony also
brought to light the continued problems faced by coolie owners in their attempts to control a new force of indentured labor. Ultimately, Ou resisted
by running away, though fugitive coolies like Ou were often recaptured by
rancheros and dogs, or by patrols and soldiers. The only manner of temporarily controlling Ou appears to have been chaining. Unlike Ou however,
those who succeeded in escaping were not represented in the testimonies
and are not represented in marronage studies, thus leaving a gap in knowledge regarding how Chinese might possibly have formed, joined, or collaborated in maroon communities. (However, the testimonies do include
references to attempts to form organizations of coolies across plantations
and covert resistance in the form of alliances with sympathetic "foreign"
officials, as discussed in the previous chapter on the petitions).

Besides his own resistance, Ou Rong also mentioned having known
"eight people who hanged themselves." The accounting of suicides is a
prominent feature of the testimonies. Given its preponderance, suicide had
undeniable effect upon those who *witnessed* these acts. Like the witness petitions, suicide accounts conveyed a desire to bear witness for those who did
not survive and revealed conditions that contributed to overtly violent resistance. He Aying succinctly listed the types of suicide, which were commonly described throughout the testimonies: "There were people who
hanged themselves or cut their throats; there were people who took poison
or drowned themselves in the river" (Petition 73). Chen Ming observed
those who dashed their heads against a well: "People cut their throats,
jumped into the river, or smashed their heads to the well; some who wore

shackles and suffered a wrong took poison" (Petition 9). Li Wencai even detailed how dead persons were retrieved: "I witnessed people hanged themselves in the woods, and people who jumped into the well were taken out of the well by an iron hook" (Deposition 116). It is tempting to read such accounts of suicide as narrations of despair in a history of exploitation. As summed up in a petition by Wang Hua and companions: "The pain and sorrow are so unbearable that we have no release until death" (Petition 42). Or perhaps, this pattern could be read as a cultural (Chinese) predisposition toward suicide, a misguided analysis at best. The South African paper *Transvaal Weekly Illustrated* once featured such a presumption, in regard to the local suicide of a coolie who protested the discriminatory Asiatic Law Amendment: "The Chinese ethics of suicide are certainly incomprehensible to the European."[6] However, Leung Quinn, leader of the Chinese passive resistance movement at Transvaal and a colleague of Gandhi, responded that he "was not aware of suicide being common in China. The Chinese regarded human life as valuable and only ended it when they are driven to desperation by much the same causes as induce suicides amongst Europeans."[7]

Positing a cultural predisposition for suicidal depression is unsatisfactory, most obviously in regard to testimonies that suggest suicide as collective protest and workplace sabotage. These accounts included the witnessing of suicide as group acts. A nineteen-year-old student when he was abducted and shipped to Cuba, Wen Changtai recounted as follows:

> *I witnessed nine workers who hanged themselves, one who jumped into a hot sugar cauldron, twelve who died because they were flogged so hard that their flesh festered and had maggots, and some who ran into the mountains and starved to death. I do not even know whether some people are still alive or not after they escaped from the sugar plantation. I saw lots of human bones while working on the sugarcane fields. I witnessed some workers who were bitten to death by the manager's dogs. . . . Once I saw seven people kill themselves by jumping into a well. Countless people hanged themselves or were beaten to death. White people here treat Chinese worse than dogs." (Deposition 18)*

The testimony of group suicide (seven people jumping into a well) potentially raises the macabre question as to how this act was planned and executed. Yet a history of the Chinese in Cuba mentions a similarly disturbing incident of fourteen coolies who committed group suicide on a plantation called "Dos Marias."[8] Henry Auchincloss noted another incident, this one concerning the predicament of a coolie owner in Cuba who sought measures against coolie suicides. The owner found that his "coolies were destroying themselves at the rate of two per day or more" and that one "eccentric Celestial climbed atop the highest chimney on the hacienda and hung himself in full view of the entire body of his colleagues." The owner responded to this public display with a spectacle of his own, by burning the coolie body "in full view of the entire plantation" and scattering the ashes "to the winds."[9] This incident suggests the coolie body as also a body of public spectacle, not only as colonized labor but also as a culturally and racially signified body. The struggle for power here depends on cultural subjugation, as the owner did not mete out physical punishment; instead, he sought to deeply violate Chinese cultural beliefs, which do not espouse the scattering of body and spirit.

That some suicides were committed as collective action and as public display suggests that a dimension of protest, and not simply a predilection for despair, was inherent in the patterns of coolie suicide. At certain times, coolies declared they would rather die than submit to the outrage: "Several workers who had been constantly beaten hanged themselves because they could not bear the humiliation and rage" (Deposition 58). One of the most frequently mentioned methods of suicide could be found in the workplace, where coolies would sometimes jump into the "hot sugar pot"— a sugar cauldron kept at extremely high temperatures to boil and purify the sugar. Chen Guanzhi's testimony typified the accounts of "sugar pot" suicide: "I witnessed lots of people who committed suicide by jumping into the sugar pot, jumping into the refinery machine, hanging themselves and jumping into the well. . . . Also I saw two people chained together, for they tried to run away. They still needed to work, and the manager hit them severely. Then these two people couldn't take it anymore so they jumped into the sugar pot together. I witnessed that as well" (Deposition 816). The sugar purification process, in which a hot cauldron was crucial, was a worksite process that coolies and slaves manned in the sugar house or sugar mill, in addition to their arduous labor in the cane fields. In *el ingenio*, there would have been a series of hot pots or a sugar train. Richard Henry Dana once described this process in the following manner: "From the last defecator, the juice is passed through the trough into the first cauldron. Of the cauldrons, there is a series, or, as they call it, a train, through all which the juice must go. Each cauldron is a large, deep copper vat, heated very hot, in which the juice seethes and boils."[10] Suicide by jumping into a seething boiling cauldron would have disrupted the immediate sugar processing and could be read as a gruesome act of protest and workplace sabotage, as it had an undeniable effect upon witnesses and disrupted the worksite.

In some cases, other forms of workplace sabotage and resistance were implied. Testimonies of "mysterious" incidents of fire in the sugar refineries or mills were conspicuous enough to suggest their being veiled references to forms of sabotage and resistance. For example, at the Las Cañas plantation, Chen Yiyou noted that "the plantation caught fire twice before, and everyone else and I tried to put off the fire. But the manager suspected that someone set the fire, so he investigated for a long time but he could not find any evidence. How the fire was started has remained mysterious until now" (Deposition 938). Others mentioned similar fire incidents caused by unknown parties. Another coolie stated that "the wood floor in the sugar plantation caught fire. The manager said the fire was set by a man from Xiangshan. He denied it" (Deposition 729). One coolie emphatically denied his involvement in a fire in the following manner: "Once I was beaten extremely hard because the overseer thought I set a fire in the sugar plantation. But I am truly innocent" (Deposition 197). Chen Dezheng also asserted his innocence, yet called attention to such conflagrations when he stated that "the plantation got fired twice. I was shocked and woke up to help others put off the fire. I don't know what caused the fire" (Deposition 439). Some testifiers even described worksite killings as "accidental," As in the case of Li Hui who claimed that he unintentionally killed his overseer: "The overseer hit me with a handspike. I took that handspike and pushed him; however, the overseer fell into the sugar-cooking pot. I did not mean to kill him." (Deposition 67)

Alongside "accidents" and acts of sabotage, overt confrontation emerges as one of the most noticeable patterns in the depositions. Testifiers indicated that their propensity to act, often collectively, was prompted by witnessing suicides and deaths. They were moved by righteousness but also by self-preservation. As one coolie put it, his group killed the overseer because "we saw many people were beaten to death on the sugar plantation, so eleven of us talked and concluded that if we did not kill the overseer, we would end up being beaten to death by him" (Deposition 503). Chen Asan came to a similar conclusion: "We'd rather risk our lives killing him than be killed by him. So we beat him with hoes. The white overseer was injured and died after seven days" (Deposition 715). In other cases, young, healthy Chinese laborers were incensed by the abuse not only directed toward themselves, but also toward those who appeared weak, handicapped, or old. Zhu Afu described the accumulating outrage, intensified by the suicide of a fellow coolie who was brutalized by an overseer: "Three workers and I were so angry that we beat the overseer with hoes. He died that night in the ward" (Deposition 559). After eight years of labor, Liang Agui exploded under the hot sun upon seeing the manager beat two people: "At my eighth year, in May it was so hot, but I still did not dare to stop working. But the manager still said we didn't do our jobs well and beat two people severely. I was so angry. I beat him to death with my hoe" (Deposition 880). Similarly, the case of "Hung Aguang" is a good example of how Chinese workers witnessed the abuse and suicide of a fellow coolie and were then motivated to collectively seek justice:

Hung Aguang couldn't stand the torture and ran away, but he was caught. He was locked up and beaten so hard that he bled all over. He still had to wear chains at work . . . They barely gave him any food. He was so hungry that he ate sugarcane on the sugarcane field, and when the overseer spotted him eating the sugarcane, he was beaten again immediately. Hung Aguang hanged himself. . . . Then more than twenty workers went to the official and complained; they said they did not want to work in that sugar plantation anymore. (Deposition 670)

Comparable to Huang Shirong's account is Lai Axi's account (Deposition 659). Lai elaborated on the same incident but placed greater emphasis on protest. He emphasized that the Chinese would go to one official who did nothing and then went to a second official, with the manager following close behind. In this instance, twenty coolies protested plantation conditions, although in the end, this obviously did not change their circumstances. Nevertheless, Huang and Lai pointed to this protest as a defining moment that motivated them to openly seek legal redress, despite legal routes being overwhelmingly depicted by the coolies as corrupted. The words of former sailor Chen Amu typify the accounts of resistance through legal routes, with outcomes that apparently worsened their situations: "On the sugar plantation, I have been treated atrociously. I am hit all the time.

Last year I was hit so hard that I could not take it, so I went to the local officer and sued the owner. But the owner bribed the officer with money and reclaimed me back. I was shackled for months, and I was treated more horribly than ever" (Deposition 905).

The propensity to appeal to legal process may have stemmed from the cultural tradition of legal institutions in China; but the coolies were also aware of being categorized as "contract" laborers who supposedly had some legal recourse (also see previous chapter).

The awareness of this rhetorical and legal differentiation, as contract labor and not slave labor, was also accompanied by feelings of outrage and humiliation. The Chinese, even those who were not of elite backgrounds, believed their stations to be above that of manual laborers, and certainly that of slaves; they thought of themselves as more like visiting craftsmen. As one coolie stated, "In China, I have been to shipyards in Shanghai and Fujian, where we treated foreign craftsmen with reason and courtesy. I can't believe that when we Chinese work abroad, we have to suffer torture like this" (Deposition 881). In a related form, humiliation was expressed out of national pride, with Chinese describing their subjugation as a synecdoche of China's weakness under foreign incursions and imperialisms. This was particularly evident in the common accounts of nakedness and queues being cut off when being sold, such as farmer Chen Aji's description of being hit "because I refused to cut my hair off" and Lin Abang's memory of humiliation upon being sold: "Chinese people who were sold in the Selling People House in Havana were forced to take off all their clothes in order to be examined whether they were healthy and strong or not. They were treated just like bulls and horses. Chinese people here were not only physically abused and tortured, but also mentally humiliated" (Depositions 4 and 74). Further compounding their feelings of humiliation and injustice was the devaluing of Chinese language, as Chen Abao recounted: "Because I could not understand the language, I was beaten a lot" (Deposition 217). Chinese ethnic identity and the rhetorical differentiation for "contract" labor did not translate into social privileges, and according to the Chinese, quite the opposite.

However, humiliation was most pointedly detailed in accounts of subjugation as spectacles, and coolies recalled the ensuing rage that such treatment spawned. "They humiliated us in every possible way," said coolie Wu Asan (Deposition 397). The spectacles of their enslavement encompass what Saidiya Hartman calls the quotidian and "benign" acts of entertainment, as well as the brute violence wrought under the master and white audience.[11] Slave revelry, which Hartman gives as an example, was also entertainment for the master who watched slaves and commanded them to dance and sing. Although the testimonies do not suggest a history of theatricality and performance in the brief generation of coolie labor, accounts similar to Wu's do depict forms of spectacular subordination or theaters of subjugation, such as the ritual of denigration administered to Chinese at the Flor de Cuba plantation: "Every Chinese who was locked up was forced by the manager to bark like dogs and bleat like sheep. If we refused to do so, we would be beaten severely. They humiliated us in every possible way. Sometimes I do not even have clothes to wear. My life here is like a living hell" (Deposition 397). The forced imitation of dogs and sheep served to reduce Chinese to the level of domesticated animals. Similarly, coolies recounted the humiliation of having to plead and beg for various privileges but most of all, for their freedom papers. Though unlike the spectacles of beating and physical domination, the recurrent spectacles of begging extended relations of domination and subjection.[12] Chen Gu stated, "I begged them on my knees to return my freedom paper," although he was hauled off instead to an official workshop (Petition 22). Deng Asi, consigned to prison after being framed for "forgery" of a freedom paper, stated the following: "I begged them to release me many times, but they refused" (Petition 46). Xie Zhiren, unable to write his name in Spanish and dependent upon the will of his master, "begged the master to write down my name and ask for a paper" (Petition 71). In some cases, coolies begged for other coolies, as in the case of one who begged for his friend's release, after his friend attempted to escape a cruel master but was later caught and locked up (Petition 17). Depictions of pleading and begging, however, were as frequent as depictions of confrontational violence. The pleas of coolies alongside patterns of confrontation underscore the different forms of resistance that were in fact related. Coolies "turned" from begging and pleading to taking sick or, in some cases, to plotting the murders of their overseers, such as described in Liang Lianqing's blunt recounting: "Once two other workers and I were all sick and asked to rest, but the overseer denied our request and still required us to work. Moreover, he beat us severely. So three of us killed him with hoes in the sugarcane field" (Deposition 1010).

The accounts of resistance expose conditions of "contract labor" as both sites of struggle for domination over unwilling subjects and as sites of racialized pleasure and abasement. One coolie quoted the sentiments of his third owner, an especially cruel man, who said, "I did not buy you to work for me; I bought you because I want to beat you" (Deposition 199). Yuan Aan described an overseer who "was so mean that he actually enjoyed beating us" (Deposition 120). Another named Chen Ajin, formerly a ship carpenter, described the torture inflicted upon him at the will of his overseer: "One time, I told the overseer I was sick. He said I was faking it and told four people to truss me up, take off my pants, and beat me two hundred times. My flesh festered. Then I was put in shackles and still had to work. But that was not over. They came back at night and forced salt and orange juice into my wounds. I almost died of the pain" (Deposition 120). Coolie torture and abasement further extended to entertainment at the hands of "little white and black children," who would throw stones at coolies upon seeing them in the streets (Deposition 144). Accounts revealed the features of *subordination as spectacle* and the exercises of power conscripted the least powerful of the social spectrum, that being children and the coerced participation of both Africans and Chinese. In a ritual of abasement, one owner forced Chinese to drink the urine of female African slaves, as recounted by a coolie named Liang Aren: "Later I was sold to a sugar plantation where I was always beaten. The owner was atrocious. If the [Chinese] worker was sick, the owner would ask a black woman to urinate and then force the worker to drink it. If the worker drank the urine, then he would be considered really sick and could have a rest. Otherwise, he had to keep working." (Deposition 175)

This ritual-as-spectacle turned upon mechanisms that inscribed racial and gendered hierarchy. Liang was subjected to drinking urine, but more specifically, to drinking the urine of a black female slave, which was constructed or *presented* by white management as the lowest or most denigrated form of the body (the act of drinking urine itself, outside this particular historical context , is not necessarily "humiliating"). In this scenario, the male Chinese coolie was coerced into a status "inferior" to that of a black female slave and thereby humiliated—an act which would have been effective if made as an example, or spectacle, for others. A momentary saving face or saving of "manhood" would have been perpetrated through the coolie's refusal of black femaleness. The enactment of this rite reproduced the ideology of white superiority/black inferiority, with the Chinese coerced into participating in a racist schema, thus coercing an en-

tire social body more effectively than an actual whipping. The black female slave, meanwhile, was subjected to humiliation by urinating (for the
satisfaction of the owner) in a spectacle that debased both her and the
coolie and that simultaneously induced antipathy, disgust, and the prurient
desire of the spectator. Rather than whipping the coolie into submission,
another form of violence, the spectacle of humiliation, effectively inscribed and reproduced hierarchies of domination and inferiority in the
social body, and promoted interracial anxiety and conflict through racially
charged and gendered violence.

Daily terror also emerged in theaters of racial, gendered, and sexualized acts, such as the daily terror of being gang-whipped, inflicted upon
Chen Afu. Chen, abducted and sold to Cuba at age eleven, described being
regularly abused by an overseer who liked to beat him while he was held
down by four "others": "I was sold to a sugar plantation to herd horses.
The overseer was very mean and hit me a lot, for I was young among most
workers here. He would ask four other people to push me down to the ground,
take off my pants, and hit my bare bottom with cane" (Deposition 12). Rituals of terror and abasement were described by Chinese as attempts to
break them psychologically and physically. Beyond the daily whipping
and chaining, these methods took several forms: cultural and sexual subordination in racialized contexts (such as hair being cut off, being beaten
for not speaking Spanish, clothes taken off, being held down and having
their pants taken off, being beaten for "pleasure," being forced to drink the
urine of a black slave, and being told to imitate animals), psychological
and physical terrorism (the preponderant use of attack dogs, pouring salt
into wounds, pouring boiling water on the body, cutting off ears, chopping
off fingers, public torture, stripping off clothes), coercion through imminent disposability (the threat of being arbitrarily beaten to death like the
"others," being told that they could be disposed of at any time, and being
told that they would be sold into a worse situation), and withholding (of
food, water, and most of all, freedom papers).

Cruel punishments were made visible and marked the coolie as a subjugated body. An ear chopped off, feet gnawed by dogs, flesh festering with
maggots, fingers chopped off, skin burned—all revealed the bodily visita-
tions of domination meant for long-term display. Cruel acts on the part of
the owners such as ordering attack dogs to bite coolies (dogs obviously
had to be trained to do such things), terrorizing and gang-whipping a boy

in the field, and forcing a man to drink urine, all comprised a litany of the perverse realities beneath contract labor, "transition," and "moderniza-tion." Appearing before the commission, coolies offered their bodies as evidence. Said Han Qingduo,"I am often beaten cruelly. There are a lot of scars on my body and please examine them now" (Deposition 717). Liang Ayou explained his obvious deformity as follows: "Once I left the store and didn't work for a day, and when I came back, the owner unexpectedly locked me up and cut off one of my ears" (Deposition 851). Bu Ahou wit-nessed the use of attack dogs upon a fellow coolie: "The white manager and the white overseer asked four dogs to bite his feet; his feet were bitten until they festered and he could no longer walk anymore" (Deposition 808).[13] Wang Changtai described twelve of his peers who died "because they were flogged so hard that their flesh festered and had maggots." An-other described how the overseer seized a knife and chopped off four of his fingers, and another described how boiling water was poured on him (Depositions 1035 and 1139). While powerful and startling as descriptions of domination and resistance, even more intriguing is what these testimo-nies suggest in terms of the economic models of "transition" from slavery to a free society. The nature of these episodes underscores the imperatives of *retrenching* a particular racial order, especially when coolies threatened that order. Coolies continually reminded the slave-owning class of the pressure to transition from slavery to wage labor or free labor. This was not only an economic arrangement but a cultural arrangement as well. As Orlando Patterson and Demetrius Eudell have emphasized, slavery was a cultural institution, and, the ending of slavery and the project of "emanci-pation" was not only a "transition from slave labor to wage labor" but could be "described in terms that understand slavery as a system of social relations—indeed, as a cultural system."[14] The most visible embodiment of transition in Cuba was the coolie. Thus, coolies had to be kept in check, subdued, and violently marked. Brought directly into a culture and labor system of race-based slavery, coolies were nonwhite figures—they were neither white, black, nor mulatto—who limned the possibility of becom-ing a free and "foreign" force. Coolies represented a new challenge to co-lonial authority, Catholicism, creole culture and language, and a race-based hierarchy of slavery. Commentary from a prominent planter at the time, Domingo Aldama, illustrated local sentiments regarding Chinese as po-tentially problematic in terms of maintaining a certain cultural and racial order. He argued that introducing *el chino* to Cuba would cause problems in terms of "race, color, religion, and sentiments" and further warned against their adding yet more potentiality to black revolt.[15] Given their demonstrated rebelliousness, the Chinese coolies did raise the specter of insurrection, and furthermore, stoked the potentiality of alliances between the coolie and slave. In the midst of the thirty-year war for Cuban independence, increasing external and local pressures toward abolition, and technological changes in sugar processing, the Chinese were not only a disruptive force but also *represented* "transition," a historical moment that they described as a micro-struggle of violence.

THE PECULIAR FATALITY OF COLOR

The Chinese were a disruptive force at every turn, just as they were hypermobile from site to site. For example, Wang Dacheng, who "worked in many places," was transferred twelve times over a ten-year period (Deposition 241). At the macro and micro level, the mobile coolie continually retested the boundaries of a worksite and its social, cultural order, and confronted what one writer called "the peculiar fatality of color." Marked as inferior subjects, the Chinese described racist attitudes that foregrounded their subjugation and compared themselves to black slaves having white owners. Expressions in the testimonies stress that both Africans and Chinese were relegated to the lowest social strata. The depositions contained similar observations. One coolie noted that "when I first arrived here, there were six hundred workers, who were black and Chinese. Now there are only four hundred workers left. The black people work the same as Chinese, who are beaten and locked up as well" (Deposition 643). Another simply concluded, "On the sugar plantation, they treated black persons and me in the same way" (Deposition 244). Another coolie observation went as follows: "Black and Chinese are locked up in the same cell. At night, we have to wear shackles and in daytime we wear foot chains to work," and as yet another succinctly put it, "two cells, one for black persons and one for Chinese. And both blacks and Chinese in cells wear shackles" (Deposition 231). The Chinese perceived that they and Africans were placed in similar predicaments of inferiority. One statement by Chen Aer encapsulated a mapping of racial economy: "White men treat us Chinese as black slaves" (Deposition 216). The "white men" and the "black slaves" were the bases of comparison and polarity in the spectrum of racial power within which the Chinese were inserted. However, the coolies perceived themselves as more like black slaves than white men. On this point, James Williams Steele, American consul in Matanzas, made an interesting observation regarding Chinese, Africans, and the hierarchy of color:

> *When a negro who has killed an overseer one morning is led out and shot the next, when you may go out in the street and take the census of the chain-gang and find in one division of it sixty Chinamen, eighteen negroes, and no white men, and when you know at the same time half a dozen men who have testified absolutely to the intentional and premeditated killing of people before the fiscal, and know that the subjects of this uncontradicted testimony went free, and when this kind of thing passes under your observation for years, and nobody ever denies it, and everybody considers it a matter of course, it begins to seem as though there were a peculiar fatality in color and accompanying poverty.*[16]

Of course, the "peculiar" fatality in color and accompanying poverty was not unique to Cuba. But moreover, Steele's observation suggests the preponderance of Chinese in the lowest social strata. The coolies consistently described themselves as far from the owning class, which in their depictions consisted of white men, though one also mentioned a white female owner (Deposition 846). They located forms of ultimate authority as embodied by whiteness, commonly referring to "the white man," "the white manager," "the white owner," "the white official," and some cases, the "owner's wife." In no instance were Africans described by the coolies as owners. Rather, the testimonies indicate the particular feature of black overseers assigned to oversee coolies. The Chinese referred to "black people" as "slaves" or "black overseers." As one coolie explained, "Black people are slaves, who don't get paid" (Deposition 729). Furthermore, Chinese made note of the generational aspect of African slavery, pointing out that offspring of coolie-slave unions would also be slaves, as one Cai Xiang exclaimed, "I saw some Chinese have children with black women, and their children will still be owners' slaves" (Deposition 1054). Another Chinese laborer recollected a fellow coolie who married an African woman and pondered whether their child would be a slave (Deposition 1081). These brief mentions of coolie-slave unions, unfortunately too brief to

draw further conclusions, revealed the ambivalence of coolie-slave relations as conflicted yet enmeshed. Some testifiers emphasized this ambivalence when they divulged covert collaborations between slave and coolie,
despite overtly antipathetic acts against each other. The account by He Lin
underscored the covert passing of information:

> *One day, the overseer beat Li De to death in the sugarcane field and
> buried him there. Four blacks assisted him, and even officials did not
> know it. I did not see it, but the blacks told me. I have been in the sugar
> plantation for three years. Then nine of us made up our minds; we beat
> the overseer to death. We were sent to jail in Havana. We stayed there
> for two years and then were sent to a sugar plantation. We worked there
> for four months. Then the manager heard that we had beaten an over-
> seer to death, so he sent us to jail in Sagua la Grande where we stayed
> for another two years. (Deposition 769)*

In another example, Lai Axi recounted an African slave who sabotaged the Chinese, yet later shared information about the incident secretly: "One night when we were pressing sugarcane, a black slave put an
iron in the sugar refinery machine and accused of us trying to break the
machine. . . . Later, the black slave told me secretly that the manager told
him to put that iron in the machine." (Deposition 216)

More often than not, however, the Chinese often regarded their social
status as similar to that of slaves; but sometimes they felt less privileged
than slaves, and therefore of lowest social status. Period tracts of scientific
racism offer a counterpart to the testimonial depictions of "lowest" social
status. One Cuban medical doctor, Benjamín de Cespédes, issued a study
(1888) that ranked the races of Cuba according to sexual behavior and
prostitution. This study ranked the sexual relations between Chinese at
the very bottom (below prostitution between people of color (black), mi-
nors, and men). Apparently the doctor witnessed prostitution between
Chinese men, which he deemed the ultimate act of sexual "abomination"
and innate racial "inferiority."[17] Relegated as a group to inferior status,
coolies also described experiencing their oppression in keenly racialized
terms. "Black and white here all treat Chinese badly," said Wu Axiang.
"They always kick us, if they see us walking on streets" (Deposition 114).
According to coolie accounts, racial hierarchy was reinforced in daily

treatment but most keenly felt in terms of daily necessities and privileges that were granted or denied. Most of the coolies would not survive to see generations of descendants, let alone survive the next month or year. The "mundane" was described in terms of struggle. Getting sleep, getting food, and the preponderance of death emerged as overwhelming concerns. The Chinese repeatedly described being hungry, and in some cases, they described the starvation deaths of other coolies. "Some [Chinese] got sick and died because they did not have enough food to eat," declared Liu Guangcai of the Concepción plantation (Deposition 727). "I am always hungry here," said He Asi, "and I have been beaten a lot. I am treated worse than animals" (Deposition 376). Aforementioned Huang Shirong spoke of a coolie who desperately sought something to eat: "He was so hungry that he ate sugarcane in the cane field, and when the overseer spotted him eating the sugarcane, he was beaten again immediately" (Deposition 670). Likewise, Lin Abang observed, "If people were caught for taking a little food during working time in the sugar plantation, they were forced to wear shackles" (Deposition 174). One Chen Long described how he snuck sugar water to sustain himself when working in the mill or refinery, "When I make the sugar, I can drink some sugar water to allay my hunger; if I do not make the sugar, I have nothing to eat" (Deposition 977). There were 709 deponents who described being in a constant state of hunger. And 953 deponents described being surrounded by death.

The examples of Xu Shaolin and Pen Wendao are most interesting because of their positions as cooks on plantations—a position that would have allowed the *most* access to food. Pen exclaimed that the Chinese "who work on the sugarcane field can't have enough food and are hungry all the time" (Deposition 829). Xu Shaolin described not only his experience with food deprivation but also the role of food in *racial division*:

> There used to be forty-seven Chinese in the group, and now only fifteen are left. We are treated badly. They beat us and do not give us food. . . . Although I work as a cook, I cannot leave here even for a moment. If I leave only for a few seconds, they will beat me, just like the laborers who plant sugarcane on sugar plantations. . . . Although I work as a cook, I still do not have enough food to eat. Even though some food gets left, it is given to the black people and not me. . . . People in Cuba already got used to enslaving the black slaves, and they

treat Chinese worse than black slaves. This does not make any sense.
(Deposition 855)

Starvation, much like death and burial rites, was experienced by coolies as inseparable from the politics of race-based privileges. In those terms, coolies compared themselves to slaves, and ultimately concluded that Chinese status was more in line with dogs. Death was featured in the testimonies as not only related to daily survival but also to cultural practices, as Chinese believed that the denial of burial rites led to eternal unrest. The concern with burials (and food), inextricable with the racial context in which deprivation emerged, was a node of racial strife. The coolie observations on this point are best exemplified by a coffin maker, Guo Amei, on the Flor de Cuba plantation, who declared the following: "Here dead Chinese won't be buried with coffins, but blacks are. I know, because my job is to make sugar cases and coffins" (Deposition 713). Another coolie made a typical observation: "I see the Chinese workers do not have a coffin upon death. They do not allow people to ask and do not allow friends to see the dead off. He (the owner) will cry if his puppy dies. We are truly not better than the dog" (Deposition 694). Chinese compared their treatment to that of dogs; but more often they felt they were treated worse than dogs, since dogs were at least mourned by their owners. The Chinese compared themselves unfavorably to slaves because they witnessed slaves being buried in coffins (though one might question whether some slaves, or perhaps less privileged slaves in the social hierarchy, might not have been discarded as the Chinese were). Due to the importance of ancestral worship and the importance of clan lineage in Chinese culture, the successful completion of funeral rites marked the critical moment of cultural and generational continuity. Elaborate burial rites and proper placements of burial sites in Chinese tradition involved practices that had been in place for thousands of years. The deep sentiment attached to the funeral emerged not only due to cultural practice, but also as a practical index of social importance and status. The lack of rites, and moreover, the manner in which this occurred, created deep-seated resentment among the Chinese for what they understood as their debasement as a group. Even baptism and conversion to Catholicism apparently did not ensure proper burial. The coolie testimonies often ended with the embittered refrain, "Chinese are buried like dogs." Testimonies by Huang Afang, Li Achang, Wu Zhangsi, Pan Wendao, Lu Zelin, and Chen Amu, provide examples of common observations made in the overall testimonies:

When the Chinese died, they were buried like dogs. (Deposition 413)

If Chinese died here, their bodies would be discarded into a big hole, which is not far from the jail. And that hole is especially for dead Chinese. (Deposition 523)

I witnessed Chinese who were buried like dogs without coffins. (Deposition 577)

After Chinese workers die, their bodies won't be buried in graves. Instead, their bodies will be just discarded around. We are not allowed to help bury those dead Chinese. (Deposition 829)

If Chinese died, their bodies would be discarded into a huge hole. The hole can contain four, five people and sometimes more than ten . . . And later the hole would be covered with mud. (Deposition 864)

The food here is not enough, and we have to work every day from three in the morning to twelve at night with only two hours for meals and rest . . . And we even have to work on Sundays . . . If Chinese died here, they will not be buried in coffins. (Deposition 905)

Coolie experiences were steeped in the racial divisiveness of slavery, with Chinese and Africans being pitted against each other. Wen Azhao observed that "black people were asked to drag and discard these dead bodies" (Deposition 50). Or as the aforementioned He Lin described, "four blacks" were recruited by the overseer to bury a coolie (killed by the overseer). The treatment of coolie deaths emerged in ways that emphasized the coolies' low status yet also revealed the white recruitment of enslaved Africans in the process of Chinese death and disposal, further reinforcing and antagonizing racial conflict.

STRUGGLE BEFORE SOLIDARITY: "ONE DAY WE COULDN'T TAKE IT ANYMORE"

Did the Chinese coolies and Black slaves transcend the racial divisions in their struggles for freedom? Is there evidence of a Walter Rodneyite vision of crossracial solidarity arising from shared oppression of labor? One simple answer would be "yes": There emerged solidarities, especially in consideration of covert and collaborative resistance in bondage, of Chinese and Black insurgencies that formed in the wars for independence, and of interracial social relations, of which some Afro-Chinese descendants are among famous figures in Cuban cultural and political history. Juan Jiménez Pastrana's important work has underscored the significant roles of Chinese *mambíses*, and a recollection of twentieth-century Cuban revolution by three Chinese Cuban generals acknowledges the significance of an earlier history of Chinese insurgence.[18] The 1874 testimonies, however, revealed the underside of solidarity and the ugliness of racial conflict in the context of slavery. Unlike Rodney's history of the working people of Guyana, in which he recounted Asian-African conflicts as not characterized by fatalities, the micro-history before and during the solidarity between Asian and African people in Cuba was raw and brutal, of fatal intensity and human cost.[19] The coolies' representations of interracial conflict disturb commemorative renderings of third-world solidarities, and they expose a more complicated and challenging history of struggle in the context of multiracial bondage.

In the twist of contract labor married to slavery, coolies resented slaves for having higher social status, and slaves resented coolies for being "not slaves." The following excerpts from Gao Alun and Yu Yecheng, respectively, provide examples of the grim consequences of racialized polarities under conditions of extreme exploitation.

When I arrived at the sugar plant, there were one hundred Chinese there. After eight years, there were only thirty left. Most of them died. . . . After fulfilling my contract, the owner detained me for four months in order to make up the time I used to be lazy while working. After the four months, he detained me for another three months. He declared he would give me twelve dollars a month. But he only gave me four dollars total in the first month and eight dollars the second month. So I refused to work. The second day, I and another nine workers went to a local officer, but he said we were runaways and sent us back. Back at the sugar plant, we were tied up in the middle of the night and beaten. The white overseer didn't stop lashing us until he was too tired to hit us anymore. I still have scars all over my body, which can be examined. Then we were locked up, and each of us was watched by a black person, who ordered us to cut grass. The grass was very tall, and we couldn't walk fast because of being chained; so the black people beat us. And then two of the Chinese thought it was hopeless, so they used knives to stab two blacks. One of the black people died, and the Chinese were beaten by the blacks and were wounded. The two wounded Chinese were then sent to the ward; we eight were still left cutting grass. One of the Chinese was beaten so hard and seriously wounded, and he died the next day. Then the owner asked the local officer to come and escorted seven of us to the yamen. The local officer asked me about my injuries and treated me. After two days, I was sent to a sugar plantation somewhere else. I have worked there for twenty days with no payment and bad food. Then I refused to work because in my heart, I did not feel I should be punished. Later, I was sent to the official workshop in Matanzas . . . (Deposition 536)

After six years, there came a new manager who was extremely brutal. So the blacks and some newly arrived Chinese worked together and killed the new manager. The owner spent some money and told the officer that the blacks didn't kill the manager, but instead said we ten Chinese, who were about to fulfill our contracts, did it. So we were sent to a jail in Cardenas. One of us refused to admit to the crime, so he was beaten to death. (Deposition 612)

Such coolie testimonies described conflict as a life or death struggle steeped in racial politics. In Gao's account, a white overseer punished coolies for disobedience by putting the coolies under the control of black slaves, an arrangement which exploded into a fatal conflict. Yu, on the other hand, described the collective action of Chinese and Africans; yet, the integrated group became divided along racial lines. As a third example, the aforementioned Lai Axi told his story of a vengeful white manager who punished the Chinese for flaunting authority by pitting Chinese against Africans. Such tales exposed the intimacy of racialized antipathies with racialized complicities. In each recounting, the exercise of domination was channeled through the division between the Chinese and Africans. Plantation owners and managers undermined Chinese and African actions of solidarity, as in Yu's account, and disposed of troublesome Chinese as a method for destabilizing racial alliances and solving conflicts cheaply. Thus, the Chinese were disposed of for reasons of economic efficiency but in ways that were racially defined and divisive. "Economic efficiency" was revealed as interwoven with racial coercions and control therein.

In the schema of colored power, "black" was portrayed by coolies as the *in-between,* the middle, and the racial divide between yellow and white. The slave was rendered as intermediate between contract labor and ownership. This coolie perspective that "people here think Chinese are worse than black slaves" (Deposition 144), is an inversion of racial narratives of the Americas, which foreground the black-yellow-white and slave-immigrant-ownership progression as constructed through the lens of immigration, modernization, and liberal politics. At the same time, the coolie depictions of slave-overseeing were still couched in terms that highlighted ultimate authority as consistently white. Most obvious in the testimonies was the coolie struggle against white authority. You Asi perceived the corruption of power as stemming from the owner as evidenced by the following testimony:

On my way to sell fish, I was kidnapped by four people to a small boat. They hid me in the bottom of the boat and took me to Heji Pigpen in Macao. I was given a contract and one foreign dollar. In the eleventh moon of the ninth year of Xianfeng (December 1859), I was shipped to Havana and I stayed there for two months. Afterward, I was sold to a sugar plantation in Colon with forty people. But after seven days, one man was beaten to death. His name is Chen Agou and he was from Fujian. He was beaten because he was sick and weak in the feet. I was hit a lot. One day I was beaten so hard that I even passed out for a while. But later I came back to life. We worked from three in the morning to eleven at night. After eight years, except me only nineteen people survived . . . Three people from Nanhai hanged themselves, and sixteen people died of illness . . . The owner asked managers and overseers to beat me. He said, "even if one is beaten to death, I still have money to buy another ten peo-ple." He was really mean and evil. (Deposition 240)

You Asi observed that the owner "asked managers and overseers to beat" him. Another coolie, Chen Qiguang, remarked upon subordination under a racial hierarchy of owner, manager, and overseer: "The owner treats us horribly; the black overseer and the white manager hit us a lot and torture us as much as they want" (Deposition 719). In another exam-ple, Lai Yasi indicates how the owner espoused brutality and promoted the perception among Africans that Chinese were disposable: "I remembered two years ago a Chinese was beaten to death and his body was discarded into the sea. Then some foreign soldiers saw his body and drag it to shore. After investigating, they knew this man used to work in this sugar refin-ery. Although the owner denied it, we all know he used to work with us. But the local officer didn't keep investigating the incident. The owner of-ten said to the black overseer, "you can just beat Chinese laborers as hard as you want; if one is dead, I can always buy two more" (Deposition 812). Chinese-African relations, dialogically constituted within a specific his-tory of extreme exploitation, necessarily included the "dialogic third" of the white owner, whether actually present in the testimony or not. In fact, the "owner" was not always physically present on the plantations, as one coolie noted, "Black overseers also often beat people fiercely. Someone gets wounds all over his body. The owner comes here once or twice every year. In the sugar plantation, the manager takes charge in everything" (Deposition 977). The social order of the plantation, as depicted in the tes-timonies, emerges as some combination of the following: white owner, white manager, white overseer, black overseer, Chinese overseer (rare), black slaves, Chinese foreman, and Chinese coolies. Beyond the owners, managers and overseers had great influence over whether a coolie would be disposed of and how. The coolies made references to both white and black overseers, describing the relationship between coolie and overseer as fraught with tension. Coolies went to lengths, however, to further elab-orate on their black overseers, remarking upon especially brutal relations between them. As Yuan Aishan put it, "Black overseers are the most bru-tal ones" (Deposition 378). Due to the racial economy of slavery, Chinese would have viewed their being placed under Africans as a more humiliat-ing subordination, being dominated by not only white owners and manag-

ers but also working under black slaves and overseers. In the social order
of slavery and in the ideologies of white supremacy, black persons were
considered in slave society as inferior. Thus, in the chain of power, the
placement of coolies under black persons signified being reduced to "less
than slaves." Given the hierarchies of race on the plantation, owners utilized this particular mode of racial subordination as a form of discipline
and punishment, such as in Gao Alun's aforementioned testimony, which
described being placed under a black overseer as further punishment for
refusal to work: "The white overseer didn't stop lashing us until he was
too tired to hit us anymore. I still have scars all over my body, which can
be examined. Then we were locked up, and each of us was watched by a
black person, who ordered us to cut grass." Through this racial lens, an
even deeper resentment was manifested between two subjugated groups,
with Chinese resenting the black overseers who had power over them.
Couched in the context of a mixed labor economy, the Chinese were confounded by the social contradiction of their labor assignation as "contract
labor" versus their social reality "as less than black slaves." The particular
resentment against blackness is suggested in certain forms of expression,
as some testifiers framed their remarks as rhetorical questions rather than
as statements: "Why" should blacks be better than Chinese and "why"
should "we" be less than "they"? Other remarks indicated perplexity, such
as "it doesn't make any sense" or "have you ever heard of such a thing."
Thus the increased rage of coolies against black overseers came about
partly—or precisely—because they were elevated as a group to positions
of superiority over Chinese. In turn, a black overseer likely harbored resentment of coolies as a nonslave, nonwhite group with a supposed wage.
Simultaneously and crucially, black overseers would have had to *prove
their (racial) fitness* for the job by forcing the Chinese into submission.
Some illustrations of this are as follows:

> *A black overseer, named Phillip, hit us ever more severely. After more
> than three years, nineteen of us were beaten severely by Phillip and
> hated him so much. One day we couldn't take it anymore and killed him
> with hoes. (Deposition 432)*

> *The black overseer was really brutal and hit us all the time. Once
> four of us couldn't take it anymore, so we killed the overseer. We*

*knew if we didn't kill him, he would beat us to death in the end.
Therefore, we did not feel bad about killing him. Four of us were sent
to a jail in Colon for sixteen months, and then we were sentenced to
jail in Havana for ten years. To me it is equally miserable to be in jail
and in the sugar plantation. . . . I'd rather die than stay in Cuba.
When I killed the overseer, I thought they would sentence me to
death. (Deposition 574)*

*A black overseer hit us a lot. Four of us decided to kill him, and then
we stabbed him with knives. Later we came before the local officer
and gave ourselves up. The officer sent me back to the sugar plant
and asked the owner about the situation. Later during the trial, I admitted the crime and was sent to a jail in Colon. (Deposition 550)*

*After more than one year, the black overseer was becoming more outra-
geous. We five people would rather give up our lives than be bullied by
him any longer, so we killed him. (Deposition 312)*

*We are treated poorly on the plantation. Four black overseers hit us all
the time. I have been beaten and worn shackles four times so far. Two of
the times, I didn't make any mistakes, but the overseer reprimanded me.
I tried to explain to him, but the overseer got upset and locked me up,
which meant I wasn't allowed to talk back. I was also locked up once for
leaving the plantation and another time for feeling sleepy at work. I
worked with another thirty Chinese, but only eight of them are left now.
(Deposition 690)*

In the black overseer/Chinese coolie arrangement, one subjugated
person or group had to assert and maintain authority over another—although always under the auspices of the dialogic third, a white owner.
Take the case of one black overseer, "Phillip," who was charged with
overseeing nineteen (and perhaps more) Chinese, a situation ripe for ex-
plosion. And the last example depicted black oversight as not only a single overseer but as representative of a racial stratum of power over
Chinese. The executions of coolies for killing black or white overseers
further underscored the racial hierarchy. The respective testimonies by

Li Qi and Lin Asheng provide examples of the conflict this hierarchy created:

> *Once four people killed a black overseer, and were arrested and locked in cells in the sugar plantation. After six months, two of them were hanged; two were shot. Every worker witnessed that. I don't know whether officials have investigated that or not, but in fact, none of us workers have ever been asked to show up in court. (Deposition 345)*[20]

> *After five months, six of us beat a white overseer to death with hoes. We were sent to the local officer; three of us were shot. I and two other guys were sentenced to jail for ten years. (Deposition 955)*

The testimonies concerning Chinese subordination and the cleaved relationship between Chinese and Africans, particularly in the coolie-overseer arrangement, complicate a romance of interracial solidarity and its convergence with revolution. While not dismissing the resistant alliances that were eventually formed, both on the plantation and in the long-lasting insurgencies for independence, this reading of conflict complicates a progressive narrative of resistance and transracial solidarity, and highlights the conflicted nature of interracial relations formed under bondage. The coolies conveyed a consciousness of their collective lot as subordinated labor in a racialized context, with many of those incidences being subordination under African slaves or overseers.

A reading of interracial relations becomes further nuanced with a reading of *Chinese* intraracial conflict. The Chinese labor force was fraught with intragroup conflict when white owners elevated Chinese into positions of punitive power against their own. Chinese foremen emerge sporadically as prominent figures in the testimonies. They were occasionally mentioned in the position of the lead coolie, as foremen who functioned mainly as translators because of an ability to communicate, however marginally, with the overseer or manager. In a handful of instances, Chinese foremen were characterized as reasonable. Yet in other cases, such foremen could assert themselves in brutal ways. In those cases, it might be assumed that the Chinese bore the abuse by Chinese foremen because of cultural commonalities or racial solidarity; but the testimonies revealed that, in fact, the Chinese resented —and sometimes murdered—their Chinese foremen. Thus, the exploitation system functioned not only by turning Chinese against Africans but also by turning Chinese against Chinese. Conflict took place not only against black overseers but also against Chinese foremen. For example, note the following testimonies:

> *When I first got here, I was beaten a lot. Later I was assigned to be a foreman. I didn't want to hit people, but the manager asked me to do so all the time. If I didn't hit Chinese workers, I would be locked up and beaten by the manager. As a result, I hit lots of workers. Once while I was asleep, a worker, who was beaten by me before, chopped my face. I was almost dead. (Deposition 555)*

> *Last year we had a Chinese overseer in the sugar plant. He treated people badly and was killed later. (Deposition 977)*

> *The Chinese overseer often beat us.... Six of us beat him to death. (Deposition 897)*

> *Once a Chinese overseer from Fujian asked a white to lock me up, I stabbed him with a knife. I stabbed him twice in the neck and twice in the chest, but he didn't die. (Deposition 864)*

The perception of racial and cultural betrayal is suggested in the Chinese-Chinese relationship, as the Chinese overseers survived by exploiting their "own," and in those instances, descriptions were of Chinese turning against Chinese. The testimony by the Chinese foreman, Zhang Yi, revealed his assignment to be racialized; he was promoted exactly because he was Chinese and because he was deemed capable of meting out punishment *against* his "own." Like black overseers, the Chinese foremen were compelled to preserve their positions and to survive as long as possible in their circumstances. The racialized politics of "selling out" in a system wherein survival turned upon exploiting one's "own," is further contextualized by the repeated, embittered accounts of coolies who testified that they felt betrayed by fellow Chinese who initially sold them to white foreigners in coolie traffic. On three fronts of Chinese-Chinese, Chinese-African, Chinese-White relations, the testimonies suggest complicated motivations for dominance and resistance, and ethnic schisms within the coolie and slave labor force. Notwithstanding the basic battle to survive, their depictions of resistance were invariably contextualized by the racialized mind-sets and practices that created their bondage to begin with.

A consideration of racialized mind-sets raises the possibility of cultural preconceptions of blackness and slavery embedded in Chinese cultural views *before* their arrival in Cuba. In the entire body of testimonies, none indicated or referred to relations or encounters with black persons before arrival in Cuba. In China, neither a system of generational black slavery nor a mass migration of African people had existed. Still, it is entirely possible that the coolies were aware of images of black slaves and racial discourses regarding slavery before exposure to black slaves in Cuba. Not enough has been written or explored on the subject of black slavery as it was viewed in China, though recent studies indicate that early African-Chinese encounters included two different patterns: One was of reciprocity and mutual respect, and another was of slavery. In the extraordinary history of Chinese navigation overseas, Louise Levathes documents epic and extensive court-sponsored expeditions of the Muslim Admiral Cheng Ho, or Zheng He, who undertook his voyages from 1405–1433.[21] At one point, his enormous fleet arrived on the coast of Africa and engaged in a respectful exchange, and even fulfilled one mission of safely returning African emissaries to their land. The African emissaries had earlier ventured to China and presented gifts to the Chinese, including African animals such as the giraffe.[22] Early Africans thus arrived in China as diplomats on one hand, and on the other, as slaves. There is evidence that small numbers of African slaves were introduced to China via Arab traders.[23] Janet Abu-Lughod discusses the cosmopolitanism of southern China at this time and the presence of people from various parts of the "world system," not the least of which were the Arab traders who formed a "sizable Muslim merchant community."[24] The traders brought slaves with them and installed them as domestic servants. Subsequently, there are indications that dark-skinned slaves were posted as guards to homes of the wealthy Chinese.[25] In Chinese literature, dark-skinned slaves emerged called K'un-lun-nu, with Kunlun becoming a popular figure in the *Legend of K'un-lun-nu*.[26] A tracing of the Kunlun history and its representation from the Tang era has been undertaken by Victor Cunrui Xiong, who noted that "Kunlun" in fact refers to the Malay peninsula, where dark-skinned people lived. Still, he concluded that Kunlun slaves of the Tang, in fact, referred to people from Africa.[27] This literary figure and its relation to Chinese attitudes reemerges in recent examination of African-Asian histories. In her long view of the history of Africa and global interaction, Maghan Keita recently examined African-Asian and African-Chinese interactions and the historiographic literature that exists on the subject(s). She noted that the presence of Africans in China may be registered in three ways: "African artifice and goods, the African and Africa imagined, and Africans as the people they were and are." In her analysis, she is in agreement with Philip Snow, who produced a monograph on early African-Chinese encounters, and Samuel Wilson, who also examines the subject, albeit less extensively.[28] Keita referred to the black Kunlun figures that emerge in the literature of the Tang era (618–906 C.E.) and, according to Snow, are portrayed in a specific context: "[They] speak Chinese, behave like Chinese and are treated by their Chinese owners with every sign of respect. The Kunlun are no common servants. They are unfailingly heroic and resourceful." Yet Keita, in agreement with Snow, asserted that a shift in attitude occurred, brought on by the increased presence of Arab merchants and slaves, and that "the values that had informed the Kunlun—the African, the black, the slave—shifted as well. They came to be characterized in the same manner that masters regarded most subject populations: servile and, many times, subhuman." Still, it is unclear when, how, or to what extent this shift occurred. The Zheng He voyages were abruptly stopped during the Ming Dynasty (1368–1644 C.E.), a ban was implemented regarding maritime trade, and relations with foreign powers were halted. This was a reversal of such magnitude that scholars today are still pondering the historical reverberations.[29] Any traffic in African slaves would have ceased. Given Keita's useful survey of historiographic sources on the subject, the relatively slim body of scholarship on African slaves in China and the extent of their presence, the lack of evidence specifically locating Chinese attitudes in this regard, it is difficult to define the pre-Cuba "roots" of Chinese coolie attitudes toward Africans. However, it is possible to infer Chinese attitudes toward dark skin and thus, blackness. Dark-skinned slaves in China included dark-skinned Chinese, Malays, and Indonesians. Historical studies indicate that all groups were utilized as servants and slaves. Serfdom in Chinese society was hereditary and perpetual and was in place until its dissipation in the eighteenth century. In this respect, "blackness" or dark-skinned labor was associated with bondage and peasant labor, and notions of perpetual servitude were naturalized in Chinese culture. Chinese systems of bondage and serfdom carry their own historical particularities and characteristics that cannot be homogenized with the Atlantic slave system, though it could be said that the Chinese cultural history of bondage and that of dark-skinned peoples, combined with vestiges of the "Kunlun" slave, may have informed Chinese with notions of "blackness." Coupled with associations of dark skin with manual labor, there was the Chinese tradition of the gentry and aristocracy being marked by non-manual labor, less exposure to sun, and fair skin. Furthermore, nineteenth-century European and American imperialism in China, and the coolie traffic, was conducted under long-running discourses of race and colonialism. The Chinese populace was outraged by the traffic and public riots ensued (see Chapter 1, "Historical Context").

Public denunciations of the coolie traffic involved comparison to African slavery, including denunciations issued not only by Chinese but also by Westerners in China. One journal of the period, edited by W.A.P. Martin, declared the following: "Even though Chinese are hired as contract laborers; in fact, they are treated as slaves with no difference from the blacks of Africa."[30] Therefore, testimonies from Chinese in Cuba offer no direct evidence of their preconceptions regarding blackness; yet the nature of "attitudes" is that they are naturalized into acts, texts, and expressions. The cultural and material histories of slavery and serfdom, the history of both Chinese and non-Chinese slaves, and the impact of European attitudes could have served as pretext to racial perceptions in the 1874 testimonies.

THE COST OF DOMINATION: "THE CROWD FOUGHT BACK"

A prominent feature of labor histories concerns the cost of production. Most striking in this history is not only the cost of production, but also the high cost of domination. Here, "cost" is put forward in terms of life and limb. Underlying this rather apparent interpretation of cost is an examination of domination, revealed as uneven, penetrable, and subject to daily resistance by coolies. There are 953 oral testimonies (or 81 percent of the total oral testimonies) that described the omnipresence of death contextualized by a numbing litany of punishment, retaliatory killings, and suicides. The coolies were cut off from their families in China, with little hope of returning. They were without enough food and lived with the dread of an unsettled death or no funeral, and most of all, there was a heightened arbitrariness and expendability to their lives. As a result, the coolie relationship to management was marked by volatility. The myth of return that arguably sustained immigrant "sojourners" abroad haunted the coolies in Cuba. But these coolies expressed the dawning realization that, in fact, they were permanently trapped and would never see home again. Thus, many felt they had nothing to lose: "How dare a Chinese worker dream of going back to China?" (Petition 2) This predicament of unending bondage combined with a high mortality rate led to the preponderance of explosive resistance and chaos. Luo Aji described the life-or-death struggle in the sugar field: "In the fifth year, I was sent to cut grass with Huang Axing and Chen Aye. Because we didn't cut one branch, the overseer hit Axing with a whip. Then Axing turned around, the manager tried to cut his neck with a machete. So Axing immediately took that machete and chopped off the manager's hand. Then Aye injured the manager's head with his sickle. I did not do anything, but I was also sent to jail with them" (Deposition 431). The implements of slave driving and hard labor made appearances throughout the testimonies in the form of whips, chains, clubs, axes, hoes, knives, machetes, and guns. This "weaponry of work" was not only wielded by managers and owners but by the coolies themselves. For example, the weaponry of work appears in Huang Azhang's account: "The overseer wanted me to bribe him, so he made me wear shackles and hit me severely with cowhide all the time, and sometimes he hit me with a club. Lin Ayou and I could not bear this humiliation and bullying, and besides, our lives were in danger, so we killed the overseer. I used an ax, and Ayou used a machete" (Deposition 447). He Afa also describes the omnipresence of slavery's implements and their violent use:

> There are two meals of corn everyday. We work from two in the morning to one at night. The time for us to eat and sleep totally is no more than five hours. If we got up slowly or walked too slow or too fast, we would get whipped. The whip is made of a big slice of leather, so using it to beat us makes our skin crack and blood flows out. There is a cell in the sugar plantation which is usually full of people with neck locks, foot locks, and shackles. I had an internal injury, so I was the one who most

often got beaten. In the sugar plantation, I saw by my own eyes that Zhang Awang, who came from Guangdong, could not stand the torture anymore and hanged himself. There were two people from Qiongzhou City in Guangdong who committed suicide by swallowing opium. I was beaten countless times. Once a manager who beat us relentlessly for days, took out a machete and wanted to slash us. Then the crowd fought back and slashed him to death instead. (Deposition 883)

Testimonies such as these depicted combative struggles in daily interaction and revealed the precariousness of controlling bonded labor. The candid and graphic nature of their words is surprising as is the pattern of remorseless and open admission, as it would seem to foreclose any possibility of liberation or redress before an official body. In these cases, these testimonies could be read as mass indictments of the system, rather than as pleas for help. The cheapness of contract labor and the easy replacement of that labor were manifested in disposability and mobility becoming methods of control over labor. Owners discarded coolies by weeding out resistant or unproductive coolies though punishment or death. Or, in some cases, coolies were simply passed off to the official workshops or other plantations and were cheaply replaced. The basic premise of control yoked "disposability" with "domination." One of the most powerful tools of control was the freedom paper system, which was manipulated by management and used to hold the coolie hostage to the potentiality of freedom. Yet, the high turnover and attrition of coolies and the seemingly endless deferment of freedom also produced enraged workers. Coolie Guan Ashou detailed their frustration, echoing testimonies of other coolies: "The overseer beat us so severely that some of us were beaten to death. Even though we fulfilled our contract, we couldn't get our freedom papers. So we'd rather kill the overseer now than be beaten to death by him later. It is much better to be put in jail than in the sugar plantation." (Deposition 504) Coolies fought back in situations marked by temporal compression, with testifiers stating that their time was limited and freedom was not forthcoming.

The life-or-death struggle and its component of fear pervade the testimonies: There was not only fear expressed by coolies but the fear that pervaded management. Managers and overseers, whose jobs were to maintain order and increase labor production, literally risked their lives in their struggle to extract labor from "voluntary labor." As one Zhong Jinxiu declared regarding his manager, "I tried every means to kill him" (Deposition 679). The daily dealings of management, as portrayed in the testimonies, reveal the strain of attempting to control a mass group that was resistant. As one Zhu Arui emphasized, "The manager used to treat us ferociously. Later a few overseers were slashed to death, so now he treats us a little bit better" (Deposition 877). While coolie labor has been understood as a category of efficient labor used in a transition from slavery to free labor, here the coolies reveal the resistance of such a force. Authority was depicted as teetering on a line that was constantly tested. In some cases, coolies described management as panicked. Wang Mujiu recalled, in the following testimony, his overseer firing madly into the crowd:

> *We worked from four in the morning to one at night with two hours break for us to eat in between, but the food was always not enough. Because the work was so intense and toilsome, I reported the situation to the officer. The officer asked the owner to give me a smaller workload and enough food to eat. The owner promised to do so in front of the officer. But soon as we got back, he locked my feet with shackles for seven months. When I was in shackles, I had to continue working. Sometimes I was too tired to work, and he would lash me and lock me up again. I was asked to cut sugarcane. The overseer furiously beat me all the time. Once I could not stand it any more, so I stabbed his arm using a knife. Then the white man started to fire his gun madly, and a few people in the same group with me got injured. Afterwards, they sent six of us to prison in Havana. (Deposition 625)*

One He Lin described how "nine of us made up our minds" to kill an overseer and how a subsequent owner hastily passed them off upon hearing of their crime.

In repeated examples, the Chinese decided with collective forethought to rid themselves of particular managers or overseers. Overt resistance included confrontation and sometimes fatalities, but there were also organized assassinations of the overseer, the manager, or both. Assassinations would involve the collective act of a select few, or would involve twenty Chinese, or in some instances a "crowd" of Chinese. Wu Zhangsi detailed the "deal" made among his group: "Sixteen people hated the overseer a lot and we made a deal; if the overseer hit us again, even if he just hit one of us, together we would beat him to death. Then we killed him and all of us were arrested and sent to jail in Colon. Three of us died in the cell, two were transferred to jail in Havana, and eleven were bought back by the owner. . . . Of those involved, four of us did not actually kill that overseer. But we were still locked up and beaten severely by the owner" (Deposition 577). And another coolie, Wu Jin, described the action taken by a group of ten: "Working for one and half years, I was hit a lot by a black overseer. One day ten of us decided to kill him with the machetes we used to cut sugarcane. Then we turned ourselves in and were sentenced to jail for ten years" (Deposition 920). Other examples of "assassination" testimonies include those such as Yuan Aying's, which described the mass act of twenty coolies who kill their manager: "His rule was we had to work day and night, and we had nothing to eat. I worked there for thirty-five days and could not stand it anymore. Totally twenty of us did it—we slashed the white manager to death" (Deposition 868). Mo Agang's following testimony recounted that five coolies "worked together and fought back" by bludgeoning the overseer to death:

> The owner and the manager were wicked people. The food was only potatoes and corns and which is not enough food to eat. When we need to press the sugarcane, we work from one in the morning to ten at night. If we do not need to press the sugarcane, we work from three in the morning to eight at night. In the sugar plantation, they use leather whips to beat us. After working in the sugar plantation for a year, I saw three people hanged themselves and five people swallowed opium to kill themselves. There were five people in my group—because five of us often got beaten by the overseers—we have wounds all over the body. One day when we were working in the sugarcane field, he started to beat us again. We worked together and fought back. We used hoes to beat him to death. The owner sent five of us to the jail in Cardenas, where we stayed for eight months. And then I was transferred to Havana and sentenced to jail for ten years. Now I have been in the jail for four and a half years. In the jail, I wear four different shackles. The officer in the jail assigned me to roll the tobaccos. I have to roll three packs of tobaccos, about sixteen thousand tobaccos. I have to work day and night in order to finish my workload, as I will get beaten if all the work is not finished. The food is only conjee, and I do not have enough food

to eat. Working here, I suffer less wear and tear of the weather com-
pared to working on the sugar plantation, but the humiliation is the
same as on the plantation. (Deposition 868)

As punishment, Mo ended up in prison. Still, Mo's captors remained fearful of him, as he was required to wear four shackles while he did daily forced labor. The fear of "Mo" exemplified the fear of the coolie, who embodied the first social and economic experiment to mitigate the rising costs of slave trade, yet was clearly resistant to labor "efficiency." One could not point to a more extreme pattern of counterproductivity than workers retaliating against their managers and overseers, whether they were black, white, or Chinese. In some cases, there were workers on one plantation killing "several" overseers in sequence. Selections from other testimonies provide further details of violence and its contexts:

The first manager was nice, but after three years, there came a new
manager, who is white. He beat us all the time. Not being able to bear
this anymore, a group of new workers killed that manager. (Deposition
868)

The manager treated me badly, and I couldn't take it anymore, so I
talked to another worker about how I had to kill the manager. One day
the manager came and told me to work night shift; I killed him with a
kitchen knife. (Deposition 264)

Ten of us couldn't take his bullying and torture anymore, so we tried to
kill him. But he did not die, only was injured. (Deposition 442)

Five of us were beaten severely for two days in a row, and we were in-
jured seriously on heads and faces. And our eyes were injured too. You
can still examine our scars. We were so angry that we fought back and
killed him. (Deposition 734)

Nineteen of us suffered a lot. One day the manager again hit people for
no reason; we tried to calm him down, but he tried to kill us with a long
knife. So we fought back and killed him with hoes. (Deposition 873)

Yet the Chinese were not always executed for these murderous acts—obviously, there were those such as "Mo" who survived to recount their term of imprisonment. As one prisoner noted, "After three years, I and another two who also hated the overseer stabbed him to death with knives, because he bullied us a lot. But a white man witnessed this, and we were arrested and sent to the local officer in Matanzas" (Deposition 909). Given that testimonies underscored the need for control by management, it would seem illogical that violent resisters be allowed to survive. Resisters' lives were spared in part because coolies represented the possibility of profit *beyond* the onsite production. The testimonies regarding deadly resistance point to the overarching lure of profit. As flexible labor, Chinese were resold in a cycle of further profiteering. This recycling amounted to immediate profit for sellers of coolies and further production in the tobacco and sugar industries. Like Li and Mo's accounts (above), coolies were sent to jails as captive labor with high yields. Li and Mo described their quotas as fifteen to sixteen thousand cigars (or cigarettes) per week. Li Hui, earlier mentioned as one who "accidentally" killed his overseer, also provided an important glimpse of coolie prison labor in the following account:

> *When we needed to press sugarcane, we worked from three in the morning to twelve at night with half hour of rest for meals. Other times, we worked until ten at night. After working for six years, one day at eleven at night I felt sleepy while cooking the sugar, so the sugar got burned. The overseer hit me with a handspike. I took that handspike and pushed him; however, the overseer fell into the sugar-cooking pot. I didn't mean to kill him. But the manager sent me to the local officer, who sentenced me to prison for ten years . . . Later I was sent to another prison in Habana, where I stayed for seven years so far. In the prison, being a tobacco-roller, I have to turn in fifteen thousand tobaccos a week to the officers. And I can earn one dollar by rolling extra five thousand tobaccos. The food in jail is not enough; however, I would rather stay in prison than in the sugar plant. In the sugar plant, I had to work all day and night long; the workload was heavy, and I was hit severely. (Deposition 67)*

Han Yanpei, described a similar quota: "In the jail, those who are in the tobacco workshop need to make twenty-six hundred cigarettes per person per day" (Deposition 219). Over six working days, this quota would have amounted to fifteen to sixteen thousand per week. Over seven working days, this would have amounted to eighteen thousand per week. Thus, "jail" was a site of production in a chain of sites that contract labor circulated through. "Jails" and "workshops," with this kind of captive yield, and the liquidity of coolie labor and resale, need to be considered in analyses of contract labor and its uses.

———

The extraordinary details of the testimonies—from those young and old, of different work sites and locations, and from those who attested to their own experience but also bore witness to the circumstances of others—emphasize the experience of so-called transition from slavery as volatile, unstable, precarious, and brutal. Why was the experience of "contract labor" of such brutal nature? One most obvious reason was profit and the systemic pursuit of it—a motive most clearly exposed in the petitions. Perhaps Wang Guijie's account is the most chilling, as it matter-of-factly depicted profiteering from the coolie traffic: "I got sick when the ship arrived at Havana. I lived in a ward and then was sold to a clinic in Matanzas. The owner of the clinic always bought sick people and cured them, so he could sell them after they got better" (Deposition 481). Wang's offhand description of Chinese being healed so they could be sold describes not only the capture of body for the purposes of forced labor but also the colonized body as future investment and commodity. Suggested in this and the remaining testimonies were two apparently contradictory impulses that buttressed this first massive influx of Asians to this hemisphere, one being the imperatives of profit and the utility of the "raced" body, and the other being the fear of the racial differences that such profit thrived upon. The threat of a new racial body and the destabilization of a preexisting racial and social order resulted in the need to redraw lines of domination and control. One Chinese Cuban of contemporary times recounts that, in the past, the Africans were called *niche* (equivalent to "nigger"), and the Chinese were called *narra*.[31] In the testimonies, fear of the Chinese was accompanied by the impulse to divide Chinese from Africans—and in some cases, Chinese from Chinese. As a new social body, the coolies emerged and complicated an already conflicted social theater of *de color* when color was primarily defined along lines of blackness and whiteness.

The heightened intensity of conflict, and the compressed nature of shortened lives under disposable exploitation, raise singular questions about forms of resistance and "community" under conditions of expendability. The testimonies suggest the mass acts of testimony as constituting a political community in itself. The tropes of witnessing and naming, the desire to speak for the dead, the prevalence of group perspective ("we," "us," and "our"), and the narrating of collective actions, signal the forming of collective identity in the act of giving testimony. The petitions (particularly the mass petitions) emerge as extraordinary forms of collective resistance through writing, and the depositions reveal the highly charged acts of testifying against great odds, with some testifiers indicating that they spoke not only for themselves but for others who had no means of communicating. Repeated tropes and themes, frequently appearing phrases and refrains, common locations and contexts, locally formed coolie language to describe and make sense of a bewildering system—all contributed to the making of an overarching coolie narrative(s), rather than simply a massive assortment of unrelated statements.

Other questions remain as to how testimony-giving directly affected the coolies after 1874. How did this historical moment of testifying affect their subsequent perceptions and actions? How did it affect their views of themselves and their futures? What effect did this event have upon the coolies' subsequent relationship with cultural identity and nationalist sentiments? Was there any correlation to the numbers of coolies who continued to join the war for Cuban liberation? How did the testimony affect the views of local Cubans toward coolies, if it did? Is there evidence that links this episode of testimony to subsequent liberatory politics, both in Cuba and elsewhere? These questions remain unanswered here. For example, exact numbers and the tracking of coolies who joined the independence wars were not recorded, though there is evidence of their mass participation. The testimonies and the commission report eventually led to the official end of coolie trafficking to Cuba but did not liberate coolies already in bondage. The last coolies in bondage would not be freed until the African slavery system underwent a slow demise in Cuba via a transitional patronage system in the 1880s.

Furthermore, there is no extant autobiographical or self-representational writing that has been left to us from the coolies, outside of their self-representations in 1874. As such, I do not suggest these testimonies as the über-source that represents experiences of all Chinese in Cuba at the time, especially as the history of Chinese in Cuba extends from the mid-nineteenth century until today and has various social genealogies. However, there is a fascinating piece of self-representation by a second generation Afro-Chinese author. He provided a narrative of the coolies as freedom fighters who emerged from slavery, but he ultimately portrayed them as marginalized figures of blackness amid the subsequent rise of a merchant class. A new generation of Chinese Californians had arrived, and this would change the landscape. In this rare history of community, this author made the first attempt to comprehensively historicize the Chinese in the wake of bondage and did so in a transnational context. Dedicating his work to the coolies, yet paying homage to merchants and new immigrant success, he ambivalently cast coolie history under the shadow of new capital while also undermining dominant paradigms of modern immigrant success along the lines of race and labor. Ultimately, his work bridges the yawning narrative gap that opens after 1874 and offers a unique and vexing perspective to the question of what happened to the "coolie." We move now to the second generation and examine the vagaries of politics in the narration of "coolie-to-immigrant."

5

AN AFRO-CHINESE AUTHOR
AND THE NEXT GENERATION

This was a strange and striking exhibition of power. Two or three white men, bringing hundreds of Chinese thousands of miles, to a new climate and people, holding them as prisoners, selling their services to masters having an unknown tongue and an unknown religion, to work at unknown trades, for inscrutable purposes! . . . The constant question is—will they remain and mix with the other races? Will they be permitted to remain? Will they be able to go back? . . . coolies are to be met with everywhere, in town and country.[1]

—*Richard Henry Dana, author of* To Cuba and Back *(1859) and* Two Years Before the Mast *(1869), upon his visit to a coolie market*

Richard Henry Dana, the prominent lawyer, abolitionist, and writer, posed a most vexing question regarding Chinese labor of the Americas: Would the Chinese mix with other races? After Dana's trip in 1859, coolies continued to appear in "town and country" and indeed, they did "mix" with other races. One of these descendants would write a densely informative book on the coolies and on the immigrants who arrived after the coolie trade ended. Born in 1860 during the slave and coolie era in Cuba, Antonio Chuffat Latour emerged as a second generation Afro-Chinese who witnessed the rise of Chinese presence in Cuba, the insurrectionary wars for Cuban independence, the abolition of slavery, and American occupation. Several decades later, at the age of sixty-seven, he published a history that linked all of these events in his rare text *Apunte histórico de los chinos en Cuba* (1927).[2] Covering the 1840s–1920s, utilizing interviews and data (including 114 photographs) drawn from several provinces in Cuba, Chuffat documented a social history of the Chinese in the wake of slavery and abolition. A buried footnote in Cuban scholarship since its appearance, his work has never before been subjected to critical review.

ANTONIO CHUFFAT LATOUR
Source: Apunte historico de los chinos en Cuba. Habana:
Molina, 1927

In modern scholarship, the most comprehensively articulated approaches to the Chinese in Cuba have examined the "unfree" on one hand
and the "free" on the other. Between these two histories is a weak link.
How did the coolies *become* merchants—or did they? Would these two social histories presumably coalesce under an umbrella ethnic sensibility of
"Chinese-ness"? What of the Racial Contract that subsumed Chinese as
enslaved labor; how was it operative vis-à-vis a free immigrant class?
More pertinent to Chuffat's work is this question: What were the rich heterogeneities of color and class, social realities, and cultural hyrbidities that
contribute to this lacuna of "transition" from a slave society to free society? The "transition" from coolie to merchant has been loosely defined as
a consequence associated with coolies who became free "entrepreneurs"
through finishing or getting free from their contracts—thus, the beginnings of immigrant community (although the previous chapter problema-
tizes this progression).[3] *Community*, implied here as the outlines of free
society and its institutions, naturally foregrounds the merchant who is the
purveyor of capital exchange and the sponsor of institutions that provide a
visible permanency that presupposes an examination of such communities.

Merchants had the means to produce representations of their histories, communities, and institutions, and could attest to their cultural history. However, Chuffat's work suggests a more class-based history, featuring the indentured coolie who limned free society in racialized and ambivalent ways.

Divided into two parts, *Libro Primero* (eight chapters) and *Libro Segundo* (eleven chapters), Chuffat's narrative falls into a chronology of the coolie and postcoolie eras. Chuffat described social and cultural formations that were marked by historical events but also riven by lines of class and color. He also described the Chinese with ethnic and political differences formed amidst inter-Americas cultural flows and racial politics. He understood the coolies as forerunners of Chinese migration even though recognition of their contributions was marginalized under their newly arrived free counterparts. The new generation, in his view, were the inheritors of the coolie sacrifice, and furthermore, of the slave. In his introduction, it was to the coolies, Chuffat said, that his work was dedicated, and in his text's final words, he reiterated the significance of the coolies as ancestors. "Blackness" and subalternity, and its ambivalent relation to Chinese identity, threaded the work. Chuffat was the first to consistently portray Chinese social history as connected to the legacy of blackness. During the 1920s and 1930s, as in earlier decades, no other literary or historiographic work on Chinese diaspora directly examined black and Chinese social histories as conjoined. Earlier, the Cuban patriot Gonzalo de Quesada wrote a brief but important piece on the Chinese contribution to the independence wars, which likened Chinese conditions to slavery, but the essay's main focus was on the Chinese contribution to a united, national Cuban independence.[4] One of Chuffat's main contributions was his unique portrayal of Chinese as not only agents in freeing themselves from a colonial slavery system but also as creative agents of cultural forms and hybridizations.[5] This perspective regarding the coolies offers a complement to the coolie testimonies and suggests the social transformations that followed after the coolie era.

On several fronts, Chuffat's study was a remarkable and highly unusual approach for its time. His approach resulted in bridging the social histories of the slave, the coolie, and the immigrant. In the larger area of the Caribbean, the Chinese coolie did not occupy the main subject of literary or biographical texts produced during the nineteenth and early twentieth centuries, although the coolie did appear as the subject of colonial papers, investigations, and personal accounts by white observers of coolie trade. For Chuffat, a work on the coolie legacy and hybrid cultural forms might have been a natural sequence to apprehending the unique questions of color presented in his experience of colonial transition and the construction of ermergent national identity. Still, with his publication appearing in the 1920s, Chuffat's preoccupation with the *coolie* was idiosyncratic and counter to the prevalent social ideas of Chinese diaspora, wherein social and cultural representations were dominated by intellectuals and free immigrants—the coolie was simply absorbed into a new history of "Chinese immigrants." Chuffat's simultaneous linking and de-linking of free social history and unfree labor offered an alternative view into the makings of diasporic class. In his narrative, the unfree and racialized laborer emerged as the "ancestor" but was intraethnically subordinated. Chuffat offered an understanding of diasporic freedom as ambivalently yet necessarily linked to subaltern labor.

Today, Chuffat's work stands as a valuable reference for the history of new free Chinese society that flourished during Republican Cuba.[6] Observations concerning the new free Chinese of the merchant period, and the Californians and their profound influence, are informed by Chuffat's documentation of the period. His text can be looked at in relation to current scholarly approaches to diasporic formations. For example, Yen Ching Hwang adroitly linked the coolie episode to the emergence of an *overseas Chinese* discourse, a discourse which continues to be considered (and debated) in any study of Chinese migrations. Hwang traced the role of coolies as nation-subjects crucial to the shaping of sovereignty that limns a modern China. Denise Helly, while mainly concerned with coolie history, examined the subsequent rise of a Chinese merchant class from the standpoint of *ethnic social formation*. She argued that the formation of the Chinese merchants as an ethnic social group arose from a combination of contradictions in slavery economy, colonial and racial ideologies, and cultural and ethnic practices. Juan Pérez de la Riva paid special attention to the rise of the California Chinese and the influx of their formations and capital in an emergent community in Cuba. He also examined the formation of a Chinese merchant group as one of *regional and transnational* politics. José Baltar's views, in agreement with Pérez de la Riva and Helly on varied points, paid special attention to *cultural organizations* and

Chinese clan societies that gave rise to and structured community.[7] Chuffat's work is relevant to all of these approaches to immigrant Chinese: overseas Chinese, Chinese as ethnic social group, as regional/transnational diaspora, and as cultural organizers.[8] However, my critical reading of Chuffat focuses upon an alternative method of reading his history *Apunte histórico* and includes some attention to his own biography. The text's methods strongly suggest a *veiled narrative*. Through a narrative analysis, a subversive and rich narrative of color and power emerges.

THE SUBVERSIVE AND THE TRANSLATOR

Apunte histórico de los chinos en Cuba was presumably, at first glance, a work on the Chinese, not an autobiography about the author nor a work about black struggle. But the book was indeed multifaceted. Chuffat's unique text could be read as an autobiography within a biography of the Chinese community, and as a critical narrative of liberalism within an immigrant-contribution narrative. What follows is an examination of Chuffat's written and visual text, with focus upon the significance of this publication as a social event: black-authored book and the cultural politics it presents. Secondly, there is a critical review of particular aspects raised in the textual content (aspects of language, religion, liberatory politics, and gender). This two-part approach thus begins with a look at Chuffat himself as a worthwhile subject of study. He was a second generation Afro-Chinese descendant who wrote about the Chinese diaspora, born and educated before the abolition of slavery. He spoke Spanish and Chinese, served as translator and intermediary for the Chinese community, and he was a black activist who was described as a "very bad agitator" by the American military. How would the politics of such a biographer complicate a reading of his narrative and contribute to the study of race, labor, and diaspora? If anyone was ideally positioned to interpret the history of blacks and Asians, precisely during the slave and coolie era and its aftermath, it was Chuffat. However, Chuffat's own politics and the narrative construction of his text suggest a veiled narrative, and it is from that perspective that a rich, compelling view of the coolie and cultural identity emerges. Chuffat's text is most interesting for three reasons: authorship, form, and content.

As an author with a modicum of status in Cuba, Chuffat was sited in the crossroads of Chinese and black social histories, a familiar cultural intertwining that is characteristic of Cuba, the Caribbean, and Latin America. The world-renowned Cuban surrealist Wilfredo Lam (1902–1982) comes to mind, as does Eugene Chen (1878–1944).[9] Chen, born and raised in Trinidad, was a creole lawyer of the family name Acham and served as Foreign Minister of Republican China and as Sun Yat-Sen's personal advisor and secretary until the latter's death. The legendary "Graciela" (Graciela Perez), descendant of a coolie and known as the first lady of Afro-Cuban jazz, gained international fame performing abroad with Machito and his Afro-Cuban Jazz Orchestra. These are only a few of the many important historical figures of Afro-Chinese cultural histories. But Chuffat's authorship is an uncommon event because he identified himself specifically as a "black man" in a Chinese context, and he had an ability to parlay his background into important positions in different social sets. There are few available details of Chuffat's life and politics, but those details offer a complex portrait of a black Cuban patriot whose was equally proud of both his African and his Chinese roots.

Documents indicate that Chuffat was active in the politics of black empowerment. A 1907 American army intelligence document, from the Chief of the "Military Information Division," places Chuffat on a list of nineteen black subversives who were part of a group organizing against American occupation. A memorandum sent from the headquarters of the Army of Cuban Pacification, addressed to the American Chief of Staff, notes that these nineteen were working together with an agent of Juan Gualberto Gomez:

> [He]is spending a great deal of time traveling around the island making political trouble among the negro people. . . . His real purpose here seems to be that of organizing the negroes into one party for the purpose of securing a more equal distribution of government positions between the blacks and whites. He is not at all satisfied with the present government nor the outlook for the near future. The Americans, he says, must not be allowed to remain here longer. The following negroes of this vicinity are considered to be very bad agitators and citizens. . . . While the people (whites) are greatly alarmed over the negro situation, I doubt that the negroes are preparing to take up arms against the present

government. It seems to me that they are organizing a strong political party. This organization may lead to trouble later.[10]

On the list of those "very bad agitators" was Chuffat. Earlier, Chuffat's political sentiments already appeared in his correspondence to the black independence leader Juan Gualberto Gomez. In a letter from Chuffat to Gualberto dated December 16, 1898, six days after the Treaty of Paris had been signed to cede Cuba to American control, Chuffat wrote of his admiration for Gualberto and his sacrifices. He put himself at Gualberto's service and volunteered himself unconditionally, stating that there was not a black person in Cuba who did not recognize and celebrate Gualberto's invaluable judgment: *"No habra un negro en Cuba que no lo reconosca y celebre su valioso criterio. . . . En espera de su contestacion tiene la alta honra de ponerse á sus órdenes y de ofrecerse incondicionalmente, no el niño de ayer, sino el hombre negro que piensa."*[11] Chuffat's support of Gualberto offers some idea of Chuffat's own politics. Juan Gualberto Gomez was a journalist, abolitionist, and Afro-Cuban revolutionary. Born in 1854 to slaves who had bought their freedom, Gualberto was often spoken of in the same breath as Antonio Maceo and especially associated with Jose Martí. Gualberto supported the rebels fighting the Spaniards in the independence wars, and he was eventually imprisoned and deported for his activities. He was publisher of the newspaper for black solidarity, *La Fraternidad*, and openly and vigorously opposed the Platt Amendment (concerning the American annexation of Cuba).[12] Directly relevant to Chuffat's correspondence here is Gualberto's leadership of the *Directório Central de Sociedades de la Raza de Color* (the Central Directory of the Societies of People of Color), which assembled all the local black and mulatto societies on a political platform.[13] Chuffat appeared to be a local political organizer, as he signed his letter with the title of "Presidente de la raza de color de Distrito de Colón y Yaguaramas." Regretfully, little is known at this time about Chuffat's activities vis-à-vis the rise of the Partido Independiente de Color and the repressive massacre of Afro-Cubans in 1912. Nonetheless, Chuffat's signature as "district president" for the local party of color is indicative of his active presence in political organizing for Afro-Cubans.

Another connection Chuffat had to Gualberto might have been a personal one. Chuffat and Gualberto were educated at the same private school for persons of color in Havana. Given their ages, they were only four years apart, and it is possible that they were schoolmates. *El Colegio "Los Desamparados" de la raza de color*, as described by Chuffat (or elsewhere referred to as *Nuestra Señora de los Desamparados*, or "Our Lady of the Abandoned"), was in fact a well-known school under the direction of the poet and journalist Antonio Medina y Céspedes.[14] At the age of twelve, Chuffat had come from Jovellanos to attend the school and worked by delivering mail for a well-connected Chinese firm, Lam y Compañía.[15] He would have been one of the few young persons of color who would receive such an education during the 1870s. According to one estimate, one-tenth of free children (with the majority being free whites), went to school in Cuba during this time.[16]

By the time Chuffat had reached age seventy-two he counted revolutionaries, merchants, and statesmen as his friends. In 1932, in a letter he wrote to the Cuban Secretary of State, Orestes Ferrera, he signed off as *su viejo amigo* (your old friend).[17] Ironically, Chuffat's book was also dedicated to Rafael Martínez Ortiz, a leading proponent of *realismo plattista*, the Plattist politics espousing accommodating of the United States, which Gualberto opposed. Martínez was a leading Cuban statesman who bore many titles by the time of Chuffat's publication. Martínez authored the two-volume work, *Cuba, los primeros años de su independencia*, which is now a classic text of Cuban history from a particular perspective, that documents the critical transition to independence under American influence.[18] Chuffat's work can be read as a *foil* to Rafael Martínez Ortiz's work. The two opening photographs of Chuffat's book, one of Martínez and the other of Chuffat, present a great irony. Martínez's writing exemplified one kind of Latin American thinking that viewed national formation pragmatically, in terms of realities under a dominant regional power (i.e., the Americans and the Platt Amendment). Martínez's exhaustive history of Cuba mentioned nothing about Chinese, Blacks, Mulattos, ex-coolies, or ex-slaves in the struggle for liberation and building of nations, but his work did expound upon the need for relocating the indigenous people so their land could be appropriated. Formed along the traditional model of "history and the individual," fashioned around developments of state, Martínez's story of Cuba was diametrically opposed to that of Chuffat's. In Martínez's model of Cuban history, the founding of nations was accomplished by great leaders and men of industrial power, such as the American railroad tycoon William Van Horne. Van Horne became president of the Cuba Railroad Company, and Martínez praised him for building the Cuban railroads.[19] Alongside this narrative of Cuba, Chuffat's work is startling for its departure from this model and is made more pronounced when comparing the visual narrative. Martínez's history contained dozens of photographs of white male figures but no photographs of either Chinese or blacks. Chuffat would do the opposite—and he would also include some photographs of women. While Martínez focused on great white men, Chuffat focused on those who were excluded. While Martínez made no mention of social justice, Chuffat elaborated upon disparity and racism. Chuffat's work was subversive in comparison.

Why would Chuffat dedicate his book to Martínez? Several factors may be attributed to this, not the least of which was the politics of censure and sponsorship. First, Chuffat produced text at a time when book publication was exceptional and necessitated sponsorship. Chuffat's role as a black author was exceptional to the history of print culture. When Chuffat was born, the Cuban illiteracy rate was 80 percent, and by the end of the nineteenth century, the rate was still 75 percent.[20] Those who could read and write were in the minority, and the possibility of a black author publishing a book was even smaller. Chuffat's book-length articulation is particularly significant given literary culture and the economy of book publishing at that time. True, there were black writers in Cuba who preceded Chuffat. These included Juan Francisco Manzano (whose slave narrative was published in London in 1839 and would not be introduced in Cuba until 1937), the free mulatto poet Placido (penname of Gabriel de la Concepción Valdés, executed in 1844 after being accused of conspiracy by the Spanish colonial government), and Afro-Cuban poets who had work published in volumes such as Francisco Calgano's 1868 anthology. Still, even with the overthrow of the Spanish colonial government in 1898 (when Chuffat would have been thirty-eight years old), and in the republican era that followed, blacks who had published books in Cuba and the former Spanish Americas were still a rarity.[21] Late nineteenth- and early-twentieth-century literary culture in Cuba was shaped by *tertulias* (literary and intellectual circles) and by elite societies that arose from the sugar system.[22] Varied in their political expressions, such groups still functioned under government scrutiny and faced the practical questions of financing and publishing works, with book runs of a few hundred at most. Book publishing was limited, and journals, newspapers, sheets, pamphlets, and booklets were the more popular forms of print. Limiting factors for the book market in Cuba included low literacy rates, lack of institutional support, constricted distribution, government surveillance, cultural control by the sugar oligarchy, and market realities that were formulated as a result.[23] Judging by the social economy of literary circles, the sugar elite, and ingrained colonial hierarchy—it is not surprising that few books by black men or women were published. Moreover, harsh censorship was applied to narratives that depicted the brutality of slavery.[24]

The possibilities of black authorship rested upon the politics of sponsorhip. Self-publication, sponsorship by funded circles, and subscription would support limited publication runs (as in Chuffat's case). Of crucial significance to understanding Chuffat's work as social production is its sponsorship by the merchants. Through their sponsorship and subscriptions, the book's publication was realized, particularly through the efforts of wealthy Chinese merchants, José Cordova, and Ramón Anón, owner of a tobacco factory.[25] In this respect, sponsored literary and historical writing of the Chinese diaspora offers reference points to Chuffat's work, including Chinese Benevolent Association histories and yearbooks.[26] Like an association "yearbook," Chuffat's book was funded by the Chinese community and offered a narrative beholden to them. Thus, there are the careful mentions of individuals and their contributions, the narrative arc of immigrant-contribution, and the moral and economic justifications of their presence. Homages to the Chinese Chamber of Commerce and various societies and to merchants, bankers, diplomats, entrepreneurs, and portraits of society filled Chuffat's commissioned text. Like a sponsored "yearbook," the book contained a hallmark section of photographs, which offered a gallery of photos depicting upstanding merchants and diplomats in formal dress.

As a young black man, Chuffat became an official translator for Chinese bankers and merchants; but Chuffat became primarily an observant commentator who was self-taught and learned social skills through his own ingenuity. His tropes of social observation, autodidactic capabilities, and especially speaking, writing, and oration, are also characteristic tropes of the slave narratives and black writings of empowerment. Speaking and writing emerged as a preoccupation for Chuffat. At age twenty-one, he and other young men of color, or *"varios jóvenes de color,"* sought out a

distinguished Englishman who was known for his progressive politics toward Chinese and blacks, in hopes that he would teach them proper English.[27] The proper use of language and especially the use of proper
castellano (old fashioned term for proper Spanish), Chuffat noted, was of
special value and marked one's social status. The transformative use of a
racially and culturally liminal position in a slave or postslave society is
laid bare in the author's biography. An electoral census in 1907 listed
Chuffat as *mestizo*, a term that was regularly applied to persons of a Chinese and African mixture.[28] The listing indicated his occupation as "interpreter," living in barrio Aduana, in Cienfuegos, in the province of Santa
Clara. The census noted that he could read, write, and had some professional or academic title: *"sabe leer; sabe escribir; poseé título profesional o
académico?"* In his writing, Chuffat identified himself as black and *de
color* (of color). Chuffat spotlighted his efforts and referred to himself in
third person as Cuban, as a person of color, as Antonio Chuffat, and as a
young man, author, and author of a book: He identified himself as *"Antonio Chuffat," "el joven," "el autor," "el autor de este libro;"* and he counted
himself among the *"negros"* and *"jóvenes de color."* Chuffat also foregrounded another Afro-Chinese figure, Manuel Capestany Abreu, by
placing his photograph in the front of the book's visual gallery of the Chinese merchant community. Chuffat noted Capestany's use of excellent
Spanish and his fame as an orator. Capestany was prominent enough to remain recorded today in Cuban encyclopedic biographies as having been a
distinguished Senator of Las Villas. He was also an ardent advocate of the
Chinese, and was the son of a respected Chinese banker who was also
Presidente de la Colonia China in San Juan de los Remedios. The examples of Chuffat and Capestany call attention to the crossing of social
boundaries before and during the Republican era, as Chinese-African descendants became visible and ascendant in Cuba's multiracial context.
Chuffat's inclusion of black men in the photographs of the Chinese of
Cuba—and the occasional mentions of black women (mentioned as freed
slaves or spouses of coolies)—mark the multicolored context of Cuban
history but also point to the porous and transformative nature of diasporic
culture.

   Chuffat revealed that his social and business appointments were made
for specific reasons, such as his language abilities, his being native Cuban,
and his ability to get along with a certain clientele.[29] Chuffat's narrative

implied that his cultural and racial hybridity, in contrast to "purity" (pure Chinese), would be advantageous, as he was both "Chinese" and "native Cuban." In a twist of the common stereotype of Chinese as middleman, Chuffat was the black middleman between the Chinese and well-heeled white Cubans. By virtue of his racial and cultural mixture, he was able to position himself as indispensable to the Chinese whose livelihood depended upon doing business in a multiracial society. Chuffat had a foothold in three realms of cultural identity that overlapped in his work: He functioned as a man of color, as a Cuban, and as a participant in the Chinese community in Cuba. Chuffat had access to those politics through his father but also through another relative. Sketch portraits of two of Chuffat's relatives are included in the book: Antonio Chuffat senior and Agustín Chuffat Lyon. Agustín was possibly Chuffat's half-brother whose mother was named Lyon (while Chuffat's mother's name was Latour). Agustín bore little resemblance to Antonio, was sent to China at one point, and was educated in Europe. Given the history of Chinese merchant societies, it is possible that Antonio Chuffat senior had two "wives" in his lifetime, one being Chuffat's African mother. The other wife might have been *china* (perhaps with the last name Leong, which would be the same pronunciation as "Lyon") who was already married to Chuffat senior before his arrival to Cuba, or was someone he sent for later in his life. Or perhaps she was *cubana*. There is no sufficient evidence to make any exact determinations in these scenarios. Nevertheless, given the photograph of Chuffat, he clearly represented the dark-skinned side of the family. Chuffat was both an insider and outsider vis-a-vis Chinese "community." This liminal position was communicated in his keen observations of color and of the Chinese community as privileged but subject to discrimination—yet also transmitting their own discriminations in various forms. His intimate knowledge and critiques of diasporic politics were exposed in detailed accounts of the Chinese merchant community and of a class of Chinese officials (who arrived in the postcoolie era, as part of the 1876 treaty). Chuffat discussed their capital investments and travels, their interactions with a myriad of non-Chinese social groups, internal conflicts and social spats, family arrangements and gossip, and even the particular dress and cut of prominent individuals' suits. Chuffat elaborated upon their activities with earnest praise and sometimes with dry humor and cutting irony.

The history of his extensive participation in Chinese affairs forms a complement to his life as a black activist. On the one hand, he was educated in a school for black children, represented a black constituency, corresponded with one of the most prominent black activists of the time, and his writing would reveal his preoccupation with slavery's legacy, *los negros,* and their oppression. On the other hand, he knew the Chinese language and held a number of official positions among merchant elites: *Ex-Profesor y Traductor de la Colonia China de la Habana 1885, Ex-Secretario del Consulado Chino de Colon y Jovellanos en 1892, Ex-Secretario de la Unión Comercial China de Cienfuegos 1901, Ex-Inspector de Sanidad, Jubilado, Actual Secretario Traductor del Partido Nacionalista de China "Kuo Min Tang" de Cienfuegos* (translator and teacher of the Havana Chinese community, Secretary of the Chinese consulate for Colón and Jovellanos, Secretary of the Chinese Business Union of Cienfuegos, Inspector of Sanitation of Cienfuegos, and Secretary/Translator of the "Kuo Min Tang" (Guomindang) party of Cienfuegos).[30] His title of secretary in the Partido Nacionalista/KMT signaled participation in transnational and regional politics that went to the heart of Chinese communities, especially during the period of Sun Yet Sen. As Kathleen Lopez, Mauro Triana, Miriam Herrera Jerez, and Mario Castillo Santana have noted extensively, the Chinese in Cuba identified themselves along lines of transnational politics during this period.[31] This took place when Chinese diaspora communities across the world were divided and passionate regarding the possibilities of a Chinese Republic. And Chuffat's participation signaled his footing in diasporic politics of the Chinese merchant society and, moreover, his value as a translator. As a politically active member, translator, and representative of the Chinese community and commercial interests, Chuffat also referred to his visits with the president of Cuba. Chuffat also served as liaison and representative for a range of occasions and travels, including an appointment to the well-established import company "Weng On" (possibly a branch of one of the oldest Chinese transnational firms "Wing On," though it is not clear from Chuffat's Spanish transliterations). The company was frequented by members of the Cuban aristocracy and sent him as a representative to Panama and Costa Rica on their behalf.[32] Chuffat's revelations unfold in a text that included cultural, political, and global and local economic contexts.

As translator and communal historian for the Chinese in Cuba, Chuffat assumed cultural authority and access to a diasporic community that was otherwise dominated by Chinese who did not consider themselves black. Given the transnational politics of cultural capital, and local and legal politics of racial discrimination, the avenue of diasporic identity for the Chinese merchants was their self-identification as "overseas Chinese."[33] A letter from the Chinese Chamber of Commerce, included in Chuffat's book, laid open their cultural and strategic identification as patriotically Cuban; but most of all they identified with the overseas Chinese, whom they thought deserved to be recognized and treated as foreign business persons. Moreover, the cultural authority of Chuffat as an official representative of the Chinese was itself a rare historical occurrence. In the nineteenth and early twentieth centuries, historically public claims of blackness as part of Chinese representation were rare, or perhaps unprecedented. Chuffat was exceptional in terms of his unique position as a biographer of the Chinese during this time; but he was even more exceptional for the subtext on slave/coolie subalterity which he managed to imbed in his text. Chuffat's appointments were contextualized by Cuba's interracial social history, and the eventuality of his importance in the making of Chinese representation is a reflection of Chuffat's self-positioning, cultural capital, and his strategic abilities to travel and "translate" between two social groups.

THE MOTLEY TONGUE: HETEROGENEITY AND HYBRIDITIES

Chuffat's text is motley tongued in its narrative construction and in its portrayal of community as heterogeneous. The text is a hyperhybrid of various genres, and all these aspects formed a dialogic narrative, including Chuffat's excerpts from newpapers of varied political leanings, treaties, legal decrees, folklore, interviews, autobiographical meanderings, diary excerpts, anecdotes, gossip, poems, anecdotes, photographs/portraits, captions, quotations from individuals and other works, and letters, including one in the original Chinese. The text is an unusual unfolding of history as not only heterolingual but also as intimate and public. At moments, Chuffat's history seemed based on the gathering of recollections and communal memories that accrued into an overwhelming task. He would recall one person's biography after another and then, as if out of breath, would say ". . . and there is more that I can't recall" (". . . *y otra mas que no re-cuerdo*").[34] The narrative yielded shifting perspectives such as first person, first person plural, third person, with Chuffat occasionally referring to himself in third person. He featured both Spanish and Chinese language in the book, including one entire letter in Chinese and a poem that he presented in his own transliteration from Chinese into Spanish, followed by his own translation of it. As written and visual text, Chuffat's presentation of heterogeneous history and the heterolingual way of telling it made for an unwieldy narrative.

The heterogeneity of *Apunte histórico* suggests a writing that resisted norms of genre but also suggests multiple readings and interpretations. The seeming ruptures of Chuffat's narration prompt a remarkable opening up of its epistemic possibilities. The inclusion of multimedia materials created "outside" perspectives, *implied* narration, and a dialogic narrative, which often arose from Chuffat's consistent strategy of contradicting his stated views by presenting alternative views by "other" people or by abruptly inserting a newspaper article that opposed his previous statements. The work's intertextuality or intratextuality produced incongruities that offer the most intriguing undercurrent of political views in Chuffat's work. Alongside the field interviews that Chuffat conducted and included is his inclusion of "official" discourses of the law and diplomacy, "verified" newspaper accounts, "published" views and counterpoints of invested Chinese and Cubans, "photographs" of diplomats and community leaders, "interviews" and firsthand accounts, excerpts from a "diary," and reprinted presentations of legality and state in the form of "contracts," "decrees," "treaties." Each written and visual form comprised a discourse of representation that connotes some sort of *epistemic validity and form*. They legitimated, confirmed, contrasted, embellished, or subverted what Chuffat was saying, thus raising questions about what he *appeared to be saying*. The divergent views suggested that behind the veil of diasporic promotion was a multiedged sword of critique. Therefore, it is difficult to characterize this work in terms of form, though for lack of a better term, it could be a called a creative history or a "communal biography," based upon strands or notes of different social groups brought into a grouped narrative. Perhaps due to the text's very unconventionality and its contradictory political messages, Chuffat's work has remained a buried yet repeated footnote.[35]

Chuffat stated in his prologue that his ostensible purpose was to *only* present the good examples, so as to leave the past behind: *"Me propongo por sola finalidad, los buenos ejemplos, borrando de le mente todo el pasado . . ."*[36] His text offered a well-crafted banner of model minority examples: passive, hardworking, loyal, amiable, obedient (Chuffat's terms). Such words complemented those of the Spanish government, which assessed Chinese labor trafficked to Cuba based upon their experience in the Philippines. In a Royal Order in 1847 the Spanish saw the Chinese as essentially docile, industrious, and thus well-suited for importation.[37] Chuffat's homage to the Chinese was also in civilized terms, as a people with rich culture, literature, deities, and a history of centeredness as the Middle Kingdom. At the heart of his introduction was a retracing of the Chinese as the most culturally superior and refined of all humankind yet unprepared for Western modernity and its barbaric colonialism. This was followed by Chuffat's illustrations of the Chinese ability to assimilate and learn from Europeans, with the implication that modernity had arrived for better or worse. Most striking, however, was Chuffat's explicit analysis of the aspirations of the successful Chinese minority. According to Chuffat, these aspirations included an incomparable dedication to assimilation and to imitating European customs: *"Buscaban la asimilación hacia el blanco, con una perseverancia incomparable. Imitaban todo lo bueno de las costumbres Europeas . . . se considera blanco y basta."* In the end, they consider themselves white, he says.[38] From this early statement of Chuffat's, contradictions and doubleness began to appear. The model of Asiatic aspiration to whiteness is directly undercut by Chuffat's explicit views of Chinese being linked to resistance and liberation, not assimilation. When the "Law" does not rectify injustice, he once declared, "some would say they (Chinese) have to rebel."[39] He further castigated liberalism, adding that those who boasted of humanitarian and progressive politics were the same ones lynching and burning black people alive: *"No fueron sólo españoles los que intentaban mantener la esclavitud de los negros, ni que trataran despiadadamente a los esclavos. Hubo otros que fueron peores, que los linchaban y quemaban vivos, para jactarse luego de humanitarios y progresistas"*[40] ("It was not only the Spaniards that attempted to maintain the slavery of blacks, nor the only ones that treated the slaves mercilessly. There were others that were worse, that would lynch them and burn them alive, to later boast themselves as being humanitarian and progressive.") Chuffat's project satisfied the needs of one social set, displaying the outward characteristics of the model minority immigrant narrative, yet was transformed. He adroitly inserted another narrative, one that encompased himself, the coolie, the slave, antislavery, antiracism, social justice, and an ironic view of class ascendance in the wake of the coolie and slave eras. In a unique merging of two genres, the *immigrant-contribution chronicle* and *anti-slavery literature*, an alternative narrative was produced. Chuffat viewed himself an outsider to the metiér of historical writing and also was aware of the uniqueness of his contribution. He described himself as writing with no specific training and emphasized that he wrote with great effort, difficulty, and time. He wrote that it would be impossible for a single book to ever capture the whole "truth" of a people or nation. It would take an extraordinary book of many pages (*"un libro de muchas paginas, extraordinario,"*) and one of abundance and brilliance to tell "the truth" of what has passed.[41]

Chuffat's portrait of *"el chino"* belies any sweeping categorization of an immigrant group and its history, which he depicted along differing lines of struggle and political identity. Chuffat's book brought together subjects for study ostensibly under the premise of national origin, with the Chinese appearing in Chuffat's work as also having migrated and transmigrated from Hong Kong, Macao, Britain, Peru, Mexico, California, and New York. Chuffat included one particularly interesting photograph of a Chinese businessman and author wearing full Mexican garb complete with hat. Chuffat's work revealed that the diverse Chinese population fell on all sides of the charter of emerging nationhood and that they employed a range of strategies that were both resistant and participatory. Chuffat's text revealed a profusion of identity markers applied to Chinese in Cuba, and here are some of his examples:

administrators, Asians, authors, bankers, blacksmiths, brothers, businessmen, gentlemen, captains, carpenters, cart pullers, comics, countrymen, criminals, Cubans, deserters, doctors, editors, the elderly, escapees, financiers, the forgotten, the free, gentlewomen, girls, immigrants, insurgents, insurrectionaries, intermediaries, ladies, laborers, indentured laborers, laborers who completed their contracts, laborers who recontracted, laborers in prisons, mechanics, men, merchants, millionaires, commanding officer, orphans, owners/sellers of contracts,

owners/managers of work gangs, undocumented passengers, patriots,
the rich, runaways, residents, sculptors, secretaries, slaves, soldiers,
statisticians, stevedores, subjects, women, work gangs, workers, coal
workers, writers, vendors.

Chuffat offered a rich mapping of a heterogeneous social history, one that showed a great breadth of color and class and varied political and social positions in the colony. In Chuffat's recounting, the Chinese were present in all areas of Cuban cultural politics and economy, with roles that escape generalized representations of "minority" populations and imply multiplicity in diasporic formation that was made up of both free and unfree Chinese. Chuffat brought to light wide socioeconomic disparity—with "millionaires" on one hand, and "orphans" and "the forgotten" on the other.

Chuffat described Chinese in urban locations, others in rural locations, some in highly concentrated Chinese areas, some in mostly black areas, and others in mainly Chinese and white contexts. His fieldwork included interviews with scores of individuals and visits to various provinces to collect data, including Matanzas, Cienfuegos, Havana, Santa Clara, Camaguey, and Oriente. Chuffat carefully noted that the Chinese were concentrated in Havana (Regla, Casa Blanca, Jaruco, San Julián de Güines, Hoyo Colorado, Guanajay and Batabanó); in Matanzas (Matanzas, Cárdenas, Colón, Jovellanos, Cimarrones, Recreo, Macagua, Unión de Reyes, San José de los Ramos, Limonar, Corral Falso, Calimete and Manguito); in Santa Clara (Sagua la Grande, Quemado de Güines, Corralillo, Sierra Morena, Santo Domingo, Cruces, Lajas, Cienfuegos, Palmira, San Juan de los Remedios, Caibarién, Isabela de Sagua, Cifuentes and Camajuaní). Lesser numbers were present in Camagüey and in Oriente. Chinese labor included those in all sectors of the economy, Chuffat emphasized. He also noted that they were pervasive in the tobacco industry in Havana. There were also carpenters, bricklayers, blacksmiths, carriers, and longshoremen. In Casa Blanca, they loaded and unloaded coal. In Regla, Chinese carpenters and cart pullers worked on boxing and transporting sugar.[42]

Chuffat's writing on the diversity of Chinese social life is most interesting for its portrayals of a *motley tongue*. Chuffat took issue with the common stereotype of Asians as being homogenous, participating in the same causes and thinking the same thing. This was erroneous, he noted, as the

Chinese would often treat each other not as brothers but as foreigners, since China actually consisted of different regions with different dialects. Often some Chinese couldn't even understand one another, as he explained in the following passage:

> *There existed the belief that all Asians were homogenous, supposing them to be participants of one same cause, of only one idea and the same thought. This is an error, because not one Chinese understands another Chinese, when he is of a different region. The Chinese when they did not understand or comprehend each other, then appealed to the means of thousands of signs to accomplish whichever action that they would have the necessity for, from each other. From there developed, the little love that they had for one another, because they did not consider each other to be their fellow countrymen, they were not his brother, and they treated each other as if they were foreigners.*[43]

Chuffat's observations regarded different ethnic dialects of the Hakka and the Cantonese as well as Chinese Cuban pidgin language. Modern linguistic scholarship has addressed the topic of Chinese use of Spanish language in Cuba to varying degrees, including the scholarship of John Lipski, Clancy Clements, Sergio Valdés Bernal, and Beatriz Varela.[44] Chuffat, however, depicted Chinese-Spanish pidgin language as a racial veil employed by Chinese coolie freedom fighters. Previous to Chuffat's representation was Gonzalo de Quesada's paean to the *chinos mambises*, which included brief renditions of their statements, some of which were declarations made famous in pidgin. In a similar vein as de Quesada, but more purposefully drawn, Chuffat's rendering of pidgin as a subversive language is figured alongside his descriptions of strategic language used among coolies and merchants under sociolinguistic regimes. The social stations of the diverse Chinese population were directly linked to a multilingual ability in at least Chinese and Spanish, with some able to speak Chinese, Spanish, English, and sometimes French. Refinement in proper *castellano* and skills in English and French were often presented as cultural capital in a society of transnational trade, commerce, and "modern" postslavery culture. Repeatedly, Chuffat stressed the importance of speaking Spanish with "precision," and that it was looked upon "admirably." To speak perfect Spanish ("*Habla perfectamente el castellano*") and to acquire European languages was a measure of education and social status. At the same time, *pidgin* appeared as a stonewalling tactic. When advantageous or "convenient" for business, merchants would speak Spanish, or they would exclaim "me no speak Spanish" (the rough equivalency of Spanish pidgin to English pidgin): *"Era ocurrentes; cuando les convenía hablaban español, y cuando el negocio no les convenía, exclamaban: 'Mi no sabe jabla español.' De ahí no los sacaba nadie."*[45] The veiling of themselves as nonspeakers of Spanish circumscribed situations when advantageous.

What of those with vastly different relations to power, as in the case of coolies who did not speak Spanish well? Chuffat's renderings of pidgin were empowering representations that appear considerably earlier than pidgin representations in contemporary literatures.[46] Chuffat recounted an anecdote concerning Chinese coal workers who used the Spanish language to assist Cuban rebels, yet they switched to pidgin to stonewall Spanish authorities. Forty-six rebels had approached Chinese laborers who offered enough food to feed them and refused payment.[47] Soon thereafter, one hundred Spanish troops arrived in the area and interrogated the same Chinese about the presence of rebels. Yet the Chinese feigned ignorance with exaggerated pidgin and denied knowledge of any rebel presence. Chuffat's reenactment illustrated strategic use of language in contexts of resistance The passage of pidgin Spanish is provided here for Spanish readers, although it is impossible to provide an equivalent in pidgin English (pidgin in bold):

"Serian las ocho y media de la mañana, cuando se presento por el callejón que venia de Cárdenas, una fuerza de cien hombres de caballería, de la Guardia Civil, al mando de un Comandante; hicieron alto frente a las casa del chino. El Comandante llamo al chino y le pregunto: "Tu chino, no ha pasado alguien anoche por aquí"? "No seno Capitán, pa me no sentí gente pasa." "Tu viste un grupo de insurrectos armados esta mañana que venían de Varadero?" "Yo no mila gente suleto tiene arma por la mañana. No seno, pa mi no sabe, ta trabaja quema carbón." "Tu solo estas aquí en la casa?" "Si seno Capitán, pa hace comida pa mi paisano, otro gente ta trabaja quema carbón." El chino era ladino, engaño hábilmente al Comandante. El Comandante le dijo al Capitán: "Vamonos de aquí: este chino es un estupido, nadie

lo entiende." El Comandante tomo el camino otra vez, que había traído, sin resultado de la investigación que había practicado. Esta vez, le toco al chino engañar al blanco en pleno día, 'como si fuese chino.' Todo un señor Comandante de la Guardia Civil, fue engañado como un chino."[48]

By stubbornly claiming, in pidgin, to know nothing, *"pa mi no sabe,"* Chiong obstructed interrogation and simultaneously seized upon the stereotype of the ignorant slave and coolie. In fact, Chuffat noted, as a general rule, that when Chinese were interrogated by soldiers, they would stonewall in this manner, using pidgin expressions such as, "me no speak Spanish" or *"pa mi no sabe jabla panol."*[49] The perceived inferiority of the coolies and the perceived *impossibility of understanding* play directly into the thickly racialized perceptions between white and nonwhite. Chuffat lauded this exchange in racialized terms, as it meant "gaining an upper hand over the white man in plain day": *"Esta vez, le toco al chino engañar al blanco en pleno día, 'como si fuese chino'."* Not stopping there, Chuffat went on to emphasize that even a commander of the civil guard could be outwitted by a Chinese: *"Todo un señor Comandante de la Guardia Civil, fue engañado como un chino."*[50] In these passages, Chuffat's phrase *fue engañado como un chino* is a play on a common Cuban colloquialism that arose in reference to the Chinese in Cuba and connoted a person who has the ingenuity to "get the better of a situation like a Chinese": *"engañar a uno como a un chino"* or *"los engañaron como a un chino."*[51]

Pidgin emerges here as a racial veil through social mimesis. Chuffat provided a follow-up to this episode in which the Cuban rebels returned to the same site as refuge again. The Chinese communicate again, in perfect Spanish, to the Cuban rebels. In Chuffat's narration, the Chinese employed languages selectively, in concert with cultural perceptions and stereotypes. The extended episode was an example of what is now called "code-switching" in contemporary critical studies of minoritized language. As a non-European minority group, the Chinese were disempowered in a European language system, and as Chuffat noted, were often ridiculed for allegedly being eccentric due to their pidgin speech, causing laughter among the Cubans and Spaniards: *"Escogiendo siempre los lugares adecuados a su carácter dado a lo raro y excéntrico, causando risa a los cubanos y españoles.*"[52] This eccentricity would serve as a foil in the face of overwhelming force; in this case, the overwhelming force was the Spanish military. In examples such as these, the motley tongue operated as a force in racial politics and was more than a cultural curiosity of ethnic localization. De Quesada also depicted pidgin in the context of resistance. The famed Chinese rebel named Juan Anelay, mentioned by Chuffat, was described by de Quesada as denouncing injustice in pidgin, or what might be termed his motley tongue, or *"abigarrado lenguaje."* His lengthy declamations ended with a famously valiant cry in pidgin upon death, when he was captured and lashed to a tree: *"Viva Cuba libe!"*[53] Another source documented the case of a capitán Juan Cuan who, while breathing his last, declared in pidgin that no Spaniard could best a Chinese Cuban rebel (*"Pañol no pue con lo chino cubano insulecto."*)[54] Apparently, some coolies, according to Chuffat, also utilized the stereotype of the impossible-to-understand Chinese to resist compulsory service with the Spanish forces by demonstrating little knowledge of Spanish. The Spanish then decided not to include them.[55] Chuffat remarked that the Chinese hated the Spanish and swore at them, *"Say Kuey,"* which was Cantonese for "damn whitey."[56]

Chuffat's anecdotes on pidgin also illustrate the politics of class and material values. In describing the legendary "Médico Chino," the doctor Cham Bom-Bia who cured many Cubans, Chuffat emphasized the doctor's reputation for willingness to cure those of all colors, rich and poor. Contemporary Cuban folklore invariably includes Cham Bom-Bia as a celebrated Chinese character.[57] According to Chuffat, Cham would tell his patients in pidgin, "If you have money you pay. If you do not have money, I always give medicine to poor people," (*"Si tiene dinelo paga pala mi. Si no tiene no paga, yo siempre le da medicina pa la gente poble."*)[58] Chuffat's quoting of Cham Bom-Bia in pidgin lends a populist characterization to the image of a Chinese doctor.

Language also unfolds in Chuffat's portrayals as the vehicle utilized by one racialized people to protest the treatment of another oppressed group. Chuffat noted a series of verses published by Chinese writers and poets in Cuba who protested black oppression. This series commenced in 1881 and included poems written in Chinese by writers such as "Kan Shi Kon," "Li Chi Son," "Hay Kau Lim." Chuffat transliterated "Kan Shi Kon's" poetry from Cantonese into Spanish. Chuffat's role as translator is enacted but made more striking by his choice of an antislavery poem written in Chinese:

> *Hat Min Gan Ga" (Cara negra, diente de plata) "Toy pok ton un hay yan" (Lo maltratan como si no fuese persona) "Sen mai mon" (Despierta del letargo) "Go sion ni chi yau" (Yo deseo tu libertad) "Yun lin" (Rompe la cadena) "Go sion ni fac tak" (Yo deseo tu felicidad) "Chiok Fi" (Vuela como el parajo) "Shi Chung Chay" (Muera el tirano) "Chan sen pen tan" (Viva la democracia) "Chi yan-Chi yau" (libertad, libertad) "Go shion" (Yo lo anhelo).*[59]

An approximate English translation of the above would read as follows: "Black faces, silver teeth/They mistreat him as if he were not human/ Wake up from lethargy/I desire your freedom/Break your chains/I desire your happiness/Fly like a bird/Down with tyranny/Long live democracy/ Freedom, freedom/I yearn for this."[60] The author became founding editor of the semiweekly Chinese newspaper, the *Voice of the People*, (*La Voz del Pueblo*), which was established in 1882 in Havana. The fashioning of Chinese writing in solidarity with black oppression suggested another meaning of Chinese community. The contributions of Cham Bom-Bia, Kan Shi Kon, and the coolie freedom fighters were struggles for social justice. The language of *immigrant-contribution chronicle* transformed in these cases to actions directly addressing oppression, examples that offer a greater dimension to the capital and material contributions of the immigrant in the Americas. The artfulness of Chuffat's representation is in its manifestly political nature and in the articulation of social differences and solidarities.

The pidgin language of the *chinos mambises*, the populist Chinese doctor, and the radical poetry of the Chinese newspaper editor, stands at odds with what Chuffat represented as the official language of empire. As a creative device, Chuffat imagined the motto of colonial government and presented it as quotation:

> *This was his motto: "If you are Chinese or black, you will have over you the rough burden of slavery; you do not have rights and have many obligations to fulfill. I will maintain you in the most strict and intentional ignorance, so that a shameful submission shall be a given. Under my*

dominion, you will not be a man; you will be an object, a thing of the society in which you live.[61]

In his creative imagining, the "voice" of colonial empire speaks directly to coolie and slave. Declarative and rational in its tone, the voice of empire is in contrast to the dodge and weave of pidgin and the poem of social consciousness. Mongrel language destabilized the clarity of domination.

Naming and renaming were other aspects of language that emerged in Chuffat's narrative. While coolies and slaves were often named after their masters or given Christian names in Spanish, merchants were able to choose their names. Naming and its critical role in the signifying and tracing of cultural formation, is of particular significance in the twists of colonial, multilingual society. The social practice of having two or three names in different (or the same) languages, foregrounded the strategic links of identity and person. This, among other reasons, makes Chuffat's genealogies of even more interest. Chuffat recounted persons having several names, in Chinese, Spanish, English, and in shorthand appellations, with some being known by as many as three names and some by nicknames. Chi Pan was one of the earliest Chinese to establish himself in what became Havana's *barrio chino*, and he was also known as Pedro Pan and as Pedro Pla Tan.[62] Another was Lan Si Ye, also known as Abraham Lan and as Abraham Scull.[63] The multiple identities of "Chi Pan" and "Lan Si Ye" are complicated conventions of naming yet clearly correspond to various avenues of identity construction. Such cross-cultural knowledge and encyclopedic accounting of social standing in Chuffat's narrative provide a wellspring of data for social history and also reveals Chuffat's subject position as translator of hybrid social identities.

Hybrid cultural forms are also depicted in Chuffat's tracing of religious practices. Rites involving homage to color and justice emerge in descriptions of transculturated local celebrations of two principal Chinese gods, Guan Gung (God of War) and Guan Yin (Goddess of Compassion), which Chuffat translated to Spanish as *Kuang Kong* and *Ku Yam*. Both Guan Gung and Guan Yin emerged as principal deities in Chinese diasporic communities worldwide. Local legends about these Chinese gods took on forms of Cuban folklore and reflected coolie history. As Chuffat explained, one local legend of "Ku Yam" (Guan Yin) originated in Caibarién, a coastal city near Santa Clara. A Chinese named "Li Yon" was walking on the beach when he spotted an apparition of a beautiful woman aglow in a silk gown, carrying a basket of jasmine. The image was interpreted as a visitation from Guan Yin who had come to save her enslaved children: "Since they saw her the Chinese believed that the precious image was none other than the goddess of beauty, that had come from China to save her children who suffered the rigor of slavery."[64] The emphasis of this local Cuban legend lay in uplift from slavery. Chuffat brought attention to another local legend featuring "Kuan Kong" (Guan Gung) in a version originating from Cimarrones, Matanzas, the province with the largest numbers of coolies. In fact, Chuffat was the first to record in detail the transculturated practices of "Kuan Kong" in Cuba, referred to in later studies of Cuban religion. Not surprisingly, the coolies worshipped Guan Gong, a figure of great courage, whose deification was based upon a general's heroic deeds in the classical Chinese epic *Romance of the Three Kingdoms,* which took place during the Han dynasty. Known as the Chinese God of War, and in some cases as the patron saint of martial arts, the legend of Guan Gong took on localized meaning. In Chuffat's recollection, the spirit of Guan Gong enters the body of one Chung Si and speaks counsel to the Chinese in Cuba. He counsels the Chinese to share rice with the needy and to treat others fairly. In China the legend of Guan Gong emphasized teachings of honor, courage, justice, and integrity. Guan Gong's counsel in Cuba, however, highlights his views regarding race, as he declares that the Chinese have their gods, as do whites, blacks, Indians, and Malays, but the true God is not white, Chinese, black, Indian, nor Malay, but is an omnipotent God: "*El chino tiene su Dios, el blanco, el negro, indio, malayo, cada cual tiene su Dios. El Dios verdadero no es blanco, chino, negro, indio, ni malayo. Es Dios Todopoderoso.*"[65] The local emphasis on ethnic catholicity bears the mark of the Cuban context and is enfolded in a Chinese folk religion that historically appealed to the masses. According to Chuffat, large-scale fiestas dedicated to "Kuan Kong" took place in Cuba during the month of August. The worship of Guan Gong is now ensconced in the Cuban Yoruba religion today (a religion of African roots), syncretized with the worship of the Spanish-Catholic Santa Bárbara and the African Changó.[66] In Cuban rituals, Guan Gong is known as "Sanfancón," appearing as the diety in red colors and carrying a large Chinese scimitar.

Chuffat's recollections of *Kuang Kong* and *Ku Yam* emphasize the transformative nature of their local manifestations and local legacy of coolie history. Yet Chuffat's elaboration upon Chinese folklore included his noting of its marginalization in Cuban society. In one episode, he notes that a Roman Catholic priest attempted to shut down festivities and rites to Guan Gong, believing this to be pagan practices of the coolie and slave.[67] While Chinese practiced rituals of Guan Gong and Guan Yin, they were coerced into converting to Catholicism. In the 1874 testimonies, coolies expressed resentment toward religious conversion and also indicated that they were required to convert to Catholicism if they were to gain their freedom papers. The master's permission and baptism were also required for any coolie requesting permission to marry. And conversion and baptism were required for residence papers.[68] Furthermore, coolies added that in practice, conversion and getting a "godfather" sponsor still offered no guarantees in getting free and staying free from bondage.

Chuffat also offered a positive example of conversion, as socially advantageous and desirable on moral grounds. This example involved a coolie named Crescencio, also known as "Cencerro," who was baptized and then married "*Cristina de Africa*," referred to as another slave, "*otra esclava*," of their master Don Mariano Gobel. Gobel apparently supported marriages among his slaves as a principle of moral education.[69] The coolie Cencerro became Cencerro Gobel and would eventually rise on the plantation from coolie to *caudrillero*, a manager of coolies.[70] Chuffat also noted that the Chinese were baptized by their masters and would celebrate this with much pomp. From this, he noted, came the extinction of Chinese names, with the exception being those who were not baptized and who preserved their original names: "*Eran bautizados por sus amos, celebrándose los bautizos con gran pompa. De ahí la extinción de los apellidos chinos; salvo excepción de algunos que no eran bautizados, y conservan su nombre primitivo.*"[71] In the colonial languge of civilizing non-Christians, Chuffat suggested that conversion was more beneficial than harmful. Still, through this anecdote, Chuffat pointed to key aspects of the *coolie* and not the *merchant*: the Chinese had masters, lived among slaves, were subject to Christian conversion, but utilized this to raise their status.[72] Chuffat's noting of religion also included reference to mixing between Chinese and indigenous peoples in a village of *semi-indígenas*. Calling these *nativos* ignorant and unbaptized, Chuffat employed racist language. Clearly, Chuffat's antiracism did not include a critical examination of racist attitudes towards indigeneity. Although, in the same breath, he proudly pointed out that Chinese insurrectionaries chose to live there, obviously worked there, and had their children there.[73] Typical of Chuffat's writing are these vexing contradictions that suggest he spoke from multilayered consciousness: He wrote as a *negro-chino* activist, but he also functioned as a sponsored translator/writer for the rising Chinese merchant community, which did not position itself as black, *de color*, or subaltern.

LIBERATION, SOLIDARITY, AND "SOCIO-POLITICAL ADULTERY"

Narratives of emancipation in the Americas have been preserved and most often told on the Atlantic template of white and black, metropole and colony. The Chinese participation in the wars for liberation spanned a remarkably long period of thirty years, with their presence from the very beginning of *la Guerra de los Diez Anos* (Ten Years' War of 1868–1878) through *la Guerra Chiquita* (Little War of 1878–1879) to the end of *la Guerra de Independencia* (War of Independence1895–1898).[74] Some served in all three wars. Culled from the margins are recountings that document and humanize Chinese fighters and reveal their unique characteristics as individuals in the position of being rebels and fugitives in a nonnative land. Other than Gonzalo de Quesada's account, Chuffat's rendering would be among the early elaborations of Chinese as resistant agitators against their oppression and participants in a revolution in the Americas. His account underscored the sustained mobilization of Chinese rebellion on a mass scale. By inscribing the Chinese into a broad representation of insurgent war and its base of enslaved labor, Chuffat preserved what little-known details there are about Asians as vital antislavery agitants in colonial economies of the Western hemisphere. Political history reveals that Cuban independence was a revolution of different agendas and factions, not all necessarily wedded to antislavery or multiracialism.[75] But for the Chinese, the struggle for Cuban liberation was the struggle for freedom from slavery, and their stake in it was on grounds linked to self-emancipation. In 1870 the Cuban rebel government promised liberty to any *chinos* and *negros* who joined the insurrection against Spain.

However, before the 1870 declaration, both coolies and slaves were already escaping the plantations to join in force. Despite the *ranchadores*, ubiquitous manhunters whose job was to capture runaways, *los chinos* responded to the call for insurrection within the first days.[76]

The Chinese, as one Cuban commander put it succinctly, were sacrificed on the front lines and never complained about it.[77] Charged with breaking open the Spanish lines, one can infer Chinese losses to have been extremely high.[78] Chuffat's recounting of Chinese freedom fighters emphasized their pervasiveness. Writing in homage, he pointed out the most memorable leaders in the movement, indicating each person's province, rank, name, and service. Their provinces were not the provinces of China, but were provinces of Cuba:

> ... *entonces suenan los nombres inmortales de los chinos Juan Díaz, en las Villas, y sucesivamente, Francisco Moreno; Comandante Antonio Moreno, que murió heroicamente en el campo de batalla; Juan Anelay que avanzando hacia Oriente con su fuerza, se bate con los bizarros soldados españoles. En Remedios, el chino Crispín Rico en Camaguey el Comandante Sian, estos a las ordenes del General González; Pablo Jiménez, que estaba a las ordenes del gran patriota Coronel Francisco Carrillo; el joven Teniente Tancredo, valiente y atrevido que orgulloso ostentaba sus galones de Teniente del Ejercito Libertador de Cuba; en Camagüey, el Capitán Bartolo Fernández, que ingreso en las filas del insigne General Julio Sanguily, y perteneció a la primera Compañía del Regimiento de Camagüey, Segunda División. En Oriente aparece el Capitán José Tolón con su fuerza, y de cuatro a cinco mil chinos, secundan el movimiento revolucionario. En Trinidad, el Capitán José Bu con gran ahínco prestaba sus servicios, y todos se mostraban siempre fieles a las ordenes del Gran Caudillo Máximo Gómez; de los patriotas Antonio Maceo, Ignacio Agramonte, Julio Sanguily y de los grandes procures de la epopeya . . ."*[79]

This rhythmic incantation calls out combatant names and their feats, with an emphasis upon their coming from every corner of Cuba: "*En Las Villas . . . En las Remedios . . . En Camagüey . . . En Oriente . . . En Trinidad . . .*" Chuffat went on to draw his portraits of the freedom fighters from interviews of Comandante Jesús Crespo, Sargento Crispín Rico,

Capitán Bartolo Fernández, and the journal of Coronel Rosendo García. From these sources, Chuffat retold encounters with Chinese troops in formations of hundreds and thousands. Among many examples, sergeant Crispín Rico described his battalion of four hundred Chinese troops, characterizing them as indentured laborers who were fighting for a Cuban "motherland."[80] Capitán Bartolo Fernández recounted being among five hundred Chinese troops in battle.[81] Fernandez was keen to point out that Chinese forces served across the board, some being brought under legendary generals of Cuban independence, including General Napoleón Arango, General Maximiliano Ramos, General Calixto García.[82] The Captain José Tolón and his forces, along with four to five thousand Chinese, made their critical appearance in Oriente, a pivotal region in the launching of insurrection.[83] The Chinese also served in key roles as leaders and strategists, such as Captain José Bu who was personally entrusted with crucial decisions by the famed General Maximo Gomez.[84] Though scores distinguished themselves as leaders on the battlefield, such as Antonio Moreno, José Tolon, José Bu, Sebastián Sian, among many others, there were countless *mambises chinos* whose names would never be recorded.[85] Records reveal that the Chinese were present at all levels, as soldiers, corporals, sergeants, lieutenants, captains, commanders. Chuffat emphasized their ubiquitous participation, from doing grunt work such as clearing paths with machetes to assuming leadership roles.[86] He noted that there were Chinese captains, majors, and Chinese throughout the Cuban forces: *"En todas las fuerzas cubanas, había chinos capitanes; comandantes, y de todo lo que encierra un ejercito organizado."*[87] Others were active recruiters who risked going into plantations to recruit coolies and slaves into rebel forces, such as one captain Francisco Moreno.[88]

Chuffat reserved his use of the inclusive "we" and "us" to refer to those who, in his view, belonged to the Cuban nation. The Cubans included himself, the slaves, the coolies, revolutionary soldiers, and those who worked in favor of ending slavery and advancing Cuban independence. Those who contributed to the "cause" were also Chinese merchants—who, as Chuffat noted, contributed capital and engaged in passive subversive acts—and Chinese intellectuals who were antislavery supporters in Cuba. These were the "peaceful" Chinese "who worked for the independence cause."[89] This diverse Chinese population included subversive free Chinese and militant

Chinese, who converged upon anticolonial agitation. However, Chuffat offered unique observations concerning the divergence of class and race after liberation. First, he elaborated upon the realities of coolie life. In his veiled narrative, the divide of race and privilege emerges, and identity appears formulated along lines of struggle. Chuffat portrayed the coolie struggle as being more closely linked to the slaves' plight than that of their Chinese cousins, the merchants. Refrains of joined struggle in bondage appeared frequently in Chuffat's phraseology of *"chinos y negros"* and *"los negros y chinos esclavos."* As a body politic, he indicated that the coolies followed a different path than that of their free Chinese counterparts. The coolies had outwardly become *cimarrones* (runaways) and *mambíses* (freedom fighters) in a national struggle that they also claimed for themselves, which, in this context, would be the coolie paradigms of diasporic ethnicity. The coolie emerges as a contrary cultural figure compared to ethnic images of immigrant culture predicated upon business, societal and familial institutions, and social advancement. In grim terms, Chuffat described the living conditions of *los chinos* in *los barracones*, bleak structures that imprisoned the slaves and coolies, sometimes using shackles and stocks, with no light or ventilation.[90] Chuffat described the great *barracón*, rising up majestically like a dark, filthy, and unsanitary prison, where the Chinese slept like "convicts." In the center of the barracks were the stocks, where those who were being punished would sleep with their feet shackled. In the morning, the foreman would beat them twenty-four times while the rest of the slaves were awoken with eighteen rings of bells. The *barracón*, he went on, was a horrible cavern that stood for the vengeance and barbarity of the colonial government. Chuffat asserted that the coolie system was, in reality, slavery with all its features: *"en realidad era una esclavitud simulada con todo el rigor."*[91] Chuffat also noted that after coolies completed their initial eight-year contracts, they were forced to recontract again, or they were pressed into forced labor in public works.[92] Chuffat's narrative of coolie life included disconcerting observations of collective action, such as a haunting incident in which fourteen coolies committed joint suicide on one night on the plantation *"Dos Marias."*[93] The struggle of coolie life contrasted with his descriptions of Chinese merchant society of *"nobleza,"* *"gran importancia,"* *"de gran prestigio en las sociedad cubana."* The immigrant culture of social representation was a sharp contrast to the life of bondage for the coolies.

With passionate exclamations throughout his book, Chuffat described how *"chinos"* and *"negros"* resisted by becoming runaways. Chinese runaways, *chinos cimarrones*, were part of Chuffat's larger picture of Chinese whom he described as being trapped in slavery, in a "circle of iron." With pronounced disgust, Chuffat described slave catching and slave catchers, or *ranchadores*, to be one of slavery's "fascinating truths."[94] He described slave catchers as "ex-convicts" who were "coarse," "delinquent," "insolent," and "vulgar." Futhermore, he added, these men were "instruments of and weapons of the government."[95] In the eyes of these manhunters, a black person was regarded as nothing, but a Chinese was regarded as even less: *"Para los ranchadores un negro era nadie; un chino menos."*[96] Chuffat's denunciation of slave catching emphasized the systemic nature of slavery and its empowerment of lower-class Cubans over the Chinese and blacks. He described their struggle to throw off the "enormous yoke" and "chains" of their bondage.[97] On one hand, Chuffat earlier reiterated the constructed image of coolies as promoted by labor agents: obedient workers and models of virtue on the sugar plantations.[98] On the other hand, Chuffat recounted their disobedience, contrariness, and unhesistant acts toward self-liberation. Chuffat's double-language reflected the doubleness of the Chinese as *figured* and the Chinese as *lived*.

Chuffat also depicted distinct experiences of the coolies in comparision to the merchants. The coolies struggled as resistant rebels, whereas the merchants strategized as model minorities, though neither path could provide exclusive strategies for survival. In between those paths lay Chuffat's diverse portrait of Chinese, Africans, creoles and Europeans in shifting states of power and lack thereof: Some of the creoles and Europeans were friends of colored Cubans; some of them were rich and others were not. They appeared in relation to *negros y chinos* as shared allies or enemies, such as one "Marques de San Miguel" who, according to Chuffat, opposed the liberty of the Chinese and was an enemy of blacks and Chinese alike.[99] In Chuffat's narration of Chinese social history, blackness was a constant presence—intersectional, comparative, syncretic, and antipathetic. After independence, Chuffat pointed out the disparities between *los negros* and *los chinos*, which would widen as Chinese merchant society rose and black society endured oppression after liberation. Although Chuffat celebrated the conjoinment of *los negros* and *los chinos* as a cultural politic of solidarities, he chronicled the ensuing divisions of class and race. His portrait of coolies and slaves could lend itself to liberation romanticism; but Chuffat's narratives are punctured by an equally realist portrait of the divisive power of capital and the designs of race once independence was achieved. He emphasized the debilitating effects of racism and its endemic effects that continued *after* slavery. Comparing the fate of blacks and Chinese, he offered an acerbic analogy of Spain as a matron having left a legacy in the Americas of children from two fathers, the result being "socio-political adultery": *"A España le pasó en América particularmente en Cuba, como augusta matrona con hijos de diferentes padres. De ahí, el adulterio social politico."*

Immediately preceding (and following) accounts of Chinese merchant society, Chuffat would often insert commentary on society's underprivileged classes. Sometimes Chuffat would juxtapose the privilege of new Chinese with the poverty of the black people. He pointed out the following: the prohibition of blacks from public parks, jobs, and schools. Chuffat's analogy of "adultery" and his account of continued racism toward Afro-Cubans emphasized the betrayal of blacks and mulattoes despite revolutionary ideals (or despite what historian Aline Helig has called "the myth of racial equality" in Cuba's postabolition history).[100] While blacks were barred from getting their education, he asserted that Chinese were mathematicians and merchants prepared by China. They were versed in reading, writing, numbers, and moreover, the Chinese in Cuba had access to social advancement, were treated better than the native Cubans, and given favored status. He emphasized that they were allowed to frequent public establishments and ride in the first car of the railway.[101] Although benefits of liberation reached others, he wrote, black Cubans' conditions remained poor, and they were, figuratively, still in stocks and shackles. Furthermore, he claimed blacks were being taught not to succeed, since success would mimic the "pretensions" of the Chinese. Chuffat had commented on how many times blacks had been told not to aspire to the pretensions of the Chinese: *"Cúantas veces se decía al negro, 'no aspira, no tiene pretensiones como el chino.' "*[102] Chuffat's recounting (and his palpable resentment) suggests the disturbing casting of Chinese as intrusive interlopers and as a competitive minority.[103] However, Chuffat ultimately points to the systemic cause of inequity. Rather than blame new immigrants, he emphasizes the role of colonialism's legacy and the failure to provide education: *"Como las iba a tener, si el Gobierno Colonial los mantenía para sus fines en las mas estricta ignorancia?*"[104] Throughout his work, Chuffat emphasized that systemic racism and engendered ignorance led to black oppression. Even on the subject of the independence wars, Chuffat's resentment is evident in his remarks regarding the pattern of white command over black troops.[105] He further noted that those blacks who served the Spanish side suffered ill-treatment and mockery.[106]

COOLIES AND CALIFORNIANS

While the freedom fighters undertook the ultimate sacrifices for independence, 1898 would mark the end of one era but the beginning of another, that being American occupation of Cuba. The next century would bring other struggles for the Chinese of Cuba, with their rise and fall in fortunes contingent upon immigration laws, transnational ties, world wars and revolutions, strategic alliances, and later, sweeping changes of the Castro era.[107] Chuffat stressed that blacks remained in poverty, coolies were forgotten, *chinos mambíses* were unrewarded, and later, Chinese merchants were forced to justify their presence amidst discriminatory immigration laws that were being enforced anew in 1926, despite their apparent social gains. By the time of Chuffat's writing there were some 35,000 Chinese in Cuba. A 1926 law was passed that directly descended from a 1902 American military order to exclude Chinese, similar to laws already in effect in the United States. Appended to Chuffat's history was a letter from the Chinese Chamber of Commerce addressed to the president of Cuba. The letter protested the 1926 immigration restrictions, which were being renewed via "*Decreto* 570." The situatedness and security of these rising minority merchants became vulnerable to the ever-changing environment of transnational politics, nationalism, and the labyrinth of a creolized yet racially segmented economy. Besides nationalist rationales for an exclusion policy regarding the Chinese, the Cuban case was also an example of transnational legal policy. Although the episteme "transnational" in studies of immigration often focuses on the politics between so-called receiving and originating countries, such as Cuba and China, this instance involved countries bound by regional and global politics: Cuba, United States, and China. Cuba's pre-1959 immigration policies directly related to preferences and investments of the United States. Therefore, the subject of Chinese diaspora as it relates to Cuba is directly linked to

American empire. During the American occupation of Cuba, Chinese immigration was first restricted under American Military Order 155 of 1902, which was specifically directed at the Chinese and would lead to a series of laws in Cuba addressing Chinese exclusion. The same year of 1902 saw the renewal of the Chinese Exclusion Act in the United States (originally passed in 1882). As part of the American intervention in Cuban civil and foreign affairs, which was institutionalized via the Platt Amendment, the Chinese were restricted under policies that were subsequently adopted by the Cuban government. Nevertheless, while there was a decline in Chinese immigration to the United States and to Cuba under the exclusion policies, new Chinese, mainly from China, the United States, and Mexico, still managed to enter Cuba.[108] Cuban scholars point to a rise in illegal immigration as being a result of the exclusion acts and immigration through uneven application.[109] The exclusion regulations had made exceptions for those of certain status to enter, such as merchants, diplomats, and students. Moreover, during World War I, labor was needed in the Cuban republic—and once again, Chinese labor was brought in. Thus, the exclusion of the Chinese was never wholly or uniformly applied. However, after World War I, the declining economy, exacerbated by the oncoming Great Depression, led to renewed focus on immigration, with particular focus on the Chinese. The collapse of Cuba's sugar market also contributed to that country's decline as a desirable immigrant destination. Cuban immigration reports indicated that from 1929–1934, total immigration fell by 83 percent compared to the preceding four years 1924–1928.[110] In regard to the Chinese, the Cuban government retrenched its 1902 restrictions with the aforementioned law passed in 1926, declaring that its original intentions had been subjected to "twisted interpretations leading to an abnormal situation that needed urgent attention."[111] The new decree of April 1926 reasserted the original terms and enhanced them with greater supervisory and regulatory measures. Among other things, certificates of residence for the Chinese would be limited to a maximum period of twenty-four months.

The use of exclusion against the Chinese in Cuba was not an aberration in the history of immigration. Before 1926, immigration laws of exclusion against the Chinese had already been implemented in the United States, Canada, and Australia. Exclusionary tactics against Chinese (including discriminatory entry taxes, denial of residency permits, and barriers against naturalization) were in force in New Zealand, and violent expulsion was utilized in Mexico. The rush to complete the book and respond to the decree of 1926 is palpable in the last chapters of Chuffat's book, with its abrupt style, untidy writing, and hasty tone.[112] A response by the Chinese Cuban representative bodies (*"La Cámara de Comercio China de Cuba"*) and the Association of the Chinese Colony of Cuba (*"Asociación de la Colonia China de Cuba"*) added an outwardly political mission to Chuffat's publication. Their letter, presented in Chuffat's text, argued for better treatment of Chinese under immigration law and rested its argument on a bi-fold representation of a transnational "community." The letter traced a direct lineage from Cuban independence to transnational privilege—from the freedom fighter to the merchant—presenting a linked diptych of social segments, yet the letter made no mention of coolie labor or its significance.[113] The response from the Chinese offered a glimpse into the strategies of a minority that was racialized as Others.

The letter explained that Chinese merchants were a passive, nonviolent community who contributed to society without political interests or political ambitions. Infused with declarations of loyalty to Cuba, the letter invoked Cuban patriots Jose Martí and his colleague Gonzalo de Quesada. Martí had written at length about American racism against Chinese in New York and San Francisco, and he also condemned the coolie regulations in Cuba as those of patent slavery, exclaiming: *"Que iba de él a la esclavitud?"*[114] De Quesada wrote about the Chinese *mambíses* and their sacrifices in his essay "Los chinos y la revolucion cubana."[115] By invoking Martí and de Quesada, the letter offered a portrait, albeit a bifurcated one, of the Chinese as squarely within the tradition of Cuban patriotism. On one hand were the Chinese rebels. On the other were merchants who differentiated themselves as "model, peaceful residents." Such a figuring operated complementarily. The portrayal emphasized both groups as substantiating loyalty in different ways. There was the insurgent on one hand, the apolitical merchant on the other. The claiming (yet "Othering") of the freedom fighter, and the careful differentiating between *those* Chinese and *these* Chinese, was an implicit division of social class and political culture, with *those* Chinese being a history of liberation, and *these* Chinese being the culture of capital and social representation. The Chinese, simultaneously domestic and foreign, contextualized in a transnational space, framed their arguments along lines of difference. Their arguments revealed that the commercial associations pragmatically capitalized on their standing as transnationals from a *different* socioeconomic class than the freedom fighter. The merchants appealed for consideration as foreign transnationals in business. Their arguments, substantiating a history of patriotism, loyalty, and social contributions, required an inclusion of the freedom fighter. However, their arguments concerning contemporaneous legal status and societal value also required a departure from domestic politics, and instead, they needed an emphasis on their standing as transnational foreigners who occupied a vital economic role. An argument was made for "special consideration to the Chinese merchants, with the same rights and perogatives as other foreign merchants established in Cuba, of all other countries."[116]

No mention was made of the coolies as being the first Chinese in Cuba, a mass migration that dwarfed the subsequent migration. No mention was made of the coolies' contributions to the Cuban economy. Memories of coolie exploitation and violent resistance were repressed in favor of the more savory legends associated with freedom. Yet, according to the 1899 census, only 13 percent of the Chinese were identified as merchants, while 73 percent remained day laborers and servants.[117] Chuffat dissected the rise of the new Chinese by noting that after the Ten Years' War of 1868–1878, their social ascension was accomplished by foreign influx, *extranjeros*. By 1874 there were already more Chinese immigrants in Cuba than in the state of California.[118] And by the turn of the century, five thousand Chinese would arrive in Cuba from California.[119] One cannot help but register the irony of their departure from exclusionary politics in the United States and their arrival to what eventually became exclusionary politics in Cuba. The rise of a free Chinese class was deemed possible and undesirable decades earlier, when parties in Cuba desired to "prevent them from constituting an independent race or class in the Island."[120] Ramon de la Sagra and his commission of 1866–1867 examined the "Chinese Question" and their rising numbers. And in the committee's conclusions pertaining to Spain, they indicated their desires to safeguard a white Cuba and make sure the Chinese presence would be transitory and not excessive or permanent. Emphasized above all, was that any additional influx of blacks would be undesirable. In their considerations they noted the disruptions caused by an abundance of Chinese in California and the Philippines.[121]

Having already experienced both the welcoming potentials and harsh realities of a "host" society, these *californianos* would have arrived in Cuba with an awareness of their precarious positions. With the cumulative legal and social barriers erected against them in the United States, the *californianos* looked to Cuba for new possibilities. From the viewpoint of social history, in a sense, this aspect of Cuban history was also an aspect of California history, and vice versa. As Cuban anthropologist José Baltar Rodriguez has pointed out, the *californianos* and their descendants would reshape Chinese presence in Cuba to one of social standing and influence, creating a new hierarchy.[122] Their societies were constructed around business property, landowning, and investment; they thrived upon activities involving labor management, imported goods, trade, relations of financial interest, transnational identity, and familial ties. Chinese cultural capital, representing and signifying transnational connectedness, was essential to their survival and profitable to their businesses. In 1866–1867 the first Chinese merchants, or *los primeros comerciantes*, appeared, and the first Chinese association was formed, called "Kit Yi Tong." The year 1870 heralded the first bankers and merchants arriving from San Francisco.[123] The "*primeros chinos comerciantes de San Francisco de California, de los Estados Unidos de América*" spilled over the pages of Chuffat's recounting.[124] Coolies, however, were marginal in the politics of social representation. Within merchant society were dozens of ethnic and clan societies—key organizing systems in Chinese diasporas. Chuffat described only one association as embracing both free and unfree Chinese: the "Hen Yi Tong" (*Los Hermanos*).[125] According to Chuffat, this society defined its goal as a brotherhood for both "slaves and free."[126] Given Chuffat's political commitment to coolies and slaves, this is the only brotherhood society that he indicated as explicitly incorporating unfree peoples.

With the new influx of American capital also came transplanted cultural practices and social patterns, including rivalries between groups of Chinese New Yorkers and Chinese Californians. The transmigrated rivalry was displayed as a "mutual hatred," with a rivalry in trade between Hong Kong and North America. Their rivalry and different dialects led Chuffat to humorously suggest that speaking to one about the other was like a Russian speaking to a Chinese about a Spaniard.[127] The new immigrants also established an array of institutions that formed a thriving cultural society. Those societies of the 1870s established banks, newspapers, import companies, business associations, and cultural institutions such as theaters. The first theater was established in 1873 by four Chinese from San Francisco and featured opera. Other theater openings followed, with actors arriving from San Francisco in 1875, giving nightly performances and Sunday matinees. Another theater in Cienfuegos was described as having a Chinese orchestra.[128] Chuffat described widely popular organized festivals and parades in different parts of Cuba, some lasting days at a time and enhancing the status of the wealthy Chinese underwriting the costs. Years after Chuffat's notations, these festivals would take on new forms as part of a Cuban carnival, with elaborate segments sponsored by Chinese communities and with Chinese musical instruments, such as the Chinese cornet, which has since become integral to Cuban music today.[129] Chuffat also noted that a Chinese cemetery was established. Thus, the Chinese carved a place for themselves in public space and elevated their social standing to one fortified by visible and lasting cultural institutions.

Chuffat's use of humor made for subversive asides that underscored the particularities of class politics. He named the millionaires, wealthy merchants, opulent contractors, landowners, business firms, and families. Chuffat's use of florid praise seemed not unusual given the customs of class and patronage, yet its voluminous repetition was combined with exaggeration and social commentary. Chuffat described the new Chinese as cultivated, multilingual, rich, and opulent. Referring to them as distinguished gentlemen, Chuffat provided details on the merchant class with formulaic consistency—names, education, family lineage, marriage and children, business establishment, amount of capital. It seemed as if no one was left out in Chuffat's accounting. He dwelled upon their social events with respectful language and interest, yet also noted their self-important habits characterized by pomp and circumstance, or *"excesiva pompa."*[130] He admired their acumen and success, yet he poked fun at their spendthrift relatives, using English to impart wry connotations. He noted the brother of a wealthy Chinese American who descended from a powerful family in San Francisco. Upon arriving in Cuba, the brother quickly spent five thousand American dollars and was, as Chuffat described, a social butterfly, party man, and a "true Gentleman" and "Sportsman."[131] Sarcastic humor was most palpable in a recounting of the first Chinese chamber of commerce, or *La Càmara de Comercio China*. Chuffat acknowledged the coalescence of a business class and its institutions, yet also poked fun at social politics. As Chuffat recounted, the chamber undertook a scheme for all middlemen to fix uniform rates on imported goods. The result was, as Chuffat dryly noted, everybody undercut each other mercilessly. Chuffat's anecdote included dialogue that took place with all the formal solemnity and foreswearing of a court case, with members swearing by various gods to never break their promises. The language included swearing before the God of Heaven, the God of Hell, to the day of death, and there was swearing to uphold the truth or have one's head cut off. Yet Chuffat notes that those who were foreswearing were the worst offenders. As an aside, he tells of association member Che Kin Chun's laughable rationalization that it was possible to make duplicitous oaths and escape consequences because Chinese demons were afraid of crossing the water. And as Chun pointed out, it (Cuba) was very far. Chuffat's deadpan response was as follows: "You're right, it is very far," or "*Tenía razón Che Kin Chun; es muy lejos.*" Chuffat's punchline, a play on a Cuban colloquialism associated with the Chinese, is only made more humorous by his dryly noting that the organization closed the same year it opened.

Chuffat's knowledge of affairs both private and public extended to his chronicles of business. With language radically different than that used to describe coolie life, Chuffat provided an unsparing measure of merchant life through capital investments, revealing private transactions with figures such as $6,000 in American gold, and $5,000, $10,000, $50,000 in pesos: "*con un capital de sesenta mil pesos oro Americano . . . con un capital de cincuenta mil pesos . . . con un capital de diez mil pesos . . . con up capital de cinco mil pesos.*"[132] Chuffat recorded dealings in the tens of thousands of pesos and even a million: "*con un capital de ochenta mil pesos . . . con un capital de un millón de peso.*"[133] Chuffat revealed the importance and extent of capital in a growing minority group that created social ties through transnational commercial networks and entrepreneurial activity. He recorded business activities and establishments of partnerships and firms, including the establishment of grand transnational firms such as "Weng On" and "Lam y Compañía," with the latter's main branch in Hong Kong. Lam y Compañía was Chuffat's first employer, headed by Sr. Tung Kong Lam who came to Havana via the United States, where he apparently studied business.[134] The Chinese who arrived via the United States emerged as a socially mobile segment in Cuba; they represented themselves not as manual laborers but as merchants with the means to relocate and invest.[135]

The ex-coolies participated in this new social venture and growth in cultural community. They pioneered this next wave by becoming street peddlers or *vendedores ambulantes*. One American had observed the following: "Here he is now, a regular thorough going 'John Chinaman,' who, after having served out his term as a coolie on perhaps some large estate, has become imbued with the ambitious desire of becoming a merchant . . . with a bamboo yoke carried over his shoulders, and pendant from the ends of which hang two large round baskets filled with crockery of all kinds. Clad in thin wide pantaloons, a blue dungaree shirt, with a broad palm-leaf hat on his head, and his feet thrust into loose heelless slippers, he perambulates the streets, seeking to tempt the cautious housewife into purchasing something from him . . ."[136] In 1858 three Chinese appeared to be the first to attempt entrepreneurial activity beyond street peddling: One opened a small eatery, another opened a fruit stand, and a third opened a grocery.[137] However, the coolie entrepreneurial activity of opening vegetable and fruit stands and small eateries (*"pequena casa de comidas"*) was of a different scale than the commercial firms and banks of new immigrants who entered under different conditions, with savings and transnational ties. The bamboo yoke of small entrepreneurial activity represented a chasm of difference from the more privileged establishment of bank partnerships and import companies. Studies show that most ex-coolies were hardly well-off financially; they were, in fact, found working in the plantations, in areas of manual labor, domestic service, railways, docks.[138] Many ex-coolies barely subsisted, and the sight of Chinese beggars on the streets (some being blind) was becoming common.[139] Some were observed as homeless, living in caves in Matanzas.[140] Some were observed as being social pariahs because of leprosy, and others were observed as workers and indigents at railways.[141] In a mapping of a new free society, the notion of a formerly unfree labor class rising to socioeconomic success is, in this case, an assumption borne by the lack of differentiation among distinct social groups. Once categorized as runaways, criminals, murderers, and rebels, the coolies arose from a different social history than those from diasporic "societies of representation."

The mapping of a social history, however, is admittedly made simplistic by a binary dissection of diaspora into merchants and coolies. The ex-coolies and merchants negotiated between themselves in the formation of work gangs. The decades-long transition to post-Spanish Cuba opened an unprecedented window for Chinese entrepreneurship in the labor market. This opportunity contributed to the making of a monied class of Chinese brokers who immersed themselves in the labor economy as managers of coolies. Free Chinese stepped in to harness and resell coolie labor to the sugar mills, or *ingenios*, and former coolies also became foremen and managers themselves. This pattern coincided with the increased need of *ingenios* to find reliable sources of labor. This need prompted the rise of the Chinese *contratistas* (contractors) and the *caudrilleros* (labor bosses). The Chinese middleman, often stereotyped as either the broker of trading goods and commodities or the cultural comprador, emerged as the new boss for coolies. By buying soon-to-expire contracts and hiring out coolies from work gangs, back to the *ingenios* (sugar mills) and plantations, the Chinese contractor formed another segment of the political and cultural economy. The new intraethnic structure for renting out labor and for management of workers resulted in profits that took the Chinese into new social roles. Chuffat was the first to bring the Chinese *cuadrillas* (work gangs) into historicized context when he described their initial formation and then their proliferation in the Cuban landscape. The social hostility of free Cuban society also made work gangs the viable option from the perspective of coolies. In free society, coolies were commonly beaten, stoned, or captured and rebonded by police who conscripted them to public works or rented them out as labor.[142] Coolies were consigned to or joined work gangs, as a place of refuge from the law and an alternative to the violence of free life. It could also be said that this type of labor ownership may have improved life for coolies and ex-coolies, as it opened possibilities for negotiation of group labor power. However, that negotiation was contextualized by the degree of leverage and coercion. The 1874 testimonies included accounts by Chinese in work gangs who told of their vulnerabilities: They suffered owners who refused to pay, intragroup disputes with managers, and the collusion of police who arrested and resold them. The coolies emerged from an oppressive culture of slavery and high mortality, and they were destitute (and often physically impaired) and disadvantaged in terms of social capital compared to their free kinsmen. The colonial government cracked down on Chinese work gangs and banned them in 1871. In the 1880s, however, when slavery was abolished, the work gangs appear to have at least temporarily flourished with government cooperation, for which Chuffat provides a lengthy list of the organizers.[143]

Chuffat notes that his wealthy relative Agustín Chuffat and Agustín's associates organized a society to form the first Chinese work gangs, beginning in the province of Cienfuegos. The first work gang was formed in November 1870 in Macagua, at the *Ingenio "Sociedad."*[144] Chuffat described the hierarchy as consisting of contracted Chinese laborers (*chinos contratados*) and their foremen (*caudrilleros*) on the bottom, then above them were the labor bosses (*caudilleros*). The most privileged social actors, in Chuffat's account, were the contractors (*contratista*), merchants (*comerciantes*), and bankers (*banqueros*), all of whom made up a social circle of local ownership and local officials at the top of the social hierarchy. The 1880s marked the rise of the Chinese landowners and immigrants ("*los chinos hacendados y colonos*"),[145] the contractors ("*los chinos contratistas*"),[146] the merchants and agriculturalists ("*los chinos comerciantes y agricultures*"),[147] and the import firms ("*las casas importadores*").[148] The rise of a series of Chinese contractors on the sugar mills, or "*una serie de Contratistas Chinos en los Ingenios*," also contributed to the acquiring of property, and some became landowners, or *hacendados*.[149] Alonso Solis was a successful contractor who became a rich landowner. In 1879 he became the first Chinese to purchase a plantation and later went on to accumulate even more land. Early on he made the profitable decision to incorporate modernized machinery. Thus began his ascent as the most influential Chinese landowner in Cuba.[150]

Chuffat illuminated this rise of the Chinese through ethnic labor management. But he also highlighted opium selling, an aspect of intraethnic exploitation that emerges through his veiled presenting of "other" people's opinions. The narrative displacement, though not quite ventriloquism, subverted any pretense of neutral observations. Chuffat described the opium trade as a lucrative and significant business—wholesale and retail by Chinese merchants—that exploited labor. This included opium and the utensils for its use.[151] The opium was then sold to coolies by *caudrilleros* and *contratistas*. The selling of opium by labor management to coolies manifested a kind of racial wage, as opium use was pushed to Chinese laborers specifically. Chuffat's inclusion of these details is noteworthy, given Chuffat's role as community translator (given that opium use was not well regarded). He further praised those who were not involved in opium, such as the Hakka, whom he characterized as not liking opium orgambling, and further described them as being men of integrity: "*El Ja Ka, no le gustaba el opio, ni el juego, eran hombres íntegros.*"[152] In the preface of the book, Chuffat had reminded his readers that opium had already been exploitively traded in China.[153] It is not difficult to discern this theme of exploitation in his later mentions of opium being sold on a grand scale to coolies in Cuba. He noted several plantations and owners that practiced the opium trade, such as the plantations of *Santa Isabel* de Carlos la Rosa, *Nena* de Araujo, and *Santa Maria* de Carrillo. He went on to name Chinese firms that were involved in the selling.[154] In a recounting of opium selling, Chuffat's own critique of opium emerged in a quotation of a friend he "admired," José Yu Ki, an American-born Chinese from San Francisco who became a wealthy financier in Cuba. Yu Ki apparently remarked that the English maintained ignorance among the Malays with opium, and similarly, the Spanish controlled the blacks with drums: "*Los ingleses mantienen en la ignorancia a los malayos, con el opio, y los espanoles a los negros con los tambores.*"[155] The general import of his comment, which obviously referred to parallel racial exploitations, was a measure of Chuffat's own veiled criticism.

Still, merchant society is itself revealed as also disparate in social standing and as still vulnerable to discriminations and disparities, which were highlighted by Chuffat's anecdotal devices. In one anecdote, Chuffat recalled a wealthy woman of Cuban aristocracy, a Sra. Dona Matilde de León de Marín, whom he described as educated and refined. Knowing the idiosyncratic value of porcelains from China and Japan, she acquired a priceless piece of chinaware at little cost from Chinese clerks who were ignorant of the value of their own goods.[156] Satisfied with the bargain, she told Chuffat that she had never seen such a plate in Paris or London. While told in a humorous manner, the seemingly harmless charm of aristocratic pastimes becomes tarnished with the subtext of coloniality and the hierarchic construction of "value." In that process, Chuffat positioned himself as being the intermediary of this transaction. Chuffat took part in the humor; but at the same time, Chuffat the author undermined that very humor by his framing of the episode. In other instances, Chuffat pointed out the vulnerabilities of the Chinese merchants in terms of ethnically segmented markets, with Chinese investing in other Chinese—some surviving and others being demolished. As landowners paid Chinese contractors on credit or with promissory notes, and as Chinese contractors paid Chinese storekeepers by the same means, the storekeepers were particularly vulnerable when the sugar market experienced downturns and the economy was disrupted by the independence wars. Commercial losses were irretrievable for Chinese stores, banks, and businesses in an economic chain directly dependent upon the sugar mills and ethnic coinvestments. Chuffat marked 1885 as a "financially disastrous" and "funereal year" for the Chinese.[157] The death of a famed chino, "el Médico Botánico," and his subsequent public funeral would mark the ill-fated tone of the year. Other enterprising merchants would be wiped out due to wars and natural disaster. One such unfortunate merchant was Sr. Lamier (Atak), who settled with wife and family and then lost everything during the independence war. Two very successful businessmen, Su Weng and Choy Sang, owned and ran several businesses only to be ruined by the war.[158] Some would lose everything in the hurricane of 1888 that destroyed vast areas of western Cuba.[159] Chen Chi Jo was one of these unfortunate hurricane victims (and was also a consular agent for Chinese affairs) who then returned to New York and died in misery.[160] Other merchants perished in the disaster, such as one Señor Revuelta and his entire family, and there were others who would go unidentified.[161]

Chuffat's study of Chinese merchant society, interestingly enough, included free Chinese women in his communal biography, however sporadically. His slim glimpses indicated a certain social agency of these women. From 1861 to the 1920s, Chinese women comprised a very scarce 0.17 percent to 0.45 percent of the Chinese population, only jumping to 2.76 percent in the 1920s (reaching a high of 4.09 percent in the 1950s).[162] Chinese women appeared in Chuffat's text as part of the merchant community, whereas black women appeared in relation to coolie marriages and in the context of slavery. Successful merchants were described as being heads of families and as joining the institution of marriage in particular ways, being married to either "*cubana*" or "*china*" women, and as having their children well educated in Cuba or Europe. Women were mentioned with an elaboration of their standing in society, implying the prestige they brought to their husbands. Chuffat hardly mentioned women in the main body of his text. However, his appendix of photographs and captions was revealing. As visual biography, this segment suggested the importance of women in the building of a new merchant society and a free diasporic class. Women, few as they were, appeared prominently in nine photographs with their husbands and children. And two of the women stand alone. Their visual presence was indicative of their primary importance as symbols of class privilege, via the institution of heterosexual marriage, familial lineage, children, and property. The new Chinese who had accumulated enough capital were able to bring over their families from the United States or bring their wives from China, though some married fair-skinned *cubana* women. Captions for each photograph contained details emphasizing their education and social prestige. These captions were often written in a descriptive style that was extremely respectful, such as the one regarding "Señora Doña Hortensia Chang," the spouse of a merchant. Sra. Chang was described as a distinguished, illustrious woman who descended from an aristocratic family in China. She came to Cuba at a very young age, and studied and spoke "admirable" Spanish.[163] Given the historical context, this kind of biography raises questions. What distinguished, aristocratic family would send their daughter to Cuba at a young age, to a place where so few women emigrated? The narrative reveals possibilities for the reinvention of women's biographies and roles. At the least, their heightened prominence demonstrates the social valuing of women as crucial to the building of immigrant society. Young female children were also included and photographed in ways that reflected their elevated value in a society wherein children (girls or boys) were a scarcity. For example, Sra. Chang's daughter Dulce Maria was described with the same attention as the boys, having received an education and excelling in piano studies. Consistently, the women were described in terms that indicated their relative independence and accomplishments. One such woman was Sra. Celia Lig, described as a successful tailor and embroiderer who was fluent in Spanish.[164] All the women appeared in stylish haircuts, Western dress and shoes, sometimes with watch and jewelry (except for one woman who appeared in Chinese garb and was described as a recent betrothal), and carried Western names such as "Esparanza," "Blanca," "Angela," and "Herencia." The men and children also wore Western clothing (although there are photographs of consular officials in formal Chinese garments). These women, and their roles in displaying social prestige, were integral in the self-representation of a new social segment engaged in society-building via commercial viability and buttressed by the institution of family and its social networks. Even when not pictured, captions and brief mentions in the main text alluded to the importance of women, such as Luisa Polo, described as a woman of high regard, or "*mas alta consideración y respecto.*"[165]

———

Chuffat wrote of the excitement that arose during the visit of the 1874 commission. Providing newspaper excerpts, Chuffat proclaimed that the arrival of the high-level Chinese commissioner "Chin-lan-pin" (Chen Lanbin) signaled a new era for the Chinese in Cuba.[166] The arrival of Chen Lanbin in Havana occurred when Chuffat was fourteen years of age and was attending school in Havana. There is, however, no evidence in Chuffat's text that indicates that Chuffat actually read the commission's report. Most likely he had not. The report was not published in Spanish nor was it published in Cuba (not surprisingly). In fact, the report was not available as a public document. Therefore, if Chuffat's work is read as counterpart to the testimonies and the commission report, it provides a fascinating chronological portrait that follows a history that preceded and overlapped his formative years. Obviously, the specter of the coolie shadowed Chuffat's consciousness into the twentieth century and would form a complex legacy for the next generation of Chinese in the context of postslavery and independence. Even though his writing was sponsored by a social set of elites, Chuffat engaged in a veiled class analysis and seized the opportunity to articulate, for the first time, the overlapping social aspects of the slave, coolie, and merchant. At that time, he was one of the few black writers to be published and one of the few Chinese to be published in the diaspora. And it seems Chuffat was the only one to provide this period glimpse of the transition from unfree to free society.

CONCLUSION:
OLD AND NEW MAPS OF COOLIES

It made you feel queer to see so many gaunt, wild faces together. The
beggars stared about at the sky, at the sea, at the ship, as though they had
expected the whole thing to have been blown to pieces. And no wonder!
They had had a doing that would have shaken the soul out of a white man.
But then they say a Chinaman has no soul.[1]

—Typhoon *by Joseph Conrad*

In 1900–1901 Joseph Conrad wrote *Typhoon*, a short piece of fiction inspired partly by Conrad's own experiences in the South China Sea. Regarded as one of the finest examples of maritime fiction in literary history,
this novella has been appreciated with classic themes in mind: man versus
nature, man versus the sea, democratic rule versus authoritarian rule, and
language and order.[2] There is, however, a peculiar aspect to *Typhoon*. As
Captain MacWhirr and his crew battle an epic storm, below deck are two
hundred human beings with whom they simultaneously do battle. Under
the hatches is a "regular little hell" that fills the crew with dread, fear, and
exhaustion. That is, below the hatches are kept two hundred Chinese coolies. The coolies attempt to get out from below, or as the first mate describes it, "The hatchway ladder was loaded with coolies swarming on it
like bees on a branch. They hung on the steps in a crawling, stirring clus-
ter, beating madly with their fists the underside of the battened hatch . . ."[3]
Faced with the chaotic situation, an anxious boatswain pleads with his
first mate: "Don't you go in there, sir." With "trembling hands," the first
mate takes the boatswain's advice and manages to refasten the hatch.

The coolie cargo was "the extraordinary complication brought into the
ship's life at a moment of exceptional stress by the human element below
her deck," noted Conrad.[4] Yet the plea of Conrad's boatswain—"Don't you
go in there"—is also Conrad's narrative strategy for figuratively managing the incorrigible coolie, by suppressing and containing the very presence that is recruited to enhance the dramatic tension of the story. The
struggle to contain the coolie (and what the term "coolie" might represent), literally and metaphorically under deck, is presented in a manner

that dehumanizes the coolies and shifts the "real" human dilemma to that of the crew and its fate. Thus, the struggle of the coolies (as "bees") is displaced by the struggle and assorted foibles of the crew (as human). The crew's fear of a beelike swarm suggests the historical struggles to control Chinese labor, historically perceived to be a "yellow horde" rife with homosexuality in South Africa, criminality in San Francisco, and disease in Hawaii. The Spanish eventually viewed the coolies in Cuba—who had become more unmanageable than they had anticipated—as a mass of "thieves, rebels, suicides, and homosexuals."[5] One Conrad critic perceptively suggests that the "counter-order" of the Chinese on the *Typhoon* represents a chaos of "effeminacy, homo-eroticism, and gibberish."[6] The subalterity of the coolie is dealt with in Conrad's narrative construction in the following two ways: There are heightened descriptions of coolie containment but also the suppression of coolie individuality. Nameless and wordless, the coolies are suppressed foils for the above-deck protagonists. The most curious moment of conflict and heightened anxiety converges, however, in an instance when a *coolie speaks*. "Suddenly," goes the tale, "one of the coolies began to speak . . . The light came and went on his lean, straining face; he threw his head up like a baying hound . . . his mouth yawned black, and the incomprehensible guttural hooting sounds, that did not seem to belong to a human language, penetrated Jukes [the first mate] . . ."[7] The speaking coolie is the most vexing figure of the novella, with his "mouth yawning black" like a forbidding vortex of incomprehensibility and inhumanity.

In my introduction, I posed the following question: What were the perspectives of the coolies? Unlike the Conrad story, the testimonies presented in this study provide counterfigures to coolies portrayed as swarming "bees" or incomprehensible "brutes." The oral and written accounts compose complex and overarching narratives, as well as a rich, varied collection of individual perspectives. In retrospect, the testimonies constitute an archetypal linchpin for narratives of global migrant bondage. The "old map" of coolie testimonies, which described encounters with an innovatively exploitative and transnational form of mass labor, is thematically linked to new mappings of global exploitation. The narratives and concerns of the nineteenth-century coolie were a prelude to what is now a contemporaneous story of "new slavery." In particular, the disclosure of "contract" as a cloaking institution and as a globalizing legal structure for a new form of slavery was put forward by coolies in 1874. And now the concept of "contract" appears in contemporary arguments regarding modern-day "new slavery" under global capitalism. Three forms of slavery continue to flourish under global capitalism: chattel slavery, debt peonage, and contract slavery (not mutually exclusive).[8] The contract has emerged as a tool to "conceal enslavement," Kevin Bales has contended, thereby engendering "contract slavery."[9] Despite pronouncements regarding a borderless world, the new global indentured laborer, or new "coolie," transgresses a highly bordered world of (il)legalities, (non)citizenry, and contracts, now refashioned as highly efficient panopticons of labor control, exploitation, and public surveillance wedded to corporate exigencies.

One of the more publicized incidences of new coolie labor involved seventy-two Thai women who were held captive by armed guards in a California sweatshop, behind razor-wire fences, until discovered in a police raid in 1995.[10] Similar to age-old plantation systems of control and bondage, laborers attested to being literally imprisoned in the workplace and forced to purchase necessities from their captors. This was after being paid only sixty cents per hour, thereby further indebting and bonding themselves. When discovered, the women were then penalized for being "illegal" labor and imprisoned again, this time by the American Immigration and Naturalization Service. Yellow prison uniforms and bail bonds were imposed. The case exposed what the Department of Labor finally admitted was not unusual practice. In common with the coolie testimonies of 1874 is the pervasive role of the contract as a state of explicit, implied, or even "involuntary agreement" in which wage and debt can be wielded by empowered parties against the contracted as mechanisms for new slavery. The testimonies from the coolies in Cuba featured their ferocious struggle with an earlier hybrid form of bondage that demonstrated dual characteristics of chattel slavery and transnational disposable labor underpinned by instruments of legality and voluntarism—in other words, papers and contracts.

I have argued that although the testimonies of the 2,871 coolies could be examined as a varied assemblage of individual accounts, when read together in crosstextual context they reveal narrative patterns and thematic particularities that, in effect, comprise a "coolie narrative." The coolie struggle with "contract" and the "paper chase" (in which coolies were *not* preoccupied with the "search for identity"—a predominant explanatory lens for describing the social travails of twentieth- and twenty-first century Asian diasporic social formations and cultural productions) calls attention to mass resistance *against* modern and systemic instruments of identity-making, surveillance, and bondage.[11] I end with the suggestion that if examined in relation to both past and contemporary narratives of global indentured or slave labor, the coolie narrative and its themes could be seen as archetypal in a long lineage of literature on slavery, freedom, and now modern slavery. The tropes and concerns of the 1874 testimonies recur as motifs in more recent investigative studies and creative representations of human trafficking and bondage.[12] Representations of the new "coolie" experience, creatively represented, emerge in two related examples: an epic poem representing contemporary migrants who died in passage and the artwork of imprisoned migrants featured in a national exhibition. "Song of Calling Souls: The Drowned Voices from the Golden Venture" (1998) by Wang Ping is an epic poem about the clandestine passage of Chinese being sold into labor. This poem was based on an actual event in which migrants endured a catastrophic, world-traversing journey that claimed ten lives and ended at the New York harbor. Reminiscent of the coolies in Cuba, the speakers in "Song" mourn unmarked deaths and unrecorded fates. "Voices" and "words" call out to the reader/audience: "pigs chickens dogs snakes,/whatever it was they called us./ Our bodies not ours,/sold to 'snakeheads' for the trip. . . . On the boat/we were close,/ hundreds of us in the hold jammed in and in./Here we live even closer,/six bodies in one hole,/the earth sifting into our common grave . . . Please, oh please/call out our names . . . even if you can't say them right. . . . even if you don't know our origin or age . . . Please, oh please/call us."[13] In this evocation of a new coolie passage, the trafficking of persons like pigs or dogs, the tortuous journey in the hold, and the urgent call for names (even if only partly known or in another language), are reminiscent of the earlier narratives of 1874. And like the coolies in Cuba, who referred to themselves as caged birds that were denied their freedom and stripped of their families, the "drowned voices" in this poetic recounting say the following: "Our women and children still awaiting our return. But here we are, nameless, in life and after life, apart. Our song is the crane calling in her cage when she thinks of her young toward nightfall." The poem alludes to the ensnarement and tragic end of migrants lured by a "promise, a golden dream." The poem exposes the underbelly of this imagined contract, which includes a contract of body. Starting with a pact with "snakeheads" who demand upwards of $30,000 per head for the passage, the indebted and illegalized cargo remain enslaved to their owners until someday, if they survive long enough, they turn enough profit to be set free. The "contract" is thus a relationship of debt-bondage and "voluntary" exploitation with an undertow of brutality that accompanies exploitation premised upon disposability.

Over a century earlier, in the mediated form of testimony, the coolies in Cuba recounted their fates with the concentrated purpose of recording their names, memorializing the passage, claiming the dead, and representing an otherwise hidden history of a new slavery. Although the historical and political circumstances of their bondage certainly cannot be conflated with all histories of bonded migration, their narratives raise enduring questions and tropes, some of which appear in the poem "Song of Calling Souls." The journey of the "drowned voices" of the Golden Venture is allegory for other "ventures" of global migrant labor that both preceded and followed this journey. In this case, nearly 300 Chinese "illegals" were stowed aboard ship, which ran aground.[14] Survivors were picked up and imprisoned ("detained"). In the end, only a few dozen eventually gained visa status. After two years, 180 remained in prisons. Others were deported to China, with well-grounded fears of punishment once they returned. A dozen were sent to South America. After almost four years, 52 remained in York County Prison in Pennsylvania where they constructed 10,000 papier-mâché sculptures from magazine pages, paper, toilet paper, and newspaper. As a result, the Museum of the Chinese of the Americas mounted an exhibition of the work, which was eventually showcased at the Smithsonian Institute, the country's premier institution of Americana. Five of the artists were granted residency on the basis of "extraordinary artistic ability."[15] One of the specially featured sculptures was an eagle on a branch, with the painted words "Fly to Freedom" and "Made in York County Prison." The migrants of this "Golden Venture" were literally prisoners of freedom. The supreme irony of the exhibition's title, "Fly to Freedom," is difficult to miss. It pays homage to the American Dream and the transformation of suffering through art; yet the event arises from a tortuous and fugitive passage on a coolie ship, with cultural production taken from its prisoners.

Representations of new coolie traffic have also recently emerged from documentary sources such as an investigative written history and a documentary film. *Forbidden Workers*, an in-depth study by Peter Kwong, is an investigative history that exposes the systemic exploitation of new illegal labor from China and their self-identification as the new coolies. They bitterly compare themselves to the nineteenth-century coolies taken to the "New World": "We are the piglets—*zhu-zha*—of the twentieth century."[16] The documentary film *Behind the Labels* by Tia Lessin also exposes modern coolie labor and features interviews with the laborers. Their testimonies bear resemblance to the old map of 1874, with the primacy of "contract" being a chief focus of their struggles. In Lessin's film, the sweatshop laborers of Saipan (the Northern Mariana Islands, American commonwealth territory) describe their contracts as promising a wage and certain conditions of labor. Yet they describe the tactics of corporations to void contracts, including the withholding of wages and papers, debt-peonage, confinement behind guarded gates, enforced isolation from the "outside" and microsurveillance of the body—including punitive measures for going to the bathroom or speaking. Predominately Filipina and Chinese women, these modern-day coolies detail their resistance in the face of repressive measures toward migrants as foreign bodies and disposable labor: They describe their cultural and linguistic disempowerment, and the collusion among government agencies, which acted as conflict-of-interest guarantors of the contract institution. The bottom-most migrant contract laborers could be called "new coolies," maximally exploited and controlled as contract laborers under transnational programs of foreign recruitment or anti-"illegal" labor. The concerns and struggles of new coolies seem eerily linked to some of the same struggles that were engaged and narrated in the initial mass experiment with transnational contract labor in nineteenth-century Cuba, in which efficient exploitation of laborers took place via "slaveholding" rather than "slaveowning."[17]

In creative representations, the "coolie" is perhaps most prominently portrayed in Caribbean fiction and poetry (aside from the significant body of Caribbean scholarly literature). These creative productions focus primarily on the subsequent generations and diasporic culture of the Indian coolie, and to a much lesser degree, the Chinese coolie.[18] The relatively sparse creative reimaginings regarding the Chinese coolie is partly the consequence of Chinese coolie migration to the Caribbean having involved comparatively fewer numbers than Indian coolie migration (leading to a marked difference in the degree of social and political presence in parts of the Caribbean today). Joyce Johnson has noted a pattern in Caribbean literature, of "registering the Chinese presence without focusing on Chinese characters as individuals."[19] A few examples of creative representations of the Chinese *coolie* (as the shopkeeper and the merchant are more commonly historicized and figured),[20] have emerged in novels by Patricia Powell, Margaret Cezair-Thompson, and Cristina Garcia (and forthcoming, a novel by Ruthann Lum McCunn). The first two works are set in Jamaica and the latter is set in Cuba. In varying degrees, each work constructs the figure of the Chinese coolie but with very different creative representations of coolie history. Cezair-Thompson creates "Ho Sing," who arrived in Jamaica on the *Prince Alexander* (*Prinz Alexander* was, in fact, a German coolie ship that arrived in 1884) and eventually ends his years as patriarch of a rainbow-colored family. Garcia offers a coolie protagonist named "Chen Pan" and extends the story line to generations later, when Chen's great-great-grandson ends up in Vietnam. Powell offers a creative portrayal of the coolie as a metaphor for subalternity and resistance. In Powell's novel, the protagonist "Lowe" arrives as a female coolie stowaway from China. Lowe hides her femaleness and passes for a male, and her lover in Jamaica hides her African lineage and passes for white. While in a clandestine lesbian relationship, the two marginally survive under social strictures of race, sex, and gender.

Among the fictional and poetic confrontations with the legacy of East Indian coolie migration is the significant work of David Dabydeen, including his poetry collection, *Coolie Odyssey*. His poems present an interlaced heritage of "jettisoned slaves," "cane chewed and spat from coolie mouth," the indigenous "Amerindian," and colonial exploitation in "The Old Map." Dabydeen's old map is a metaphor for the cultural inheritance of a mixed history of subjugation under colonial empire. Another example of a creative, historically based representation of the Indian "coolie" emerges in the novel *Last English Plantation* by Jan Lo Shinebourne, which is one of several literary works that scholarly critics have addressed in critiques of "coolie-ness."[21] Shinebourne's story concerns a girl named June of Indian (and of lesser narrative focus, Chinese) heritage, coming of age in Guyana during the last gasp of the British colonial era and the beginnings of Guyanese self-determination. June resists the colonial mind-set of the British education system and that of her mother who shouts the following: "Turn into a coolie! You used to be a coolie and I manage to turn you into a civilized person, now you want to turn coolie again!"[22] The claims of the British Commonwealth transmute as inherited colonial loyalties and hierarchies of culture. June's mother insists "this is the West Indies, not India, not Africa, not China, the West Indies! We are British!"[23] An exegesis regarding the colonized mind is obviously suggested, but more striking is Shinebourne's approach to an often-told narrative of national independence and liberation, with primary focus placed upon the struggles of "woman" and "coolie." The novelistic and poetic interpretations of "coolie" and "coolie-ness" are further amplified by yet another creative approach to Indian coolie history and subsequent cultural transformation, called "coolitude," proposed by poet Khal Torabully. With parallels to "negritude" and creolité, Torabully has undertaken a cultural and philosophical aesthetic that takes the coolie passage as its extended metaphor.

These creative mediations and documentary representations of "coolie"—historical and contemporary, Indian and Chinese—and the philosophical meditation upon "coolie-ness," comprise a field of counternarratives on the coolie that are incommensurate with global depictions of the coolie in the marketplace of leisure, humor, fashion, and style. One anecdote concerning a twentieth-century global icon of glamour gives some illustration of the commodification of "coolie" as colonial pastime. Apparently, a "black doll" and a "Chinese doll" made by Lenci, famous maker of what are now collectible antique dolls, were Marlene Dietrich's most treasured possessions. Greatly attached to them, she could not travel or even appear on a movie set without the pair of dolls (the Chinese doll was acquired as a "companion" for the black doll). They also appeared with the famed Dietrich in her films and publicity photos. In an interview on her initial visit to the United States, Dietrich once referred to her Chinese doll as "my little Chinese."[24] While the dolls could be arguably described as African and Chinese, and not necessarily as slave and coolie, it is precisely the history of subjugation and the pastime of colonialism that provides the necessary pretext for fetishizing the Africans and Chinese. The childlike quality of the "black" and "Chinese" dolls and Dietrich's affectionate possession of them, especially as a public spectacle, effectively recast the slave and coolie as racial (or racist) kitsch.

Now, the coolie is figurative shorthand for labor kitsch and an advertising mnemonic for the rehearsal of colonial and classed nostalgia. "Coolie wear" is featured on the runways of cosmopolitan fashion, sold as middle-class humor, and appears as a pedestrian tradition in party costume wear.[25] The privileged fetishizing of the coolie sidesteps the political history of labor struggle and anticolonial resistance, similar to what Dorinne Kondo has called fashion's "power-evasive celebration."[26] The coolie is present on the horizon of entertainment and consumer culture but recalled in ways that assuage and humor a history of bondage, once described as "worse than death" by coolies in 1874.[27]

NEW MAPS AND PROBLEMS

The coolie testimonies contained a certain dark irony. The "regular little hell" of Conrad's tale was described as "hell on earth" by coolies in 1874, who upon recounting the bizarre and ghastly nature of their experience, asked this question: "Who ever heard of such a thing?" Their question and its profound connection to contemporary questions of freedom and exploitation point to new directions, areas, and methods of inquiry. The hearing of "such a thing" requires a new map, not the least of which is a journey into hybrid methodology. Here I share some of the research challenges faced in this project, with some digressions into detail that the reader might tolerate and find useful. A new mapping of the coolie narrative is contingent upon a new map for approaching, researching, and theorizing diasporic and transnational subjects. I was forced to adopt methods of research and interdisciplinarity that make possible such an investigation, such as the use of sources in multiple languages, of different cultures, and across multiple disciplines. The difficulties of reading these thousands of testimonies snowballed into practical challenges and theoretical conundrums in the "translation" of cultural and material histories, textual and historical consistencies, and of course, difficulties in grappling with the act of translation as an epistemologically loaded act that could not be confused with "equivalence." What I offer in this study is not a transparent "translation" (as translation theorists would contend there is no such thing) but what Lydia Liu calls a third epistemological event, which I recognize as constituting another body of knowledge naturally structured by its own logic, limitations, flaws, and by what Naoki Sakai would deem cultural politics unavoidably at work in the representation of translation itself. I initiated this study with a desire to read original testimonies by those in bondage and not simply via third-hand reports about testimonies. In fact, the commission's report in 1874 contains erroneous transcriptions when crosschecked with the testimonies, including numerous errors in names and in testimony content. Besides excerpting the testimonies and suppressing others, the commission report thus perpetuated its own "error" in translation and mediation, as is the nature of all reports. The power of the testimonies and the process of attempting to locate, contextualize, and read them has been a truly humbling experience. There has also been the challenge of engaging Antonio Chuffat Latour's next-generation work, which is hybrid in form and language, not to mention veiled and vexing in so many ways.

A double process occurred for this project. The first process entailed the translation of the materials. The second process involved the combined quantitative and qualitative analysis. One naturally informs the other—all are inseparable, dialogic and simultaneous. For the coolie testimonies, rather than go with a partial sample, I realized that a complete sampling was needed, given the startling claims that appeared in the early viewing of the materials. Within this two-step process, a supertriangulated process occurred in which the terms and concepts raised by the Chinese coolies in Cuba needed careful consideration in the following simultaneous contexts: Chinese culture, migration conditions, Cuban history, labor economies, colonial histories of the Caribbean and Latin America, maritime histories, sugar economy and plantation societies, linguistic history and etymologies, literary traditions and genres of testimony, literatures of indenture and slavery, testimonial and investigatory histories, histories of race and racialization, and philosophies of bondage and freedom. Simply, the claims being made in the testimonies were incommensurate to previous conclusions drawn from existing scholarship in any one of these areas. But their claims made sense and raised key questions in a multilinear intersection of all of these areas.

What did the coolies mean by "slave," "contract," and "freedom"? And what did Chuffat mean by "Chinese," "Black," and "Cuban"? After all, are not these terms culturally specific and locally defined? Meanings travel, transform, and take on other meanings. A more challenging question is how do *their* uses of the terms contribute, transform, and expand to present understandings of these terms (and discourses)? This line of inquiry is an example of the long threads of theoretically, philosophically, methodologically, and historiographically driven interrogations demanded by the material. The reading of this material was, in the deepest sense, a "literary" reading, with an acute awareness of the opaqueness, thickness, and slipperiness of narration. The "details" were overwhelming, yet eventually emerged as pronounced and pivotal in reading the politics as not only an individual protest but also as part of a web of relations and cultural locations. For example, was a certain testifier talking about dollars in Chinese currency or Cuban currency? What year was the testifier talking about (as currency and its values changed)? Was the testifier speaking of silver, gold, paper? When the testifiers talked of time, were they referring to the lunar calendar or the Gregorian calendar? They might have been referring to the dynastic calendar, an agricultural calendar (as some spoke of the days and nights in terms of "watches"), or the "stem-branch" system, consisting of ten heavenly stems and twelve earthly branches (which appeared in some of the testimonies)? When a testifier said he was age seventeen upon arrival, did he mean seventeen according to the Chinese calendar or the Western calendar (by which gauge he would have been age sixteen)? All of the above ways of telling time were present in the testimonies, and the challenge was not only to reconcile these different systems but also to read these details as reflective of the testifier's perspectives, culturally and temporally located. Concepts of time, money, and place, for example, became crucially important given the great emphasis of testifiers upon perversions of the contract, some of which led to critical insight into the nature and location of their resistance. Were they talking of the same person, the same event, the same law, the same location, or the same owner? If so, how were their perspectives the same or different, and how were their tellings presented? If the body of testimonies were disaggregated according to date of arrival, age of testifier, ethnic origin, social class, location of bondage, type of labor, and so on, how would that affect the apprehending of "perspective"? And from this knowledge, what could one deduce about the politics of self-representation and strategic narration?

In some instances, terms were provincial colloquialisms and idioms reflecting the localized nature of language and the provincial origins of the testifier. At other times, a testifier made allusion to a legend or historical figure. What was the original myth and how did this expand or even subvert the apparent narration? Furthermore, these testimonies were written in classical Chinese language and without punctuation, sometimes rife with ancient terms no longer in use or no longer found in modern Chinese lexical references. As a result, the text (especially the petitions section) is difficult to parse even for an educated Chinese reader, who would need several secondary references. Even then, such a reader would be frustrated, as some of the terms were pidgin forms of Spanish and English that were directly related to Cuban culture, geography, and sugar history. After all, many terms were newly and resourcefully conceived by the Chinese *after their arrival in Cuba* in attempts to describe the new world they faced. The frustrating nature of reading these materials points to the very nature of writing and reading as historically, culturally, temporally, and spatially situated, and to the opaqueness of meaning and translation. For example, the repeated references to a "sugar pot" became significant in the context of the sugar mill, the technologies of sugar processing, the racialized space of the worksite, and then the terrible significance of jumping into a boiling cauldron as a method of public sabotage and suicide. The many references to knives made little sense unless put in the context of sugar and the basic tool of sugar labor, the machete. The repeated concentration of authority in the manager and the overseer (and the dominant references to black overseers) seemed overdrawn unless contextualized by the local history of absentee-ownership in Cuba. Owners commonly lived off the plantation and took up residence in the cities, further contextualized by Cuba's history of railroads, which facilitated and increased the trend during that period.[28]

Such interdisciplinary challenges are also epistemological and methodological challenges facing not only this project but also diasporic and transnational studies at this moment. With these as brief examples, I cannot overemphasize the need for *collaborative* study, given the nature of interdisciplinary, multilingual work. Whereas the commission report contains a wealth of excerpts in English, I sought the complete and primary testimonies. The translations were the result of my locating the testimonies and then forming a team of Chinese translators who carried out translations of the testimonies into English. We underwent many interrogations, additions, reversals, and revisions over the years, and some of this research turned upon lively transcultural debate, including struggles over the nature of poetic translation. Without this collaboration, the project would have been impossible. For a fuller and more nuanced reading of Antonio Chuffat Latour's Spanish-language text, I consulted Spanish translators. The text presented unique challenges in terms of its literary meanings. Chuffat used Cuban colloquialisms of the period as well as awkward prose and flourishes that revealed his attempts to present himself as an educated writer. In addition to this, however, Chuffat's text presented challenges as a transcultural text. At times, he employed Spanish approximations of Chinese (phonetically), and for example, even included his own Spanish approximation of a Chinese poem, as it would have sounded in Cantonese (a dialect of Chinese). Obviously, Chuffat's book presented challenges in tracing the origin of terms and in affirming the curious passages that were presented. He included scores of anecdotes, events, and personages, some of whom episodically appeared under both Chinese and Spanish names, or appeared under Spanish transliterations of Chinese names. Moreover, the text called for a consideration of the author's presentation of "blackness" and its relation or significance to understandings of African, Chinese, and Caribbean social histories and diasporas. Thus again, I underscore the great benefit of crosscultural, collaborative study of diasporic materials. As is convention, I respectfully acknowledge the crucial work of translators in my "Acknowledgements" section. But here, I wish to further underscore, in this brief note on research and method, the imminent need for further collaboration in diasporic studies and transparently, my reliance upon it. The cross- and interdisciplinarity of transnational work, and the multinational and multilingual nature of these fields, make these sites uniquely demanding and dense in the practical sense as well as the epistemic and ontological sense.

ADDENDUM: SELECTED PETITIONS

PETITION 2

On the fourth day of the second moon, according to Xian Zuobang (first-degree licentiate), Qin Abao, He Asi, He Aqiu, Zhang Fucai, Zhou Qing, Lü Jinyuan, Li Ajin, He Azao, Liang Agui, Liu Aguang, Wu Achang, Chen Shidong, Jin Awen (civilians) from Nanhai County, Guangdong Province:

A first-degree licentiate, I passed the prefecture examination under Master Yin, Minister of Education [of Guangdong], and became a student of the provincial academy, in the ninth year of Xianfeng (1859)[i]. In the next year, Pan Aheng, who lived in Panyu County, Foshan, told me that if I went to teach in Macao, I would be paid a hundred and twenty *yuan* each year. However, after arriving in Macao, I was abducted to work abroad. Other civilians, who lived in either villages or cities, were also abducted or deceived by gangsters hired by foreigners in Macao. Once we entered the Pigpen, we were not allowed to leave. Once we boarded the Pigship, we were not allowed to land. We were shackled and lashed according to their will. Soon we were shipped across the ocean. Once we got to the Havana Selling People House, our plaits were cut off, our clothes were changed, and people were allowed to choose and buy. Here, no matter how knowledgeable one was in China, one has to become a laborer. No matter what status one had in China, one will become a slave. If one is sold to a household to be a servant or a cook, although one still gets lashed, at least one will not be starved and will have fewer night shifts. However, not that many people are fortunate. If one is sold to work at brick kilns, bakeries, mountain hut or sugar refinery, one cannot prevent from working with feet shackled and work overnight shifts. Thousands of millionaires of sugar plantations make a profit by using this kind of cheap labor. The Chinese labors here eat food that is not even wanted by dogs and do work that is even hard for horses and oxen. We are lashed so often that our arms and legs break and bleed. Hanging, drowning, cutting throats and poisoning—all kinds of suicides take place every day among the Chinese laborers. People who were shipped earlier from Fujian or Guangdong Province signed a five-year contract. However, the contract was taken away by staff at Selling People House as soon as we arrived Havana. People who were shipped from

---

i. First-degree licentiate under the former system. After passing two exams, the first-degree licentiate was a formal student in the country. Most likely, this petition was written by Xian Zuobang and co-signed by other petitioners. The word "I" referred to Xian Zuobang himself.

Macao all signed an eight-year contract. No one knows who set down the contract period. In the earlier years, after finishing the contract, people often could spend ten *yuan* or more to find a godfather to wash heads so that they were able to get the freedom paper.[ii] Now, the officials collude with the merchants; even godfathers cannot help. If a Chinese did not have the proof issued from the owner, he could not apply for freedom paper from official.[iii] If he did not have the freedom paper, the patrol could force him into the official workshop whenever they wanted to. In Cuba, the official workshop is no difference from the prison. People with an expired contract are called "runaways" and are locked up in the workshops forever, just like being locked up in official prisons forever. They just make a conspiracy to trap the Chinese workers to work at the official workshop forever since they do not need to pay us anything and also they can skim profits by binding us. Apart from the freedom paper, there is the Walking Paper, which requires a fee to renew every year. Without that paper, one could not walk on the street. If one wanted to travel to another town, one would have to ask the local officials for Traveling Paper; otherwise, one could be put into prison. Any Chinese who are handicapped and cannot work, or are expelled by the sugar plantation, or are very old and sick in the official workshops, need a Begging Paper in order to become a beggar. The Begging Paper cannot be obtained without a fee. As to the Go-Abroad Paper, the fee depends on how much money one has in savings. It ranges from a few dozen *yuan* to several hundred *yuan*. How dare a Chinese worker dream of going back to China? We witnessed that in the year of Ren Xu (1862), soldiers suddenly arrested the Chinese who already had the freedom paper and forced them to chip stones. This was called *jiandiela*; the Chinese were forced to sign contracts again.[iv] Black overseers were so atrocious that there were cries everywhere. Thanks to the coming of an upright official in the year of Gui Hai (1863), the Chinese workers were finally released and received freedom papers so that they could earn a living. Later, once again, in the year of Xin Wei (1871), patrols intruded in the homes of the Chinese at night and took their freedom papers away, and then put them into prison, accusing them of running away from plantations. Fortunately, British and American consuls intervened, and they were released. But still, there are Chinese workers being resold into the mountains. Why are innocent Chinese so miserable here? Whenever Chinese walk in the street, they are yelled at and thrown stones at by Cuban people. If the Chinese resist, they will be beaten down by many people and be put in the jail. When the Chinese buy things from Cuban people, they are punched by the store owner if they try to abate the price. However, when local people buy things from the Chinese or have meals in a Chinese restaurant, the Chinese will be lashed if they ask

ii. "Wash head" referred to baptism.
iii. "Proof" means the proof of finishing the eight-year contract.
iv. Another term for "official workshop."

the Cubans to pay. There have been Chinese who die in these incidents. We always want to know why people from other countries come and go freely and trade fairly in Cuba; anyone but the Chinese! Why are the Chinese abused even worse than Blacks? We always think of writing letters to warn all the other Chinese not to be cheated to Cuba again; but we find no way to send them out. Luckily we have your honor here so that we can file a plaint of grievance all together.

PETITION 11

On the tenth day of the second moon, according to the petition by Zhang Luan, a military officer from Guandong, former Commandant of the Right Brigade in Tingzhou City who was awarded the rank of Brigade Commander because of military merits; Cheng Rongling, a Jiangsu native and Expectant Appointee for Police Chief of Guangxi; Mo Rongxian, a Commandant in the Jinxian County, Guangdong; Chen Xuezhou, a Squad Leader by Recommendation from Guangdong Province; Lin Guo from Zhao'an County, Fujian Province; Li Chang and Tang Meilang from Jiayingzhou City, Guangdong Province; Lin San from Changle County; Gu Xiu, Gu Song, Zou Er, Zou Sheng, Lin Si, Lin Chang, Zhang Ping, Tian Fa, Yu Yangxiu, and Lin Man from Boluo County; Zhang Fu and Liang Gui from Guishan County; Chen Shi and Lin Nan from Jieyang County; Zhang Bing from Yingde County; Xian Qiao from Xin'an County; Luo San from Xinning County; Huang Yixing from Lianpingzhou City; Peng Liang, Huang Chun, Peng Jinbao, and Du Teng from Enping County; Chen Fu from Wuchuan County (civilians):

We were born and grew up in China, having a well-off life in China.[v] Since the time of our grandpa's generation, nobody has ever heard of going abroad to make a living. The principle of running a country from ancient times is to grow in population for ten years and not worry about a large population. Rulers would only try to gather people, but not scatter people in four directions making temporary living in foreign countries, let alone let them fall into a deathtrap.[vi] But in recent decades, China is doing business with foreigners;[vii] unexpectedly there are Portuguese colluding with Spanish, also with the Chinese gangsters whose job is to abduct people. This practice originated in Xiamen and prospers in Macao. The accomplices are spread over prefectures, counties, and cities, and capture or abduct Chinese along the coastal line, and send them to the Pigpen, then ship them to Havana to sell as

v. This petition is very likely written by the four officials among the petitioners, because this petition begins with "*zhideng*," (职等) which is how lower-level officials addressed themselves while talking or reporting to higher-level officials.

vi. Unlike other petitions, the first sentences here talked about how to rule a country. They reflected the status of the author(s), who were educated in politics.

vii. In the Qing Dynasty, emperors pursued a "Closed Door" policy until 1840. The policy shut the Chinese off from the advancing world and affected how Chinese viewed both foreigners and the world.

goods. Sometimes, they cheat us by honeyed words and phrases, telling us that it is very easy to become wealthy in Cuba without working for long time. Moreover, they tell us that the ship is going to Britain, Singapore, San Francisco, or New York, and other places, so that people will not be scared. But they cast their nets in every harbor and their schemes block every road. No matter the wise or the fool, we are all trapped. All this happens because Portugal and Spain are hard-hearted and lack moral principles. They lure people into greed and perfidy. They tempt people to violate laws and to commit crimes. As a result, the kindred of good Chinese people are separated; the branches of kinship are broken off. The island of Cuba is shaped like an alligator; the toxic air is suffocating, which is totally different from the places where we have been. Sugar plantations stand like trees in a forest and miles and miles of sugar cane grow there; there are more than thousands of prisons and tens of thousands of shackles. Voices crying out wrong and bearing pain, shapes of broken skin and flesh, and suicides by cutting one's throat, hanging, swallowing opium, and drowning are by no means isolated cases. The young and strong are willing to commit crimes to become prisoners while the old and weak beg for begging papers to become beggars. Do Cubans even have sympathy for us as humans? On top of it all, most of the Cuban officials are businessmen; sugar plantation owners always collude with them. If owners use brutal punishment, officials pretend they know nothing about it. If owners beat laborers to death, officials do not ask about it. In recent years, Cuban officials held up the freedom paper and do not issue one without large fees. They expanded the official workshop and have patrols to hunt for Chinese everywhere. If a Chinese is caught, they force him to sign a contract to work. Government officials do so as a favor for businessmen, as well as getting a share of the bondage money. These officials circulate Chinese laborers to gain pure profit. In this way, the Chinese pass through many hands and become all of Cuba's slaves forever, without any hope of returning alive again. For those who have finished eight-year contract, they should be given freedom papers and released, which is obviously reasonable. Instead, they are sent to the official workshop, working with their feet chained same as murderers and other prisoners. The ones who are not supposed to be locked up are all locked up; the ones who did not run away are accused as runaways. Have you ever heard of this kind of unfair political thing in the world, in history? Several years ago, because of no doctors for illness, no graveyards for the dead,[viii] no way to send letters home, and no definite date to return home, the Chinese planned to set up an association with donations from every port and elected directors. Some righteous foreigners were willing to help. Unexpect-

viii "No graveyards for the dead": In China, a funeral is considered "the white joyous occasion," while a wedding is the red one. Chinese believe that people still continue on in an afterlife after death and that improper funeral arrangements can wreak ill fortune and disaster upon the family of the deceased. In ancient China, a proper funeral was a very elaborate ceremony, involving about twenty to forty procedures. It was considered an insult if a person did not receive a proper funeral ceremony.

edly, the Portugal officials wanted to break up the morale of the Chinese. They colluded with Chinese traitors and said that the Chinese would collect money for revolt. Then they persuaded the Cuban government to prevent the matter. Later, the Portugal vice-consul lured the Chinese to go to Cardenas to get fake papers. At the same time, he secretly contacted patrols to check their papers or to extort it from them. Most people who had genuine freedom papers were seized and resold to the mountains. How unfair and miserable! Just think, there are thousands of Chinese associations all over trading centers both in China and abroad. Have you ever heard any of them organizing to rebel against governments? Cuba has been in a civil war, which was caused by the Spanish, for several years. During wartime, every plantation owner forced the laborers to join the war. However, the Chinese would rather die than obey the order. They went away one after another. You can still ask around for their names now. In some sugar plantations, which were near the enemy's camp, and some workshop in La Trocha, no one ever heard of any Chinese who rebels. This is not because our Chinese are willing to requite ingratitude with kindness.[ix] It is because we come from China, a land praising decorum. We do not want to do anything immoral. Cubans ought to feel grateful and ashamed but on the contrary they started a rumor from this incident and even found a way to lock up the Chinese. Do they even have morals? Since we were children, we studied literature or martial arts so that we could earn a scholarly honor or official rank.[x] We did not even think of working overseas. Now, we are trapped on this faraway desolate land without any hope of escaping. We cannot devote ourselves to our country but disgrace her. What else can we say?[xi] Only our hearts look forward to our country as eagerly as sunflowers look forward to the sun. Only our hopes grow as pea shoots grow after being plucked. Fortunately we can welcome your honor here so that we dare to reveal our miseries. We beseech your investigation and your rescue. As quoted.

PETITION 20

On the fifteenth day of the second moon, according to the petition by the licentiate Li Zhaochun from Panyu County, Guangdong Province; Wu Er, Lin Dexiu,

---

ix. To requite ingratitude with kindness is considered to be virtuous in Chinese society.
x. "Studied literature or *wushu*": In order to become a civil officer, one must study literature and pass several examinations, and "the military examination system progressed through the same stages as its civil counterpart. . . . To become a military licentiate, or *wushengyuan*, a man had to pass the district, prefecture, and qualifying military examinations [. . .] the only difference between military and civil examinations was that the military system lacked the extra reexaminations that had been interpolated in the civilian system." See Miyazaki, 102–104.
xi. This passage expresses the desire to dedicate themselves to the service of their country, but the concern about bringing humiliation to their country is an indication of their dishonor as Chinese officials.

Zheng Deru and Ye Er from Wuchuan County; Wei Zuo from Changle County; Yuan Er and Zhang Jiu from Xingning County; Xie Fu, Pang Erxian, Zhang Chang, Zeng Jin, and Xie Yulang from Jiayingzhou City; Zhu Yuan from Yingde County; Chen Bing from Dong'an County; Li An from Leizhou City; Wen Chuchen, Yu Desheng, Tang Zisheng, Zhou Maoting, Li Wenchu, Zhou Yougui, Li Desheng, and Wen Rizhang from Xiangtan County, Hunan Province; Cao Jun from Tianjin City; Tan Decheng from Longnan County, Jiangxi Province; Wan An, Zhang Wen, and Yuan Sheng from Ji'an County; Guo Sheng from Raozhou City; Liu Ming from Jianchang Prefecture; Chen Jinyuan from Jintan County, Jiang Nan; Huang Man from Shangyuan County; Yao Si from Fengtian Prefecture; He Chang from Guilin City, Guangxi Province; Jiang Linhang, Zhang Erding, Jin Nian, Lin Bai, and Zheng Yan from Quanzhou City, Fujian Province; Wu Wanzhen from Zhangzhou City; Zhuang Jiu from Longxi County; Hong Wei, Chen Zhen, and Wu Junzheng from Nan'an County; Lin Run and Shen Chao from Zhao'an County; Xu Gao from Hui'an County; Chen Qinglai from Pinghe County; Lin Youwen from Zhangpu County; Liu Xiunian from Heyuan County, Guangdong Province; Chen Fu from Suixi County; Zhang Run from Yingde County; Zhuo San and Xi Gao from Xin'an County; Deng Jin, Zheng Ying, Mai Wen, Yang Songlang, and Huo Hao from Sanshui County; Li Bie, Ruan He, Feng Songji, He Fu, Zhao Jian, and Ou Chang from Nanhai County; Tan Lai, Mai Weixin, and Wu Lianfa from Xiangshan County; Zhong Xiu, He You, and Liang San from Xinning County; Tan Wang, Liao Ersheng, Wen Zhao, Luo Yinggui, and Zeng Jinxiu from Zengcheng County; Liang Li, Su Fa, and He Cheng from Xinhui County; Zheng Quanfu, Li Jin, Li Hai, You Shi, Yuan Wan, Yuan Qing, Cai Ji, Ou Zhi, Zhou Xin, and Wang Song from Dongguan County; Lu Yuan and Su Huaibao from Shunde County; Zhong Tian and Liu Er from Conghua County; Ye Gengxiu from Longmen County; Ling Run and Huang Yan from Panyu County; Jiang Er, Huang Zao, Chen Fu, Zou Huo, Li Xi, and Tang Hong from Boluo County; Lin Liang, Liu Chang, Lin Qun, He Baoluo, Nan Yanggu, Chen Fu, Cai Ming, Xie Guiqiu, Chen Fu, Chen Kai, Luo Yingpan, Tu Shengcai, Qiu Jinfu, He Bao, Lu Taolin, Yao Fu, Xiao Man, Shi Chang, Zhang You, and Xue Gong from Guishan County; Liu Jinbao, Li Mu, and Liu Mei from Haifeng County; Xie Quan, Li Run, Xie Xian, Li Xi, Ruan Nian, Liu Mangui, Zhang Xing, Wu Mei, Wang You, and Ruan Xi from Heyuan County; Li Chengji, and Zhang Xian from Yong'an County; Lin Lu from Lufeng County; Wu Tao from Longchuan County; Tan Dehou, He Chang, and Liang Dai from Kaiping County; Chen Zheng from Yangjiang County; Kong Long, Zheng Xia, Xiao Lian, Peng Liang, Liu Jiu, Lu You, and Zeng Genglian from Enping County; He Ming from Gaoyao County; Shen Chuan and Li Sheng from Heshan County; Wu Shui from Sihui County; Huang Jinke and Wu Fu from Gaoming County; Zhang Mao from Deqingzhou City; Chen Qushou and Zeng Hong from Haiyang County; Xiao

Mao and Zhou Dong from Chaoyang County; Lin Wangzi from Jieyang County; Fang Fu from Huilai County (civilians):

I was born in the fourth year of Xianfeng (1854).[xii] I was a first-degree licentiate, graduated from Zhangbaikui Institute.[xiii] Then I became a teacher. During an upheaval, I was deceived and told that there was teaching job in Macao. After arriving at Macao, I was forced to go abroad and later was sold to be a slave in a tobacco shop. Others of us were peasants, scholars, woodcutters, fishermen, or small retailers in China. Over the several years, one by one, we were abducted and lured to a Pigpen in Macao by Portuguese who colluded with gangsters. In the Pigpen, we were not allowed to leave. They often told us that certain people, who refused to go abroad, were beaten to death, or tied up and thrown into the sea, or left to die in a dungeon. We were so frightened as if our hearts and guts were split open. Later we were dragged to see some foreign officials. They were as ferocious as wolves and tigers. The interpreter read the contract to us ambiguously. He said that we were hired to work in places like Vietnam, Singapore, Melbourne, or San Francisco. At that time, we were still hoping for a chance to survive so as not to die immediately. Then we had no other choice but sign the contract and board the ship. We didn't know that we were sold to Cuba to be slaves for the rest of our lives and suffer so much that we would hope to die soon, but our hope has not been granted. After the abduction, for tens of years, our families have no idea of whether we are alive or dead and of our whereabouts. We remember that we were shut in the cabin or even put in the bamboo cages or locked up in irons when we were on the ship. The owners of the ship arbitrarily dragged several people out and beat them to put on a show of force. We did not know how many of our peers died on the ship because of illness, beating, thirst, or suicide by jumping into the sea when there was a chance. When we arrived at Havana, we were washed, our plaits cut, and sent to the Selling People House.[xiv] We had to wait for businessmen to select and negotiate the price. We didn't know how much we were sold for or who shared the ill-gotten gains. We were born in China, educated by our parents and finally grew up. To our surprise, we were cheated and sold by foreigners in a steady stream, who keep the bondage money. From ancient times to the present, is there anything that is more unfair than this? Cubans claim that they are merely hiring and recruiting people, or trading contracts. They never say that they are selling people to be slaves. Just think of

---

xii. This petition was written by Li Zhaochun and co-signed by other people. Therefore, "I" in this petition referred to Li himself. And "we" referred to Li and his peers.

xiii. Zhangbaikui Institute was named after the high governor of Guangzhou, Zhang Baikui. This was an official institute, where education was connected with politics. See Liu Dong 刘东, *Zhonghua wenming duben* 中华文明读本 (*Reader in Chinese Civilization*) (Beijing: Shehui kexue wenxian chubanshe, 1999), 292.

xiv. The plait was a symbol of national identity to that particular generation of Chinese. It was important especially to the ones who were loyal to the Qing Dynasty.

those people who died on the way to Cuba, would Cubans want to trade these dead people's contracts? How can the Spanish even try to deny the fact that they trade people? As to those who were sold to be slaves, only several of them were sold into stores; very few of them were sold to tobacco or coffee plantations; nine out of ten were sold into sugar plantations. The owners of sugar plantations would ask the mangers for more sugar; in turn, the mangers ask the overseers for more work to be done. They put profit-making first and do not care about laborers' lives at all. They have no concerns about whether Chinese laborers have enough rest or not, whether they are starved or not, or whether they are alive or not! For each of the two meals daily, the Chinese laborer receives four plantains. Those managers who give only three plantains for a meal are considered even more capable. We are forced to work for twenty hours a day. Those managers who could force us to work for twenty-one hours a day were considered even more capable. Beatings happen often; locking-up takes place wantonly. The ones who report an illness are beaten up and starved; the ones who work slowly are chased and bitten by dogs. Many of us die of being lashed, stabbed, and drowned. No one goes to the law against the owners. Even if so, officials merely come to take a look and get through it perfunctorily. Among us, some have had long friendships with each other since they were in their hometowns or have close relationships like young shoots of a reed, and have witnessed a murder, but would not dare tell the truth. Because if they ever did so, they would be killed immediately! Cubans always say that Chinese often kill their managers. Why would one pay one's life for killing others, unless forced by the situation? Cubans say Chinese often escape. Why would one risk life to escape, unless one could not live safely? In every sugar plantation, the Chinese laborers get four *yuan* paper currency for payment, which is worth just one silver. It is not enough for buying clothing or food in the first place. However, inside the plantation, mangers own stores, where groceries are low quality and expensive. We have to buy from them and have our salary deducted. If we buy from other places, we would be accused of running away, then our feet would be shackled while working. After the expiration of the eight-year contract, who will have enough traveling money to go back to China? In recent years, the sugar plantation owners, who are also officials in government, have set up a new harsh policy. The Chinese laborers whose contracts have expired have to be sent to the official workshops to work with feet shackled and without any payment. No matter where you work, no matter how long you work, you have to work till you die. If the former master or other people negotiate with the government officials, they can pay about ten *yuan* or more to hire labor back to the plantations, which is called "Tie-up" (bondage). However, most of the salary is submitted to the officials, according to the policy. The money that the Chinese laborers receive is just several *yuan* each month. How could we save money for traveling? As to the contracts that we signed in Macao, most of them were taken away by the plantation owners when we arrived at the plantation. The plantation owners can negotiate with officials and substitute a dead person's contract with another living person in the official workshop. That is even more miserable. The Chinese laborers here do not really like gambling, but the Spanish government schemes up gambling like "White Dove Ticket" and has tickets sold everywhere. If one wins the first prize, called "Heaven Prize," one would be allowed to buy back freedom. Therefore, everyone puts their hope on the game without knowing that this makes them even poorer! Moreover, not all of the Chinese laborers like smoking opium. Even if they do, the voyage from Macao to Cuba lasts so long that their addiction is stopped. However, policemen use opium houses to make money and use opium-smoking to extort people. So they are glad to see Chinese smoke opium. The rich people believe that if the Chinese become addicted to opium, they will not desire to go back to China because of lack of money and aspiration. That is why they like to lure the Chinese into smoking opium. The Chinese consider that they are not able to own their bodies and they are not able to own their money. Besides, everyone is forced to stay and not to go back to China. Thus, they throw off restraint, spend their money thoughtlessly and smoke more opium; there is no alternative. Otherwise, given the fact that the penalty from the sugar refineries' is extremely harsh, how would it be hard to prohibit us from smoking opium? Moreover, how could it be possible for the Chinese to ship and sell opium here? Besides, if places like stone workshops, sugar plantations, brick kilns, tobacco plantations, railroad companies, or shoe stores, owned several Chinese or more, they would set up implements for punishment. Whips, shackles, cells, and so on, these implements look the same as ones in sugar plantations. People from other countries also own sugar plantations. Sometimes, they give four silvers for payment and some rice or noodles for meals every other day. However, due to customs in Cuba, the working hours in these plantations are still very long. According to the new policy, after eight years, freedom paper will not be issued. We believe that you need to get permission from the owner of the goods if you want to sell the owner's goods, but now the Spanish collude with gangsters, trading Chinese freely. Our families do not know about it; the law is ignored. The society is so decadent that even relatives and friends try to cheat one another. The Spanish are destroying human relations and rotting people's sympathy in China. This peril has no end and is no trivial matter. We also see that people feed their horses and oxen till they are full and rest them when they are tired. Even if they do whip the animals, the whipping is only a few strikes. They never shackle their feet while yoking them. However, look at how the Spanish treat the Chinese laborer: not enough food, arduous labor, hundreds of strikes till skin is ruptured and bones are broken without any sympathy. The cells in sugar plantations are seldom empty. In the daytime the prisoners still have to work with their feet shackled. There are official workshops, which are also called Runaway Company.

The Chinese laborers who have fulfilled their contracts and have not tried to escape are still sent to these workshops. Every day, they have to chip stones and carry dirt with their feet shackled. Foreigners oversee the labor with whip and machete. Sometimes, they put on two or more shackles on the laborers' feet to make them more miserable and coerce them into signing bondage contracts for more years with rich businessmen. After the expiration of these contracts, they employ the same scheme over and over. Thus, the Spanish sell us for slaves and make a way to enslave us for the rest of our lives. We do not have any hope of surviving. Is there any brutal and vicious thing in the world worse than this? We do not know in the morning what may happen in the evening; we do not know when our lives will be ended. We just hope that this peril can be stopped so that Chinese will never come to Cuba again to suffer. Then we could die with our eyes closed.[xv] As quoted.

PETITION 25

On the twentieth day of the third moon, according to the petition by Jian Shiguang, Liang Lai, and Zhong Wen from Panyu County, Guangdong Province; Lan Ru, Huang Lichang, and Zhuang Tuo from Haiyang County; Wu Lian, Lin Yuanxing, and He Liangyi from Jieyang County; Chen Gu, Lin Zhenyang, and Zhuang Ermei from Chaoyang County; Wubao Lisan from Dabu County; Chen Yong, Liu He, Ruan Xifan, Wu You, and Pan Rui'an from Nanhai County; Xie Chang, Huang Qi, Pang Zhang, Pang Er, Ye Long, and Lin Wan from Xinning County; Li Wen, Chen Lei, Chen Mei, Liu Xian, and Hong Cai from Haifeng County; Zhu San, He Baosheng, and Huang Nan from Zengcheng County; Zeng Wu from Enping County; Hu Shou, Lu Yuan, Wu Sheng, and Liao Xi from Shunde County; Kuang Lu, Zhou Chang, and He Mengmei from Kaiping County; Yuan Gui, Chen Wuchang, Shen Fo, Dong Li'an, Zhong Mei, Zhuang Ming, Chen Song, Huang Fu, Feng Man, Huang Guanyang, Fang Lai, and Liu Gui from Guishan County; Liu Long, Zeng Guangcheng, and Chen Tian from Xingning County; Huang Hui, Wang Neng, Wu Ming, Huang Ting, and Ye Fu from Dongguan County; Zhang Guiqing, Zhang Yuelai, Jiang Er, and Wen Hua from Boluo County; Liao Yuangui from Shixing County; Huang Fu, Liu Run, Li Xi, Yuan Fu, and You Wen from Heyuan County; Li Xian from Sanshui County; Li Hui and Lun Guang from Gaoyao County; Zhang Biao from Luoding City; Qiu Huan and Wang Fengqing from Jiaying City; Zhong Chun and Zhong Ri from Fengshun County; Kong Jinhong, Deng Er, Liao Xian, Zeng Xian, and Wan Er from

---

xv. *Sibu mingmu* "死不瞑目" is an idiomatic expression that means "people die with eyes open." This saying implies that people who die with their eyes open usually die with unrequited injustice or without fulfilling their duties or wishes.

Changle County; Pei Xian from Longmen County; Wen Fu from Heshan County; Luo Chuanzeng, Luo Hai, and Liu Lian from Longchuan County; Chen Fa and Luo De from Lufeng County; Lin Zhang from Xiangshan County; Zhang Wu from Deqing County; Lin Rende from Yangjiang County; Li Cekui from Yizhang County, Hunan Province; Jia Runcheng from Ningyuan County, Hunan Province; Zhou Weiping from Jiangning County, Jiangsu Province:

We, as ordinary civilians, have little learning and we were born in ill times.[xvi] Some youths were sold here because of failure in business; some were tricked and abducted by the wicked in their prime years. The reasons why we are here are filled with misery. Nevertheless, we have fallen into this trap, how can we get away from it? We only hope that we can go back to our hometowns after the contract expires. We did not expect to work in the foreign country, and we are treated worse than prisoners. We are sinking in a strange place and living in a hell on earth. The managers act like tyrants. They seek bribes. The owners are greedy. They often overwork us day and night. Sometimes, they put shackles and handcuffs on us. They flog us brutally. It is hard to have a day without being lashed; it is hard to have a morning to take a rest. Although the contract period on paper is eight years, they never follow the contract. We are miserable for the rest of our days. Working in the cities is a little better than other places. However, the local Cubans bully us even worse than slaves. We are bound by the contract; how can we not keep firm in difficulties? When the contract expires, almost half of us have died. For those who have not died, a lot of them either become disabled or have internal injury. If you are still healthy, you will be bullied by the rich or the government officials; or will be forced to sign another contract; or will be forced to work in the official workshop; or will be put into prison. They find ways to tie us up and make us slaves forever. How atrocious and greedy those people are! Moreover, this country has set up a cruel policy, stating that Chinese who have contracts here have to covert to Catholic and find a Cuban as "godfather" after the contract expires, if they want to get a freedom paper. If no freedom paper, the Chinese would be counted as an escaped convict. People in this country are greedy and untrustworthy. If we Chinese ask them to do something, we have to speak to them nicely and give them a lot of money, give them treasures and gold, respect them as godfather, and beg them to apply for a freedom paper for us. If they agree, they will ask for a lot of money, which is said to be used to bribe government officials. Thus, there are hundreds of thousands of Chinese laborers here, whose contracts have expired; but only several thousands of them get the

---

xvi. Although the authors of this petition said that they had little learning, the petition employed a standard speech and had many references. The pattern of sentences was carefully and neatly done. This ended with praises to the Qing emperor. The reason why the authors said that they had little learning or were foolish was to show modesty and humbleness, which are considered good virtues in Chinese tradition.

freedom paper. There is an incident, which would make the listener's hair stand on end.[xvii] Cuban government officials are like greedy *qiongqi* and *taotie* at heart.[xviii] Havana police go as far as vicious tigers and jackals. They often knock at our doors at night, intrude with weapons, and seize the opportunity to rob everything; they break crates and take away all money. Even if you call out loud, your neighbors cannot help. If you fight with them, they will take money, frame a case against you, and put you into prison. Where can we voice our grievances? To whom can we inform our woes? Their avarice is like a river that can never be filled. Their desire is like a sea that can never become full. On the tenth of the ninth moon in the year of Xin Wei (1871), local rich people started a riot and put Chinese in a bad situation. The corrupted officials manipulated power for personal ends and tortured the Chinese. All of a sudden, they assembled their army, and sacked the Chinese thoroughly. They took away freedom papers by force and locked up the Chinese, using thousands of cruel corporal punishments. They forced the Chinese into bondage and into signing another contract. Countless Chinese died in this incident. At that time, life and death were both difficult dilemmas, going forward and withdrawal were both dangerous decisions. Fortunately we unexpectedly were rescued from this desperate situation by heroes from other countries. Some officials from other countries knew we were treated unjustly and came to rescue us. They asked the generals for legal justifications and questioned the magistrate for reasons. They talked with harsh words and stern looks and made the Cuban officials talk with low voices. They discussed people's comments and made the local rich tyrants bow their heads in submission. Finally, the iron lock was open; the birdcage was broken; we were like swimming fish fleeing from the fishnet, weighing favor from those countries as

---

xvii. "Making the listener's hair stand on end" (发指, *fazhi*) is a Chinese idiom, which is an expression of extreme anger.

xviii. These are mythological beasts. In Chinese mythology, *qiongqi* (穷奇) is an evil god who praises evil and censures good. It is said that *qiongqi* often visit fight scenes, where they bite off the good person's nose. If someone has done bad deeds, *qiongqi* would encourage them to do more bad deeds. Therefore, ancient Chinese would call people, who befriend evilness and shun away from goodness, *qiongqi*. It was written in the chapter of Wengong (文公十八年) from *Zuozhuan* (左传) that a worthless son of a *Shaohao* clan, who despised righteousness and worshiped iniquity had been called "*qiongqi*" by the people. *Zuozhuan* (左传) (Spring and Autumn Annals and the Commentary of Zuo Qiuming) Available at www.guoxue.com/jinbu/13jing/cqzz_006.htm. There is also another definition: "A mythological beast, shaped like a cow, has hedgehog hair, makes noises like wild dogs," in *Shan hai jing*, the ancient Chinese mythology text; "A kind of beast, shaped like a tiger, has wings. It eats humans from their heads. It has another name: *Cong Zu*," in Pu Guo 郭璞, *Shan hai jing: 18 juan* (山海经: 18 卷), (Shanghai: Shang wu chubanshe 上海: 上海商务出版社, 1937). In Chinese mythology, *taotie* (饕餮) is a human-eating beast. During the *Shang* Dynasty, Chinese used the motif of *taotie* to decorate vessels. The term first appeared in *Zuozhuan*, in the chapter of *Wengong*, as a worthless son of *Jinyun* clan who had been extremely greedy in obtaining both food and goods, and his desire was difficult to be satisfy, so people called him "*taotie*." See Zuo Qiuming. This has also been described as follows: "In the mountains of Gou Wu . . . there is a kind of beast. It has a goat's body and human face. Its eyes are under its armpits. It has tiger teeth and human fingers, named *Pao Xiao*, which eats humans," in Pu Guo.

heavy as a mountain. We were like frightened birds flying back to our nests, grasping belongings in our homes as if precious as jade. How sad it is! Yesterday our lives were threatened in an instant; how miserable it is! Hunger and cold are everywhere near. All the suffering we experienced is due to the despotic ruling of Cuban government. Now, His Majesty's kindness is like a wide ocean, extending to corners of the world. We are like grass and trees that benefit from his rain-like generosity, which is a rare grace in thousands of years. We, as ordinary civilians, are humble and foolish laborers with misfortune. Youths are trapped in a land faraway from home; adults are wasting their lives in a foreign country. We regret that we are poor and sickly. We feel woeful that the harsh government here is making more cruel policies. That is why we dare to voice our grievance to you. As quoted.

PETITION 54

On the third day of the third moon, according to the petition by Ren Shizhen from Nanhai County; Dai Renjie from Xinning County; Liang Xingzhao from Shunde County, Guangdong Province:

Back in China, Shizhen ran a *fengshui* house in downtown Guangdong.[xix] Renjie had a restaurant. Xingzhao was the owner of a paper-money store.[xx] We all had wives and children, living well-off lives. However, we were cheated onto the Pigship, forced to travel across the ocean, and sold to a sugar plantation. We had been suffering hunger and whipping for eight years. Since we had to buy food and clothes from the stores in the sugar plantation, all our payment was deducted because of that. We had thought that after eight years, when we finished the contract, we could go out to find some jobs, which would pay us a little higher than the sugar plantation did, and could earn some traveling expenses to go back home. Unexpectedly, on the day when we finished contracts, the owner of the sugar plantation sent us into the official workshop. The next day, our feet were shackled, and we were forced to repair roads like prisoners. There was no payment at all. Then some businessmen came to make a deal with the officials and the workshop. Later they forced us to sign another contract, which was called "bondage." Every month, the payment was fifteen *yuan*. However, the officials took away ten *yuan* so that we got only five *yuan*. Sometimes, we had thirty *yuan* for payment, but the officials shared twenty-four *yuan* so that we got only six

---

xix. *Fengshui* (风水) is a study of environmental balance between the people and where they live, especially their dwelling or workplace. Ren Shizhen who ran a fengshui house, earned his living by providing consultation.

xx. Paper-money stores (纸宝铺, *zhibao pu*) sell symbolic money for funeral rites and might also sell paper houses, or in the ancient times, paper servants. The family of the deceased burns these as offerings.

yuan. When the bondage contract expired, we were sent back to the official work-shop. After several months in the official workshop, we were forced into bondage again. In between, there was not even one day when we could do as we like! Not to mention that we did not have money to go back home, even if we had money, we could not go back to home because we did not have the paper for going abroad. We are about sixty years old now and cannot see the end of our suffering. We think that the foreigners must have made a lot of money by abducting us Chinese for sale. They sell each Chinese for four hundred to one thousand *yuan*. They can get about two to three hundred *yuan* as profit. By now, they must have sold more than two hundred thousand Chinese and profited millions from this business. But since we are Chinese, this money is supposed to be given to our country and shared with our families. People who come from Fujian Province or Guangzhou Prefecture mostly sign a five-year contract. However, we three had to work for eight years. Obviously they have taken away three more years payment from us. We also saw that some people who got freedom paper in the earlier years could go out to work. They can earn at least twenty *yuan* and at most sixty *yuan* a month. Now we finished the contract and did nothing wrong, but we were forced to do unpaid labor in the official workshop. If we were paid at the rate of an outside job, which is thirty *yuan* on average, how much money have they made from that and how much should they return us? When we were in bondage, officials took away a big part of the bondage money, so how much money have they taken from us Chinese and how much should they return to us? As for the fee for freedom paper, it was only less than a hundred *yuan* in the earlier years. But later, officials ask for hundreds of *yuan*. Just think about it, how much money have they taken from us? The fee for going to court, walking paper, opening-store paper, doctor's license paper, off-board paper, begging paper, and the renewal for all these paper, how much money have they gotten from us Chinese labor? And it is needless to mention the rapacity and the robbery from the precinct chief and the soldiers. Though the officials and the businessmen in Cuba have gained so much money from the Chinese labor, they do not know how to appreciate; instead, they humiliate us, trample on us, and insult us by making us slaves and treating us like animals. Have you ever heard of any other things more miserable than this in history? We heard that the Chinese government has already reconciled with those big foreign countries and those countries have already prohibited the trade of black people; why is it that nobody tries to save the Chinese in Cuba? Why? Since the Cuban officials have made ways to make us slaves over and over, we have been trapped here for seventeen or eighteen years and have already become weak. We are not really sure about our future. Maybe we will be tortured to death in the official workshop or at the bondage place; or will be expelled out and will die in the street because of sickness and aging. In all, when we die, we will have no coffin and no grave. Maybe our bones will be burned and mixed with bulls and horses' bone ashes, and then used for the bleaching of white sugar![xxi] Our sons will have their sons, and then their sons will have sons. Nobody in our family will have the chance to know where we are. How pitiful! How pitiful! As quoted.

PETITION 65

On the sixth day of the third moon, according to the petition by Tang Liansheng from Nantongzhou Prefecture; Jiangsu Province; Wu Axiao from Baoshan County; Yang Defu from Shangyuan County; Wu Alei from Tong'an County, Fujian Province; Xie Aling, Xie Ari, Yu De, Lin Danian, and Shi Ashang from Zhangzhou Prefecture; Ping Hui from Dong'an County; Gao Ayi from Quanzhou Prefecture; Shen Axiang from Zhao'an County; Li Abu from Jian'an County; Wang Ming from Jinjiang County; Chen Wangying, Zhang Chao, Lai Azhang, Weng Agui, and Qiu Asheng from Heyuan County; Peng Acai, Liao Abing, Lin Abei, Chen Aren, Chen Aguang, Pan Ahe, and Liu En from Panyu County; Luo Afang and Kuang Renlian from Conghua County; Lu Shengying from Yong'an County; Huang Acheng, Xu Akang, Chen Axian, Zhong Amei, and Zhang Axian from Guishan County; Ding Atuan and Luo Alin from Raoping County; Chen Azhang from Longmen County; Hu Axian and Li Jinxing from Heshan County; Wu Afang, Gu Ageng from Huilai County; Xu Ahui, Wang Aman, and Chen Afu from Dongguan County; Huang Aliu and Li Youke from Jieyang County; Zhu Fu from Chenghai County; He Yinghua, Chen A'er, Huang Akuan, and Feng Asheng from Enping County; Chen Axing from Dong'an County; Chen Agang from Gaoyao County; Li Zhongji, Ou Ashu, Huang A'an, Su Achang, and Yu Dazhang from Nanhai County; Chen Aman and Mai Ayi from Xiangshan County; Liu Atang, Lin Changkun, Liu Ayang, Li Ajin, Cai Daji, Ou Ashi, Wu Shaoqing, Zeng Adong, and Cai Ashun from Chaozhou Prefecture; Liu De from Leizhou Prefecture; Zhang Awang and Xiao Achang from Huizhou Prefecture; Xie Asan, Ke Guansheng, Zhong Axi, Gu Guanqie, Zhu Axian, and Zhu Alian from Boluo County; Liang Acheng, Mo Afu, Huang Axing and Lei Bai'an from Xinhui County; Hu Linbao from Zengcheng County; Huang Aheng and Tan Yuankun from Shunde County; Chen Chunfu, Luo Ayao, Zhou Yi, Wen Asi, Xiao Liangxing, Li Ade, and Zhang Ayi from Jiayingzhou Prefecture; Xie Achang and Wu Jiuru from Kaiping County; Huang Amao and Wang Aman from Changle County; Lin Ashun from Zhenping County; Li Tingling and Chen Ashi from Xinning County; Wu Arong from Pingyuan County; Pan Chenglan from Wuchuan County; Chen Suixian and Jiang Ageng from Sanshui County; Xu Ashao

---

xxi. In other petitions/depositions, it was said that by mixing a human's bone ashes with the sugar, the sugar would be whiter. In regular sugar refining, animal bone ashes, sometimes called bone char, are used to filter raw sugar juice.

from Chaoyang County; Yang Akuan from Wenchang County; Lin Achang from Qingyuan County; Wu Lianfa from Xingning County, Guangdong Province:

In the last ten years, we were abducted by the Portuguese, shipped from Macao and sold in Cuba to different sugar plantations as slaves. We are tormented in every possible way. Those who are lucky enough to survive after eight years hoped that they could go back home. But if one does not have freedom paper, one cannot apply for the Go-Abroad Paper; if one does not have the Go-Abroad Paper, one is not permitted to take a ship back to China. In earlier years, when laborers fulfilled their contract after eight years, they could implore the master to sign a Proof. Then they could find a godfather as sponsor and apply for the paper from local officials. The fee required by officials varied from half gold to fifteen gold. And the fee for Go-Abroad Paper varied from half gold to twenty or thirty gold. When the officials received the money, they always put it off from one week to the next and even for tens of weeks. If during that waiting time officials were reassigned, one would lose both one's money and paper. Even after you get the freedom paper and stay in Cuba temporarily, you have to pay about ten *yuan* to buy a Walking Paper in order to walk on the streets. This paper has to be renewed every year with several *yuan*. If the paper was lost or expired, one would be penalized heavily. Or if one wants to go to another port town in Cuba, one has to obtain a Go-to-another-port Paper from the local boss. Doctors have to apply for Doctor's Paper; beggars have to apply for a Begging Paper in order to beg. All require a fee. Small vendors have to get Open-Store Paper, which takes more time and more money to obtain. Even if you have all the papers that you should have, the street patrols could always stop you in the street; the patroller could always break into your residence to check them. Some take them away and say the paper is fake; some tear them apart and say you have no papers. They will put you into prison or the official workshop doing non-paid work with your feet and neck chained. This will last until some rich businessmen comes to declare you an "escapee" and claim you in a casual manner. You will be forced to sign another contract called "Tie-up" with the businessman. The payment is made a little high so the government officials can divide and take more than half of it. After fulfilling this bondage, you would be sent back to the official workshop to work for some time. Then you would be forced into bondage again. It is like a circle without an end, no matter how many times. The officials can have a construction project done for this entire island by not having to pay any wages. Businessmen use laborers who have finished the first contract and fill up government officials' pockets. The more associated the businessmen and the officials are, the more injustice and misery Chinese labor suffer. When we worked in a sugar plantation, we were slaves for one household. Now when we are sent to the official workshop, we are forced to be slaves for all. We are trapped and slaves for them for the rest our lives! Last year the forced labor service of La Trocha was close to a rebel camp and was very dangerous. The natural surroundings and climate were bad. Officials sent 10 percent black people and 90 percent Chinese over to work. They said after six months the contract would be completed and freedom paper would be given upon return. Except one third who died there, two thirds have come back one by one. However, instead of being given freedom paper, the returning Chinese were sent to official workshops in different cities. They regard Chinese labor as profitable commodities. Since local officials and businessmen here ill-intentioned and untrustworthy, reason cannot even be talked about. We are trapped in this faraway land so that we are at our last gasp. But we have seen businessmen and civilians from other countries come and go freely. Why have only Chinese been so misfortunate in Macao and Cuba? Misery upon misery without end. We are especially petitioning here and hope that your Honor will take pity and will try every means to save us from this extreme suffering. We would be deeply grateful. As quoted.

SOURCES

The primary source for this study comes from the petitions and depositions in the fourteen-volume set of *Guba huagong chengci* 古巴华工呈词 (Testimonies given by Chinese labor in Cuba) and the four-volume set of *Guba huagong kougongce* 古巴华工口供册 (Volumes of testimonies given by Chinese labor in Cuba). These volumes are housed in the Library of Ancient Books at the National Library of China in Beijing. In modern times, a set of the testimonies was translated into simplified Chinese, put in standard punctuated form and published in Beijing in 1984. This set, which features a quarter of the depositions, appears as part of one volume in a ten-volume series. The ten-volume series is entitled *Huagong chuguo shiliao huibian* 华工出国史料汇编 (Collection of historical sources on overseas Chinese labor). This source is out of print, but it can be found in various research libraries worldwide. (A note to researchers: The order in which these testimonies appear does not correlate to the *order of the original testimonies in the 1874 set*. Thus, researchers might be confused upon comparing the modern set and the original set.) I stumbled upon another collection of testimonies at Columbia University's C.V. Starr East Asian Library, *Guba huagong diaochalu* 古巴华工调查录 (Records of investigation on Chinese labor in Cuba). This source provides less than a quarter of the depositions. At my urging, the library digitized the material, which makes this unique source accessible to the public and can be viewed through the library portal.

As for the commission report, the English portion was republished in the United States in 1993, with a remarkable introduction by Denise Helly. The original trilingual report (English, French, and one memorandum in Chinese) was republished in Taiwan in 1970. Both of these publications are out of print but are available to view or borrow at numerous libraries worldwide. A handwritten copy of the English portion of the report can be seen at the U.S. National Archives (II) in Maryland, and found there is also intriguing correspondence among the consular officials surrounding this event. As for the text by Antonio Chuffat Latour, *Apunte historico de los chinos en Cuba* (1927), it is rare. It can be viewed at Biblioteca Nacional José Martí. Other than that, it is available for viewing at only three libraries in the world: the University of California Los Angeles, University of California Berkeley, and Miami University (Florida) libraries. Materials related to Chuffat's surveillance by the American military can be viewed at the U.S. National Archives (I) in Washington, DC. As for the nineteenth-century travel accounts, memoirs, histories, and period studies of Cuba written in English, Spanish, and French, I have made fairly transparent the numerous sources in the endnotes. As a final note, I follow this study with two volumes that provide both the original and translated versions of the entire body of testimonies (petitions and depositions) with an index and glossary.

SELECTED BIBLIOGRAPHY

Abu-Lughod, Janet. *Before European Hegemony: The World System AD 1250–1350.* New York: Oxford University Press, 1989.

Accomando, Christina. *The Regulations of Robbers: Legal Fictions of Slavery and Resistance.* Columbus: Ohio State University Press, 2001.

Alonso Valdés, Corlia. "La immigración china: su presencia en el Ejército Libertador de Cuba." *Catauro: Revista Cubana de Antropología* 1.2 (2000).

Ancheta, Angelo. *Race, Rights, and the Asian American Experience.* New Brunswick: Rutgers University Press, 1998.

Andrews, William. *To Tell a Free Story: The First Century of Afro-American Autobiography, 1760–1865.* Urbana: University of Illinois Press, 1988.

Arensmeyer, Elliot. "British Merchant Enterprise and the Chinese Coolie Labour Trade." Dissertation, University of Hawaii, 1979.

Ballou, Maturin Murray. *Due South; or, Cuba Past and Present.* New York: Negro Universities Press, 1969.

Bergad, Laird W. *Cuban Rural Society in the Nineteenth Century.* Princeton: Princeton University Press, 1990.

Bergad, Laird W., Fe Iglesias Garcia, and Maria del Carmen Barcia. *The Cuban Slave Market, 1790–1880.* Cambridge: Cambridge University Press, 1995. 162–73.

Blackmar, Frank W., ed. *Kansas; A Cyclopedia of State History, Embracing Events, Industries, Counties, Cities, Towns, Prominent Persons, etc.* Vol. 2. Chicago: Standard Publishing Company, 1912.

Blassingame, John W. *The Slave Community: Plantation Life in the Antebellum South.* New York: Oxford University Press, 1972.

———. *Slave Testimony: Two Centuries of Letters, Speeches, Interviews, and Autobiographies.* Baton Rouge: Louisiana State University Press, 1977.

———. "Using the Testimony of Ex-Slaves." *The Slave's Narrative.* Charles T. Davis and Henry Louis Gates, eds. New York: Oxford University Press, 1985.

Bodde, Derk. *Law in Imperial China.* Cambridge: Harvard University Press, 1967.

Bretos, Miguel. "Imagining Cuba under the American Flag: Charles Edward Doty in Havana 1899–1902." *The Journal of Decorative and Propaganda Arts* 1.22 (1996): 83–104.

Britain. *Report of British Consulate General.* Havana, 1 Sept. 1873.

Calcagno, Francisco. *Poetas de color.* La Habana: S.S. Spencer, 1887.

Campbell, Persia. *Chinese Coolie Emigration to Countries Within the British Empire, 1923.* London: Frank Cass, 1971.

Carter, Marina. *Lakshmi's Legacy: The Testimonies of Indian Women in 19th Century Mauritius.* Mauritius: Éditions L'Océan Indien, 1994.

———. *Servants, Sirdars, and Settlers: Indians in Mauritius, 1834–1874.* New York: Oxford University Press, 1995.

———. *Voices from Indenture: Experiences of Indian migrants in the British Empire.* New York: Leicester University Press, 1996.

Carter, Marina, and Khal Torabully, eds. *COOLITUDE: An Anthology of the Indian Labour Diaspora.* Anthem Press, 2002.

Cezair-Thompson, Margaret. *The True History of Paradise.* New York: Dutton, 1999.

Chen, Hansheng 陈翰笙, Wendi Lu 卢文迪, Zexian Chen 陈泽宪 and Jiali Pang 彭家礼, comps. and eds. *Huagong chuguo shiliao huibian* 华工出国史料汇编 [Collection of historical sources on overseas Chinese labor]. Beijing: Zhonghua shuju, 1980.

Chen, Willi. *King of the Carnival.* London: Hansib Publishing, 1988.

Ch'ien, Evelyn. *Weird English.* Cambridge: Harvard University Press, 2004.

China. *Chinese Emigration: Report of the Commission Sent by China to Ascertain the Condition of Chinese Coolies in Cuba.* 1876. Taipei: Cheng Wen, 1970.

Chomsky, Aviva, et al., eds. *The Cuba Reader: History, Culture, Politics.* Durham: Duke University Press, 2003.

Choy, Philip, Lorraine Dong, and Marlon Hom. *The Coming Man.* Seattle: University of Washington Press, 1994.

Chuffat Latour, Antonio. *Apunte histórico de los chinos en Cuba.* Habana: Molina, 1927.

———. Letter to Sr. Dr. Orestes Ferrara. 3 June 1932. Archivo Nacional de Cuba.

Chuh, Kandice, and Karen Shimakawa, eds. *Orientations: Mapping Studies in the Asian Diaspora.* Durham: Duke University Press, 2001.

Cirules, Enrique. "Algunas reflexiones sobre la presencia de los chinos en Cuba." *Catauro: Revista Cubana de Antropología* 1.2 (2000).

Clements, Clancy. *The Linguistic Legacy of Spanish and Portuguese: Colonial Expansion and Language Change.* Cambridge University Press, forthcoming.

Cohen, Jerome, ed. *Essays on China's Legal Tradition.* New Jersey: Princeton University Press, 1980.

Cohen, Lucy. *Chinese in the Post–Civil War South.* Baton Rouge: Louisiana State University Press, 1984.

Corbitt, Duvon. *A Study of the Chinese of Cuba 1847–1947.* Wilmore: Asbury College Press, 1971.

Crespo Villate, Mercedes. *Mis imagines.* La Habana: Ediciones Verde Olivo, 2000.

Cuba. Centro de Estadística. *Noticias estadísticas.* Expediente General Colonización Asiática. AHN. Ultramar. Leg. 87 (1872).

Cubilié, Anne. *Women Witnessing Terror: Testimony and the Cultural Politics of Human Rights.* New York: Fordham University Press, 2005.

Cutler, Carl. *Greyhounds of the Sea.* Annapolis: Naval Institute Press, 1984.

Cvetkovich, Ann, and Ann Pelligrini. "Introduction." *Scholar and Feminist Online* 2.1 (2003).

Dabydeen, David. *Coolie Odyssey.* London: Hansib Publishing, 1998.

Dana, Richard Henry. *To Cuba and Back: A Vacation Voyage.* Boston: Ticknor and Fields, 1859.

Deerr, Noel. *The History of Sugar, I.* London: Chapman and Hall, 1949.

———. *The History of Sugar, II.* London: Chapman and Hall, 1950.

Desnoyers, Charles A. "Chinese Foreign Policy in Transition: Ch'en Lan-pin in the New World, 1872–1882." Dissertation, Temple University, 1988.

———. "Toward 'One Enlightened and Progressive Civilization': Discourses of Expansion and Nineteenth-Century Chinese Missions Abroad." *Journal of World History* 8.1 (1997): 135–156.

Ding, Loni. *Ancestors in the Americas.* Documentary. Berkeley: Center for Educational Telecommunications, 1997.

Dookhan, Isaac. "The Elusive Nirvana: Indian Immigrants in Guyana and the Des Voeux Commission, 1870–71." *Revista/Review Interamericana* 17.3–4 (1987): 54–89.

Dye, Alan. *Cuban Sugar in the Age of Mass Production.* Stanford: Stanford University Press, 1998.

Edreira de Caballero, Angelina. *Vida y Obra de Juan Gualberto Gómez, seis lecciones en su centenario.* La Habana: R. Mendez, 1954.

Elman, Benjamin A. *A Cultural History of Civil Examinations in Late Imperial China.* Berkeley: University of California Press, 2000.

Eng Herrera, Pedro, and Mauro Garcia Triani. *Marti en los chinos, los chinos en Marti.* La Habana: Grupo Promotor, 2003.

Erenchun, Félix. *Anales de la isla de Cuba.* Habana: Imprenta de la Antilla, 1858.

Escott, Paul. "The Art and Science of Reading WPA Slave Narratives." *The Slave's Narrative.* Edited by Charles T. Davis and Henry Louis Gates. New York: Oxford University Press, 1985.

Falleti, Tulia. "Juan Gualberto Gómez: Pioneer of Afro-Cuban Political Mobilization." *A Political Atlas of the African Diaspora.* 2001. http://diaspora.northwestern.edu.

Fermor, Patrick Leigh. *The Traveller's Tree: A Journey Through the Caribbean Islands.* London: John Murray, 1950.

Fermoselle, Rafael. *Politica y color en Cuba, La guerrita de 1912.* Montevideo: Ediciones Géminis, 1974.

Ferrer, Ada. *Insurgent Cuba: Race, Nation, and Revolution 1868–1898.* Chapel Hill: University of North Carolina, 1999.

Fisher, Sibylle. *Modernity Disavowed.* Durham: Duke University Press, 2004.

Gabbacia, Donna. "The Yellow Peril and the Chinese of Europe." *Migration, Migration History, History.* Edited by Jan Luccassen and Leo Lucassen. Bern: Peter Lang, 1999.

García Pedrosa, José R. *Legislación social de Cuba.* Habana: La Moderna Poesia, 1936.

García Triano, Mauro. *Los chinos de Cuba y los nexus entre las dos naciones.* La Habana: Sociedad Cubana de Investigaciones Filosóficas, 2003.

Gates, Henry Louis. Introduction. *The Slave's Narrative.* Edited by Henry Louis Gates and Charles T. Davis. New York: Oxford University Press, 1985.

Gates, Henry Louis, and William Andrews, eds. *Pioneers of the Black Atlantic: Five Slave Narratives from the Enlightenment.* Washington DC: Counterpoint, 1988.

Gonzales, Michael. "Resistance among Asian Plantation Workers in Peru." *From Chattel Slaves to Wage Slaves.* Edited by Mary Turner. Kingston: Ian Randle Publishers, 1995.

Gonzales, Olympia. *Leyendas Cubana.* Illinois: National Textbook Company, 1997.

Griffin, Eldon. *Clippers and Consuls.* Ann Arbor: Edwards Brothers, 1938. Taipei: Cheng Wen, 1972.

Guanche, Jesus. *Componentes Etnicos de Cuba.* Habana: Fundación Fernando Ortiz, 1996.

Guha, Ranajit. *A Subaltern Studies Reader.* Minneapolis: University of Minnesota Press, 1997.

Gungwu, Wang, and Ling-chi Wang. *The Chinese Diaspora.* Vols. I and II. Singapore: Times Academic Press, 1998.

Guo, Pu 郭璞. *Shan hai jing zhuan* 山海经传 [Commentary on the legendary geography and wonders on ancient China]. Beijing: Zhonghua shu ju ying yin, 1983.

Gushu diangu cidian 古書典故辭典 [Collection of extracts from ancient books in China] ed. Department of Chinese in Hangzhou University 杭州大學中文系. Hangzhou: Jiangxi jiaoyu chubanshe, 1988.

Guterl, Matthew. "After Slavery: Asian Labor, the American South, and the Age of Emancipation." *Journal of World History* 14.2 (2003): 209–242.

Gyory, Andrew. "A Reply to Stanford Lyman." *New Politics* 8.1 (2000): 51–67.

Hall, Stuart. "Cultural Identity and Diaspora." *Colonial Discourse and Postcolonial Theory*. Edited by Patrick Williams and Laura Chrisman. New York: Columbia University Press, 1994.

Hart, Sir Robert, et al. *The I.G. in Peking: Letters of Robert Hart, Chinese Maritime Customs, 1868–1907*. Cambridge: Belknap Press of Harvard University Press, 1975.

Hartman, Saidiya. *Scenes of Subjection: Terror, Slavery, and Self-Making in Nineteenth-Century America*. New York: Oxford University Press, 1997.

He, Huaihong 何怀宏. *Xuanju shehui ji qi zhongjie: Qin Han zhi wan Qing lishi de yizhong shehui xue chanshi* 选举社会及其终结—秦汉至晚清历史的—种社会学阐释 [Elective society and its end—an explanation of sociology from Qin, Han Dynasty to late Qing Dynasty]. Beijing: Shenghuo, dushu, xinzhi sanlian shudian, 1998.

Helg, Aline. *Our Rightful Share: The Afro-Cuban Struggle for Equality 1886–1912*, Chapel Hill: University of North Carolina Press, 1995.

Helly, Denise. *Idéologie et ethnicité: les Chinois Macao à Cuba, 1847–1886*. Montréal: Presses de l'Université de Montréal, 1979.

———. Introduction. *Cuba Commission Report, 1986*. Baltimore: Johns Hopkins Press, 1993.

Hirabayashi, Lane Ryo, Akemi Kikumura-Yano, and James A. Hirabayashi. *New Worlds, New Lives: Globalization and People of Japanese Descent in the Americas from Latin America in Japan*. Stanford: Stanford University Press, 2002.

Hoerder, Dirk. *Cultures in Contact: World Migrations in the Second Millennium*. Durham: Duke University Press, 2002.

Hu-Dehart, Evelyn. "Coolies, Shopkeepers, Pioneers: The Chinese of Mexico and Peru (1849–1930)." *Amerasia Journal* 15.2 (1989): 91–116.

———. "From Area Studies to Ethnic Studies: The Study of the Chinese Diaspora in Latin America." *Asian American Comparative and Global Perspective*. Edited by Shirley Hune et al. Pullman: Washington State University Press, 1991.

———. "Chinese Coolie Labour in Cuba in the Nineteenth Century: Free Labour or Neoslavery?" *Slavery and Abolition* 14.1 (1993): 75.

———. "The Chinese Diaspora." *The Asian Pacific American Heritage*. Edited by George Leonard. New York: Garland, 1998.

———. "Chinese in Cuba." *The Chinese Diaspora*. Edited by Lingchi Wang and Gungwu Wang. Singapore: Times Academic Press, 1998.

———. "Race Construction and Race Relations." *The Chinese Diaspora II*. Ling-Chi Wang and Gungwu Wang, eds. Singapore: Times Academic Press, 1998.

———. Report in *Encounters: People of Asian Descent in the Americas*. Edited by Roshni Rustomji-Kerns, et al. Lanham: Rowman & Littlefield, 1999.

Hui, Juan Hung. *Chinos en América*. Madrid: Editorial MAPFRE, 1992.

Hui, Ong Jin. "Chinese Indentured Labour: Coolies and Colonies." *The Cambridge Survey of World Migration*. Cambridge: Cambridge University Press, 1995.

Hwang, Yen Ching. *Coolies and Mandarins: China's Protection of Overseas Chinese in the Late Ch'ing Period 1851–1911*. Singapore: Singapore University Press, 1985.

Irick, Robert. *Ch'ing Policy Toward the Coolie Trade 1847–1878*. Taipei: Chinese Materials Center, 1982.

Ishay, Micheline. *The History of Human Rights: From Ancient Times to the Globalization Era*. Berkeley: University of California Press, 2004.

Jay, W.M.L. *My Winter In Cuba*. New York: Dutton and Company, 1871.

Jenkins, Edward. *The Coolie, His Rights and Wrongs*. New York: George Routledge and Sons, 1871.

Jerez, Miriam Herrera, and Mario Castillo Santana. *De la memoria a la vida pública*. La Habana: Centro de Investigación y Desarrollo de la Cultura Cubana Juan Marinello, 2003.

Jiménez, Luis A. *El arte autobiografico en Cuba en el siglo XIX*. New Brunswick: The Ometeca Institute, 1995.

Jiménez Pastrana, Juan. *Los Chinos en la liberación de Cuba*. Habana: Instituo de Historia, 1963.

———. *Los Chinos en la historia de Cuba: 1847–1930*. Habana: Editorial de Ciencias Sociales, 1983.

———. *Los Chinos en las luchas por la liberación cubana*. Habana: Editorial de Ciencias Sociales, 1983.

Jin, Meiling. *Gifts From My Grandmother: Poems*. London: Sheba Feminist, 1985.

Jung, Moon Ho. *Coolies and Cane*. Baltimore: Johns Hopkins University Press, 2006.

———. *Song of the Boatwoman*. Leeds, England: Peepal Tree Press, 1996.

Kale, Madhavi. *Fragments of Empire: Capital, Slavery, and Indian Indentured Labor in the British Caribbean*. Philadelphia: University of Pennsylvania Press, 1998.

Keita, Maghan. "Africans and Asians: Historiography and the Long View of Global Interaction." *Journal of World History* 16.1 (2005): 1–32.

Kirkpatrick, Margery. *From the Middle Kingdom to the New World*. Guyana: Kirkpatrick, 1993.

Klein, Herbert S. *African Slavery in Latin America and the Caribbean*. Oxford: Oxford University Press, 1986.

Knight, Franklin. *Slave Society in Cuba*. Madison: University of Wisconsin Press, 1970.

Kwok Crawford, Margery. *Scenes from the History of the Chinese in Guyana.* Guyana: Crawford, 1989.

Lai, Him Mark. *Becoming Chinese American: A History of Communities and Institutions.* Walnut Creek: Altamira Press, 2004.

Lai, Walton Look. *Indentured Labor, Caribbean Sugar: Chinese and Indian Migrants to the British West Indies, 1838–1918.* Baltimore: Johns Hopkins University Press, 1993.

———. *The Chinese in the West Indies 1806–1995.* Kingston, Jamaica: University of West Indies Press, 1998.

———. "Asian Contract and Free Migration." *Coerced and Free Migration: Global Perspectives.* Edited by David Eltis. Stanford: Stanford University Press, 2002.

Laing, Alexander. *The Sea Witch: A Narrative of the Experiences of Capt. Roger Murray and Others in the American Clipper Ship During the Years 1846–1856.* New York: Farrar and Rinehart, 1933.

Lamar-Santana, Hedy. *Semblanzas de mi padre: el medico chino.* Lamar-Santana, 2001.

Lamounier, Lucia. "Between Slavery and Free Labour: Early Experiments with Free Labour & Patterns of Slave Emancipation in Brazil and Cuba." *From Chattel Slaves to Wage Slaves.* Kingston: Ian Randle Publishers, 1995.

Lau, D.C. *Mencius.* Harmondsworth: Penguin Books, 1970.

Laurence, K.O. *A Question of Labour: Indentured Immigration into Trinidad and British Guiana, 1875–1917.* New York: St. Martin's Press, 1994.

Lee, Easton. *From Behind the Counter: Poems from a Rural Jamaican Experience.* Kingston, Jamaica: Ian Randle Publishers, 1998.

Lee, Erika. "Orientalisms in the Americas: A Hemispheric Approach to Asian American History." *Journal of Asian American Studies* 8.3 (2005): 235–256.

Lee, Robert G. *Orientals: Asian Americans in Popular Culture.* Philadelphia: Temple University Press, 1999.

Lesser, Jeffrey. "Neither Slave nor Free, Neither Black nor White." *Estudios Interdisciplinarios de America Latina y Caribe* 5.2 (1994): n.p. http://www.tau.ac.il/eial/V_2/lesser.htm.

———. "In Search of the Hyphen." *New Worlds, New Lives.* Edited by Lane Hirabayashi, et al. Stanford: Stanford University Press, 2002.

Levathes, Louise. *When China Ruled the Seas.* New York: Oxford University Press, 1996.

Leveen, E. Phillip. "A Quantitative Analysis of the Impact of British Suppression Policies on the Volume of the Nineteenth Century Atlantic Slave Trade." *Race and Slavery in the Western Hemisphere; Quantitative Studies.* Edited by Stanley I. Engerman and Eugene D. Genovese. Princeton: Princeton University Press, 1975.

Lipski, John. "Chinese-Cuban Pidgin Spanish." *Creole Genesis, Attitudes, and Discourse*. Edited by John Rickford and Suzanne Romaine. Philadelphia: John Benjamins Publishing, 1999.

Liu, Dong 刘东. *Zhonghua wenming duben* 中华文明读本 [Reading materials regarding Chinese culture]. Beijing: Shehui kexue wenxian chubanshe, 1999.

Liu, Lydia. Tokens of Exchange: The Problem of Translation in Global Circulations. Durham: Duke University Press, 1999.

———. *Clash of Empires: The Invention of China in Modern World Making*. Cambridge: Harvard University Press, 2004.

Liu Yiqing 刘义庆. *Shi shuo xin yu* 世说新语 [A new account of tales of the world]. Taipei: Yiwen yinshuguan, 1964.

Lo Bartolo, Guiseppe. *Barrio Chino de la Habana, imagen del tiempo*. Panamá: Caribe Publishing, 1999.

Lodge, Henry Cabot. "The Business World Vs. The Politicians." *The Forum* (1895).

Loewen, James. *The Mississippi Chinese: Between Black and White*. Cambridge: Harvard University Press, 1971.

Lott, Tommy. *Subjugation and Bondage: Critical Essays on Slavery and Social Philosophy*. Lanham: Rowman & Littlefield, 1998.

Lowe, Lisa. *Immigrant Acts*. Durham: Duke University Press, 1996.

Lubbock, Basil. *Coolie Ships and Oil Sailers*. Glasgow: Brown, Son & Ferguson, 1935.

Luciano Franco, José. *Comercio clandestine de esclavos*. Havana: Editorial de Ciencias Sociales, 1980.

Lugo-Oriz, Agnes. *Identidades Imaginadas: Biografia y nacionalidad en el horizonte de la Guerra*. San Juan: Editorial de la Universidad de Puerto Rico, 1999.

Lyman, Stanford M. "The 'Chinese Question' and American Labor Historians." *New Politics* 7.4 (2000): 113–148.

Ma, Lawrence, and Carolyn Cartier. *The Chinese Diaspora*. Lanham: Rowan & Littlefield, 2003.

Marti, José. *Fragmentos*. Habana: Editorial Tropico, 1949.

Martin, Wilbur. *Slavery in China During the Former Han Dynasty*. New York: Russell and Russell, 1943.

Martínez Ortiz, Rafael. *Cuba, los primeros años de su independencia*. Paris: Imprimerie Artitique "Lux," 1921.

Martinez-Alier, Verena. *Marriage, Class and Colour in Nineteenth Century Cuba*. New York: Cambridge University Press, 1974.

Mathews, Robert Henry, ed. *Mathews' Chinese-English Dictionary*. Revised American ed. Cambridge: Harvard University Press, 1945.

Mattei, Andrés Ramos. *La Hacienda Azucarera: Su crecimiento y crisis en Puerto Rico*. San Juan: CEREP, 1981.

McBride, Dwight. *Impossible Witness: Truth, Abolition, and Slave Testimony.* New York: New York University Press, 2001.

McGary, Howard, and Bill Lawson. *Between Slavery and Freedom.* Bloomington: Indiana University Press, 1992.

McLagan, Meg. "Human Rights, Testimony, and Transnational Publicity." *Scholar and Feminist Online* 2.1 (2003): http://www.barnard.columbia.edu/sfonline/ps/mclagan.htm.

Meagher, Arnold Joseph. "The Introduction of Chinese Laborers to Latin America: The 'Coolie Trade,' 1847–1874." Dissertation, University of California, Davis, 1975.

Metzger, Thomas A. *The Internal Organization of Ching Bureaucracy.* Cambridge: Harvard University Press, 1973.

Mills, Charles. *The Racial Contract.* Ithaca: Cornell University Press, 1997.

Mintz, Sidney. *Sweetness and Power: The Place of Sugar in Modern History.* New York: Penguin, 1985.

Miyazaki, Ichisada. *China's Examination Hell.* New Haven: Yale University Press, 1981.

Mongia, Radhika. "Impartial Regimes of Truth." *Cultural Studies* 18.5 (2004): 749–768.

Montejo, Esteban, *Biography of a Runaway Slave.* Translated by W. Nick Hill. Edited by Miguel Barnet. Willimantic: Curbstone Press, 1994.

Montejo, Esteban, and Miguel Barnet. *Biografía de un cimarrón.* Barcelona: Ediciones Ariel, 1968.

Moreno Fraginals, Manuel. *El ingenio: complejo económico social cubano del azúcar.* Vols. 1 and 3. Habana: Ciencias Sociales, 1978.

———. "Extent and Significance of Chinese Immigration to Cuba (19th Century)." In *Asiatic Migrations in Latin America.* Edited by Luz María Martínez Montiel. Mexico: Colegio de México, 1981.

Munasinghe, Virajini. *Callaloo or Tossed Salad?* Ithaca: Cornell University Press, 2001.

Murray, David R. *Odious Commerce: Britain, Spain, and the Abolition of the Cuban Slave Trade.* Cambridge: Cambridge University Press, 1980.

Murray, Henry. *Lands of the Slave and the Free.* London: John Parker & Sons, 1855.

Naipaul, V.S. *Guérillos.* Paris: Albin Michel, 1981.

Northrup, D. *Indentured Labor in the Age of Imperialism 1838–1914.* New York: Cambridge University Press, 1995.

O'Kelly, James. *The Mambi-land or Adventures of a Herald Correspondent in Cuba.* Philadelphia: Lippincott, 1874.

Okihiro, Gary. *Margins and Mainstreams.* Seattle: University of Washington Press, 1994.

————. *Common Ground: Reimagining American History*. Princeton: Princeton University Press, 2001.

————. "Toward a Pacific Civilization." Lecture, University of Arizona, March 22, 2001.

Olney, James. "'I Was Born:' Slave Narratives, Their Status as Autobiography and as Literature." In *The Slave's Narrative*. New York: Oxford University Press, 1985.

Padura, Leonardo. "El viaje mas." *Catauro: Revista Cubana de Antropologia* 1.2 (2000): 154–155.

Palumbo-Liu, David. *Asian/American: Historical Crossings of a Racial Frontier*. Stanford: Stanford University Press, 1999.

Pan, Lynn. *Sons of the Yellow Emperor: A History of the Chinese Diaspora*. New York: Kodansha International, 1994.

Pateman, Carole. *The Sexual Contract*. Stanford: Stanford University Press, 1988.

Pérez, Louis A. *Slaves, Sugar & Colonial Society: Travel Accounts of Cuba, 1801–1899*. Wilmington: Scholarly Resources, 1992.

————, ed. *The Travel Diary of Joseph Dimock*. Wilmington: Scholarly Resources, 1998.

————. *Winds of Change: Hurricanes and the Transformation of Nineteenth Century Cuba*. Chapel Hill: University of North Carolina Press, 2001.

Pérez de la Riva, Juan. "Demografia de los culíes chinos en Cuba, 1853–74." *Separata de la Revistad de la Biblioteca Nacional José Martí* 57.4 (1966): 57–86.

————. *Contribución a la Historia de la gente sin historia*. Habana: Editorial de Ciencias Sociales, 1974.

————. *El barracón: esclavitud y capitalismo en Cuba*. La Habana: Editorial de Ciencias Sociales, 1975.

————. *El barracón y otros ensayos*. La Habana: Editorial de Ciencias Sociales, 1975.

————. *Los culíes chinos en Cuba*. La Habana: Editorial de Ciencias Sociales, 2000.

Plowman, Robert. "The Voyage of the Coolie Ship *Kate Hooper* October 3, 1857–March 26, 1858." *Prologue, Quarterly of the National Archives and Records Administration* 33.2 (2001): 87–95.

Powell, Patricia. *The Pagoda*. New York: Knopf, 1998.

Prashad, Vijay. *The Karma of Brown Folk*. Minneapolis: University of Minnesota Press, 2000.

Qiu, Pengsheng 邱彭生. "Zhenxiang dabai? Ming Qing xingan zhong de falü tuili" 真相大白?明清刑案中的法律推理 [Law and Order in Ming and Qing Dynasty]. *Rang zheng ju shuo hua, Zhongguo pian* 让证据说话, 中国篇 [Let the evidence speak]. Ed. Bingzhen Xiong. Taipei: Maitian chuban, 2001. 135–198.

Qu, Tongzu. *Local Government in China Under the Qing*. Cambridge: Harvard University Press, 1962.

Quesada, Gonzalo de. *Mi Primera Ofrenda*. New York: Imprenta de El Porvenir, 1892.

———. *Los Chinos y la independencia de Cuba*. Leipzig: Breitkopf & Hartel, 1910.

———. *Los chinos y la revolución cubana*. La Habana: Ucar, Garcia, 1946. Report reprinted in *Catauro: Revista Cubana de Antropología* 1.2 (2000): 179–191.

Ramdin, Ron. *Arising from Bondage: A History of the Indo-Caribbean People*. London: I.B. Taurus, 2000.

Ramdin, Ron, and Captain Swinton. *The Other Middle Passage: Journal of a Voyage with Coolie Emigrants*. London: Hansib Publishing, 1994.

Rawick, George P. *From Sundown to Sunup; The Making of the Black Community*. Westport: Greenwood Publishing Company, 1972.

Remington, Frederic. "Under Which King?" *Colliers*, April 1899.

Rhoads, Edward. "In the Shadow of Yung Wing: Zeng Laishun and the Chinese Educational Commission to the United States." *Pacific Historical Review* 74.1 (2005): 19–58.

Rodríguez, José Baltar. *Los chinos de Cuba*. La Habana: Fundación Fernando Ortiz, 1997.

Rodriguez La O, Raul. "Juan Gualberto Gómez and his stay in Paris (1869–1876). *Granma Internacional* (30 December 2003).

Rodríguez Pastor, Humberto. *Chinos culíes: Bibliografía y fuentes*. Lima: Instituto de Apoyo Agrario e Instituto de Historia Rural Andiro, 1984.

———. *Hijos del Celeste Imperio en el Peru (1850–1900): Migración, agricultura, mentalidad y explotación*. Lima, Perú: Instituto de Apoyo Agrario, 1989.

———. *Herederos del dragon: Historia de la comunidad China en el Perú*. Lima, Perú: Congreso del Perú, 2000.

Rustomji-Kerns, Roshni, Rajini Srikanth, and Leny Mendoza Strobel. *Encounters: People of Asian Descent in the Americas*. Lanham: Rowman & Littlefield, 1999.

Ryan, Alan, ed. *The Reader's Companion to Cuba*. New York: Harcourt Brace, 1997.

San guo zhi 三国志 [History of three kingdoms]. Compiled by Shou Chen 陈寿 Shanghai: Zhonghua shuju, 1927.

Sanders, Mark. "Reading Lessons." *Diacritics* 29.3 (1999): 3–20.

———. *Complicities: The Intellectual and Apartheid*. Durham: Duke University Press, 2002.

———. "Ambiguities of Mourning." In *Loss: The Politics of Mourning*. Edited by David Eng and David Kazanjian. Berkeley: University of California Press, 2003.

————. "Truth and Contestation." *Law and Literature* 16.3 (2004): 475–490.

Sarduy, Severo. *De Donde Son Los Cantantes*. Barcelona, Spain: Seix Barral, 1980.

Sarusky, Jaime. "The East Indian Community in Cuba." *Indenture and Exile: The Indo-Caribbean Experience*. Ed. Frank Birbalsingh. Toronto: TSAR, 1989.

Scott, James C. *The Moral Economy of the Peasant: Rebellion and Subsistence in Southeast Asia*. New Haven: Yale University Press, 1976.

————. *Weapons of the Weak: Everyday Forms of Peasant Resistance*. New Haven: Yale University Press, 1985.

————. *Domination and the Arts of Resistance: Hidden Transcripts*. New Haven: Yale University Press, 1990.

Scott, Rebecca. *Slave Emancipation in Cuba*. Pittsburgh: University of Pittsburgh Press, 1985.

Scherer, Frank. "Sanfancón: Orientalism, Self-Orientalization, and 'Chinese Religion' in Cuba." *Nation Dance: Religion, Identity, and Cultural Difference in the Caribbean*. Edited by Patrick Taylor. Indianapolis: Indiana University Press, 2001.

Schulman, Ivan A. Introduction. *Autobiography of a Slave/Autobiografica de un escalvo*. By Juan Francisco Manzano. Translated by Evelyn Picon Garfield. Detroit: Wayne State University Press, 1996.

Shen, Yansheng 沉延生 and Zhang Shouli 张守礼. "Zizhi yihuo xingzheng: Zhongguo xiangzhi de huigu yu zhanwang" 自治抑或行政—中國鄉治的回顧與展望 (Autonomy or administration—retrospect and prospect of rural management in China). June 3, 2007. http://www.chinarural.org/news_show. aspx?cols=221048&ID=28392.

Shepherd, Verene, ed. *Maharani's Misery*. Kingston: University of West Indies Press, 2002.

Sherer, Frank. "Chinese Shadows: Fernando Ortíz and José Martí on Cubanity and Chineseness." http://www.yorku.ca/cerlac/documents/chinese-shadows.pdf.

Shinebourne, Janice. *Timepiece*. Leeds, England: Peepal Tree Press, 1986.

————. *The Last English Plantation*. Leeds, England: Peepal Tree Press, 1988.

Sims, Lowery Stokes. *Wilfredo Lam and the International Avant Garde*. Austin: University of Texas Press, 2002.

Smith, Gaddis. "The *Amistad* in a Global Maritime Context." *The Connecticut Scholar: Occasional Papers of the Connecticut Humanities Council* 1.10 (1992): 37–43.

Smith, Richard, John Fairbank, and Katherine Bruner, eds. *Robert Hart and China's Early Modernization*. Cambridge: Council of East Asian Studies/Harvard University Press, 1991.

Smorkaloff, Pamela Maria. *Readers and Writers in Cuba: A Social History of Print Culture, 1830s–1990s*. New York: Garland, 1997.

Snow, Philip. *Star Raft: China's Encounter With Africa*. Ithaca: Cornell University Press, 1988.

Spivak, Gayatri Chakavorty. "Can the Subaltern Speak?" In *Marxism and the Interpretation of Culture*. Edited by Cary Nelson and Larry Grossberg. Urbana: University of Illinois Press, 1998.

Stanley, Amy Dru. *From Bondage to Contract: Wage Labor, Marriage, and the Market in the Age of Slave Emancipation*. New York: Cambridge University Press, 1998.

Steele, James Williams. *Cuban Sketches*. New York: G.P. Putnam's Sons, 1881.

Steinfeld, Robert. *Coercion Contract and Free Labor in the Nineteenth Century*. Cambridge: Cambridge University Press, 2001.

Stepto, Robert. *From Behind the Veil: A Study of Afro-American Narrative*. Urbana: University of Illinois Press, 1991.

Stewart, Watt. *Chinese Bondage in Peru*. 1951. Reprint, Westport: Greenwood Press, 1970.

Sublette, Ned. *Cuba and Its Music: From the First Drums to the Mambo*. Chicago: Chicago Review Press, 2004.

Sue-A-Quan, Trev. *Cane Reapers*. Vancouver: Riftswood Publishing, 1999.

Sun, E-tu Zen, and John de Francis. *Chinese Social History: Translations of Selected Studies*. New York: Octagon Books, 1972.

Takaki, Ronald. *Different Mirror*. Boston: Little Brown & Co., 1993.

———. *Pau Hana: Plantation Life and Labor in Hawaii, 1835–1920*. University of Hawaii Press, 1983.

Tan, Qianchu 谭干初. "Guba zhaji" 古巴杂记 [General description of Cuba]. *Xiaofanghu zhaiyu dicongchao* 小方壶斋舆地丛钞 [Travel notes of different places]. Ed. Xiqi Wang 王锡祺. Hangzhou: Hangzhou guji shudian, 1891.

Tanco Armero, Nicolas. *Viaje de Nueva Granada á China y de China á Francia*. Paris: Simon Raçon, 1861.

———. "La emigración de los colonos chinos." *Revista Contemporanea* 3.7 (1877): n.p.

Tchen, John Kuo Wei. *New York Before Chinatown*. Baltimore: Johns Hopkins University Press, 1999.

Tejeiro, Guillermo. *Historia ilustrada de la colonia China en Cuba*. Habana: Editorial Hercules, 1947.

Thomas, Hugh. *Cuba: or The Pursuit of Freedom*. New York: Da Capo, 1988.

———. *The Slave Trade*. New York: Simon & Schuster, 1997.

Tinker, Hugh. *A New System of Slavery: The Export of Indian Labour Overseas, 1830–1920*. London: Hansib Publishing, 1993.

Tomich, Dale. *Through the Prism of Slavery*. Lanham: Rowman & Littlefield, 2004.

Turner, Mary. "Between Slavery and Free Labour." *From Chattel Slaves to Wage Slaves*. Edited by Mary Turner. Kingston: Ian Randle Publishers, 1995.

U.S. Congress. "Report of the Committee on Commerce of the House of Representatives." *American Diplomatic and Public Papers: The United States and China 1842–1860.* Vol. 17, 34th Cong., 1st sess., H. Doc. 443. Washington, DC, 1–30.

U.S. Congress. "Report of the Secretary of State." *American Diplomatic and Public Papers: The United States and China 1842–1860.* Vol. 17, 34th Cong., 1st sess. Washington, DC.

Valdes Bernal, Sergio. "Los chinos desde el punto de vista linguistico." *Catauro: Revista Cubana de Antropología* 1.2 (2000): 62–63.

Varela, Beatriz. *Lo chino en el habla cubana.* Miami: Ediciones Universal, 1980.

Watt, John R. *The District Magistrate in Late Imperial China.* New York: Columbia University Press, 1972.

Wideman, John. "Charles Chestnutt and the WPA Narratives." *The Slave's Narrative.* Edited by Charles T. Davis and Henry Louis Gates. New York: Oxford University Press, 1985.

Wilson, Samuel M. *The Emperor's Giraffe and Other Stories of Cultural Contact.* Boulder: Westview Press, 1999.

Wing, Yung. *My Life in China and America.* New York: Henry Holt, 1909.

Wong, Kevin Scott. "The Transformation of Culture: Three Chinese Views of America." *American Quarterly* 48.2 (1996): 201–232.

Wu, Frank H. *Yellow: Race in America Beyond Black and White.* New York: Basic Books, 2001.

Wu, Jianxiong 吴剑雄. *Haiwai yiju yu huaren shehui* 海外移居与华人社会 [Overseas migration and Chinese societies]. Taipei: Yunchen wenhua, 1993.

———. *Shijiu shiji qianwang Guba di huagong: 1847–1874* 十九世纪前往古巴的华工 [Chinese coolies in Cuba during the nineteenth century]. Taipei: Zhongyang yanjiuyuan Sanmin zhuyi yanjiusuo, 1998.

Xiong, Victor Cunrui. "The Story of a Kunlun Slave in Tang Chang'an." *Chinese Historians* 4.1 (1991): 77–81.

Xu, Yipu 徐艺圃. "Beijing tushuguan cang Qing dang youguan huagong shiliao jieshao" 北京图书馆藏清文件有关华工史料介绍 [Introduction of materials on Chinese labor saved at National Library in Beijing]. *Ming Qing dangan lunwen xuanbian* 明清档案论文选编 [Selection of essays on profiles in Ming and Qing Dynasty]. Ed. Zhongguo diyi lishi danganguan 中国第一历史档案馆. Beijing: Dangan chubanshe, 1985.

Yang, Anand. "Images of Asia: A Passage through Fiction and Film." *History Teacher* 13.3 (1980): 351–360.

Yap, Melanie, and Dianne Leong Man. *Colour, Confusion, and Concessions.* Hong Kong: Hong Kong University Press, 1996.

Yetman, Norman. "Ex-slave Interviews and the Historiography of Slavery." *American Quarterly* 36.2 (1964): 181–210.

———. "The Background of the Slave Narrative Collection." *American Quarterly* 19.3 (1967): 534–53.

———, ed. *Life Under the "Peculiar Institution"; Selections from the Slave Narrative Collection*. New York: Holt, Rinehart and Winston, 1970.

———, ed. *Voices from Slavery: 100 Authentic Slave Narratives*. New York: Holt, Rinehart and Winston, 1970.

Yun, Lisa. "Chinese Coolies and African Slaves in Cuba, 1847–74." *Journal of Asian American Studies* 4.2 (2001): 99–122.

∨ ———. "Under the Hatches: American Coolie Ships and Nineteenth Century Narratives of the Passage." *Amerasia Journal* 28.2 (2002): 38–63.

———. "An Afro-Chinese Caribbean: Cultural Cartographies of Contrariness in the Work of Antonio Chuffat Latour, Margaret Cezair-Thompson, and Patricia Powell." *Caribbean Quarterly* 50.2 (2004): 26–34.

∨ ———. "Chinese Freedom Fighters: Bondage and Liberation." *AFRO/ASIA: Revolutionary Political and Cultural Connections Between African- and Asian-Americans*. Edited by Fred Ho and Bill V. Mullen. Durham: Duke University Press, 2008.

Zanetti, Oscar, and Alejandro Garcia. *Sugar and Railroads: A Cuban History 1837–1959*. Chapel Hill: University of North Carolina Press, 1998.

NOTES

INTRODUCTION

1. Essay on Rudyard Kipling (1942), in George Orwell, *A Collection of Essays* (New York: Harvest, 1981).

2. See debate between Stanford Lyman and Andrew Gyrory on the Chinese "Coolie Question," Stanford M. Lyman, "The 'Chinese Question' and American Labor Historians," *New Politics* no. 7.4 (2000): 113–148; Andrew Gyory, "A Reply to Stanford Lyman," *New Politics* ns 8.1 (2000): 51–67. For American middle-class formation and the anti-Chinese coolie movements, see Robert G. Lee, *Orientals: Asian Americans in Popular Culture* (Philadelphia: Temple University Press, 1999). For American foreign debate and negotiations over coolies, see Eldon Griffin, *Clippers and Consuls* (1938; Ann Arbor: Edwards Brothers; Taipei, Taiwan: Cheng Wen, 1972). For Chinese debate and negotiations regarding coolies, see Yen Ching Hwang, *Coolies and Mandarins: China's Protection of Overseas Chinese in the Late Ch'ing Period* 1851–1911 (Singapore: Singapore University Press, 1985); Robert Irick, *Ch'ing Policy Toward the Coolie Trade 1847–1878* (Taipei, Taiwan: Chinese Materials Center, 1982). For British debates over coolies, including those in South Africa, Cuba, and the West Indies, see Persia Campbell, *Chinese Coolie Emigration to Countries within the British Empire* (London, England: Frank Cass, 1971). For Peruvian debates over Chinese coolies see Watt Stewart, *Chinese Bondage in Peru* (1951; Westport: Greenwood Press, 1970).

3. Joel Benjamin et al., *They Came in Ships* (Leeds, England: Peepal Tree Press, 1998) 39–43. Marina Carter and Khal Torabully, eds., *COOLITUDE: An Anthology of Indian Labour Diaspora* (London, England: Anthem Press, 2002); David Dabydeen, *Coolie Odyssey* (London, England: Hansib Publications, 1988).

4. Tam Pui-shum, Diccionario Español-Chino/Xiu zhen Lüsong huawen hebi zidian 袖珍吕宋华文合璧字典 (Hong Kong: Xunhuan tushu fanyi bianjishe 循环图书翻译编辑社, 1915.)

5. "culi. *Adaptación española de la palabra inglesa [coolie], a su vez transcripción de la voz indostánica [quli], con que se designa en la India, China y otros países orientales a los sirvientes indígenas. Esta voz no ha sido introducida en el D.R.A.E. hasta la edición de1956 y, como antes era muy frecuente el uso de la misma palabra inglesa pronunciándola como se escribe, sigue también usándose en esa forma,"* in *Diccionario de Uso del Español*. Maria Moliner. (Madrid: Editorial Gredos, S.A. 1966), 838 vol.1. "culi. *(Del ingl. Coolie, y este del hindi kulī). En la India, la China y oros países de Oriente, trabajador o criado indígena,"* in *Diccionario de la lengua española* 481 (Real Academia Espanola, 2001). No mention in *Diccionario etimológica español e hispánico* (Madrid: Epasa-Calpe, S.A. 1985). No mention in *Diccionario crítico etimológico castellano e hispánico,* Joan Corominas y Jose A. Pascual, (Madrid: Editorial Gredos, 1989).

6. Vijay Prashad, *Everybody Was Kung Fu Fighting* (Boston: Beacon Press, 2001), 72.

7. East Indian migration and cultural formation in the Caribbean offers similarities to that of the Chinese, though obviously there are clear distinctions. There are many studies

on the role of East Indians in the Caribbean, but for those specifically on the Indian coolie trade, see (among many) Hugh Tinker, *A New System of Slavery: The Export of Indian Labour Overseas, 1830–1920* (London, England: Hansib Publishing, 1993); K.O. Laurence, *A Question of Labour: Indentured Immigration into Trinidad and British Guiana, 1875–1917* (New York: St. Martin's Press, 1994); D. Northrup, *Indentured Labor in the Age of Imperialism 1838–1914* (New York: Cambridge University Press, 1995); Madhavi Kale, *Fragments of Empire: Capital, Slavery, and Indian Indentured Labor in the British Caribbean* (Philadelphia: University of Pennsylvania Press, 1998); Ron Ramdin, *Arising from Bondage: A History of the Indo-Caribbean People* (London, I.B.Taurus, 2000); poetry by David Dabydeen, *Coolie Odyssey* (London, England: Hansib Publishing, 1988); Marina Carter and Khal Torabully, *COOLITUDE: An Anthology of the Indian Labour Diaspora*; Virajini Munasinghe examines the East Indian ethnic "estrangement from the state" in *Callaloo or Tossed Salad?* (Ithaca: Cornell University Press, 2001). Historical work with major focus upon on the Chinese coolies of Cuba include this partial list of Juan Pérez de la Riva's work: Pedro Deschamps Chapeaux and Juan Pérez de la Riva, *Contribución a la historia de la gente sin historia* (La Habana: Editorial de Ciencias Sociales, 1974, 1966); *El barracón; esclavitud y capitalismo en Cuba* (1966; La Habana: Editorial de Ciencias Sociales, 1975); "Demografía de los culíes chinos en Cuba, 1853–74," *Separata de la Revistad de la Biblioteca Nacional José Marti* 57.4 (1966): 57–86; *Los culies chinos en Cuba* (La Habana, Cuba: Editorial de Ciencias Sociales, 2000). Denise Helly, *Idéologie et ethnicité : les Chinois Macao à Cuba, 1847–1886; The Cuba Commission Report*, introduction Denise Helly (Baltimore: Johns Hopkins University Press, 1993); José Baltar Rodríguez, *Los chinos de Cuba* (La Habana, Cuba: Fundación Fernando Ortiz, 1997); Juan Jiménez Pastrana, *Los chinos en las luchas por la liberación cubana* (La Habana, Cuba: Editorial de Ciencias Sociales, 1983); Wu Jianxiong, *Shi jiu shi ji qian wang Guba de hua gong*: 1847–1874 (Taipei, China: Zhongyang yanjiuyuan Sanmin zhuyi yanjiusuo, 1998); Duvon Corbitt, *A Study of the Chinese in Cuba, 1847–1947* (Wilmore: Asbury College Press, 1971); Arnold Meagher, *The Introduction of Chinese Laborers to Latin America: the "Coolie Trade," 1847–1874*," dissertation, University of California, Davis, 1975; Marshall Powers, *Chinese Coolie Migration to Cuba*, dissertation, University of Florida, 1953; articles of Evelyn Hu-Dehart, including, "Chinese Coolie Labour in Cuba in the Nineteenth Century: Free Labour or Neoslavery?" *Slavery and Abolition* 14.1 (1993): 75 and "The Chinese in Cuba," in *The Chinese Diaspora*, eds. Lingchi Wang and Gungwu Wang (Singapore: Times Academic Press, 1998). Juan Hung Hui's *Chinos en América* (Madrid, Spain: Editorial MAPFRE, 1992) covers a wide survey of Chinese diasporas in the Americas but includes a chapter on Chinese labor trafficking to Cuba. Persia Campbell and Walton Look Lai focus mainly upon coolie traffic to former British colonies, but do include work on coolie traffic to Cuba: Persia Campbell, *Chinese Coolie Emigration to Countries within the British Empire* (London, England: Frank Cass, 1923); Walton Look Lai, *Indentured Labor, Caribbean Sugar: Chinese and Indian Migrants to the British West Indies, 1838–1918* (Kingston, Jamaica: University of West Indies Press, 1998); and *The Chinese in the West Indies 1806–1995* (Kingston, Jamaica: University of West Indies Press, 1998). For historical work specifically focused upon coolies of Peru, see Humberto Rodriguez Pastor, *Hijos del Celeste Imperio en el Peru (1850–1900)* (Lima, Peru: Instituto de Apoyo Agrarion, 1989); Watt Stewart, *Chinese Bondage in Peru* (1951; Westport: Greenwood Press, 1970); Evelyn Hu-Dehart, "Coolies, Shopkeepers, Pioneers: The Chinese of Mexico and Peru (1849–1930)" in *Amerasia Journal* 15.2 (1989): 91–116; and "Chinese Coolie Labor in Cuba and Peru in the Nineteenth Century: Free Labor or Neoslavery?" in *Slavery and Abolition* 14.1 (1993): 75; Michael Gonzales, "Resistance among Asian

Plantation Workers in Peru," *From Chattel Slaves to Wage Slaves*, ed. Mary Turner (London, England: James Curry, 1995) 201–223. There is also a body of historical work on Chinese of the West Indies, including documentation from family histories. Those that include coolie history are the following: Walton Look Lai, *Indentured Labor, Caribbean Sugar: Chinese and Indian Migrants to the British West Indies, 1838–1918* and *The Chinese in the West Indies 1806–1995;* Trev Sue-A Quan, *Cane Reapers* (Vancouver, Canada: Riftswood Publishing, 1999); Margery Kwok Crawford, *Scenes from the History of the Chinese in Guyana* (Guyana: Crawford, 1989); Margery Kirkpatrick, *From the Middle Kingdom to the New World* (Guyana: Kirkpatrick, 1993).

8. Middle-class transnationalists, "astronaut" wives, "parachute" kids, and multiple passport holders, and the social formations precipitated from these migrations are elaborated upon in Aihwa Ong, *Flexible Citizenship* (Durham: Duke University Press, 1999).

9. Though in a rare exception, Donna Gabbacia noted low-cost Italian labor in the late nineteenth and early twentieth centuries, calling them the Chinese of Europe, like coolies. In "The Yellow Peril and the Chinese of Europe," *Migration, Migration History, History*, eds. Jan Luccassen and Leo Lucassen (Bern, Switzerland: Peter Lang, 1999).

10. For contemporary theorizing on "diaspora" see Kandice Chuh and Karen Shimakawa, eds., *Orientations: Mapping Studies in the Asian Diaspora* (Durham: Duke University Press, 2001), and David Palumbo-Liu, *Asian/American* (Stanford: Stanford University Press, 1999) for insight into the deployment of "diaspora" as a frame for inquiry. This study employs the term to designate a migratory formation that can be compared to other migratory formations transnational contexts that were also linked to systems of bondage. There is also a long-standing body of work on "Chinese diaspora" and "overseas Chinese" that speaks to certain politics and debates regarding Chinese nationalisms and ethnic identity. See Wang Gungwu and Ling-chi Wang, *The Chinese Diaspora*, vols. I and II (Singapore: Times Academic Press, 1998); Lawrence Ma and Carolyn Cartier, *The Chinese Diaspora* (Lanham: Rowman & Littlefield, 2003).

11. See fn 7.

12. Loni Ding, *Ancestors in the Americas* (Berkeley: Center for Educational Telecommunications, 1997) documentary.

13. Roshni Rustomji-Kerns et al., *Encounters: People of Asian Descent in the Americas* (Lanham: Rowman & Littlefield, 1999). Lane Ryo Hirabayashi et al., *New Worlds, New Lives: Globalization and People of Japanese Descent in the Americas, from Latin America in Japan* (Stanford: Stanford University Press, 2002).

14. Erika Lee, "Orientalisms in the Americas: A Hemispheric Approach to Asian American History," *Journal of Asian American Studies* 8.3 (2005): 235–256.

15. Stuart Hall, "Cultural Identity and Diaspora," *Colonial Discourse and Postcolonial Theory,* eds. Patrick Williams and Laura Chrisman (New York: Columbia University Press, 1994), 395.

16. Gary Okihiro noted that "In the eighteenth century, the well-known Atlantic trade triangle was in fact an adjunct of the Afro-Eurasian trade in which Europeans exchanged Indian textiles and European manufactures for African slaves who produced America's sugar, tobacco, and other goods exported to Europe" in "Toward a Pacific Civilization" (paper), University of Arizona 3/22/01. Herbert S. Klein, *African Slavery in Latin America and the Caribbean* (Oxford: Oxford University Press, 1986), 141.

17. Routes of coolie trade to the West Indies and Caribbean both took place via both Atlantic and Pacific passages. See the work of maritime history by Basil Lubbock, called *Coolie Ships and Oil Sailers* (Glasgow: Brown, Son & Ferguson, 1935).

18. Hall, 398.

CHAPTER ONE

1. Among others: Cast as transition in Ong Jin Hui, "Chinese Indentured Labour: Coolies and Colonies," *The Cambridge Survey of World Migration*, ed. Robin Cohen (Cambridge: Cambridge University Press, 1995), 51; cast as transition in Dirk Hoerder, *Cultures in Contact: World Migrations in the Second Millennium* (Durham: Duke University Press, 2002), 234, 369–371; as figured in global race discourses, in Gary Okihiro, *Margins and Mainstreams* (Seattle: University of Washington Press, 1994) 37–43; as confronted by Chinese in South Africa, in Melanie Yap and Dianne Leong Man, eds., *Colour, Confusion, and Concessions* (Hong Kong: University Press, 1996); as between slave and free, black and white, Chinese in Brazil, in Jeffrey Lesser, "Neither Slave nor Free, Neither Black nor White," *Estudios Interdisciplinarios de America Latina y Caribe* 5:2 (July–December 1994); as between slave and free, black and white, Chinese in Cuba, in Evelyn Hu-DuHart, "Race Construction and Race Relations," in *The Chinese Diaspora (II)*, eds. Ling-Chi Wang and Gungwu Wang (Singapore: Times Academic Press, 1998), 78–85; as negotiated by Chinese in American postslavery, in James Loewen, *The Mississippi Chinese: Between Black and White* (Cambridge: Harvard University Press, 1971); as negotiated by Asians under black/white paradigms of American law, in Angelo Ancheta, *Race, Rights, and the Asian American Experience* (New Brunswick: Rutgers University Press, 1998); as figured in American race politics, in Frank Wu, *Yellow: Race in America Beyond Black and White* (New York: Basic Books, 2001).

2. Manuel Moreno Fraginals, "Extent and Significance of Chinese Immigration to Cuba (19th Century)," *Asiatic Migrations in Latin America*, ed. Luz María Martínez Montiel (Mexico: Colegio de México, 1981), 54.

3. Moreno, 55.

4. Jeffrey Lesser, "Neither Slave nor Free, Neither Black nor White," *Estudios Interdisciplinarios de America Latina y Caribe* 5:2 (July–December 1994).

5. Dale Tomich, *Through the Prism of Slavery* (Lanham: Rowman & Littlefield, 2004).

6. Rebecca Scott, *Slave Emancipation in Cuba* (University of Pittsburgh Press, 1985), 26.

7. Scott, 31.

8. Scott, 35.

9. Okihiro, *Margins and Mainstreams,* 37–43; *Common Ground* (Princeton: Princeton University Press, 2001), 36.

10. Juan Pérez de la Riva *Contribución a la historia de la gente sin historia* (La Habana: Editorial de Ciencias Sociales, 1974); *El barracón: esclavitud y capitalismo en Cuba* (La Habana: Editorial de Ciencias Sociales, 1975); *Demografía de los culíes chinos en Cuba, 1853–74* (1966); *Los culies chinos en Cuba* (2000).

11. Scott, 108.

12. Pérez de la Riva, *Los culies chinos en Cuba*, 214.

13. Pérez de la Riva, *Los culies chinos en Cuba*, 215.

14. Juan Huang Hui, 194. Roberto Mesa.

15. Noel Deerr, *The History of Sugar*, II (London: Chapman and Hall, 1950), 402. Also Lynn Pan, *Sons of the Yellow Emperor: A History of the Chinese Diaspora* (New York: Kodansha International, 1994), 26.

16. Lynn Pan, *Sons of the Yellow Emperor.*

17. Walton Look Lai, *Indentured Labor, Caribbean Sugar: Chinese and Indian Migrants to the British West Indies, 1838–1918* (Baltimore: Johns Hopkins University Press, 1993).

18. Lesser, "Neither Slave nor Free, Neither Black nor White"; Lucia Lamounier, "Between Slavery and Free Labour: Early Experiments with Free Labour & Patterns of Slave Emancipation in Brazil and Cuba," in *From Chattel Slaves to Wage Slaves*, ed. Mary Turner (London, England: James Curry, 1995), 195.

19. José Luciano Franco, *Comercio clandestino de esclavos* (Havana: Ciencias Sociales, 1980), 139, 159, 257.

20. Humberto Rodríguez Pastor, *Hijos del Celeste imperio en el Perú (1850–1900): Migración, agricultura, mentalidad, y explotación* (Lima, Peru: Instituto de Apoyo Agrarion, 1989); H. Rodríguez Pastor, *Herederos del dragón: historia de la comunidad china en el Perú* (Lima, Perú: Congreso del Perú, 2000); Watt Stewart, *Chinese Bondage in Peru* (Durham: Duke University Press, 1951); Denise Helly, "Introduction," *Cuba Commission Report*, 1876 (Baltimore: Johns Hopkins University Press, 1993), 20; Pérez de la Riva, "Demografía de los culíes chinos en Cuba, 1853–74"; Pérez de la Riva, *Los culies chinos en Cuba*. Pérez de la Riva estimates another 5,000 for undocumented Chinese.

21. David R. Murray, *Odious Commerce: Britain, Spain, and the Abolition of the Cuban Slave Trade* (Cambridge: Cambridge University Press, 1980), 244.

22. Consistent with past and present scholarship on coolie trade and indenture, the terms "East Indian" and "Indian" are used herein, not the postcolonial term "South Asian."

23. Hugh Tinker, *A New System of Slavery: The Export of Indian Labour Overseas, 1830–1920* (London, England: Hansib Publishing, 1993), 274.

24. Melanie Yap and Dianne Leong Man, *Colour,* 160.

25. For more on the Indian coolie trade, see (among many): Hugh Tinker, *A New System of Slavery: The Export of Indian Labour Overseas, 1830–1920* (London, England: Hansib Publishing, 1993); K.O. Laurence, *A Question of Labour: Indentured Immigration into Trinidad and British Guiana, 1875–1917* (New York: St. Martin's Press, 1994); D. Northrup, *Indentured Labor in the Age of Imperialism 1838–1914* (New York: Cambridge University Press, 1995); Madhavi Kale, *Fragments of Empire: Capital, Slavery, and Indian Indentured Labor in the British Caribbean* (Philadelphia: University of Pennsylvania Press, 1998).

26. Captain and Mrs. Swinton, *The Other Middle Passage: Journal of a Voyage with Coolie Emigrants* (1859; London, England: Alfred Bennett; London, England: Hansib Publishing, 1994).

27. Verene Shepherd, ed., *Maharani's Misery* (Kingston, Jamaica: University of West Indies Press, 2002).

28. Madhavi Kale; and Radhika Mongia, "Impartial Regimes of Truth," *Cultural Studies* 18:5 (Sept. 2004): 749–768.

29. Walton Look Lai, "Asian Contract and Free Migration to the Americas," in David Eltis, ed. *Coerced and Free Migration* (Stanford: Stanford University Press, 2002) 229–258.

30. D.J. Williamson to Secretary of State, in U.S. Consular Dispatches 1870, in Watt Stewart, *Chinese Bondage in Peru* (Durham: Duke University Press, 1951), 97.

31. Williamson, 98.

32. Walton Look Lai, *The Chinese in the West Indies 1806–1995* (Kingston, Jamaica: University of West Indies Press, 1998); and *Indentured Labor, Caribbean Sugar: Chinese and Indian Migrants to the British West Indies, 1838–1918* (Baltimore: Johns Hopkins University Press, 1993).

33. Louis A. Perez, ed, *Slaves, Sugar, and Colonial Society* (Wilmington: Scholarly Resources, 1992), xv.

34. Noel Deerr, *The History of Sugar*, I (London: Chapman and Hall, 1949), 240.

35. Herbert S. Klein, *African Slavery in Latin America and the Caribbean* (Oxford: Oxford University Press, 1986), 92.

36. Manuel Moreno Fraginals, *El Ingenio*, I (Habana, Cuba: Ciencias Sociales, 1964).

37. Jamaica gradually emancipated its slaves from 1833 to 1838.

38. Klein 93; and Moreno, *El Ingenio*, III (Habana, Cuba: Ciencias Sociales, 1986), 35–37.

39. Sidney Mintz, *Sweetness and Power: The Place of Sugar in Modern History* (New York: Penguin, 1985).

40. Denise Helly, *Idéologie et ethnicité: les Chinois Macao à Cuba, 1847–1886* (Montréal, Canada: Les Presses de L'Université de Montréal, 1979), 109.

41. Gary Okihiro draws linkages among the expansion of European imperialism and colonialism in Asia, Africa, and the Americas, the global labor economy, and the trafficking of Indian coolies, Chinese coolies, and African slaves. Gary Y. Okihiro, *Margins and Mainstreams*, 37–43.

42. Helly, "Introduction," 20. She refers to Arnold Meagher and Humberto Rodriguez Pastor.

43. *El Diario de la Marina*, La Habana, January 1, 1847.

44. Pérez de la Riva, *El barracón y otros ensayos* (La Habana, Cuba: Editorial de Ciencias Sociales, 1975), 258–59.

45. Pérez de la Riva, *El barracón: Esclavitud y capitalismo en Cuba* (Barcelona: Editorial Crítica, 1978), 92.

46. Hugh Thomas, *The Slave Trade* (New York: Simon & Schuster, 1997) 802.

47. Pérez de la Riva, *El barracón y otros ensayos*, 264.

48. Deerr, *History of Sugar,* II, 403.

49. Nicolas Tanco Armero, "La emigración de los colonos chinos," *Revista Contemporane* 3.7 (1877): 348. See original Nicolas Tanco Armero, *Viaje de Nueva Granada a China y de China a Francia* (Paris, France: Imprenta e Simon Raco y Cia, 1881). See Pérez de la Riva's critiques of Tanco.

50. Tanco, 56–61.

51. Pérez de la Riva, *El barracón*, 267.

52. Félix Erenchun, *Anales de la isla de Cuba* (Habana, Cuba: Imprenta de la Antilla, 1858), Año de 1856, BE, 1329–1334; *Memoria de la Alianza. Compania de Creditos y Seguros* (Habana, Cuba: n.p., 1866); Pérez de la Riva, *El barracón y otros ensayos*, 257; Juan Jiménez Pastrana, *Los Chinos en la Historia de Cuba 1847–1930* (Habana, Cuba: Ciencias Sociales, 1983), 50–51; Juan Jiménez Pastrana, *Los Chinos en la liberación de Cuba* (Habana, Cuba: Instituto de Historia, 1963), 25–26.

53. Erenchun*; Memoria de la Alianza. Compania de Créditos y Seguros*; Pérez de la Riva, *El barracón y otros ensayos* 257.

54. *Cuban Commission Report*, 53.

55. Laird W. Bergad, *Cuban Rural Society in the Nineteenth Century* (Princeton: Princeton University Press, 1990), 248; Pérez de la Riva, *El barracón*, 57; Juan Jiménez Pastrana; Julio Le Riverend; among others. While 124,873 were documented as sold, larger estimates (150,000) include undocumented "contraband" and Chinese from California and Mexico.

56. James O'Kelly, *Mambiland or Adventures of a Herald Correspondent in Cuba* (Philadelphia: Lippincott, 1874), 71.

57. Henry Murray, *Lands of the Slave and the Free* (London, England: John Parker & Sons, 1855), 310.

58. Pérez de la Riva, *El barracón* 92.

59. Pérez de la Riva, *El barracón*, 270. Denise Helly offers a statistic of $80 million, in her introduction, *Cuba Commission Report*, 15. Peréz de La Riva calculated the costs and overhead of coolie procurement, mortality, shipping, and approximated the overall profit from coolie sales of this period to be 25–30 million pesos. In 1975, at the time of his writing, he notes that this was equivalent to 80 million pesos.

60. Jesus Guanche, *Componentes étnicos de la nación cubana* (Habana, Cuba: Fundación Fernando Ortiz, 1996), 76.

61. This only accounts for those who were recorded.

62. Evelyn Hu-DeHart, "Chinese Coolie Labor in Cuba in the Nineteenth Century," *Slavery and Abolition* 14:1 (1993): 75.

63. Also see Okihiro, *Margins and Mainstreams*, 42, and Helly, "Introduction," 21.

64. Alexander Laing, *The Sea Witch: A Narrative of the Experiences of Capt. Roger Murray and Others in an American Clipper Ship During the Years 1846–1856* (New York: Farrar and Rinehart, 1933).

65. It was also common for ships to be bought, sold and renamed. In addition, Spanish firms began to verticalize their coolie "business" and began acquiring the ships from other countries. See Pérez de la Riva, *Los culies chinos eu Cuba*.

66. Thomas, *Slave Trade*.

67. *Cuba Commission Report*, 53.

68. *Cuba Commission Report*, 37.

69. Helly, "Introduction," 12.

70. Lai, *Chinese in the West Indies,* 6.

71. March 1895 issue of *The Forum*. "The Business World vs. The Politicians."

72. Eldon Griffin, *Clippers and Consuls* (Taipei, Taiwan: Cheng Wen, 1938, rep 1972); Lucy Cohen, *Chinese in the Post–Civil War South* (Baton Rouge: Lousiana State University Press, 1984), 22–45.

73. *Report of British Consulate General*, Havana, Sept. 1, 1873. The Americans, British, Spanish, French, and Portuguese sent the most coolie ships to the Americas. Not surprisingly, these were (or had been) active traders in slave traffic. Also see Basil Lubbock's *The Coolie Ships and Oil Sailers* (Glasgow, Scotland: Brown, Son & Ferguson, 1935), which includes European and American coolie ships.

74. Cohen; Matthew Guterl, "After Slavery: Asian Labor, the American South, and the Age of Emancipation," *Journal of World History* 14.2 (June 2003): 209–242; Najia Aarim–Heriot *Chinese Immigrants, African Americans, and Racial Anxiety in the United States 1848–1882* (University of Illinois Press, 2003); Moon Jung Ho, *Coolies and Cane* (Baltimore: Johns Hopkins University Press, 2006).

75. Cohen, 151.

76. Cast as free migration in multicultural studies, Ronald Takaki, *Different Mirror* (Boston: Little Brown & Co., 1993), 191–215. Also see debates of Stanford Lyman and Andrew Gyrory: Stanford M. Lyman, "The 'Chinese Question' and American Labor Historians," *New Politics* ns 7.4 (Winter 2000): 113–148; Andrew Gyory, "A Reply to Stanford Lyman," *New Politics*, ns 8.1 (Summer 2000): 51–67.

77. Marshall Powers, *Chinese Coolie Migration to Cuba*; dissertation (University of Florida 1953), 177.

78. Lisa Yun, "Under the Hatches: American Coolie Ships," *Amerasia Journal* 28.2 (2002): 38–63.

79. Franklin Knight, *Slave Society in Cuba During the Nineteenth Century* (Madison: University of Wisconsin Press, 1970), 119.

80. For example, the Aspinwalls. Pérez de a Riva, *Los culies chinos en Cuba*, 137. Griffin, 199. The Howland and Aspinwall families were involved in coolie traffic and resisted American resolutions to condemn coolie traffic, including a letter to President Pierce. Howland and Aspinwall were also the owners of the ship *Sea Witch*, mentioned in this chapter. The Aspinwall family was also the main American investor in Panama.

81. Griffin, 199.

82. Griffin, 199.

83. Griffin, 198.

84. 7/23/1855 Letter by William Robertson, U.S. Consul at Havana, to Secretary of State William Marcy (enclosure in "Report of the Secretary of State" August 2, 1856) Sen. Exec. Doc. 99, Ser. 824, 34th Cong. 1st Sess., 93–94. In *American Diplomatic and Public Papers: The United States and China 1842–1860*. Vol 17, 204.

85. 8/6/1855 Letter by William Robertson, U.S. Consul at Havana, to Secretary of State William Marcy (enclosure in "Report of the Secretary of State" August 2, 1856), 204.

86. Report of the Committee on Commerce of the House of Representatives. House Report 443, Ser. 1069, 36th Cong., 1st Sess., 130. In *American Diplomatic and Public Papers: The United States and China 1842–1860*. Vol 17.

87. Report of the Committee on Commerce of the House of Representatives. House Report 443, Ser. 1069, 36th Cong., 1st Sess., 130.

88. *American Diplomatic and Public Papers,* 113.

89. *American Diplomatic and Public Papers*, 225–226.

90. *American Diplomatic and Public Papers*, 225–226.

91. Yun, "Under the Hatches: American Coolie Ships," 38–63. Also see excellent maritime history by Carl Cutler, *Greyhounds of the Sea* and see Basil Lubbock's authoritative history of coolie ships, *Coolie Ships and Oil Sailers*.

92. See fn 91.

93. Robert Plowman, "The Voyage of the Coolie Ship *Kate Hooper* October 3, 1857–March 26, 1858," in *Prologue, Quarterly of the National Archives and Records Administration* 33.2 (2001): 87–95.

94. Lubbock, 32–51. Persia Campbell, *Chinese Coolie Emigration to Countries Within the British Empire* (London, England: Frank Cass, 1971), 157. As the British began to withdraw from the Chinese coolie trade, the Hong Kong colonial administration legislated against the fitting of iron hatches and even the local production of these hatches, as ship masters had turned to making them at port and then fitting them at sea, to circumvent any cursory ship inspections.

95. Lubbock, 33.

96. Edgar Holden, "A Chapter in the Coolie Trade," *Harpers New Monthly* 29.169 (June 1864): 111. Also see in *American Clipper Ships Vol. I*, 334.

97. Gaddis Smith, "The *Amistad* in a Global Maritime Context" in *The Connecticut Scholar: Occasional Papers of the Connecticut Humanities Council* 1.10 (1992): 37–43.

98. Campbell, 156.

99. Campbell. Also see dissertation by Elliot Arensmeyer, "British Merchant Enterprise and the Chinese Coolie Labour Trade," dissertation, University of Hawaii, 1979; Tinker.

100. Campbell, 235.

101. Evelyn Hu-DeHart concludes that coolies were legally not slaves and emphasizes that actual physical treatment itself must be separated from legal status, in "Chinese Coolie Labor," 83. On the other hand, Walton Look Lai concludes in *Indentured Labor*, 266 that considerable differences in state regulated coolie labor versus private enterprises

speculator-run coolie labor raise questions as to whether coolie labor differed greatly from slavery in Cuba and Peru. Lai also questions the contradictions in the laws themselves (British and Spanish) and the nature of coercion.

102. Philip S. Foner, A *History of Cuba* (New York: International Publishers, 1962), 224; Knight, 119. Also see Duvon Corbitt, *A Study of the Chinese of Cuba 1847–1947* (Wilmore: Asbury College Press, 1971), and Arnold Meagher.

103. Julia Ward Howe, *A Trip to Cuba* (1860; New York: Negro Universities Press, 1969), 219–20.

104. José Baltar Rodriguez, *Los Chinos de Cuba* (Habana, Cuba: Fundación Fernando Ortiz, 1997), 21; Guanche, 75.

105. Helly, "Introduction"; and Pérez de la Riva, *El barracón,* 63.

106. Hu-DeHart, "Chinese Coolie Labor," 77.

107. Lai, *Indentured Labor,*193.

108. See Pérez de la Riva's body of work on the Chinese coolie of Cuba as the chief research done on this topic: "Demografía de los culíes chinos en Cuba, 1853–74" (1966); *Contribución a la Historia de la gente sin historia* (1963, 1974); *Para la historia de las gentes sin historia* (1976); *El barracón: esclavitud y capitalismo en Cuba* (1978); *Los culíes chinos en Cuba, 1847–1880* (2000).

109. *Cuba Commission Report,* 53.

110. O'Kelly, 60.

111. For information on the legal status of the Chinese, see Juan Pérez de la Riva, "Demografía de los culíes chinos en Cuba (1853–1874)"; "La situación legal del culí en Cuba," in *El barracón y otros ensayos,* 469–507, 209–45; *Tsung li ko kuo shih wu ya mên, Report of the Commission Sent by China to Ascertain the Condition of the Chinese Coolies in Cuba* (1876; Shanghai: Imperial Maritime Customs Press; Taipei, Taiwan: C'eng Wen Publishing Company, 1970); Helly, *Idéologie et ethnicité: Les Chinois Macao à Cuba*; Juan Jiménez Pastrana, *Los chinos en las luchas por la liberación cubana* 127–40.

112. Deerr, *History of Sugar* II, 403.

113. Bergad, 252.

114. Hu-DeHart, "Race Construction and Race Relations," in *The Chinese Diaspora (II),* eds. Ling-Chi Wang and Gungwu Wang (Singapore: Times Academic Press, 1998), 78–85.

115. Moreno, *El Ingenio*; and "Extent and Significance of Chinese Immigration to Cuba (19th C)," in *Asiatic Migrations to Latin America,* 53–58.

116. Scott.

117. Helly, "Introduction," 23.

118. Juan Jiménez Pastrana, *Los chinos en la historia de Cuba* 37, 57. José Baltar Rodríguez, *Los chinos de Cuba,* 34–37. More on Quesada's writing regarding the Chinese fighters in Guillermo Tejeiro, *Historia ilustrada de la colonia china en Cuba* (Habana, Cuba: Editorial Hercules, 1947). See section under "Gonzalo de Quesada . . ."

119. See Chapter 5 of this book.

120. See Juan Jiménez Pastrana, *Los chinos en las luchas por la liberacion cubana*; Antonio Chuffat Latour, *Apunte histórico de los chinos en Cuba* (Habana, Cuba: Molina, 1927); Gonzalo de Quesada, *Los chinos y la revolución cubana* (1892, 1946), in *Catauro: Revista Cubana de Antropología* 1.2 (2000): 184.

121. Jiménez, 84.

122. See Rodriguez's *Los Chinos de Cuba* for an examination of the postcoolie era.

123. Pérez de la Riva, *Contribución a la historia de la gente sin historia.*

CHAPTER TWO

1. Maturin Murray Ballou, descendant of Hosea Ballou (the Universalist clergyman), first editor-in-chief of the *Boston Daily Globe*, writer of several novels and travel accounts. In Ballou's *From Due South; or, Cuba Past and Present* (New York: Negro Universities Press, 1969) 276–77, excerpted in *Slaves, Sugar, and Colonial Society: Travel Accounts of Cuba* (Wilmington: Scholarly Resources, 1992), 244.

2. Yen Ching Hwang, *Coolies and Mandarins: China's Protection of Overseas Chinese in the Late Ch'ing Period 1851–1911* (Singapore: Singapore University Press, 1985), 127–128.

3. Juan Pérez de la Riva, "Demografía de los culíes chinos en Cuba, 1853-74," *Separata de la Revistad de la Biblioteca Nacional José Martí* 57.4 (1996): 31.

4. Yen Ching Hwang; and Robert Irick, *Ch'ing Policy Toward the Coolie Trade 1847–1878* (Taipei: Chinese Materials Center, 1982).

5. Newspapers used by several sides to forward agendas. See Robert Hart's directive to get the commission into the newspapers. See *American Diplomatic Papers*. See Eldon Griffin's account of missionaries. Also see Williams and Graves on missionaries' involvement in anticoolie trade politics.

6. Letter to James Duncan Campbell, October 9, 1873. In John Fairbank, Katherine Bruner, Elizabeth MacLeod Matheson, eds. *The I.G. In Peking: Letters of Robert Hart, Chinese Maritime Customs, 1868–1907*, Volume I (Cambridge: The Belknap Press/Harvard University Press, 1975), 1129.

7. Irick, 303.

8. 3/31/1874 *Diario de la Marina*, 5/7/1874 *Diario de la Marina*. Rhoads, Irick, Hwang, Desnoyers. And *all* Cuban scholarship on the Chinese.

9. He appears as "Yeh Shoo tung" in Charles Desnoyers's, "Toward One Enlightened and Progressive Civilization: Discourses of Expansion and Nineteenth-Century Chinese Missions Abroad," *Journal of World History* 8.1 (1997) 157; "Yeh Yuanchun" in Irick 297; Yung Wing as "Yeh Shu Tung," *My Life in China and America* (New York: Henry Holt, 1909), 197; all referring to the same person.

10. Desnoyers, 157.

11. Desnoyers, 157. Appears as "Luther H. Northrop" in Cuban newspaper 3/18/1874 *Diario de la Marina*.

12. Of Hartford, in Desnoyers, 157. Listed as "Henry J. Terry" in *Diario de la Marina* 18 March 1874.

13. Desnoyers, 157.

14. Edward Rhoads, "In the Shadow of Yung Wing: Zeng Laishun and the Chinese Educational Commission to the United States," *Pacific Historical Review* 74.1 (Feb 2005): 42. Robert Irick 298. Irick lists Zeng as part of the delegation, though Rhoads indicates Zeng went ahead of delegation for preparatory work. Yung Wing wrote his own account of events; his recounting is shaded by his animosity to Chen Lanbin and by historical inaccuracies pointed out by historians such as Irick.

15. *Diario de la Marina* 7 May 1874

16. Desnoyers (emphasis on Yeh) 158; Rhoads (emphasis on Zeng for laying groundwork for the group) 42; Irick (emphasis on Yeh, who would receive appointment in Chen's staff as first Chinese minister to the United States, and as secretary of the first embassy to the United States, Spain, and Peru), 298.

17. Denise Helly says the 18th. But Cuban newspaper *Diario de la Marina* 18 March 1874 reported port arrival one day after actual arrival, which would have been March 17.

18. Irick, 301.

19. Yung Wing claimed to have been to Peru and had completed his report before Chen Lan Pin completed his on Cuba, but Edward Rhoads notes Yung Wing was in Peru after Chen Lan Pin had already completed his trip to Cuba in "In the Shadow of Yung Wing," *Pacific Historical Review* 43. Watt Stewart places Yung Wing in Peru in September of 1874, in Watt Stewart, *Chinese Bondage in Peru* (Westport: Greenwood Press, 1970), 201. For more on Yung Wing see Kevin Scott Wong, "The Transformation of Culture: Three Chinese Views of America," in *American Quarterly* 48.2 (1996): 201–232.

20. Yung Wing, *My Life in China and America* (New York: Henry Holt, 1909).

21. Desnoyers, "Toward One Enlightened and Progressive Civilization: Discourses of Expansion and Nineteenth-Century Chinese Missions Abroad," *Journal of World History* 8.1 (1997): 141.

22. K. Scott Wong insightfully troubles the ideologically constructed binary of "Eastern" tradition versus "Western" progressivism. "The Transformation of Culture: Three Chinese Views of America," in *American Quarterly* 48.2 (1996) 201–232. Desnoyers also troubles these dualities in relation to Chen Lanbin and Yung Wing in "Chinese Foreign Policy in Transition: Ch'en Lan-pin in the New World, 1872–1882," dissertation, Temple University, 1988.

23. Desnoyers provides the most concentrated effort to provide some background on Chen, though details are largely about Chen's professional background post-1872, with the most focus upon his official role in the forming of foreign policy and the perceptions of that role from various historical actors. See Charles Desnoyers's "Chinese Foreign Policy in Transition: Ch'en Lan-pin in the New World, 1872–1882." Yung Wing provides some comments on his perceptions of Chen as a colleague, with thinly veiled antagonism toward him as a Confucian traditionalist, in Yung Wing, *My Life in China and America.* Chen himself wrote brief comments on his work in the States, revealing nothing of his experience in Cuba or any biographical details. See Chen Lanbin 陈兰彬 *"Shi mei ji lue"* 使美记略, in *Xiaofanghu zhaiyu dicongchao* 小方壶斋舆地丛钞, ed., Wang Xiqi 王锡祺 (Hangzhou: Hangzhou guji shudian, 杭州古籍书店, 1891).

24. Desnoyers, *Chinese Foreign Policy,* 56–59 and private correspondence with Desnoyers 9/28/05 in which he reconfirms his finding.

25. John R. Watt. *The District Magistrate in Late Imperial China* (New York: Columbia University Press, 1972), 200–221.

26. Lü, Zhixing (吕志兴). *Songdai fazhi tedian yanjiu* (宋代法制特点研究, Studies of Characteristics of Juridical System in Sung Dynasty) (Chengdu shi: Sichuan daxue chubanshe, 2001); Qiu, Pengsheng (邱彭生), *"Zhenxiang Dabai Ming Qing Xingan Zhong De Falu Tuili"* (真相大白明清刑案中的法律推理, Law and Order in Ming and Qing Dynasty). http://www.legal-history.net/scholar/2004-9/200494200737.htm; Qu, Tongzu, *Local Government in China Under the Qing* (Cambridge: Harvard University Press, 1962); Derk Bodde, *Law in Imperial China* (Cambridge: Harvard University Press, 1967); Thomas A. Metzger, *The Internal Organization of Ching Bureaucracy* (Cambridge: Harvard University Press, 1973).

27. *Essays on China's Legal Tradition,* ed. Jerome Cohen (Princeton, NJ: Princeton University Press, 1980), 92–98.

28. Lex Heerma van Voss, introduction, *International Review of Social History* Vol. 46 Supplement S9 (Dec. 2001): 1–10.

29. *International Review of Social History* Volume 46 Supplement S9 special issue (December 2001): 1–235.

30. *Report of the Commission Sent by China to Ascertain the Condition of Chinese Coolies in Cuba* (1876; Shanghai: Imperial Maritime Customs Press; Taiwan: Ch'eng-wen Publishing, 1970): 90.

31. See Zulueta Foundation, Marshall Powers, and Pérez de la Riva.

32. Gallenga, *Pearl of the Antilles* (London: Chapman and Hall, 1873), 91–106, excerpted in *Slaves, Sugar, and Colonial Society,* ed. Louis Perez (Wilmington: Scholarly Resources, 1992), 83.

33. Decree of December 13, 1872 stipulated the membership ratio. See "Memorandum concerning legislation of Spanish and Colonial Governments regarding Chinese Immigrants." Report of the Commission.

34. Commission Report, 90–91.

35. *Report of the Commission Sent by China to Ascertain the Condition of Chinese Coolies in Cuba.* Question L.

36. *Report of the Commission Sent by China to Ascertain the Condition of Chinese Coolies in Cuba* (1876; Shanghai: Imperial Maritime Customs Press; Taiwan: Ch'eng-wen Publishing, 1970).

37. See National Archives papers, letter from Otin.

38. Irick, 303.

39. Related nineteenth-century diplomatic relations and the political backdrop for coolie trade also are described in greater detail by historians such as Robert Irick and Yen Ching Hwang. Coolie-related conventions, also described by Hwang and Irick, as well as by Juan Pérez de la Riva and Juan Huang Hui. Also Juan Huang Hui, *Chinos en America* (Madrid: Editorial MAPFRE, 1992) chapter on "Actitidues de los gobiernos chino y español respecto a la inmigración china en el siglo XIX)."

40. Ranajit Guha, *A Subaltern Studies Reader* (Minneapolis: University of Minnesota Press, 1997), 34–62.

41. Gayatri Chakavorty Spivak, "Can the Subaltern Speak?" in *Marxism and the Interpretation of Culture,* eds. Cary Nelson and Larry Grossberg (Urbana: University of Illinois Press, 1998), 217–313.

42. For recent interrogations of testimony and testimonial forms, including image and video, see "Public Sentiments," *Scholar and Feminist Online* 2.1 (Summer 2003), special issue on testimony, trauma, representation, archives. Especially, "Introduction" by Ann Cvetkovich and Ann Pelligrini, and "Human Rights, Testimony, and Transnational Publicity" by Meg McLagan.

43. For a history of ideas that lead to present day discourses of human rights, see Micheline Ishay, *The History of Human Rights: From Ancient Times to the Globalization Era* (Berkeley: University of California Press, 2004). For critical interrogation of testimony in relation to discourses of human rights and ethics, see Anne Cubilié, *Woman Witnessing Terror: Testimony and the Cultural Politics of Human Rights* (New York: Fordham University Press, 2005). For study of testimony as framed by universal human rights, see Mark Sanders, "Ambiguities of Mourning," *Loss: The Politics of Mourning,* eds. David Eng and David Kazanjian (Berkeley: University of California Press, 2003), 77–98, esp. 79.

44. K.O. Laurence 7, 18. Isaac Dookhan, "The Elusive Nirvana: Indian Immigrants in Guyana and the Des Voeux Commission, 1870–71" *Revista/Review Interamericana* 17.3–4 (Fall/Winter 1987): 56.

45. Isaac Dookhan, 56.

46. Radhika Mongia, "Impartial Regimes of Truth," *Cultural Studies* 18.5 (Sept 2004), re: the "Dickens Committee Report."

47. Mongia, 761; Marina Carter, *Lakshmi's Legacy: The Testimonies of Indian Women in 19th Century Mauritius* (Mauritius: Editions L'Océan Indien, 1994); Carter, *Servants, Sidars, and Settlers: Indians in Mauritius* (New York: Oxford University Press, 1995); Carter, *Voices from Indenture: Experiences of Indian Migrants in the British Empire* (New York: Leicester University Press, 1996).

48. Madhavi Kale, *Fragments of Empire* (Philadelphia: University of Pennsylvania Press, 1998).

49. Kale, 10.

50. Kale, 10.

51. Kale, 134.

52. Mongia, 761.

53. Carter, *Voices from Indenture: Experiences of Indian Migrants in the British Empire*, 1. Also see Carter, *Lakshmi's Legacy: The Testimonies of Indian Women in 19th Century Mauritius*; Carter, *Servants, Sidars, and Settlers: Indians in Mauritius*.

54. Carter, *Voices from Indenture*, 2.

55. Carter, *Voices from Indenture*, 229.

56. Meg McLagan, "Human Rights, Testimony, and Transnational Publicity," *The Scholar and Feminist Online* 2.1 (Summer 2003): Public Sentiments.

57. Richard Smith, John Fairbank, Katherine Bruner eds., *Robert Hart and China's Early Modernization* (Cambridge: Council of East Asian Studies/Harvard University Press, 1991), Preface xvii. According to Irick, the questions were fashioned by Robert Hart, in Irick, 299.

58. Most recent critical work on testimonies of the Holocaust is represented in two special issues of *Poetics Today* "How Testimony Communicates" 26.2 (Spring 2006) and "The Humanities of Testimony" 27.2 (Summer 2006). Also see the work of Lawrence Langer, including *Holocaust Testimony: The Ruins of Memory* (New Haven: Yale University Press, 1991).

59. Henry Louis Gates, Introduction in Charles T. Davis and Henry Louis Gates eds., *The Slave's Narrative* (New York: Oxford University Press, 1985).

60. James Olney, " 'I Was Born': Slave Narratives, Their Status as Autobiography and as Literature," in *The Slave's Narrative*, 152.

61. Henry Louis Gates and William Andrews, eds., *Pioneers of the Black Atlantic: Five Slave Narratives from the Enlightenment* (Washington DC: Counterpoint, 1988), 1–29.

62. William Andrews, *To Tell a Free Story: The First Century of Afro-American Autobiography, 1760–1865* (Urbana: University of Illinois Press, 1988); Robert Stepto, *From Behind the Veil: A Study of Afro-American Narrative* (Urbana: University of Illinois Press, 1991). John Blassingame, *The Slave Community; Plantation Life in the Antebellum South* (New York: Oxford University Press, 1972).

63. Dwight McBride, *Impossible Witness: Truth, Abolition, and Slave Testimony* (New York: New York University Press, 2001), 151–172.

64. Deposition 225

65. John Blassingame, *Slave Testimony: Two Centuries of Letters, Speeches, Interviews, and Autobiographies* (Baton Rouge: Louisiana State University Press, 1977); Norman Yetman, ed., *Life Under the "Peculiar Institution": Selections from the Slave Narrative Collection* (New York: Holt, Rinehart and Winston, 1970); Norman Yetman ed., *Voices from Slavery: 100 Authentic Slave Narratives* (New York: Holt, Rinehart and Winston, 1970); Norman Yetman, "The Background of the Slave Narrative Collection," *American*

Quarterly 19.3 (1967): 534–53; and Yetman, "Ex-Slave Interviews and the Historiography of Slavery," *American Quarterly* 36.2 (Summer 1984): 181–210.

66. Paul Escott, "The Art and Science of Reading WPA Slave Narratives"; John Wideman, "Charles Chestnutt and the WPA Narratives," John Blassingame, Using the Testimony of Ex-Slaves" in *The Slave's Narrative*; Norman Yetman, "Ex-Slave Interviews."

67. Christina Accomando, *The Regulations of Robbers: Legal Fictions of Slavery and Resistance* (Columbus: Ohio State University Press, 2001), especially ch. 5.

68. Mark Sanders mentions "factual and forensic truth" in "Truths and Contestation," *Law and Literature* 16.3 (Fall 2004): 475–490

69. Mark Sanders discusses "tired oppositions of law and literature" in "Truths and Contestation," 475–490.

70. Mark Sanders, *Complicities: The Intellectual and Apartheid* (Durham: Duke University Press, 2002. He teases out the "enfoldedness" and "complicity" in testimony-giving and -receiving, with special attention to the women's requests for the dead.

71. Herbert S. Klein, *African Slavery in Latin America and the Caribbean* (Oxford: Oxford University Press, 1986), 99. Klein provides 1863 as an example, with Havana and Matanzas accounting for 70 percent or 512,000 tons produced during *zafra*. With Las Villas, the sugar production of all three areas would be over 70 percent of total.

72. *Report of the Commission,* Question XLI. The commission based its figure from the 1872 Cuban census and added an additional 11,332 from British records for Chinese who subsequently departed from China to Cuba. Rebecca Scott provides comparable figures for Chinese population in 1872, at 58,400, with 24 percent *cumplidos* (those who had fulfilled their contracts), but not including the additional Chinese who arrived after 1872. 90,101. Denise Helly also notes the same figure of 58,400 for 1872, not including the subsequent numbers who arrived after 1872. Helly, 137.

73. *Report of the Commission*, based upon British and Cuban figures. Also see Pérez de la Riva, 192–184; Duvon Corbitt, and Antonio Chuffat Latour. See Cuban Census, 1872.

74. Drawn only from depositions.

75. Helly, *Idéologie et ethnicité: les Chinois Macao à Cuba, 1847–1886* (Montréal: Presses de l'Université de Montréal, 1979), 72.

76. Calculation based upon figures from Herbert Klein, *African Slavery in Latin America and the Caribbean* (New York: Oxford University Press, 1986), 95.

77. Oscar Zanetti and Alejandro García, *Sugar and Railroads: A Cuban History* 122–123.

78. *Report of the Commission*, "Despatch."

79. Pérez de la Riva, 58.

80. Persia Campbell, *Chinese Coolie Emigration* (London: Frank Cass, 1923), 111.

81. Pérez de la Riva, "Demografiía de los culies," *Separata de la revista de la Biblioteca Nacional José Martí* 57.4 (1966): 17.

82. Juan Jiménez Pastrana, *Los chinos en la historia de Cuba* (Habana: Editorial de ciencas sociales, 1983), 58. Features ads from *Diario* and *Gaceta de la Habana*.

83. Félix Erenchun, *Anales de la isla de Cuba* (Habana, Cuba: Imprenta de la Antilla, 1856–61): 1329, in Marshall Powers, 90.

84. Ong Jin Hui "Chinese Indentured Labour: Coolies and Colonies," *The Cambridge Survey of World Migration*, ed. Robin Cohen (Cambridge: Cambridge University Press, 1995): 51; Denise Helly, foreword, *Cuba Commission Report* (1986; Baltimore: Johns Hopkins University Press, 1993); Dirk Hoerder, *Cultures in Contact: World Migrations in the Second Millenium* (Durham: Duke University Press, 2002), 369–371; Ronald Takaki,

Different Mirror (Boston: Little Brown & Co., 1993): 191–215; Robert Kent "A Diaspora of Chinese Settlement in Latin America and the Caribbean," *The Chinese Diaspora*, eds. Laurence Ma and Carolyn Cartier (Lanham: Rowman and Littlefield, 2003): 117; Evelyn Hu-Dehart; and Walton Look Lai.

85. Zanetti and García, 122.

86. Robert Lee, *Orientals: Asian Americans in Popular Culture* (Philadelphia: Temple University Press, 1999), for American discourse and public imaginary regarding coolie labor; John Kuo-Wei Tchen, *New York Before Chinatown* (Baltimore: Johns Hopkins University Press, 1999), on the "Chinese Question" in the United States and coolies, esp. Chapter 8; Gary Okihiro, *Common Ground: Reimagining American History* (Princeton: Princeton University Press, 2001) on coolie as sexualized figure, esp. Chapter 4; Philip Choy, Lorraine Dong, Marlon Hom, *The Coming Man* (Seattle: University of Washington Press, 1994), for American images of the coolie; Persia Campbell, *Chinese Coolie Emigration to Countries Within the British Empire* (1923; London: Frank Cass, 1971) for British parliamentary debates and Chinese coolie in former British colonies; Erika Lee, "Orientalisms in the Americas," in *Journal of Asian American Studies* 8.3 (September 2005): 235–256, on anti-Chinese campaigns of Canada, United States, and Mexico.

87. *Report of the Commission.*

88. For tracing of the yellow peril discourse over several centuries, see Gary Okihiro, *Margins and Mainstreams* (Seattle: University of Washington Press, 1994), especially chapters 1, 2, and 5. Also see John Kuo Wei Tchen, *New York Before Chinatown,* and Robert Lee, *Orientals.*

89. Frank Sherer, "Chinese Shadows: Fernando Ortíz and José Martí on Cubanity and Chineseness," 5. Available at http://www.yorku.ca/cerlac/documents/chinese-shadows .pdf.

90. Brij Lal, *Girmitiyas: The Origins of the Fiji Indians*, 70.

91. Depositions 327 and 555 mention coolies from Vietnam, Deposition 555. Deposition 617 mentions Manchu "bannermen" among the coolies. Manchu bannermen were given special legal and economic privileges in China.

CHAPTER THREE

1. Edward Jenkins, *The Coolie, His Rights and Wrongs* (New York: George Routledge and Sons, 1871), 142.

2. *Report of the Commission*, 91.

3. *Mathews' Chinese-English Dictionary* [Mathews, R. H. (Robert Henry)] (Cambridge: Harvard-Yenching Institute, Harvard University Press, 1945). Edition: Rev. American ed., 3d. printing. 61–78.

4. http://saturn.ihp.sinica.edu.tw/~mct/html/2010.htm. The document submitted by civilians to the officer before a lawsuit was called "zhuang" (狀), instead of "bing"; though Chen chose the word "bing" perhaps due to the petitions being submitted by his lower-level assistants as reports to him. http://saturn.ihp.sinica.edu.tw/~mct/html/2013 .htm.

5. "闻得大人到此特来寓面秉" (wende daren daoci te laiyu mianbing). British officials took issue with the term in their dealings with China, as some interpreted *bing* as indicating a kind of subordination. Lydia Liu, *Clash of Empires* (Cambridge: Harvard University Press), 51–53.

6. Deposition 19. For more examples; see Depositions 4 and 110.

7. Of note, this person's name in Chinese means "Tolerate everything."

8. *Diario de la Marina,* 2/26.

9. *Diario de la Marina,* 2/4.

10. *Diario de la Marina,* 2/26.

11. Pérez de la Riva, 187.

12. Pérez de la Riva, 187.

13. Pérez de la Riva, *Los culies chinos en Cuba.* 217–218.

14. Regulations of 1868. The term "apparatus of protection" also appears in K.O. Laurence's study of Indian indenture in Trinidad, *A Question of Labour* (New York: St Martin's Press, 1994), 167.

15. 71st article.

16. 77th and 78th article.

17. Decree of 1860, Section III.

18. Depositions 420, 691, 749, 762, 809, 841, 859, 923, 937, 943, 1019, 1048, 1050, 1085, 1096, 1108, 1153, 1171, and others.

19. Li, Dingkun 李丁昆, ed, *Han ying cige duibi yu fanyi* 汉英词格对比与翻译 (Wuhan: Huazhong Shifan daxue chubanshe 华中师范大学出版社, 1994) 415, 442.

20. D.C. Lau (translated), *Mencius* (Harmondsworth: Penguin Books, 1970) 95–96.

21. Mark Sanders, "Reading Lessons," *Diacritics* 29.3 (Autumn 1999): 17.

22. Laurence, 17.

23. Amy Dru Stanley, *From Bondage to Contract* (Cambridge: Cambridge University Press, 1998), 35.

24. Stanley, 59.

25. See language of 1860, 68, 71 in the commission's report, under Regulations and Decrees.

26. Carole Pateman, *The Sexual Contract* (Stanford: Stanford University Press, 1988), 146–147, 71.

27. Pateman, 146.

28. Robert Steinfeld, *Coercion Contract and Free Labor in the Nineteenth Century* (Cambridge: Cambridge University Press, 2001), 26.

29. Steinfeld, 238.

30. Tommy Lott, *Subjugation and Bondage* (Lanham: Rowman & Littlefield, 1998), 116.

31. Lott, 123.

32. Mills, 26.

33. Deposition 144 and Petition 51.

34. Charles Morris, *Our Island Empire: A Handbook on Cuba, Puerto Rico, Hawaii, and The Philippine Islands* (Philadelphia: J.B. Lippincott, 1899), 110.

35. Stanley, 98–137.

36. Hartman, 138.

37. Viranjini Munasinghe, *Callaloo or Tossed Salad?* (Ithaca: Cornell University Press, 2001), 74.

38. K.O. Laurence, *A Question of Labour* (New York: St. Martin's Press, 1994), 16.

39. Foucault, "The Subject and Power," in *Michel Foucault: Beyond Structuralism and Hermeneutics,* by Hubert L. Dreyfus (Chicago: University of Chicago Press), 1982.

40. Deposition #225, petition #37.

41. The use of "resistance yet complicity" is distinct from that theorized by Mark Sanders who examines intellectuals and notions of responsibility-in-complicity, such as in his analysis of Zola's infamous public letter "J'accuse."

42. Dale Tomich, *Through the Prism of Slavery* (Lanham: Rowman & Littlefield, 2004), 31.

43. Peter Kwong, *Forbidden Workers* (New York: New Press, 1997). Ko-lin Chin, *Smuggled Chinese* (Philadelphia: Temple University Press, 1999).

44. Memorandum on Legislation of Spanish, regarding the Chinese, in Report of the Commission.

45. Charles Mills, *The Racial Contract* (Ithaca: Cornell University Press, 1997).

46. Regulations of September 14, 1872.

47. Commission Report, Appendix Materials.

48. Helly makes reference to 1849, 1852, 1854, 1860, 1862, 1868, 1872 (264). The report mainly examined codes of 1860 and subsequent measures stemming from it. Pérez de la Riva and Hui highlight legislation of 1854 and 1860, though Pérez de la Riva also refers to 1853, 1854, and 1858. Also see Report's Appendix materials.

49. Pérez de la Riva, Hui, and the commission, cited these as the most extensive. See Report "Memorandum, Regulations" for full text of the legislation.

50. Report, "Memorandum, Regulations."

51. Pérez de la Riva *Los culíes chinos en Cuba*, 219–221.

52. Called "depots" in the report. Instead, this study translates the literal term used by the Chinese, "official workshop."

53. Regulations of 14 September 1871.

54. Pérez de la Riva *Los culíes chinos*, 183–84.

55. Officials in China were an extremely small part of the population. The number of officials was only 10,000. Even if "scholars" (*shiren* 士人) and the lowest level of scholars, *shengyuan* 生员 were included, the number of officials was usually less than 1% of the population and sometimes only one in a of thousand. According to Gu Yanwu, the total number of *shengyuan* 生员 in China was about 500,000 in the late Miang and early Qing period. According to Zhongli Zhang, until the 19th century and before *Taiping tianguo* 太平天国 (Taiping Heavenly Kingdom), the total number of *shengyuan* 生员 was approximately 740,000, which was only 0.18% of all China's population. After the Taiping Heavenly Kingdom, the total number of *shengyuan* 生员 was about 910,000, which was 0.24% of all China's population. China's gentry were 1,100,000 before Taiping Heavenly Kingdom and 1,400,000 after Taiping Heavenly Kingdom. It was still no more than 1% of China's population. After Taiping Heavenly Kingdom, including their family members (5 persons/per gentry), the gentry were no more than 3% of the population. The total number of gentry was a little more than 1 million (*shengyuan* 生员, the lowest level, was 70 percent of them) in the late Qing period. Including their family members, this was about 1.3 percent of China's population. He Huaihong 何怀宏, "*Xuanju shehui ji qi zhongjie: Qin Han zhi wan Qing lishi de yizhong shehuixue chanshi*" 选举社会及其终结__秦汉至晚清历史的—种社会学阐释, (Beijing: Sanlian shudian 北京三联书店, 1998). Shen Yansheng 沈延生 and Zhang Shouli 张守礼, "*Zizhi yi huo xingzheng: Zhongguo xiang zhi de huigu yu zhanwang*" 自治抑或行政—中国乡治的回顾与展望 Available online at: http://unpan1.un.org/intradoc/groups/public/documents/APCITY/UNPAN007919.pdf

CHAPTER FOUR

1. Excerpt of W.M.L. Jay [Julia Louisa M. Woodruff], *My Winter in Cuba* (New York: Dutton and Company, 1871), in Louis A. Perez, ed., *Slaves, Sugar, and Colonial Society: Travel Accounts of Cuba 1801–1899* (Wilmington: Scholarly Resources, 1992), 74.

2. See James Scott's study on conditions and forms of resistance: *Weapons of the Weak: Everyday Forms of Peasant Resistance* (New Haven: Yale University Press, 1985); *Domination and the Arts of Resistance: Hidden Transcripts* (New Haven: Yale University Press, 1990). Also see his early book *The Moral Economy of the Peasant: Rebellion and Subsistence in Southeast Asia* (New Haven: Yale University Press, 1976).

3. Howard McGary and Bill Lawson, *Between Slavery and Freedom* (Bloomington: Indiana University Press, 1992), 54.

4. Ronald Takaki, *Pau Hana: Plantation Life and Labor in Hawaii 1835–1920* (Honolulu: University of Hawaii Press, 1983), 127–152.

5. George Rawick, *From Sundown to Sunup* (Westport: Greenwood Publishing Company, 1972), 97. Rawick also noted that slave struggles were "rarely epic, though they were real and often successful in limited terms," in Rawick, 101.

6. Melania Yap and Dianne Leong Man, *Colour, Confusion, and Concessions* (Hong Kong: Hong Kong University Press, 1996), 149.

7. Yap and Leong Man, 149.

8. Antonio Chuffat Latour, *Apunte histórico de los chinos en Cuba* (Habana: Molina, 1927), 36.

9. Henry B. Auchincloss, "The Chinese in Cuba," *The Hunt's Merchants Magazine and Commerical Review* vol. LII, Jan-June 1865, 186–192; in Marshall Powers's *Chinese Coolie Migration to Cuba* (University of Florida 1953) dissertation, 137.

10. Richard Henry Dana, *To Cuba and Back* (Boston: Ticknor and Fields, 1859), excerpt in Louis A. Pérez, *Slaves, Sugar and Colonial Society: Travel Accounts of Cuba, 1801–1899* (Wilmington: Scholarly Resources, 1992), 61.

11. Sadiya Hartman, *Scenes of Subjection: Terror, Slavery, and Self-Making in Nineteenth Century America* (New York: Oxford University Press, 1997), 42.

12. Hartman, 42.

13. Deposition 808, also see Deposition 124: "I met a policeman and he asked to show him my freedom paper. He then claimed that my freedom paper was fake. I defended myself, and he then sent the dog to bite me."

14. Demetrius Eudell, *The Political Languages of Emancipation in the British Caribbean and the U.S.* (Chapel Hill: University of North Carolina Press, 2002), 9.

15. Marshall Powers quoting Aladama, in Powers's *Chinese Coolie Migration to Cuba* (University of Florida 1953) dissertation, 128.

16. James Williams Steele, *Cuban Sketches* (New York: G.P. Putnam's Sons, 1881), 150–152 as excerpted in *Slaves, Sugar, and Colonial Society: Travel Accounts of Cuba, 1801–1899* (Wilmington: Scholarly Resources, 1992), 144. Biographical detail regarding James Williams Steele, in Frank W. Blackmar, ed., *Kansas: A Cyclopedia of State History, Embracing Events, Institutions, Industries, Counties, Cities, Towns, Prominent Persons, etc., Volume II* (Chicago: Standard Publishing Company, 1912), 763.

17. Jill Lane, *Blackface Cuba 1840–1895* (Philadelphia: University of Pennsylvania Press, 1995).

18. Juan Jiménez Pastrana, *Los chinos en las luchas por la liberación cubana* (La Habana, Cuba: Editorial de Ciencias Sociales, 1983). Armando Choy, Gustavo Chui, and Moisés Sío Wong, *Our History Is Still Being Written* (New York: Pathfinder Press, 2005), 59–62.

19. Walter Rodney, *A History of the Guyanese Working People* (Baltimore: The Johns Hopkins University Press, 1981).

20. Depositions 555 and 345. Related: Mentioned four coolies killing a black overseer of the plantation.

21. Louise Levathes, *When China Ruled the Seas* (New York: Oxford University Press, 1996). Also Janet Abu-Lughod, *Before European Hegemony: The World System AD 1250–1350* (New York: Oxford University Press, 1989), 321.

22. Samuel M. Wilson, *The Emperor's Giraffe and Other Stories of Cultural Contact* (Boulder: Westview Press, 1999).

23. Wilbur Martin, *Slavery in China During the Former Han Dynasty* (New York: Russell and Russell, 1943), 93.

24. Abu-Lughod, 304.

25. Wilbur Martin, 93.

26. See Fang Li and Xiaofeng Huang, *Taiping Guangji* (Taipei, Taiwan: Xinxing Shuji, 1973), an extensive compilation in the Taiping Years (976–983) of about seven thousand stories published before and in the first years of the Song Dynasty.

27. Victor Cunrui Xoing, "The Story of a Kunlun Slave in Tang Chang'an," *Chinese Historians* 4.1 (1990): 77–81.

28. Maghan Keita, "Africans and Asians: Historiography and the Long View of Global Interaction," *Journal of World History* 16.1 (March 2005): 1–32. Samuel M. Wilson, *The Emperor's Giraffe and Other Stories of Cultural Contact* (Boulder: Westview Press, 1999). Philip Snow, *Star Raft: China's Encounter with Africa* (Ithaca: Cornell University Press, 1988).

29. Abu-Lughod, 321–348.

30. William Alexander Parsons Martin, *Zhongxi wenjian lu* 中西闻见录 (Nanjing: Nanjing gujiu shudian 南京古旧书店, 1992).

31. Armando Choy, et al., *Our History is Still Being Written: The Story of Three Chinese-Cuban Generals in the Cuban Revolution* (New York: Pathfinder, 2005), 68.

CHAPTER FIVE

1. Richard Henry Dana, in Aviva Chomsky et al, eds., *The Cuba Reader: History, Culture, Politics* (Durham: Duke University Press, 2003), 79. Also see the original, one of the most influential travel accounts of Cuba, *To Cuba and Back: A Vacation Voyage* (Boston, 1859).

2. Antonio Chuffat Latour, *Apunte histórico de los chinos en Cuba* (Habana: Molina, 1927).

3. Denise Helly, Juan Pérez de la Riva, José Baltar Rodriguez, Miriam Herrera Jerez and Mario Castillo Santana (co-authors), Mauro García Triano, Duvon Corbitt, Evelyn Hu-Dehart.

4. Gonzalo de Quesada, *Los chinos y la revolución cubana* (1892, 1946), in *Catauro: Revista Cubana de Antropología* (2000) 1:2, 179–191. Gonzalo de Quesada, *Mi primera ofrenda* (New York: 1892).

5. Borrowing from Viranjini Munasinghe's distinctions between the generative concept of "creators" as versus bearers of culture, though she makes the distinction as contextualized and problematized by nationalist conceptions of "creole," in her study of Indo-Trinidadians and national identity in *Callaloo or Tossed Salad* (Ithaca: Cornell University Press, 2001).

6. Chuffat is footnoted in the scholarship of the following scholars on Chinese of the postslavery period: Juan Pérez de la Riva, Duvon Corbitt, Denise Helly, José Baltar Rodriguez, Miriam Herrera Jerez and Mario Castillo Santana (coauthors), Mauro García Triano, and Kathleen Lopez. For example, José Baltar Rodriguez, capitulo I, *Los Chinos de Cuba*

(Habana: Fundacion Fernando Ortiz, 1997); Duvon Corbitt: *A Study of the Chinese in Cuba;* Miriam Herrera Jerez and Mario Castillo Santana: *De la memoria a la vida publica* (La Habana, 2003); Mauro García Triano, *Los chinos de Cuba y los nexus entre las dos naciones* (Habana: Sociedad Cubana de Investigaciones Filosóficas, 2003); Kathleen Lopez, "One Brings Another: The Formation of Early-Twentieth Century Chinese Migrant Communities in Cuba," in Andrew Wilson, ed., *The Chinese in the Caribbean* (Princeton: Markus Winters Publishers, 2004): 93–128.

7. Additionally, one might consider the view of Orlando Patterson. Although not directly related to the specificities of Cuba, Patterson argues that Chinese merchants in Jamaica emerged as a social, occupational group due to a *niche economy* and not necessarily due to Chinese cultural norms or practices.

8. To be clear, Yen Ching Hwang does not refer to Chuffat as a source.

9. Lowery Stokes Sims, *Wilfredo Lam and the International Avant Garde* (Austin: University of Texas Press, 2002).

10. RG 35, Entry 1007, Records of U.S. Army Overseas Operations and Commands 1898–1942, Army of Cuban Pacification 1906–1909, Correspondence of Military Information Division 1906–1909.

11. Letter, *"Cartas dirigidas a Juan Gualberto Gómez por Antonio Chuffat Latour, fechadas en la Habana a 14 y 16 diciembre 1898,"* Archivo Nacional de Cuba, Fondo Adquisiciones, leg. 16, exp. 921.

12. Donna Wolf, *The Cuban Gente de Color and the Independence Movement* 1879–1895 (1975); Rafael Fermoselle, *Politica y Color en Cuba, La Guerrita de 1912* (Montevido: Ediciones Geminis, 1974); Angelina Edreira de Caballero, *Vida y Obra de Juan Gualberto Gómez* (Habana: R. Mendez, no date); Raul Rodriguez La O, "Juan Gualberto Gómez and his stay in Paris (1869–1876)," *Granma Internacional* December 30, 2003; Tulia Falleti points out, however, that he did not support the armed rebellion of Afro-Cubans in the "race war" of 1912 in which 3,000 or more Afro-Cubans were killed, "Juan Gualberto Gómez: Pioneer of Afro-Cuban Political Mobilization," *A Political Atlas of the African Diaspora*. Hugh Thomas has a more skeptical view, implicating Gualberto as a great but corrupt black leader, in his book *Cuba: or The Pursuit of Freedom* (New York: Da Capo, 1988, 1971), 522–525.

13. In July of 1892, nearly 3,000 representatives from about seventy societies met in Havana.

14. Chuffat, 43.

15. Chuffat, 43. Raul Rodriguez La O, "Juan Gualberto Gómez and his stay in Paris (1869–1876)" *Granma Internacional* December 30, 2003.

16. Hugh Thomas, *Cuba: Or the Pursuit of Freedom* (New York: Da Capo Press, 1998), 285.

17. Antonio Chuffat Latour to Sr. Dr. Orestes Ferrera, Archivo Nacional de Cuba, Fondo: Donativos y Remisioners, Caja: 380, Num: 12, cartas dirigidas a Orestes Ferrera. 3 junio 1932.

18. Rafael Martínez Ortiz, *Cuba, los primeros años de su independencia* (Paris: Imprimerie Artistique "Lux," 1921).

19. Martínez , *Cuba, los primeros años de su independencia* , 297–298.

20. Pamela Maria Smorkaloff, *Readers and Writers in Cuba: A Social History of Print Culture, 1830s–1990s* (New York: Garland, 1997), 5, 21.

21. Manzano is the main and rare example of slave narrative and black writing in nineteenth-century Cuba. Manzano's autobiography was sponsored by abolitionists and published in English in London, 1836, and not published in Cuba until 1937, ten years after

the appearance of Chuffat's book. See Luis A. Jiménez, *El arte autobiográfico en Cuba en el siglo XIX* (New Brunswick: The Ometeca Institute, 1995), and Ivan A. Schulman's Introduction in the bilingual edition, Evelyn Picon Garfield translator, Juan Francisco Manzano, *Autobiography of a Slave/Autobiografía de un esclavo* (Detroit: Wayne State University Press, 1996). The mulatto poet Placido was known as a popular poet in nineteenth-century Cuba. His work has been both praised and denigrated from varying political and cultural angles. See Francisco Calcagno, *Poetas de color* (Havana: 1868, 1887). See Sibylle Fisher, *Modernity Disavowed* (Durham: Duke University Press, 2004), 77–106; Edna Rodríguez-Mangual, *Lydia Cabrera and the Construction of Afro-Cuban Identity*, (Chapel Hill: University of North Carolina Press, 2004), 16–17.

22. Smorkaloff provides a social history of Cuban print culture, which includes Chuffat's period, in *Readers and Writers in Cuba: A Social History of Print Culture, 1830s–1990s*. See Chapters 1–3 in particular. Agnes Lugo-Ortiz traces patrician literary societies that ultimately shape nineteenth-century literary production in Cuba, focused upon white writers and white readership, and pedagogical and moral concerns. *Identidades Imaginadas: Biografía y nacionalidad en el horizonte de la Guerra (Cuba 1860–1898),* (San Juan: Editorial de la Universidad de Puerto Rico, 1999). See Chapter One.

23. Smorkaloff, Chapters 2 and 3.

24. Sibylle Fischer, *Modernity Disavowed* (Durham: Duke University Press, 2004), 108–109.

25. Chuffat, 157, 119.

26. No substantive critical analysis has been done on the Chinese community yearbook as a *genre*. However, see Him Mark Lai's examination of benevolent association materials, and his historicizing of community press and representational organizations (including benevolent associations), though focused on formation in U.S. context, *Becoming Chinese American: A History of Communities and Institution* (Altamira Press 2004).

27. Chuffat, 84.

28. Lista Electoral. Municipio de Cienfuegos. Provincia de Santa Clara. Censo de Septiembre 30 de 1907. In Exp. 14476, leg. 261, Fondo Secretaría de Estado y Gobernación, Archivo Nacional de Cuba.

29. Chuffat, 105.

30. Chuffat.

31. Miriam Herrera Jerez and Mario Castillo Santana examine these politics in the Chinese Cuban community at length in *De la memoria a la vida publica* (La Habana, 2003). Kathleen Lopez "One Brings Another: The Formation of Early-Twentieth Century Chinese Migrant Communities in Cuba," in Andrew Wilson ed. *The Chinese in the Caribbean* (Princeton: Markus Winters Publishers, 2004), 93–128.

32. Chuffat, 105.

33. For further elaboration upon the discourse of "overseas Chinese," see Laurence Ma and Carolyn Cartier, eds., *The Chinese Diaspora: Space, Place, Mobility, and Identity* (Lanham: Rowman & Littlefield, 2003); 10, 52, 56, 12, 30, 196. Wang Ling-chi and Wang Gungwu, eds., *The Chinese Diaspora* Volume I (Singapore, Times Academic Press, 1998) 1–13. See Yen Ching Hwang *Coolies and Mandarins: China's Protection of Overseas Chinese During the Late Ch'ing Period (1851–1911)* (Singapore: Singapore University Press, 1985) for the development of overseas Chinese discourse as emergent modern policy in Qing period, China.

34. Chuffat, 96.

35. José Baltar Rodriguez, capitulo I, *Los Chinos de Cuba* (Habana: Fundacion Fernando Ortiz, 1997); Juan Pérez de la Riva; Duvon Corbitt, *A Study of the Chinese in Cuba;*

Miriam Herrera Jerez and Mario Castillo Santana, *De la memoria a la vida publica* (La Habana, 2003); Mauro García Triano, *Los chinos de Cuba y los nexus entre las dos naciones* (Habana: Sociedad Cubana de Investigaciones Filosóficas, 2003).

36. Chuffat, 5.

37. Duvon Corbitt, A *Study of the Chinese in Cuba, 1847–1947* (Wilmore, Kentucky: Asbury College, 1971), 5.

38. Chuffat, 15–16.

39. Chuffat, 25.

40. Chuffat, 49.

41. Chuffat, 123.

42. Chuffat, 17.

43. Chuffat, 94.

44. For linguistic analysis of Chinese pidgin in Cuba, see John Lipski "Chinese-Cuban Pidgin Spanish," in John Rickford and Suzanne Romaine, eds., *Creole Genesis, Attitudes and Discourse* (Philadelphia: John Benjamins Publishing, 1999), 215–233. Clancy Clements argues that from the standpoint of linguistic analysis, the manifestation of Spanish spoken by Chinese coolies should be characterized more accurately as "naturalistic second language acquisition" and not pidgin, in *The Linguistic Legacy of Spanish and Portuguese: Colonial Expansion and Language Change* (Cambridge University Press, forthcoming). Sergio Valdes Bernal delves into Chinese dialects in Cuba and uniquely Chinese pronunciations of Spanish, "Los chinos desde el punto de vista linguistico," in *Catauro: Revista Cubana de Antropología* (2000) 1:2. Beatriz Varela examines Chinese inflected terms in Cuban vocabulary in *Lo chino en el habla cubana*.

45. Chuffat, 31, 61.

46. During Chuffat's time, there were some instances of representing pidgin in Cuban theater, though as caricature and for comedic effect. Sergio Valdes Bernal, "Los chinos desde el punto de vista linguistico," in *Catauro: Revista Cubana de Antropología* (2000) 1:2. 62–63. Chinese pidgin as a marker of localism-yet-unassimilability was frequently referred to with overtones of exoticism, parody, or noted as a colorful addition to local culture.

47. Chuffat, 101.

48. Chuffat, 101.

49. Chuffat, 61.

50. Chuffat, 98–101.

51. See various usages in Beatriz Varela, *Lo chino en el habla cubana*, (Miami: Ediciones Universal, 1980), 44; Sergio Valdes Bernal, "Los chinos desde el punto de vista linguistico," in *Catauro: Revista Cubana de Antropología* 1:2 (2000): 68; Juan Pérez de la Riva, *Contribución a la historia de la gente sin historia* (Habana: Editorial de Ciencias Sociales, 1971), 136. Interpretations have varied. Denise Helly suggests a usage that still stems from Chinese experience in Cuba, which means to be duped into something, as in the Chinese having been duped into false contracts: "des colonos asiatiques: ils le dupèrent comme un Chinois (lo engañaron como a un Chino)" in Denise Helly, *Idéologie et ethnicité* (Montréal : Presses de l'Université de Montréal, 1979), 269.

52. Chuffat, 31.

53. Jiménez, 92, quoting Gonzalo de Quesada. *Mi primera ofrenda* (New York: 1892); Tejeiro, *Historia ilustrada de la colonia China en Cuba* (Habana: Editorial Hercules, 1947): unpaginated text, section under "Gonzalo de Quesada . . ."

54. Jiménez, *Los chinos*, 110, from Juan del Pueblo (pseud.), "Un chino que puede ser presidente de la República," *La Semana*, La Habana, marzo 19, 1930.

55. Chuffat, 54.

56. Chuffat, 54. Literally means "stupid ghost," but such a literal equivalent does not communicate its meaning. It is more accurately translated into English as "damn whitey."

57. References to the Médico Chino are common in Cuban folklore of the nineteenth and early twentieth centuries, particularly any reminiscences involving Chinese presence. For a summary, see Olympia Gonzalez, *Leyendas Cubana* (Illinois: National Textbook Company, 1997), 63–68. This legend has expanded to include other "médico chino" types and biographies, such as Hedy Lamar-Santana's recollection of her father, *Semblanzas de mi padres (el médico chino)* (Lamar-Santana, 2001).

58. Chapter 7.

59. Chuffat, 89.

60. Chuffat, 89.

61. Chuffat, 23.

62. Chuffat, 17 and 49.

63. Chuffat, 17 and 49.

64. Chuffat, 87. Also referred to as Quan Yin, Kwan Yin, Kuan Yin, Gwan Yin, Guan Yin in English transliterations.

65. Chuffat, 87. Frank Scherer examines San Fan Con in "Sanfancón: Orientalism, Self-Orientalization, and 'Chinese Religion' in Cuba," *Nation Dance: Religion, Identity, and Cultural difference in the Caribbean,* ed. Patrick Taylor (Indianapolis: Indiana University Press, 2001).

66. Guan Gong, also referred to as Guan Gung, Gwan Gung, Kuan Kong, Kwan Kong, Kuan Kung, in English transliterations. Referred to as Kuan Kong, Cuang Con, and Cuan Kung in Cuban studies. Lisa Yun, interviews in *barrio chino,* 1998, with participants of the religion. Also see José Baltar Rodriguez, *Los Chinos de Cuba* (Habana: Fundacion Fernando Ortiz, 1997), 173–184; Leonardo Padura, "El viaje mas" in *Catauro: Revista Cubana de Antropología* 1:2 (154–155), Mercedes Crespo Villate, *Mis Imagenes* (Habana: Ediciones Verde Olivio, 2000), 72–73. For photographs of Guan Gung/San Fan Con, see Giuseppe Lo Bartolo, *Barrio Chino de La Habana, imagen del tiempo* (Panama: Caribe Publishing, 1999), 80. Frank Scherer examines San Fan Con in "Sanfancón: Orientalism, Self-Orientalization, and 'Chinese Religion' in Cuba," *Nation Dance: Religion, Identity, and Cultural difference in the Caribbean,* ed. Patrick Taylor (Indianapolis: Indiana University Press, 2001).

67. Chuffat, 91–92.

68. 1860 Royal Decree Section II, *Cuba Commission Report.*

69. Chuffat, 38.

70. Chuffat, 97.

71. Chuffat, 18.

72. In terms of marriage, Cuban society was permissive to the idea of coolie marriages to blacks but opposed to coolie marriages with whites, though in some rare instances this was accomplished. Verena Martinez-Alier, *Marriage, Class and Colour in Nineteenth-Century Cuba* (New York: Cambridge University Press, 1974), 76–79; Evelyn Hu-Dehart, "Race Construction and Race Relations," in Roshni Rustomji-Kerns, et al., eds., *Encounters: People of Asian Descent in the Americas* (Lanham: Rowman & Littlefield, 1999), 109. Hu-Dehart notes the case of Julian Guisen, whose case involved some manuveurings of the system for him to marry a white woman and remain in Cuba. His contract was sold to the priest who then transferred it to the white wife, who then petitioned authorities to release Guisen from the remainder of his contract.

73. Chuffat, 46.

74. See Juan Jiménez Pastrana, *Los chinos en la historia de Cuba* (La Habana : Editorial de Ciencias Sociales, 1983), Chapters V and VI.

75. Ada Ferrer characterizes the mixed politics of Cuban independence, "ambivalently defined as anti-slavery and multiracial" (although she does not examine Chinese insurgency) in *Insurgent Cuba: Race, Nation, and Revolution 1868–1898* (Chapel Hill: University of North Carolina, 1999).

76. Jiménez 84.

77. Chuffat, 26.

78. Enrique Cirules, "Algunas reflexiones sobre la presencia de los chinos en Cuba," *Catauro: Revista Cubana de Antropología* (2000) 1:2. 29.

79. Chuffat, 22–23.

80. Chuffat, 27.

81. Chuffat, 28.

82. Chuffat, 29.

83. Chuffat, 22.

84. Chuffat; Corlia Alonso Valdés, "La immigración china: su presencia en el Ejército Libertador de Cuba," *Catauro: Revista Cubana de Antropología* 1:2 (2000): 128; Jiménez Pastrana. Also troops of 500 Chinese served under Maximo Gómez, see Enrique Cirules, "Algunas reflexiones sobre la presencia de los chinos en Cuba," *Catauro: Revista Cubana de Antropología* 1:2 (2000): 29.

85. From sources other than Chuffat, recollections reveal that the freedom fighters' escapades became local legend, with many only known by their Spanish names, and even then, perhaps just by their first names. This was the case of one Chinese corporal known as "José," known for his bravery and sardonic statements in battle. He was also a member of General Antonio Maceo's personal escort. Mauro García Triano, *Los chinos de Cuba y los nexus entre las dos naciones* (Habana: Sociedad Cubana de Investigaciones Filosóficas, 2003), 175. Juan Jiménez Pastrana, *Los chinos en la historia de Cuba* (La Habana: Editorial de Ciencias Sociales, 1983), 120, 123.

86. Chuffat, 61.

87. Chuffat, 61.

88. Chuffat, 29 and 36.

89. Chuffat, Preface.

90. Chuffat, 20–21.

91. Chuffat, 58.

92. See also Persia Campbell, Pérez de la Riva, Jiménez, Helly.

93. Chuffat, 36.

94. *Ranchadores* also termed *ranchadeores* in Spanish. Esteban Montejo's *Biografía de un cimarrón* also describes the *ranchadeore* component of slave society: "Since the cimarrón was a slave who had escaped, the masters sent a posse of rancheadores after them. Mean guajiros with hunting dogs so they could drag you out of the woods with their jaws . . . When a slave catcher caught a black, the master or the overseer gave him an ounce of gold or more. In those years, an ounce was like saying seventeen pesos. Who knows how many guajiros were in that business!" Esteban Montejo, ed. Miguel Barnet, trans. Nick Hill, *Biography of a Runaway Slave* (Willimantic: Curbstone Press, 1994), 47.

95. Chuffat, 25. Also see 38.

96. For the slave catcher, a negro was nothing, Chinese were even less.

97. Chuffat, 15.

98. Chuffat, 124.

99. Chuffat, 34.

100. Aline Helg, *Our Rightful Share: The Afro-Cuban Struggle for* Equality 1886–1912 (Chapel Hill: University of North Carolina Press, 1995).

101. Chuffat, 62.

102. Chuffat, 62.

103. Such social analysis shares similarities with popular rhetoric behind contemporary black/Asian conflict in other parts of the Americas. Jeffrey Lesser, "In Search of the Hyphen," in Lane Hirabayashi et. al., eds., *New Worlds, New Lives* (Stanford: Stanford University Press, 2002), 38–39. Lisa Lowe, *Immigrant Acts* (Durham: Duke University Press, 1996), 93–95; David Palumbo-Liu, *Asian/American: Historical Crossings of a Racial Frontier.* (Stanford: Stanford University Press, 1999), 170–181; Vijay Prashad, *The Karma of Brown Folk* (University of Minnesota Press), 167–170; Lisa Ikemoto, "Traces of the Master Narrative in the Story of African American/Korean American Conflict," in Richard Delgado ed., *Critical Race Theory* (Philadelphia: Temple University Press, 1995), 305–315.

104. Chuffat, 62.

105. Chuffat, 55.

106. Chuffat, 70.

107. "Chinese of Cuba" is a term used here to describe a people in loose terms of global diasporic history, as in "Chinese of Malaysia," "Chinese of Australia," "Chinese of South Africa." Contemporary Chinese in Cuba whom the author interviewed identify themselves as "cubano/a" but also call themselves "chino/a" in terms of cultural ancestry.

108. José Baltar Rodriguez, *Los chinos de Cuba* 37, Pérez de la Riva, and SELA.

109. Miriam Herrera Jerez and Mario Castillo Santana, and Mauro García Triano.

110. Figured calculated based upon: Republic of Cuba, Secretaría de Hacienda: "Inmigración y movilidad de pasajeros" (Reports for 1902 to 1934). Obtained from *Cooperación Técnica* "International Migrations in Cuba" by Rolando Garcia Quiñones, Director del Centro de Estudios Demográficos (CEDEM), Cuba. See http://www.sela.org/index from El Sistema Económico Latinoamericano (SELA) or The Latin American Economic System (SELA).

111. *Legislacion,* 563.

112. Chuffat, 112.

113. Chuffat, 175.

114. José Marti, *Fragmentos,* Apendice 2, Tomo 74, Habana: Editorial Tropico, 1949), 59–60. As quoted in Pedro Eng Herrera and Mauro Garcia Triana, *Marti en los chinos, los chinos en Marti* (Habana: Grupo Promotor, 2003), 83: "Refiriéndose al Reglamento de 1860 criticó el régimen esclavista al que prácticamente estaban sometidos los chinos al decir: '¿Que iba de él a la esclavitud?' "

115. Gonzalo de Quesada's essay appeared as *Los chinos y la independencia de Cuba* (Leipzig: Breitkopf & Hartel, 1910), *The Chinese and Cuban Independence* (Leipzig: Breitkopf & Hartel, 1925), *Los chinos y la revolución cubana (La Habana: Ucar, Garcia, 1946), Los chinos y la revolución cubana* (1892, 1946), in *Catauro: Revista Cubana de Antropología* (2000) 1:2, 179–191. Also see Juan Jiménez Pastrana, *Los Chinos en la historia de Cuba,* 37, 57; Gonzalo de Quesada *Mi primera ofrenda* NY 1892, 122–123; José Baltar Rodriguez, *Los chinos de Cuba* (Habana: 1997), 34–37. On Quesada's writing regarding the Chinese fighters, see *Historia Ilustrada de la Colonia China en Cuba* by Guillermo Tejeiro, Habana: Editorial Hercules, 1947. Unpaginated text. See section under "Gonzalo de Quesada . . ."

116. Chuffat, 175.

117. Duvon Corbitt, 92.

118. Mauro Garcia Triano, 85.

119. Juan Pérez de la Riva, José Baltar, Miriam Herrrera Jerez and Mario Castillo Santana.

120. Mary Turner, "Between Slavery and Free Labour," in Mary Turner, ed., *From Chattel Slaves to Wage Slaves* (London: James Curry, 1995), 189.

121. Triano, 80–83.

122. Baltar, 37–40. José Baltar Rodriguez, in agreement with Juan Pérez de la Riva, noted the significance of the *californianos* in creating a new hierarchy.

123. Chuffat, 18 and 31.

124. Chuffat, 32, 41, 43, 49, 57.

125. Chuffat, 18. Contemporary articles have appeared regarding the Chinese in Cuba that misquote Chuffat, attributing his description of Hen Yi Tong to another association, Kit Yi Tong.

126. Chuffat, 18.

127. Chuffat, 94.

128. Chuffat, 43, 39, 57.

129. Patrick Leigh Fermor in *The Reader's Companion to Cuba,* ed. Alan Ryan (New York: Harcourt Brace, 1997), 127–128. His account of Cuba's annual carnival in 1940s is excerpted from his original *The Traveller's Tree* (London: John Murray, 1950). Also see Ned Sublette, *Cuba and Its Music: From the First Drums to the Mambo* (Chicago: Chicago Review Press, 2004).

130. Chuffat, 91.

131. Chuffat, 114.

132. Chuffat, 62–63.

133. Chuffat, 43.

134. Chuffat, 43.

135. *Californianos* is a term coined by Juan Pérez de la Riva, though Chuffat called them *chino-americano* or described them as *chinos* from San Francisco. See also Baltar, 96. There were approximately 5,000 Chinese Californian merchants that had arrived by the 1880s. Baltar and Pérez de la Riva's assessments of this period use Chuffat as a source.

136. Corbitt, 90; quoting Samuel Hazard, *Cuba Pen and Pencil.*

137. Chuffat, 17.

138. See Corbitt, 92; Pérez de la Riva; see chapter two of this book.

139. Martin Ballou's travel account.

140. Miguel Bretos "Imagining Cuba under the American Flag: Charles Edward Doty in Havana 1899–1902," in *The Journal of Decorative and Propaganda Arts,* Issue 22, (1996): 83–104. Photograph of a homeless Chinese man in Matanzas.

141. Corbitt, 91. Leper coal workers, Frederic Remington in *The Reader's Companion to Cuba,* 67, excerpt from the original "Under Which King?" in *Colliers* April 8, 1899. Observation of Chinese brakemen on railroad, *The Travel Diary of Joséph Dimock,* ed. Louis A. Pérez (Wilmington: Scholarly Resources, 1998), 32.

142. See Chapters Two and Three of this study. Also see *Report of the Commission Sent by China to Ascertain the Condition of Chinese Coolies in Cuba, 1876* (Taipei : Cheng Wen, rep. 1970). Also see introduction by Denise Helly in *Cuba Commission Report*, (Baltimore : Johns Hopkins University Press, 1993).

143. Chuffat, 96–97.

144. Chuffat, 36.

145. Chuffat, 89.

146. Chuffat, 96.
147. Chuffat, 104.
148. Chuffat, 102.
149. Chuffat, 96.
150. Chuffat, 86, 89, 99.
151. Chuffat, 70.
152. Chuffat, 95.
153. Chuffat, 10.
154. Chuffat, 108.
155. Chuffat, 110.
156. Chuffat, 105–106.
157. Chuffat, 103.
158. Chuffat, 116.
159. Luis A. Pérez, *Winds of Change: Hurricanes and the Transformation of Nineteenth Century Cuba* (University of North Carolina Press, 2001).
160. Chuffat, 106.
161. Chuffat, 106.
162. Jesus Guanche, *Componentes Etnicos de la Nacion Cubana*, 86.
163. Chuffat, 157.
164. Chuffat, 158.
165. Chuffat, 150.
166. Chuffat, 56.

CONCLUSION

1. Joseph Conrad, *Typhoon and Other Tales* (Oxford: Oxford University Press, 1998), 80.
2. Jonathan Raban, *Oxford Book of the Sea* (Oxford: Oxford University Press, 1992), 31; Cederic Watts, introduction, *Typhoon and Other Tales*, by Joseph Conrad (Oxford University Press, 1998). For more recent interpretations see Sooyoung Chon, "Typhoon: Silver Dollars and Stars," *Conradiana* 22.1 (1990):39; Ross Forman, "Coolie Cargoes: Emigrant Ships and the Burden of Representation in Joseph Conrad's *Typhoon* and James Dalzier's 'Dead Reckoning,'" *English Literature in Transition: 1880–1920* 47.4 (2004): 398–429.
3. Conrad, 62.
4. Conrad, Introduction, *Typhoon* vii.
5. Hugh Thomas, *Cuba* (1971; New York: Da Capo Press, 1998), 188.
6. Francis Mulhearn, "English Reading," in *Nation and Narration*, ed. Homi Bhabha (New York: Routledge, 1990), 256.
7. Conrad, 80.
8. Kevin Bales, *Disposable People* (Berkeley: University of California Press, 1999).
9. Bales.
10. See Julie Su, "El Monte Thai Garment Workers: Slave Sweatshops," *Sweatshop Watch Newsletter* at www.sweatshopwatch.org; also published in *No Sweat: Fashion, Free Trade and the Rights of Garment Workers*, ed. Andrew Ross (New York: Verso, 1997).
11. David Palumbo-Liu critiques the pedagogical propensity for this approach, in *Asian/American: Historical Crossings of a Racial Frontier* (Stanford: Stanford University Press, 1999); Jeffery Lesser utilizes but complicates notions of hyphenation among Japanese Brazilians (and mentions Okinawan Brazilians) in "In Search of the Hyphen" *New*

Worlds, New Lives, eds. Lane Hirabayashi et al. (Stanford: Stanford University Press, 2002): 37–58.

12. Ko-lin Chin, *Smuggled Chinese* (Philadelphia: Temple University Press, 1999); Peter Kwong, *Forbidden Workers* (New York: Free Press, 1998); Kevin Bales, *Disposable People* (Berkeley: University of California Press, 1999); These authors are among others who discuss the human trafficking industry, which includes laborers of Asian, Latin, Caribbean, African, and Eastern European descent.

13. "Song of Calling Souls," *Nuyorasian Anthology,* ed. Bino Realuyo (Philadelphia: Temple University Press, 1999): 131–135. Reprinted from Wang Ping, *Of Flesh and Spirit* (Minneapolis: Coffee House Press, 1998).

14. *Fly to Freedom: The Art of the Golden Venture Refugees Teacher Resource Packet* (New York: Museum of the Chinese in the Americas, 2001).

15. The Smithsonian Institute exhibit "Fly to Freedom: Art of the Golden Venture Refugees" (May–September 2001).

16. Peter Kwong, *Forbidden Workers* (New York: New Press, 1997): 37–45.

17. Kevin Bales makes this distinction between forms of modern-day "new slavery" and old slavery, which was formulated upon discourses of "ownership." Chapter 1 in Kevin Bales, *Disposable People* (Berkeley: University of California Press, 1999).

18. Term distinguishing between Indian descendants of indenture and contemporary migrants, proposed by Veronique Bragard in "Coolie Woman Fictionalizing Political History: Janice Shinebourne's Memories of Violence," *Journal of Caribbean Literature* 3.1 (2003): 14. Also see Joel Benjamin et al., eds., *They Came in Ships: an Anthology of Indo-Guyanese Writing* (Leeds, England: Peepal Tree Press, 1998) and Noor Kumar Mahabir, ed., *Still Cry* (Ithaca: Calaloux Publications, 1985).

19. Scholar Joyce Johnson notes that overall, most Anglophone West Indian literature features Chinese characters only briefly. Most feature the Chinese as male and as "existing outside the power relations of creole societies . . ." in Joyce Johnson, "Representations of the Chinese in Anglophone Caribbean Fiction" in *Immigrants & Minorities* 16 (1997): 36–54.

20. See, for example, the wonderful encyclopedic collection of the Chinese of Jamaica, Ray Chen, ed., *The Shopkeepers* (Kingston: Periwinkle Publishers, 2005). Also see Victor Chang's short story of family, "Light in the Shop."

21. Veronique Bragard, "Coolie Woman Fictionalizing Political History: Janice Shinebourne's Memories of Violence" in *Journal of Caribbean Literature* 3.1 (2003): 14; Brinda Mehta, "The Colonial Curriculum and the Construction of 'Coolie-ness' in Lakshmi Persaud's *Sastra and Butterfly in the Wind* (Trinidad) and Jan Shinebourne's *The Last English Plantation* (Guyana)," *Journal of Caribbean Literature* 3.1 (2001): 111–128.

22. Jan Lo Shinebourne, *The Last English Plantation* (Leeds, England: Peepal Tree Press, 1988): 126.

23. Shinebourne, 128.

24. The dolls can be viewed at Deutsche Kinemathek—Marlene Dietrich Collection Berlin. *Deutsche Kinemathek Newsletter* Number 33 (November 1, 2001): http://www.marlene.com/news-views/news33.pdf. The newsletter, which answers queries by readers, includes a query by Judith Mayne, to which an answer is provided, including a reference to the "little Chinese." See also Mayne's article in which she theorizes about the dolls (mainly concerning the "black doll"), fetishism, and queries the implications of doll collecting for feminist studies, in "Marlene, Dolls, and Fetishism," in *Signs: Journal of Women in Culture and Society* 30.1 (2004): 1260. Maria Riva provides the anecdotes about her mother's dolls in *Marlene Dietrich: Photographs and Memories* (New York: Knopf, 2001).

25. Coolie-wear—"coolie jackets" and "coolie pants"—recurs in the globalized high fashions of Prada, Christian Dior, Yves St. Laurent, and Donna Karan. "Coolie lamps" are promoted by the lighting industry as a common staple for upscale lamp retailers. "Coolie hats" are marketed by the fashion industry, sometimes called the "classic coolie," with designers offering versions such as the "Black Coolie." "Coolie costumes" are popular rentals, utilized as another kind of blackface or yellowface. For Halloween, one could rent a "Chinese Coolie" costume for $45 (for the same price, one could also order the "Chinese Housegirl"). Family-oriented clothing chains such as Abercrombie & Fitch featured the coolie image as a humorous throwback to racial subservience, such as T-shirts that featured a coolie under the words "Wok-N-Bowl." At one point, one could buy a coolie "kit" from Urban Outfitters, a self-described "hip and trendy" international chain.

26. Dorinne Kondo, *About Face* (New York: Routledge, 1997), 16.

27. As a comparative point, see Barbara Christian's contention that the Middle Passage has practically disappeared from cultural memory, in which she refers to Toni Morrison who also makes this point. In Barbara Christian's "Fixing Methodologies: Beloved," *Cultural Critique* 24 (Spring 1993): 7.

28. Oscar Zanetti and Alejandro Garcia, *Sugar and Railroads: A Cuban History 1837–1959* (1987; Chapel Hill: The University of North Carolina Press, 1998). Hugh Thomas, 142.

INDEX

Coen, Jan Pieterzoon, 5
Cohen, Lucy, 22
Colomé, Juan A., 16
Conrad, Joseph, 229–230
contratistas, 223–224
coolie: burials, 93, 161; definition of,
xvii–xix; disposability of, 31, 85, 166,
181, 231; diversity of, 62–66, 69–70,
199, 200, 201; etymology, xvii;
language and dialect. *See* language;
in Western literature, xiv, 23,
229–230, 235; as a socially specific
designation, xvii–xviii, 66, 102, 217,
222; as mobile slave, xviii, 126,
133–135, 146; identifications, xviii, 82,
120, 137, 195–196, 234; intra-group
conflict, 169–173; involvement in
liberation, 33, 126, 142, 181, 198,
209–217; laws regulating, 5, 30, 93,
111, 134, 137, 215–217, 251. *See also*
laws and regulations; mortality rates,
7, 17–18, 134; Cuban population, 19,
32, 61, 226; price of, 17, 249; religious
coercion of, 92–93, 98, 208; renaming,
83, 206; reselling, 61, 133, 223;
runaways, 31, 33, 62, 74, 83, 136, 164,
212–13; suicide, 10, 84, 90, 147–150,
243; survivors, 30, 33, 81, 233; in the
twentieth century, xii, 22, 34, 163,
191, 196; wage of, 30, 98, 108, 134,
141, 231, 234; women, 62–64, 89,
191–193, 226–228, 231
coolie contract: xiv, xvii, 105–107;
manipulations of, xix, 5, 29, 31, 56,
71, 105–108; "new slavery," 230–231;
notion of voluntariness, 22, 30, 106,
109, 122, 230; philosophy of, xviii,
recontracting, 5, 30–31, 112, 132, 199,
212, 223
coolie labor: as alternative to African
slave, 11–13, 154, 176; in conjunction
with African slaves, xiii, 32–33;
economy, 8, 65, 167, 223; profitability,
14, 16–17, 23–24, 27, 34, 78, 179, 180,
246, 256; "new coolies," 234
coolie masters, 29–31, 153, 172, 208
Coolie Odyssey (Dabydeen), 235
coolie rebellions, 1, 18, 30–34, 145, 185
coolie ships, 9, 16, 18, 28, 116

coolie testifiers: origins of, 70, 199;
locations in Cuba, 60–61; occupations
of, 67–68
coolie testimony: "assassination testimony,"
176–179; as counternarrative, 109,
236; as exposition, 57, 107; narrative
forms of. *See* coolie petition;
obstacles of, 45–46, 88; procurement,
37, 42; as protest, 1, 53, 77, 80;
transference, 101; as transpirational,
56. *See also* oral testimony
coolie traffickers, 6–7, 14–26
Cordova, José, 192
Costa Rica, 6, 195
Crespo, Comandante Jesús, 210
St. Croix, 6
caudrilleros (labor bosses), 223–224
Cuba commission, 37–40, 49, 53, 62,
105–106. *See also* Report by the
Commission Sent by China

Dabydeen, David, 52, 235
Dana, Richard Henry, 149, 183
Davis, Charles T., 55
diasporic patterns, xix-xx, 8, 185–186,
195–197
Deerr, Noel, 13, 31
Denmark, 18
Desnoyers, Charles, 39, 41
Dietrich, Marlene, 236
Ding, Loni, xix–xx
Douglass, Frederick, 54–55, 83
Dupierris, Marcial, 16
Dutch East Indies (Indonesia), 5, 8

East Indian: coolie trade, xix, 6–10
passim, 51–52, 119, 235; coolie
narratives, 9; origins, 66; in Western
literature, 235–236
Equiano, Olaudah, 83
Escott, Paul, 58
Eudell, Demetrius, 156

Fang Tianxiang, 88, 129
Fernández, Capitán Bartolo, 210–211
Ferrán, Antonio, 16
Ferrera, Orestes, 190
Fiji, 7, 66
Foner, Philip, 29

Lisa Yun is Associate Professor of English and Asian and Asian American Studies at Binghamton University.